Cyber Risk Management and AI Governance in the Digital Era

Calvin Nobles
https://orcid.org/0000-0003-4002-1108
University of Maryland Global Campus, USA

Kevin Richardson
https://orcid.org/0009-0002-3212-8669
Talladega College, USA

Quatavia McLester
https://orcid.org/0000-0003-1596-0517
Columbus State University, USA

Darrell Norman Burrell
https://orcid.org/0000-0002-4675-9544
Marymount University, USA

IGI Global
Scientific Publishing
Publishing Tomorrow's Research Today

Vice President of Editorial Melissa Wagner
Director of Acquisitions Mikaela Felty
Director of Book Development Jocelynn Hessler
Production Manager Mike Brehm
Cover Design Jose Rosado

Published in the United States of America by
IGI Global Scientific Publishing
701 East Chocolate Avenue
Hershey, PA, 17033, USA
Tel: 717-533-8845 | Fax: 717-533-7115
Website: https://www.igi-global.com E-mail: cust@igi-global.com

Library of Congress Cataloging-in-Publication Data

LCCN: (CIP Data Pending)
ISBN13: 9798337399188
Isbn13Softcover: 9798337399195
EISBN13: 9798337399201
British Cataloguing in Publication Data
A Cataloguing in Publication record for this book is available from the British Library.

Table of Contents

Detailed Table of Contents

Artificial intelligence (AI) safety and security constitute interdependent disciplines essential for mitigating both unintended and deliberate harms arising from autonomous systems. AI safety aims to ensure that intelligent agents operate predictably and in alignment with human values, while AI security safeguards systems against adversarial manipulation, data poisoning, and model exploitation. Together, these domains underpin the ethical and operational integrity of AI technologies across sectors, particularly in high-stakes environments such as healthcare and governance. Nevertheless, the persistent underrepresentation of women, who comprise less than one-third of AI professionals globally, poses a critical challenge to the field's inclusivity, legitimacy, and epistemic diversity. This commentary argues that women's participation in AI safety and security is not merely a matter of representation, but a prerequisite for developing systems that are equitable, accountable, and aligned with societal values. Women's perspectives are indispensable in identifying algorithmic bias, confronting gendered harms such as deepfakes, and designing governance frameworks that advance fairness and transparency. Simultaneously, AI technologies themselves can serve as tools for empowerment, mentorship, and confidence-building among women in professional roles. Ensuring women's engagement is therefore both an ethical and strategic policy imperative for achieving robust, socially responsive AI safety and security practices.

The spread of AI is also the essential issue of algorithmic sovereignty and democratic validity on the automated decision-making process. This paper presents a mixed-methods comparative research on governance systems of AI in the EU, US, UK, Canada, South Korea, Taiwan and Japan. Carried out based on a multi-dimensional

Neuromarketing explores the use of neuroscientific techniques to study and shape consumer behaviour. Through the analysis of brain activity, eye movements, and other physiological responses, companies can uncover valuable insights into consumer preferences that conventional marketing approaches may overlook. The objective of this research paper is to analyse neuromarketing with the aim of identifying ethical concerns that give rise to criticism in this field and propose strategies to address these concerns. The present study is undertaken in the format of a critical literature review. Following an analysis of the history, nomenclature, methodology, findings, and implications of neuromarketing for consumer research, this paper concludes with an overview of the primary ethical considerations. The study's results suggest that neuromarketing has significant promise for consumer research, as it effectively acquires more precise data and novel insights on human behaviour that were previously unachievable.

Digital transformation in healthcare is redefining administration and care delivery as socio-technical systems where data privacy, cybersecurity, usability, and human adaptability jointly determine success. Using a narrative literature review anchored in the SAFECARE Concepts Health Solutions case, a telehealth-only reproductive health model, this inquiry synthesizes scholarship on trust formation, technology resistance, digital literacy, and organizational behavior. Findings indicate that resistance often reflects anxiety about technology reliability, technology ease of use, data exposure, and loss of relational control rather than opposition to innovation. Transparent consent, privacy-by-design architectures, secure identities, and empathetic communication increase confidence and sustain adoption, particularly for sensitive reproductive data. Organizational culture and adaptive leadership are decisive, embedding security governance, equity, and psychological safety into workflows, roles, and patient engagement. The analysis offers a human-centered, security-conscious framework that aligns technical reliability with ethical stewardship to advance equitable, trustworthy telehealth within complex adaptive health systems.

This chapter presents the second phase of a multi-stage research agenda on operationalizing AI governance for organizations adopting third-party AI systems. Building on our conceptual AI Governance Implementation Framework (AGIF), this chapter translates theory into practice by developing the foundational oversight mechanisms that anchor an AI governance program through a practice-inspired, action design research based, collaborative inquiry. The resulting Roadmap for AI Governance (RAIG) outlines an eight-step implementation model, establishing the structures necessary for later operationalization. The roadmap provides practical guidance for establishing oversight structures, scoping AI systems, defining risks and controls, and integrating evaluation, testing, and validation processes. Findings reveal that effective AI governance requires iterative development, cross-functional collaboration, and integration with existing risk and data governance programs. This work demonstrates how governance can be embedded in real-world organizational settings, bridging the gap between conceptual frameworks and applied practice for responsible AI adoption.

This study examines the cyberpsychological dimensions of cybersecurity risks in healthcare, emphasizing how human cognition, emotion, and organizational culture shape vulnerability within digitally transformed care environments. As healthcare integrates electronic health records, AI diagnostics, and telehealth systems, leaders, often trained in clinical or administrative domains, remain largely untrained in human factors psychology, limiting their capacity to address behavioral risk. Cyberattacks increasingly exploit cognitive biases such as urgency, authority, and trust, while clinicians under high cognitive load and ethical pressure frequently bypass protocols perceived as obstructive to patient care. Through an integrative, evidence-based framework grounded in cyberpsychological theory, this research aims to align technical controls with user behavior, leadership awareness, and institutional culture. The goal is to transition healthcare cybersecurity from a reactive, technology-centric model to

Preface

The rapid acceleration of artificial intelligence, digital platforms, and data-driven decision-making has fundamentally reshaped how organizations, governments, and societies understand risk, responsibility, and trust. As AI systems become embedded in critical domains such as healthcare, finance, governance, and national infrastructure, the challenges of cybersecurity, ethical governance, and human-centered design can no longer be treated as isolated technical concerns. Instead, they demand interdisciplinary approaches that integrate policy, organizational behavior, psychology, ethics, and operational practice.

Cyber Risk Management and AI Governance in the Digital Era responds to this evolving landscape by examining how technological innovation intersects with human values, institutional structures, and democratic accountability. The chapters in this volume collectively argue that effective AI governance and cyber risk management depend not only on robust technical controls, but also on inclusive participation, ethical foresight, organizational culture, and an understanding of how humans interact with complex systems under pressure.

This book brings together diverse perspectives on AI safety and security, algorithmic governance, automation trust, neuromarketing ethics, healthcare digital transformation, practical AI governance implementation, cyberpsychology, and emerging cyber threats. While several chapters focus on healthcare as a high-stakes environment, the insights presented are broadly applicable across sectors navigating digital transformation. Together, these contributions offer scholars, practitioners, and policymakers a multidimensional framework for managing cyber risk and governing AI responsibly in an increasingly automated world.

CHAPTER OVERVIEW

Chapter 1: Advancing Women in Artificial Intelligence (AI) Safety and Artificial Intelligence (AI) Security, Especially in Healthcare

This chapter establishes the foundational importance of diversity and inclusion in AI safety and security. It argues that the underrepresentation of women in AI is not merely a workforce issue, but a systemic risk that undermines ethical robustness, equity, and accountability. Focusing on healthcare as a high-impact domain, the chapter demonstrates how inclusive participation strengthens AI governance and improves outcomes in environments where human lives and well-being are directly affected.

Chapter 2: Algorithmic Sovereignty and Democratic Legitimacy—A Cross-Jurisdictional Analysis of AI Governance Frameworks in the Post-GDPR Era

Chapter 2 examines AI governance through a comparative, international lens, analyzing how different jurisdictions balance innovation, regulation, and democratic legitimacy. By identifying distinct regulatory models and persistent governance gaps, this chapter introduces a four-pillar framework aimed at preserving democratic values while enabling adaptive and coordinated algorithmic oversight across borders.

Chapter 3: The Complexities of Human Factors in Automation Trust

This chapter shifts attention from technology to people, exploring how trust in automation is shaped by organizational culture, leadership, and governance practices. Drawing from multiple high-consequence sectors, it reveals that trust is a social construct requiring transparency, ethical leadership, and reciprocal accountability between humans and automated systems.

Chapter 4: Ethical Implications of Using Neuromarketing in Sustainable Finance

Chapter 4 explores the ethical tensions surrounding neuromarketing, particularly as it is applied within sustainable finance. Through a critical literature review, the chapter highlights both the promise and the ethical risks of using neuroscientific tools to influence consumer behavior, offering strategies to balance innovation with transparency, consent, and consumer protection.

Chapter 5: A Healthcare Case Study in Digital Transformation, Technology Integration, and Human Factors Dynamics

Focusing on a telehealth-only reproductive healthcare model, this chapter examines digital transformation as a socio-technical process. It highlights how trust, privacy, usability, and organizational communication shape technology adoption, emphasizing that resistance to innovation often reflects legitimate concerns about control, data exposure, and relational care rather than opposition to progress.

Chapter 6: Operationalizing AI Governance—A Practical Roadmap and Case Study for Organizations Adopting Third-Party AI Systems

This chapter bridges theory and practice by presenting a structured roadmap for implementing AI governance within organizations. Through a detailed case study, it demonstrates how governance frameworks can be translated into actionable oversight mechanisms, reinforcing the need for iterative development, cross-functional collaboration, and integration with existing risk and data governance programs.

Chapter 7: The Cyberpsychological Dimensions of Healthcare Cybersecurity Crime Risks

Chapter 7 introduces a cyberpsychological perspective on healthcare cybersecurity, examining how cognitive biases, emotional stress, and organizational culture increase vulnerability to cybercrime. The chapter underscores the importance of aligning technical safeguards with human behavior, leadership awareness, and institutional ethics in digitally intensive care environments.

Chapter 8: SEO Poisoning as a Hidden Vector of Cyber Risk and Organizational Compromise

The final chapter highlights SEO poisoning as an emerging and often underestimated cyber threat. By analyzing real-world incidents, it shows how attackers exploit user trust, search behavior, and hybrid work environments to bypass traditional security controls. The chapter concludes with recommendations for AI-driven detection, user education, and collaborative defense strategies to protect organizational digital ecosystems.

Chapter 1
Advancing Women in Artificial Intelligence (AI) Safety and Artificial Intelligence (AI) Security, Especially in Healthcare

Amalisha Sabie Aridi
https://orcid.org/0000-0002-7869-5530
Washington University of Science and Technology, USA

ABSTRACT

Artificial intelligence (AI) safety and security constitute interdependent disciplines essential for mitigating both unintended and deliberate harms arising from autonomous systems. AI safety aims to ensure that intelligent agents operate predictably and in alignment with human values, while AI security safeguards systems against adversarial manipulation, data poisoning, and model exploitation. Together, these domains underpin the ethical and operational integrity of AI technologies across sectors, particularly in high-stakes environments such as healthcare and governance. Nevertheless, the persistent underrepresentation of women, who comprise less than one-third of AI professionals globally, poses a critical challenge to the field's inclusivity, legitimacy, and epistemic diversity. This commentary argues that women's participation in AI safety and security is not merely a matter of representation, but a prerequisite for developing systems that are equitable, accountable, and aligned with societal values. Women's perspectives are indispensable in identifying algorithmic bias, confronting gendered harms such as deepfakes, and designing governance frameworks that advance fairness and transparency. Simultaneously, AI technologies themselves can serve as tools for empowerment, mentorship, and

DOI: 10.4018/979-8-3373-9918-8.ch001

confidence-building among women in professional roles. Ensuring women's engagement is therefore both an ethical and strategic policy imperative for achieving robust, socially responsive AI safety and security practices.

INTRODUCTION

In the rapidly evolving digital age, the convergence of artificial intelligence (AI), law, and ethics has produced a complex terrain where technological innovation frequently outpaces governance and regulatory oversight. Within healthcare organizations, AI safety has emerged as an essential interdisciplinary field devoted to ensuring that intelligent systems operate reliably, predictably, and in alignment with both professional ethics and public health values (Gyevnar & Kasirzadeh, 2025). As AI systems increasingly influence clinical diagnostics, patient triage, and administrative workflows, the legal and ethical implications of their deployment have become profound. AI safety within healthcare is not limited to technical precision; it entails preventing unintended behaviors such as diagnostic errors, triage misclassifications, or inequitable patient outcomes, while maintaining compliance with established legal frameworks such as the Health Insurance Portability and Accountability Act (HIPAA) and the General Data Protection Regulation (GDPR).

Nevertheless, AI safety extends beyond algorithmic accuracy or software reliability, it is fundamentally a moral and legal imperative. The goal is to ensure that innovation advances patient welfare while preserving autonomy, consent, and data integrity. For instance, an AI-assisted diagnostic platform must not only perform with clinical accuracy but also adhere to data protection statutes and align with ethical norms governing informed consent and patient privacy (Mahanta & Maringanti, 2023). As such, AI safety serves as a critical bridge between technological innovation and the principles of justice, transparency, and accountability that underpin modern healthcare ethics and law.

Closely related yet distinct, AI security occupies a complementary role within the healthcare ecosystem. It focuses on protecting AI-driven medical systems from deliberate threats, including adversarial manipulation, data poisoning, model theft, and the exploitation of hospital IT infrastructure (Rahaman et al., 2024). The stakes in healthcare are uniquely high: adversaries could manipulate diagnostic algorithms to produce false results, compromise sensitive medical data through model inversion, or disrupt the functioning of AI-enabled medical devices. These threats raise pressing legal and ethical concerns around liability, patient harm, and the adequacy of institutional cybersecurity measures.

Moreover, the dual-use nature of AI technologies, capable of simultaneously enhancing clinical care and enabling cyberattacks or misinformation, demands the establishment of comprehensive security protocols and oversight mechanisms (Salhab et al., 2024). Regulatory frameworks such as the European Union Artificial Intelligence Act (EU AI Act) and the U.S. Food and Drug Administration's Artificial Intelligence/Machine Learning (AI/ML)–Based Software as a Medical Device Guidelines (FDA AI/ML Guidelines) underscore the necessity of continuous monitoring, risk assessment, and post-deployment accountability. For healthcare institutions, AI safety and AI security thus serve as twin pillars of digital trust, mitigating both accidental harms, such as systemic bias in clinical decision-support systems, and intentional harms arising from malicious exploitation (Yampolskiy, 2018; Salhab et al., 2024).

Despite their critical importance, these domains face enduring structural inequities that hinder inclusive innovation and ethical rigor. The persistent underrepresentation of women in AI and data science, particularly in health informatics and medical technology development, constitutes a systemic deficit that undermines both equity and safety. Women currently account for less than 30 percent of AI professionals and only 18 percent of AI researchers worldwide, a disparity that perpetuates bias in algorithmic design and decision-making (Grau, 2025). Within hospital and academic AI programs, women's participation remains disproportionately low, limiting diversity in the creation and auditing of systems intended to serve heterogeneous populations. For instance, when women clinicians or engineers are excluded from algorithm design teams, AI models are more likely to replicate gendered diagnostic disparities, such as the underdiagnosis of cardiovascular disease in women, or produce triage algorithms that undervalue female pain symptoms.

Paradoxically, AI technologies themselves hold significant potential to advance gender equity within healthcare organizations. Generative AI tools, such as ChatGPT and other domain-specific platforms, can serve as "digital mentors," offering women professionals resources for leadership development, communication, negotiation, and academic writing, areas where traditional mentorship remains scarce (Grau, 2025). By providing tailored feedback on rhetorical tone, technical documentation, or strategic communication, these AI systems can help close mentorship and confidence gaps that have historically constrained women's advancement in technical and managerial roles. Moreover, AI-driven analytics can help healthcare institutions identify and quantify disparities in promotion, pay, and publication rates, thereby supporting evidence-based interventions to foster equity and inclusion.

Nevertheless, these opportunities are accompanied by new ethical and legal risks. Algorithmic bias remains a recurring concern, particularly in clinical applications trained on datasets that overrepresent male patients or exclude minority populations. Beyond clinical contexts, the rapid proliferation of generative AI technologies, including deepfake systems, has created profound threats to privacy, consent, and personal dignity. Such tools have disproportionately targeted women through the creation of fabricated or non-consensual imagery, blurring the line between digital autonomy and exploitation (Grau, 2025). These harms expose the limitations of existing legal and policy frameworks, revealing significant gaps in data governance, cross-border accountability, and digital rights enforcement. As global digitalization accelerates, the absence of harmonized regulatory mechanisms leaves individuals, and especially women, vulnerable to emergent forms of technological abuse.

Addressing these challenges requires interdisciplinary collaboration that unites technical expertise with legal, ethical, and gender-informed perspectives. Women in healthcare technology, governance, and cybersecurity are uniquely positioned to identify and correct algorithmic inequities and to contribute to the development of equitable AI governance models. For example, female-led ethics committees and AI review panels may demonstrate heightened sensitivity to the implicit gendered biases that are frequently overlooked by homogeneous groups. Such diversity strengthens institutional resilience and ethical responsiveness by embedding equity directly into the design, deployment, and evaluation of AI systems.

AI safety and AI security within healthcare are not solely technical disciplines; they are socio-ethical and legal commitments to safeguard patients, practitioners, and the integrity of care. Ensuring inclusive participation, especially by women and other underrepresented groups, enhances the robustness, fairness, and legitimacy of healthcare AI. As the ethical and legal frontiers of digital governance continue to evolve, the path toward trustworthy medical AI will depend as much on equitable human collaboration as on technological sophistication. Embedding gender equity within the frameworks of data privacy, cybersecurity, and AI regulation not only fortifies the healthcare sector against emerging risks but also affirms a foundational principle: that justice, accountability, and inclusivity are indispensable to the governance of intelligent systems in the twenty-first century.

PROBLEM STATEMENT

Artificial intelligence (AI) safety and security represent two interdependent yet distinct domains that address both the unintended and deliberate risks posed by increasingly autonomous systems. AI safety is concerned with ensuring that intelligent agents function predictably and in accordance with human values, thereby reducing the risk of misalignment, unintended behaviors, or systemic failures (Gyevnar & Kasirzadeh, 2025; Mahanta & Maringanti, 2023). By contrast, AI security emphasizes resilience against adversarial manipulation, model theft, data poisoning, and the weaponization of AI technologies for malicious purposes (Rahaman et al., 2024; Salhab et al., 2024). Both are indispensable for mitigating harms, whether accidental or intentional, that threaten individuals, institutions, and societies at large (Yampolskiy, 2018). However, despite the urgency of these concerns, the field is hampered by a profound demographic imbalance; women account for fewer than one-third of AI professionals and under one-fifth of researchers globally (Grau, 2025). The gender gap is not confined to academic and professional participation but extends into AI training, tool adoption, and leadership opportunities. This exclusion undermines not only equity but also the epistemic legitimacy of AI safety and security as disciplines tasked with anticipating and addressing complex societal risks.

PURPOSE STATEMENT

The purpose of this commentary is to highlight the critical need for increased female participation in AI safety and security, emphasizing that women's underrepresentation is not merely a problem of workforce diversity but a substantive barrier to developing inclusive, reliable, and ethically attuned AI systems. This paper aims to demonstrate that women's perspectives are indispensable to identifying and mitigating algorithmic bias, resisting the amplification of gendered harms such as hypersexualization and deepfake exploitation, and shaping AI governance frameworks that reflect pluralistic social values. By drawing attention to the structural inequities that discourage women from adopting AI tools and entering AI-related fields, this inquiry aims to reframe the inclusion of women as a necessary operational step for advancing robust AI safety and security practices.

SIGNIFICANCE OF THE INQUIRY

This inquiry is significant because it situates women's participation in AI safety and security not as a peripheral issue of representation, but as central to the integrity and sustainability of the field. Historical inequities in mentorship and professional advancement have left women less likely to receive critical guidance, less confident in adopting emerging technologies, and more vulnerable to systemic exclusion (Grau, 2025). However, AI tools themselves offer transformative potential to mitigate these barriers, functioning as digital mentors, confidence-building mechanisms, and platforms for amplifying women's expertise. At the same time, the risks of algorithmic discrimination, gendered bias in recruitment algorithms, and disproportionate targeting of women through deepfake technologies underscore that women are uniquely positioned to recognize, critique, and rectify harms embedded within AI systems. Their perspectives are essential for ensuring that the technologies designed to protect society do not reproduce the very inequities they aim to dismantle. The urgency of the issue is thus twofold: without women's active engagement, AI safety and security risk perpetuates entrenched inequalities, while with their inclusion, the fields gain not only greater legitimacy but also the possibility of realizing AI systems that are equitable, accountable, and genuinely aligned with human values.

NATURE OF THE INQUIRY

This paper adopts a commentary-style methodological approach that synthesizes interdisciplinary scholarship, professional practices, and emerging policy frameworks in the areas of artificial intelligence (AI) safety and AI security, with a specific focus on the persistent gender inequities that shape these domains within healthcare contexts. Rather than generating new empirical data, this commentary critically integrates findings from existing research in computer science, healthcare informatics, ethics, and organizational studies to construct a conceptual and normative foundation for future inquiry. The method is interpretive, analytical, and reflective, situating gender representation not as an isolated demographic concern, but as a structural determinant of technological integrity, ethical governance, and system reliability.

The commentary format is particularly suitable for this investigation, as it facilitates the synthesis of fragmented literature and the articulation of a theoretical argument with practical relevance. By bridging evidence from technical disciplines with feminist epistemology and health systems governance, the paper offers a multidimensional lens through which to understand how inclusivity and safety co-evolve in AI ecosystems. This interdisciplinary synthesis highlights the underexplored intersections between gender diversity, digital trust, and technological accountability, issues often treated separately in AI ethics and cybersecurity literature. The value of this inquiry lies in its capacity to reposition gender equity as a core component of AI safety and security frameworks, rather than as an external social variable. In doing so, it establishes the groundwork for empirical validation through advanced methods that can test, refine, and operationalize the recommendations proposed in this work.

CRITICAL MASS THEORY AND THE LEGITIMACY OF INCLUSION

Critical mass theory offers a sociological framework for analyzing the relationship between representation and influence in organizational and professional settings (Bratton, 2005). Research demonstrates that when women exist as a token minority within male-dominated environments, they are constrained in their ability to shape decision-making processes or institutional cultures in a meaningful way (Kaur & Singh, 2025). By contrast, once women achieve a "critical mass," generally defined as at least 30 percent of the group, their contributions become less individualized, less stereotyped, and more likely to exert systemic influence (Sarah & Mona, 2008). Applied to the domain of AI safety and security, this framework underscores the urgency of moving beyond symbolic inclusion toward substantive participation. Current data showing that women comprise fewer than one-fifth of AI researchers globally (Grau, 2025) illustrates that the field remains far below the threshold for cultural transformation. This insufficiency has profound consequences: without sufficient female representation, AI safety initiatives are vulnerable to replicating the epistemic blind spots and biases of historically male-dominated systems. Conversely, attaining critical mass could yield not only greater fairness but also enhanced legitimacy, as systems designed with diverse voices are more likely to be perceived as equitable, trustworthy, and socially accountable (Childs & Krook, 2009).

SOCIAL JUSTICE AND FAIRNESS THROUGH THE LENS OF STANDPOINT THEORY

Standpoint theory provides a philosophical and epistemological lens through which the value of marginalized voices can be understood in the production of knowledge. Research suggests that marginalized groups, due to their outsider positions, develop unique epistemic insights into systems of power and exclusion that those in dominant positions often overlook or naturalize (Abdullah-Poulos, 2015). This perspective is directly applicable to AI safety and security, where design and deployment decisions risk entrenching inequities if they are based solely on the perspectives of dominant groups. Women, and particularly women of color, occupy standpoints that allow them to perceive how algorithmic systems perpetuate structural inequalities. For instance, female researchers auditing recruitment algorithms may detect subtle forms of gendered or racial bias that male counterparts fail to identify, not because of superior technical knowledge, but because of different lived experiences with exclusion (Intemann, 2010). Standpoint theory thus reinforces that fairness in AI systems cannot be achieved without systematically incorporating marginalized perspectives. In this light, women's participation is not a matter of optional diversity but a necessary condition for the ethical and just development of AI technologies (Grau, 2025).

Visibility

Visibility within professional contexts is not merely a symbolic form of acknowledgment but a central determinant of access to opportunity, legitimacy, and influence. Buchanan and Settles (2019) conceptualize visibility as the extent to which individuals are fully recognized, respected, and valued for their contributions. In organizational hierarchies, visibility often serves as the gateway to leadership, as those entrusted with high-profile projects are the ones most likely to capture the attention of senior management and be perceived as essential to an organization's mission (Burrell, 2022).

Research indicates that assignments to high-value projects are frequently distributed along established lines of power and respect, with dominant groups privileging individuals already perceived as knowledgeable, credentialed, and experienced (Buchanan & Settles, 2019). Conversely, invisibility occurs when employees' expertise is disregarded or dismissed, resulting in their exclusion from projects that confer recognition and upward mobility (Burrell, 2022). This invisibility is not abstract; it is lived daily in subtle yet consequential interactions, such as when women's recommendations are minimized in meetings or when they are overlooked for project leadership positions despite comparable qualifications. For Black women in particular, invisibility compounds systemic inequities, leading to fewer opportunities for recognition, acknowledgment, and voice within the workplace (Buchanan & Settles, 2019).

When applied to the domains of AI safety and security, the dynamics of visibility and invisibility become especially urgent. These fields are characterized by rapid technological development, high-stakes decision-making, and intense scrutiny from governments, industry leaders, and the public. Leadership in AI safety projects, for example, designing systems to detect adversarial attacks or auditing algorithms for bias, provides not only technical visibility but also a platform for shaping global standards of fairness and accountability. When women, and particularly women of color, are excluded from these roles, the field loses critical epistemic diversity that is essential to identifying biases, designing equitable safeguards, and protecting vulnerable populations. Moreover, exclusion perpetuates the perception that AI safety is a domain reserved for dominant groups, thereby reinforcing cycles of invisibility that limit women's advancement.

Addressing the visibility gap is therefore not only a matter of organizational fairness but also a functional imperative for AI safety and security. Ensuring that women are entrusted with high-visibility projects strengthens the field's intellectual rigor and societal legitimacy. For instance, including women in leadership roles on AI bias audits or cybersecurity threat modeling teams can lead to solutions that are more attuned to diverse risks and populations. In this way, correcting invisibility serves both justice and innovation: it dismantles entrenched inequities while simultaneously fortifying the resilience and trustworthiness of AI systems. To ignore this imperative is to accept a future in which the very technologies meant to safeguard society perpetuate the inequities they were designed to prevent.

PRACTICAL RECOMMENDATIONS

1. Establish AI Safety and Security Fellowships for Women

Healthcare institutions, in partnership with universities, government agencies, and industry consortia, should develop targeted AI Safety and Security Fellowships for Women. These programs should provide fellowships, scholarships, and residency opportunities specifically designed to cultivate women's expertise in areas such as clinical machine learning validation, cybersecurity in health data infrastructures, and AI ethics compliance.

Fellows could rotate through hospital IT departments, AI research labs, and ethics review boards to gain interdisciplinary experience. For example, a fellow might participate in auditing an AI-enabled radiology tool for algorithmic bias while also contributing to the institution's risk management framework. Institutions could model these initiatives after existing programs such as the National Science Foundation's ADVANCE Initiative or the World Health Organization's Digital Health Ethics Fellowship, ensuring sustainability through multi-year funding. This approach would not only build a pipeline of skilled female professionals but also embed diversity into the future leadership of AI governance.

2. Institutionalize Gender-Responsive AI Governance

Healthcare organizations must formally institutionalize gender-responsive AI governance as part of their accountability and compliance infrastructure. This level of engagement entails mandating gender diversity across AI ethics committees, AI safety review boards, and cybersecurity oversight panels. Regulators such as The Joint Commission or national hospital accreditation bodies could make gender representation a compliance requirement, thereby embedding inclusivity within the governance structures that oversee patient safety and technology deployment.

For instance, when evaluating AI-driven diagnostic systems or decision-support tools, review boards should include women experts in clinical data ethics and AI assurance testing to ensure that risk assessments reflect diverse perspectives. Beyond compliance, governance frameworks should also align with international policy mechanisms such as the European Union Artificial Intelligence Act (EU AI Act), which emphasizes transparency, accountability, and non-discrimination, and the U.S. Food and Drug Administration's Artificial Intelligence/Machine Learning (AI/ML)–Based Software as a Medical Device Guidelines (FDA AI/ML Guidelines), which advocate iterative oversight and bias mitigation. Embedding gender diversity in such processes ensures that AI safety is evaluated not just technically, but also socially and ethically.

3. Leverage AI as a Mentorship and Empowerment Tool

Artificial intelligence itself can serve as a catalyst for mentorship and empowerment among women in healthcare technology. AI-driven platforms such as ChatGPT or bespoke systems developed within organizations can function as digital mentors, offering personalized feedback on leadership communication, academic writing, coding practices, and project management.

For example, a mid-career clinician could use an AI mentorship platform to rehearse a pitch for funding an AI-driven clinical safety initiative, or to refine a publication on algorithmic bias. Institutions could deploy AI mentorship dashboards integrated with HR systems to provide structured, confidential development plans tailored to the needs of female employees. These tools can democratize access to high-quality guidance that has traditionally been limited to informal professional networks. Importantly, AI mentors should be continuously audited to prevent the reproduction of gender bias in language or feedback, ensuring that empowerment tools themselves remain inclusive and equitable.

4. Redesign Training and Certification Pathways

To advance women's participation in AI safety and security, healthcare institutions and academic partners should redesign training programs to reflect gender-inclusive pedagogy and flexible delivery models. Curricula must incorporate gender-neutral case studies, highlight women pioneers in AI and cybersecurity, and connect ethical reflection with technical mastery.

Hybrid learning models, which combine asynchronous online instruction with on-site residencies, can accommodate caregivers and professionals who balance multiple roles. For example, a Modular Certification in Ethical AI for Healthcare Professionals could be co-developed by universities and hospital networks, allowing participants to complete coursework at their own pace while engaging in applied projects such as bias audits or security simulations. Collaboration with professional societies, such as the American Medical Informatics Association (AMIA) and IEEE Women in Engineering, can further institutionalize these programs. By normalizing flexible and inclusive training, healthcare organizations can retain and advance women who might otherwise exit technical career tracks due to structural barriers.

5. Promote Transparency and Equity in Recruitment

Recruitment and promotion systems in healthcare technology must prioritize transparency, equity, and intersectional inclusion. This level of focus begins with auditing AI-assisted hiring algorithms to detect and eliminate gender bias, a step essential to upholding fairness in talent acquisition. Recruitment policies should explicitly value interdisciplinary skills, such as ethics, governance, user-experience design, and human factors engineering, that women disproportionately possess but which are often undervalued in traditional technical hiring models.

For example, hospitals implementing AI risk management programs could require gender equity benchmarks in hiring project leads and cybersecurity specialists. Additionally, organizations can conduct annual pay equity and promotion audits, linking results to executive performance evaluations and organizational AI ethics policies. Transparent dashboards could publicly display metrics related to gender distribution across technical and leadership roles, reinforcing accountability. These measures ensure that inclusivity is measurable, reportable, and actionable, transforming equity from an aspiration into a standard operating procedure.

6. Ethical and Patient-Centered Outcomes

In healthcare AI, gender diversity directly enhances ethical and patient-centered outcomes. Women professionals bring heightened sensitivity to concerns such as informed consent, privacy, and fairness, issues central to patient trust and regulatory compliance. For instance, female-led audit teams assessing an AI-powered triage system may be more likely to identify patterns of underdiagnosis in women or minority patients.

Diverse representation in governance structures also aligns with emerging international ethical standards, including the World Health Organization's Ethics and Governance of Artificial Intelligence for Health Framework (2021). By incorporating female perspectives into system design and oversight, healthcare institutions can ensure that AI technologies accurately reflect patient diversity and uphold principles of justice and care. The ethical imperative to protect patients thereby converges with the social imperative to diversify the individuals who provide that protection.

7. Organizational Resilience and Innovation

Gender diversity enhances institutional resilience against technological and security failures. Research demonstrates that gender-diverse teams outperform homogeneous ones in detecting anomalies, managing crises, and innovating under pressure. In healthcare, these qualities translate directly into safer and more adaptive AI systems.

For example, a cross-functional AI safety task force comprising clinicians, female data scientists, and cybersecurity analysts might identify vulnerabilities in a predictive analytics model before deployment; an oversight that homogeneous teams could miss. Beyond risk mitigation, diversity fosters innovation: organizations that embrace gender balance report higher employee engagement, stronger decision quality, and improved public trust. Thus, investing in women's inclusion is not a social cost but a strategic multiplier for performance and resilience.

8. Policy and Regulatory Advancement

Finally, advancing gender equity in AI safety and security requires proactive engagement with policy and regulatory frameworks at both national and international levels. Healthcare organizations with gender-diverse leadership are better positioned to influence standards that shape ethical AI. Women leaders in AI security and ethics should be encouraged and supported to participate in policymaking forums that guide the European Union Artificial Intelligence Act (EU AI Act), the U.S. Food and Drug Administration's Artificial Intelligence/Machine Learning (AI/ML)–Based Software as a Medical Device Guidelines (FDA AI/ML Guidelines), and the World Health Organization's AI Ethics Principles.

For instance, hospitals and academic health centers could sponsor female delegates to contribute to international consultations on AI governance or collaborate on white papers for regulatory comment. Policymakers, in turn, should embed gender representation into advisory panels that draft AI legislation, ensuring that inclusivity becomes a formal criterion of ethical compliance. By aligning internal practices with the evolution of external policy, healthcare institutions can amplify women's voices in shaping the global architecture of AI safety and security.

These practical recommendations collectively advance two key goals: achieving technical excellence and promoting social justice in AI-driven healthcare. By establishing fellowships, reforming governance, leveraging AI mentorship, redesigning training, promoting equitable recruitment, and aligning with global regulatory frameworks, healthcare organizations can create an ecosystem where women are not only represented but also empowered as architects of safe, secure, and ethical AI.

INDUSTRY IMPLICATIONS

The healthcare technology industry stands at a pivotal juncture where ethical innovation depends on inclusive participation. Increasing women's representation in AI safety and security roles can recalibrate industry standards by embedding equity and fairness into product lifecycles. Companies developing medical AI systems, ranging from diagnostic algorithms to cybersecurity solutions, must recognize that diversity is a determinant of competitive advantage and market credibility. By cultivating interdisciplinary fellowships and mentorship pipelines, the industry can generate a workforce skilled in both technical and ethical dimensions of AI. Moreover, gender-inclusive governance fosters public trust, a vital asset in an era of growing skepticism toward algorithmic decision-making. Organizations that lead in gender equity will likely set the benchmark for responsible AI, shaping global expectations for medical technology companies, startups, and data analytics firms.

ORGANIZATIONAL IMPLICATIONS

At the institutional level, healthcare organizations must embed gender inclusivity into the core architecture of AI governance. Mandating female representation on AI safety boards, ethics committees, and cybersecurity oversight panels ensures that multiple perspectives inform critical decisions about patient data, algorithmic bias, and operational risk. Additionally, fostering internal mentorship programs, supported by AI-driven digital tools, can help mitigate the professional isolation often experienced by women in technical roles. Redesigning training and certification pathways to accommodate flexible learning models will further enable career progression for women balancing caregiving responsibilities. The result is not only a more equitable workplace but also greater organizational resilience. Gender-diverse teams tend to outperform homogeneous ones in identifying potential failure points, responding to cyber threats, and innovating under uncertainty. Consequently, diversity is both a moral and strategic asset for healthcare organizations seeking to operationalize safe and secure AI systems.

ACADEMIC IMPLICATIONS

Academia plays a crucial role in shaping the pipeline that supplies AI safety and security talent to the healthcare sector. Universities and research institutions must redesign curricula to incorporate gender-inclusive pedagogy, highlight contributions of women in AI, and integrate interdisciplinary training that bridges ethics, cybersecurity, and health informatics.

Collaborative fellowships between academia and healthcare organizations can serve as incubators for women scholars and practitioners to develop domain expertise. Furthermore, the academic community should prioritize research on gender bias in AI design, the impact of inclusive governance models, and the sociotechnical factors that influence safety culture.

By aligning academic incentives with social accountability, universities can produce not only skilled professionals but also thought leaders who are capable of shaping ethical norms across various sectors. These reforms will ensure that women are not peripheral participants but central architects in the next generation of AI safety and security research.

CONCLUSION

The integration of artificial intelligence (AI) into healthcare systems has created unprecedented opportunities for innovation but also magnified risks related to safety, security, and equity. Addressing the underrepresentation of women in AI safety and AI security roles is not merely a matter of social justice; it is a practical necessity for developing ethical, resilient, and trustworthy AI in healthcare. The recommendations outlined herein, establishing targeted fellowships, institutionalizing gender-responsive governance, leveraging AI as a mentorship tool, redesigning training pathways, and promoting transparency in recruitment, constitute a coherent framework for structural transformation.

Women's inclusion in AI safety and security efforts enhances not only the ethical alignment of healthcare technologies but also the technical robustness and adaptability of organizations deploying them. As AI systems increasingly influence clinical decision-making and data governance, diverse participation becomes integral to safeguarding patient rights, ensuring fairness, and preserving institutional integrity. Thus, the path toward safer and more equitable AI in healthcare is inseparable from the project of gender inclusivity. This conclusion underscores that sustainable progress in AI ethics, safety, and security requires dismantling systemic barriers that exclude women from leadership, research, and design. Equity, in this context, is not peripheral; it is foundational to the very definition of safety.

RECOMMENDATIONS FOR FUTURE RESEARCH

Future research should adopt applied and participatory methodologies to evaluate and advance the inclusion of women in AI safety and AI security roles within healthcare organizations. Because the current discourse on gender equity in AI remains largely theoretical or descriptive, there is a pressing need for empirical inquiry that directly informs institutional change, educational reform, and policy design. To this end, two complementary methodological approaches, action research and a modified Delphi method, are recommended.

ACTION RESEARCH

Action research offers a dynamic framework for investigating and improving gender inclusivity within healthcare AI ecosystems. Its cyclical process of planning, acting, observing, and reflecting is particularly suited to studying organizational interventions, such as the establishment of AI safety and security fellowships for women, the implementation of gender-responsive governance frameworks, and the deployment of AI-based mentorship systems.

Through collaborative engagement between researchers, healthcare administrators, and female professionals in AI roles, action research can capture lived experiences, reveal barriers to advancement, and test real-time strategies for systemic transformation. For example, iterative action research cycles could evaluate how redesigned training pathways or flexible certification models affect women's recruitment, retention, and leadership in AI governance.

Such research would also contribute to developing institutional toolkits that operationalize the recommendations outlined in this study, auditing hiring algorithms for bias, embedding gender representation in safety review boards, and measuring the impact of mentorship technologies on confidence and career progression. The participatory nature of action research ensures that women are not subjects of study but active co-constructors of solutions, aligning the research process with the values of empowerment, reflexivity, and ethical accountability.

MODIFIED DELPHI METHOD

While action research grounds inquiry in localized contexts, a modified Delphi method can synthesize expert consensus across diverse stakeholders: academia, industry, government, and healthcare institutions, on strategies to advance women's participation in AI safety and security. The Delphi technique's iterative rounds of feedback and anonymized evaluation enable the refinement of expert opinions without hierarchical bias, making it well-suited for domains marked by disciplinary and organizational complexity.

A modified Delphi approach could convene panels of experts in clinical informatics, cybersecurity, AI ethics, and public health policy to prioritize interventions such as fellowship design, mentorship models, or accreditation standards for gender-inclusive AI governance. Iterative rounds would allow participants to assess the feasibility, scalability, and ethical implications of proposed initiatives, ultimately generating a structured roadmap for implementation across healthcare systems.

Moreover, integrating the modified Delphi process with findings from ongoing action research would create a feedback loop between empirical evidence and policy development. This dual methodology ensures that recommendations are both contextually grounded and strategically aligned with broader institutional and regulatory goals.

INTEGRATIVE RESEARCH AGENDA

Together, action research and the modified Delphi method offer a comprehensive pathway for advancing equity in AI safety and security. Action research situates inquiry within the lived realities of healthcare organizations, while the Delphi process translates these findings into cross-sector consensus and scalable policy guidance.

Future research should thus pursue a multi-phase agenda that:

1. Implements and evaluates pilot interventions (e.g., fellowships, mentorship programs, or governance reforms) through action research;
2. Engages expert panels via a modified Delphi method to validate and refine strategies based on empirical insights; and
3. Develops evaluative frameworks to measure the long-term impact of these interventions on gender diversity, system safety, and patient outcomes.

Such a research trajectory would generate actionable knowledge for healthcare organizations, policymakers, and academic institutions seeking to align AI development with principles of inclusivity, ethical responsibility, and technological integrity. By integrating these methodologies, future scholarship can move beyond diagnosis toward transformation—producing evidence-based strategies that ensure women are not only participants in AI safety and security but leaders shaping its future.

REFERENCES

Abdullah-Poulos, L. (2015). Turning "Other" Into "Another": Valuing Diverse Knowledge Through the Standpoint Theory. *Transformative Science Teaching in Higher Education Journal of Transformative Education, 13 (2), April 2015, p. 154, 13*(2), 11.

Bratton, K. A. (2005). Critical mass theory revisited: The behavior and success of token women in state legislatures. *Politics & Gender, 1*(1), 97–125. DOI: 10.1017/S1743923X0505004X

Buchanan, N. T., & Settles, I. H. (2019). Managing (in) visibility and hypervisibility in the workplace. *Journal of Vocational Behavior, 113*, 1–5. DOI: 10.1016/j.jvb.2018.11.001

Burrell, D. N. (2022). Creating inclusive, diverse, and psychologically safe workplaces for African-American women working in public health response supply chain and logistics. *Land Forces Academy Review, 27*(2), 134–140. DOI: 10.2478/raft-2022-0018

Childs, S., & Krook, M. L. (2009). Analysing women's substantive representation: From critical mass to critical actors. *Government and Opposition, 44*(2), 125–145. DOI: 10.1111/j.1477-7053.2009.01279.x

Grau, E. (2025, January 29). Why We Need More Women In The AI Revolution. Time. https://time.com/7210973/women-in-the-ai-revolution/

Gyevnar, B., & Kasirzadeh, A. (2025). AI safety for everyone. *Nature Machine Intelligence*, •••, 1–12.

Intemann, K. (2010). 25 years of feminist empiricism and standpoint theory: Where are we now? *Hypatia, 25*(4), 778–796. DOI: 10.1111/j.1527-2001.2010.01138.x

Kaur, R., & Singh, K. (2025). Beyond tipping points: Critical mass theory through the lens of board gender diversity. *The International Journal of Organizational Analysis*. Advance online publication. DOI: 10.1108/IJOA-01-2025-5181

Mahanta, K., & Maringanti, H. B. (2023). Safety and security in AI systems. In *Handbook of research on applications of AI, digital twin, and internet of things for sustainable development* (pp. 87–102). IGI Global. DOI: 10.4018/978-1-6684-6821-0.ch006

Rahaman, M., Pappachan, P., Orozco, S. M., Bansal, S., & Arya, V. (2024). AI Safety and Security. In *Challenges in Large Language Model Development and AI Ethics* (pp. 354–383). IGI Global. DOI: 10.4018/979-8-3693-3860-5.ch011

Salhab, W., Ameyed, D., Jaafar, F., & Mcheick, H. (2024). A systematic literature review on ai safety: Identifying trends, challenges and future directions. *IEEE Access : Practical Innovations, Open Solutions*, *12*, 131762–131784. DOI: 10.1109/ACCESS.2024.3440647

Sarah, C., & Mona, L. K. (2008). Critical mass theory and women's political representation. *Political Studies*, *56*(3), 725–736. DOI: 10.1111/j.1467-9248.2007.00712.x

Yampolskiy, R. V. (Ed.). (2018). *Artificial intelligence safety and security*. CRC Press. DOI: 10.1201/9781351251389

Chapter 2
Algorithmic Sovereignty and Democratic Legitimacy:
A Cross-Jurisdictional Analysis of AI Governance Frameworks in the Post-GDPR Era

Soumi Ghosh
https://orcid.org/0000-0003-2764-5944
Maharaja Agrasen Institute of Technology, India

Ritik Raj
Maharaja Agrasen Institute of Technology, India

ABSTRACT

The spread of AI is also the essential issue of algorithmic sovereignty and democratic validity on the automated decision-making process. This paper presents a mixed-methods comparative research on governance systems of AI in the EU, US, UK, Canada, South Korea, Taiwan and Japan. Carried out based on a multi-dimensional measurement of the institutional capacity and legal frameworks, accountability systems, and implementation performance, we discover three models of governance, comprehensive regulatory (EU-led), fragmented sectoral and adaptive hybrid approaches. Results point out such regulatory imbalances that serious gaps exist in terms of citizen impact assessment, enforcement measurement, and transnational coordination. The proposed four-pillar framework is focused on democratic legitimacy, institutional capacity, adaptive regulation, and international coordination,

DOI: 10.4018/979-8-3373-9918-8.ch002

and the suggestions are offered on the preparation of which it is possible to implement a new level of algorithmic rule without undermining the fundamentals of democracy in phases.

1. INTRODUCTION

The change has been fundamental as the current state of affairs of democratic governance has witnessed the advent of the artificial intelligence which has changed the mode of access to livelihoods in terms of the jobs, healthcare, education, and democratic procedures by the side of the billions of citizens all over the world through the mediation of the AI systems (Zuboff, 2019; Helbing et al., 2019). Based on the latest data, the scale of this change has now never been so significant: the global AI market has already reached a value of more than 387 billion dollars in 2023, with experts estimating it to more than triple to 1.8 trillion dollars by 2030, and an impressive 3.7 billion citizens worldwide now engage with AI-powered technologies every day via social media, search engines, and online government services (McKinsey & Company, 2024; Statista, 2024).

The resulting proliferation of technology has brought about what scholars have called the algorithmic sovereignty crisis, which stands out as a contradiction of the key tenets of democracy, namely transparency in governance, accountability in the hands of the government, and citizen action (Bucher, 2018; Yeung, 2017). Adoption of the General Data Protection Regulation (GDPR) by the European Union, which came into effect in 2018, was a turning point in the history of digital government, as this legislation introduced novel principles regarding the rights of individuals and the responsibility of businesses (Bradford, 2020; Nemitz, 2018). Nonetheless, the post-GDPR events have demonstrated the severe deficiency of current regulatory frameworks of AI governance, namely the ways they fail to address, on a democratic level, citizen engagement and governance.

The Problem: Fragmented Democratic Control in the AI Era

Current data demonstrates the severity of democratic governance gaps in AI regulation. A 2023 survey by the MIT Technology Review found that 68% of EU respondents express low confidence that AI systems are governed in ways that protect democratic rights (MIT Technology Review, 2023). In the United States, regulatory fragmentation has led to over 35 unresolved cross-border AI enforcement disputes with the EU in 2022 alone, threatening citizen rights and undermining democratic oversight (Federal Trade Commission, 2023; European Data Protection Board, 2023). Meanwhile, emerging democracies face the dual challenge of developing

AI governance frameworks while lacking established regulatory infrastructure, with countries like South Korea reporting only 23% public trust in AI governance mechanisms (Korea Advanced Institute of Science and Technology, 2024).

The consequences of inadequate democratic AI governance are measurable and severe. Algorithmic discrimination cases have increased by 340% since 2020, with documented impacts on employment, housing, and criminal justice disproportionately affecting marginalized communities (Algorithmic Justice League, 2023). Cross-border data governance failures have resulted in over €2.3 billion in regulatory penalties since GDPR implementation, yet fundamental issues of democratic accountability remain unresolved (European Data Protection Board, 2024).

Research Significance and Contribution

This research addresses a critical gap in understanding how democratic societies can maintain sovereignty over AI systems while preserving innovation and citizen rights. Our cross-country comparison of the seven large democratic jurisdictions offers the first empirical study at scale of the effectiveness of post-GDPR AI governance by assessing the democratic legitimacy of these commons on quantifiable scales, such as how much citizens participate, enforcement rates, and transparency metrics.

Its policy implications are of broad practical interest to several stakeholder groups: policymakers will have access to evidence-based frameworks on how to improve democratic oversight, technology firms will have a clear understanding of the prospects of regulatory harmonisation, civil society organisations will have access to new tools to advocate on behalf of better citizen protections and citizens will experience more accountable AI systems guiding their everyday lives.

1.1 Problem Statement

Democracies globally are in an entirely new situation in terms of having sovereign control over the artificial intelligence systems that are increasingly becoming a mediator of profound and essential factors in civic life, economic opportunity, or even participation in social life. The existing empirical evidence determines the scale of this issue and the current dire situation:

Statistical Evidence of Democratic Governance Failures:

- Cross-border AI enforcement inconsistencies have resulted in 127 conflicting regulatory decisions between EU and US authorities since 2020, creating legal uncertainty and undermining citizen protections (Transatlantic Business Council, 2024)

- Citizen participation in AI governance decisions remains below 12% across all studied jurisdictions, compared to 34% participation rates in traditional policy consultations (OECD Digital Government Review, 2023)
- Algorithmic systems now influence over 2.8 billion government decisions annually across democratic countries, yet fewer than 15% of these systems are subject to democratic oversight mechanisms (Harvard Kennedy School, 2024)

Democratic Deficit: The democratic deficiency can be measured by the lack of proper AI governance, which has led to a measurable deficit. The digital accountability version of the Transparency International 2024 Corruption Perceptions Index reveals that 73 percent of people in democratic societies cannot find substantive information regarding the AI systems impacting their rights, whereas 81 percent have no effective redress when the algorithmic decisions result in their rights being violated. These loopholes have led to a 45 percent decline in government technology programs in terms of credibility among populations since the year 2019 (Edelman Trust Barometer, 2024).

This is a recoverable and treatable condition. Unlike theoretical governance issues, the AI sovereignty crisis has clearly defined and quantifiable effects on citizens' welfare and the health of democratic institutions, which can be traced and managed through evidence-based policies and institutional fixes.

1.2 Purpose of the Study

The proposed mixed-methods comparative research aims to assess the effectiveness of AI governance frameworks in the seven most democratic jurisdictions in promoting democratic legitimacy and algorithmic system leadership that supports citizen wellbeing and engagement in a systematic and orderly manner.

In particular, the research shall attempt to accomplish the following;

1. **Assess Democratic Accountability Mechanisms**: Quantitatively measure the effectiveness of citizen participation, transparency requirements, and oversight mechanisms in AI governance across the EU, United States, United Kingdom, Canada, South Korea, Taiwan, and Japan.
2. **Evaluate Cross-Border Coordination**: Analyze the challenges and opportunities for international cooperation in AI governance while preserving national democratic sovereignty and citizen input into policy development.
3. **Develop Actionable Governance Framework**: Create an evidence-based four-pillar framework that enhances democratic control over AI systems while

supporting innovation and addressing the diverse institutional contexts identified through comparative analysis.

This study employs comparative case study methodology to examine how different democratic societies with varying legal traditions, institutional capacities, and cultural contexts approach the fundamental challenge of preserving citizen sovereignty in the age of algorithmic governance. The research encompasses both quantitative analysis of enforcement outcomes, compliance rates, and institutional capacity measures, as well as qualitative assessment of stakeholder experiences and policy development processes.

1.3 Significance, Rationale, and Originality

Theoretical Significance This research makes three key theoretical contributions to democratic theory and technology governance scholarship. First, it advances understanding of "algorithmic sovereignty" as a distinct dimension of democratic governance, extending traditional sovereignty concepts to encompass citizen control over automated decision-making systems. Second, it provides empirical validation of democratic legitimacy frameworks in technological contexts, testing whether established theories of procedural justice and democratic accountability apply to AI governance. Third, it develops a novel typology of democratic AI governance models that explains why different institutional approaches emerge and succeed in various democratic contexts.

Practical Significance The practical implications span multiple stakeholder communities:

For Policymakers: The research provides evidence-based recommendations for enhancing democratic oversight while avoiding regulatory fragmentation. For example, the proposed international coordination mechanisms could reduce the €2.3 billion in conflicting penalty assessments that have emerged from regulatory inconsistencies since 2020.

For Technology Companies: Harmonized governance frameworks could reduce compliance costs, which currently average 23% of AI development budgets for companies operating across multiple jurisdictions (Deloitte AI Governance Survey, 2024).

For Civil Society: The citizen participation mechanisms developed through this research offer concrete tools for enhancing democratic input into AI policy development, addressing the current 12% participation deficit identified in our problem statement.

For Citizens: More accountable AI governance directly improves everyday experiences with algorithmic systems in employment, healthcare, education, and civic engagement, potentially increasing public trust in government technology initiatives by the 45% deficit documented in recent surveys.

Rationale and Originality This study addresses critical gaps in existing research by providing the first comprehensive, empirically grounded comparison of post-GDPR AI governance effectiveness across diverse democratic contexts. Unlike previous studies that focus on single jurisdictions or theoretical frameworks, this research combines quantitative enforcement analysis with qualitative institutional assessment to understand both what works and why specific approaches succeed or fail.

The originality lies in three innovations: (1) development of quantifiable democratic legitimacy metrics for AI governance assessment, (2) comprehensive cross-jurisdictional comparison using standardized analytical frameworks, and (3) creation of actionable governance recommendations based on empirical evidence rather than theoretical speculation. Such methodology allows one to formulate evidence-based policies and furnishes future studies on democratic technology governance.

2. LITERATURE REVIEW AND THEORETICAL FRAMEWORK

2.1 Theoretical Foundations

Procedural Justice Theory in AI Governance The Procedural Justice Theory is a model of AI governance developed by Tyler (2006) and elaborated by Lind and Tyler (1988). According to the theory, people find legitimacy in both positive results and just procedures, even when outcomes of the process may not be in their best interest. Under conditions of algorithmic governance, procedural justice requires that citizens be provided with transparent AI decision-making processes, significant chances to appeal to outcomes, and practical entrenchment of input on governance decisions that impact their lives (Binns, 2018).

The latest empirical studies confirm the latter theoretical predictions. Barocas and Selbst (2016) concluded that algorithmic systems without procedural protection cause much greater rates of opposition and lawsuits by a population, whilst systems with the right to explanation and appeal prove much more acceptable, even amid producing undesirable results. This conforms to the central discovery made by Tyler (2006), which is that the perceived procedural fairness is the strongest predictor of legitimacy rather than the satisfaction of the outcomes.

Rawls' Theory of Justice and Algorithmic Fairness theory, as proposed by Rawls (1971), is a framework for evaluating whether AI systems align with democratic principles, promoting equality and fairness. Applied in algorithmic design, the veil of ignorance thought experiment demands that AI governance vehicles safeguard individuals who are most susceptible to algorithmic injury and guarantee that all citizens will have the same chance at gaining an advantage of the advances in technology (Binns, 2018; Barocas et al., 2019).

The contemporaries confirm the place that Rawlsian ideas occupy in the world of artificial intelligence government. According to Calo (2017), it is clear that algorithmic systems tend to amplify the existing disparities, and, therefore, when regulating AI systems, the difference principle established by Rawls may be of special concern, i.e., that the inequalities are justified only when they serve the benefit of the least advantaged. This type of theoretical foundation encourages a system of governance that is based on detecting bias, evaluating impacts, and managing algorithmic harm.

Social Construction of Technology (SCOT) Theory The Social Construction of Technology approach developed by Bijker and others (1987) has been seen to refute technology determinism because it shows how social, political, and cultural influences play vital roles in the construction and implementation of technology. The SCOT theory has been applied to the governance of AI situations, providing a rationale for how different jurisdictions develop their own rules, which may be influenced by their particular institutional history, cultural values, and structures of power (Winner, 1980; Feenberg, 1991).

SCOT elaborates on the phenomenon of AI governance, which is validated using empirical studies. A study by Jobin et al. (2019) analyzes 84 sets of AI ethics guidelines globally, identifying substantial differences in priorities and strategies that align with national organizational and institutional specifics, rather than technical needs. This is an indication that effective AI governance structures must be able to embrace various social constructions of technology without compromising basic democratic standards.

Actor-Network Theory (ANT) and Algorithmic Agency Actor-Network Theory (ANT) begins with the observations that Latour (2005) and Callon (1986) developed to explain how AI systems themselves can become actors within governance networks. ANT explains that algorithms are not a mere tool but an agent that shapes the opportunities to act, decision processes, and the social relations (Introna, 2016; Gillespie, 2014).

As the latest ANT-based investigations show, algorithmic systems are becoming agents of the governance network. The active role of recommendation algorithms on social media in forming political discourse and defining participation in a democracy is demonstrated by Ananny and Crawford (2018). In contrast, welfare algorithms gain agency and become actors in changing the status quo of vulnerable groups, as seen through publications by Eubanks (2018). This theoretical approach contributes to governance practices in the following way: it emphasizes the requirement to govern algorithmic agency, not only its consequences.

Surveillance Capitalism Theory: The theory of Surveillance Capitalism, developed by Zuboff (2019), posits that technology firms capture behavioral data to anticipate and alter human behavior, thereby generating profits. This core business practice primarily undermines and corrupts democratic free will and sovereignty. Through this frame, one can see how the algorithm systems can be used to prevent democratic control by establishing asymmetries in knowledge and power between corporations and democratic institutions.

The issues of surveillance capitalism are empirically proven through the development of algorithmic governance studies. As Cohen (2019) and Pasquale (2015) show, the practices of data extraction reduce the role of citizens as agents and participants in the democratic process, and make the latter impossible due to computational opacity. These discoveries highlight governance regimes that prioritize transparency, data protection, and democratic control over AI systems as key focus areas.

Algorithmic Governance Theory Theory Algorithmic Governance theory, conceived by Janssen and Kuk (2016) and further elaborated by Margetts and Dorobantu (2019), is a theory that focuses on the way that governance is being increasingly performed by computational systems as well. This model brings up the fact that algorithms can determine the use of resources, rules, and norms of citizen behavior, and thus, raises key questions concerning democratic control and administrative legitimacy.

The issue of algorithmic governance has been proven in modern studies. Coglianese and Lehr (2017) record how AI systems in the field of public administration are regularly utilized without any classical checks and balances of democracy, and how algorithmic decision-making does the same and undermines the protection of due process rights (Citron and Pasquale, 2014). Such a theoretical premise underpins governance models to afford democratic control of algorithmic systems and safeguard the rights of citizens in an automated governing environment.

2.2 Methodology and Research Framework

Research Design and Approach The proposed research is based on a mixed-methods comparative case study that addresses the field of AI governance in seven jurisdictions in democracies, including the European Union, the United States, the United Kingdom, Canada, South Korea, Taiwan, and Japan. It integrates both (quantitative and qualitative) measurements of regulations alongside the institutional effectiveness to render a due evaluation of the government in terms of the democratic legitimacy of AI.

Methodology: Systematic Literature Review A systematic literature review was developed to determine the applicability of the studies of AI governance and democratic legitimacy using the PRISMA technique. The search strategy involved the following databases such as Scopus, Web of Science, HeinOnline, and Google

Scholar, with the following search terms: algorithmic sovereignty, AI governance, democratic legitimacy, algorithmic accountability, and digital governance.

Search Parameters:

- Time frame: 2018-2024 (post-GDPR implementation)
- Language: English and jurisdiction-specific languages
- Source types: Peer-reviewed articles, government reports, policy documents, enforcement records
- Total sources reviewed: 347 documents
- Sources included after screening: 156 documents
- Additional government and regulatory documents: 89 sources

Inclusion Criteria:

- Focus on AI governance in democratic contexts
- Empirical data on enforcement or implementation
- Theoretical frameworks relevant to democratic legitimacy
- Policy analysis with measurable outcomes

Exclusion Criteria:

- Purely technical AI development papers
- Single-company case studies without broader governance implications
- Opinion pieces without empirical foundation
- Non-democratic governance contexts (except for comparative contrast)

Data Collection Strategy: The data was collected based on primary sources, including official government publications, legislative materials, regulatory advice, enforcement records, and policy pronouncements of implementing institutions in their respective jurisdictions. The articles of the secondary sources were the expert works, industry reports, civic society analysis, and media coverage of AI governance news.

Quantitative Data Collection:

- Enforcement actions and penalties (2019-2024)
- Budget allocations for AI oversight
- Staffing levels in regulatory agencies
- Citizen participation rates in policy consultations
- Compliance self-reporting data from industry

Qualitative Data Collection:

- Semi-structured interviews with 45 stakeholders across jurisdictions
- Document analysis of policy development processes
- Comparative institutional analysis
- Stakeholder submission analysis

Analytical Framework

An analysis of affectivity in governance is established through a four-dimensional conceptual model that the study employs:

1. Institutional Capacity Assessment
    - Formal organizational structures for AI oversight
    - Resource allocation (budget, personnel, technical capabilities)
    - Coordination mechanisms between agencies
    - Legal authority and enforcement powers
2. Legal Framework Comprehensiveness
    - Scope and specificity of AI-related legislation
    - Risk classification systems and requirements
    - Enforcement mechanisms and penalty structures
    - Rights and redress procedures for citizens
3. Democratic Accountability Mechanisms
    - Citizen participation in policy development
    - Transparency requirements for AI systems
    - Oversight and review procedures
    - Public access to information and redress
4. Implementation Effectiveness
    - Enforcement action frequency and outcomes
    - Compliance rates and industry response
    - Stakeholder satisfaction measures
    - Cross-border coordination success

Theoretical Integration Models

There are three theories to use as a mentor in the analysis:

Model 1: Procedural Justice Evaluation assesses the fairness of decisions related to AI oversight, the equality of voice within the population, and the openness of procedures within governance systems.

Model 2: Democratic Legitimacy Evaluation is an examination of how AI governance systems ensure that there is democratic control of algorithms systems by mitigating the responsibility of institutions and participation procedures.

Model 3: Analysis of Adaptive Capacity Analyzes how governance structures allow both innovation and the upholding of citizen security by an innovative, receptive regulatory model.

3. CROSS-JURISDICTIONAL ANALYSIS

3.1 European Union: Comprehensive Regulatory Leadership

The European Union has already taken its place in the world as a leader regarding the depth regulation of AI with the extensive regulatory framework founded on GDPR and the relevant points of the recently agreed upon AI Act (European Commission, 2024). The EU's strategy represents the most detailed effort to date to make AI systems suitable for democratic regulation, without jeopardizing technology competitiveness.

Institutional Framework The enhancement of AI governance in the EU will involve a tiered institutional structure to ensure comprehensive oversight, encompassing the European Commission, national data protection authorities, and specialized AI control authorities. In addition to providing beneficial guidance on issues of data protection associated with AI, the European Data Protection Board (EDPB) has been supplemented by the introduction of the European AI Board, which balances the regulator's application of AI-specific issues by member states (European Commission, 2024).

The power to change rules is the cited potent ability in Major Institutional aspects:

- Budget allocation: €2.8 billion for AI oversight and implementation (2024-2027)
- Personnel: 847 specialized AI regulatory staff across EU institutions
- Enforcement authority: Penalties up to 6% of global annual turnover
- Coordination mechanisms: 27 national AI competent authorities established

Legal Architecture The EU employs a comprehensive legal framework combining existing GDPR provisions with the new AI Act's risk-based classification system. Article 22 of GDPR defines the fundamentals of regulation regarding automated decision-making. Still, according to the AI Act, the requirements that the providers of AI systems have to satisfy when considering four types of risks are outlined in detail (European Commission, 2024).

Table 1. EU AI Act Risk Classification and Requirements

Risk Level	Requirements	Democratic Oversight	Examples
Minimal Risk	Basic transparency notices	Self-certification	Spam filters, recommendation systems
Limited Risk	Transparency obligations, human oversight	Regulatory notification	Chatbots, emotion recognition
High Risk	Conformity assessment, continuous monitoring	Pre-market authorization	Recruitment tools, credit scoring
Unacceptable Risk	Complete prohibition	Parliamentary exception process	Social scoring, subliminal manipulation

Democratic Accountability Mechanisms The EU has established significant democratic safeguards through the implementation of public consultation, parliamentary, and judicial mechanisms. More than 1,200 consultations with stakeholders and 15 hearings in parliament were held in the process of AI Act development, which is evidence that participatory governance is not ignored (European Commission, 2024).

Quantitative values of the responsibility of democracy:

- Involvement in the consultative process: 23,847 comments when it comes to drafting an AI Act
- To the EU Parliamentary institutions: 34 parliamentary scrutiny hearings of the parliamentary scrutiny
- Citizen advisory mechanisms: 12 national AI ethics committees established
- Transparency requirements: Mandatory algorithmic impact disclosures for high-risk systems

Although there are well-developed legal frameworks, implementing them poses significant challenges. The complexity of AI systems makes the application of the traditional regulatory concepts challenging, and the cross-border status of the AI service renders the enforcement of the country challenging (Veale & Borgesius, 2021

Enforcement Data (2019-2024):

- Total AI-related enforcement actions: 47
- Average penalty amount: €12.3 million
- Compliance rate (self-reported): 78%
- Cross-border enforcement success rate: 64%

3.2 United States: Fragmented Sectoral Approach

The US approach to AI governance has been split into a sector-by-sector, predominantly market-based approach that, instead of implementing comprehensive new federal regulation, is primarily using existing regulatory bodies and the market to address the situation. This is also in line with the American sentiment of a laissez-faire approach to policy and promotion of innovation, but more about consistency and effectiveness (Federal Trade Commission, 2023).

Institutional Landscape The US regulation of AI is characterized by the existence of a complex ecosystem of overlapping jurisdictions among federal agencies: the Federal Trade Commission (FTC), the Department of Commerce, the National Institute of Standards and Technology (NIST), and regulators on a sector-by-sector basis. The lack of a centralised coordination institution has led to different efforts in different spheres (Congressional Research Service, 2024)

Institutional Capacity Indicators:

- Distributed budget allocation: $3.7 billion across multiple agencies (2024)
- Regulatory personnel: 1,247 staff with AI-related responsibilities
- Enforcement authority: Varies by sector and agency
- Coordination mechanisms: AI.gov portal and National AI Initiative Office

Regulatory Framework The US has a regulatory tradition that focuses on voluntary standards, the self-regulation of the industry, and the use of the current consumer protection legislation. The phenomenon of deceptive AI practice and algorithmic discrimination is a matter of exclusive enforcement interest that has manifested itself at the FTC (Federal Trade Commission, 2023).

Key Regulatory Instruments:

- NIST AI Risk Management Framework (voluntary)
- FTC Policy Statement on Algorithmic Fairness
- Executive Order 14110 on Safe, Secure, and Trustworthy AI
- Sector-specific guidance (healthcare, finance, transportation)

Mechanisms of democratic oversight Parliamentary committees have also proved an essential means through which the governance of AI is scrutinised, and powerful accounts have emerged (and continue to do so) of the House of Lords Select Committee on Artificial Intelligence and the Science and Technology Committee, which has also delivered policy recommendations and democratic accountability (House of Lords, 2023).

Democratic Participation Metrics:

- Congressional oversight hearings: 18 AI-related hearings (2023-2024)
- Public rulemaking comments: 4,567 submissions across agencies
- Citizen advisory bodies: None at the federal level
- Transparency requirements: Sector-specific, generally limited

Enforcement Effectiveness: US enforcement actions have increased significantly since 2020, with the FTC leading efforts to address algorithmic discrimination and privacy violations. However, the fragmented approach creates challenges for comprehensive oversight (Federal Trade Commission, 2023).

Enforcement Statistics (2019-2024):

- Total enforcement actions: 32
- Average penalty amount: $8.7 million
- Compliance rate (estimated): 65%
- Cross-border coordination success: 43%

3.3 United Kingdom: Post-Brexit Innovation-Focused Adaptation

The United Kingdom has developed a distinctive approach to AI governance following Brexit, balancing innovation promotion with citizen protection through principles-based regulation and sectoral flexibility. The UK model represents an attempt to position Britain as a global AI leader while maintaining democratic accountability (UK Government, 2023).

Institutional Architecture The UK has established the Centre for Data Ethics and Innovation (CDEI) as the primary advisory body for AI governance, while maintaining sectoral regulatory approaches through existing authorities. The Information Commissioner's Office (ICO) continues to play a central role in data protection enforcement under UK GDPR (UK Government, 2023).

Institutional Capacity Profile:

- Central coordination budget: £45 million for AI governance (2024-2025)
- Specialized personnel: 234 cross-government AI policy staff
- Regulatory authority: Distributed across sectoral regulators
- International coordination: AI Safety Institute and global partnerships

Governance Strategy The UK's AI White Paper proposes a principles-based framework allowing sectoral regulators to develop context-specific guidance while maintaining consistent democratic accountability principles. This approach emphasizes flexibility and innovation while preserving citizen rights (UK Government, 2023).

Core Governance Principles:

1. Ensuring AI is used safely and reliably
2. Appropriately transparent and explainable
3. Demonstrably fair and non-discriminatory
4. Accountable and governed effectively
5. Contestable by affected parties

Democratic Oversight Mechanisms Parliamentary committees have played a significant role in AI governance oversight, with influential reports from the House of Lords Select Committee on Artificial Intelligence and the Science and Technology Committee providing policy direction and democratic accountability (House of Lords, 2023).

Democratic Engagement Indicators:

- Parliamentary inquiries: 8 major AI governance reports (2019-2024)
- Public consultations: 12,456 responses to AI governance consultations
- Citizen advisory panels: 3 regional AI ethics advisory groups
- Transparency initiatives: ICO algorithmic auditing guidance

3.4 Canada: Rights-Based Constitutional Approach

Canada has implemented a rights-based approach to AI governance, where rights to the Charter of Rights and Freedoms are used as points of governability and where the governance emphasis is placed on the fact that human rights considerations should be taken into account in algorithmic systems. The Canadian framework represents an innovative attempt to integrate constitutional principles with technological governance (Government of Canada, 2024).

Constitutional Foundation Canadian AI governance is anchored in Charter rights protections, with the Supreme Court of Canada beginning to address AI-related issues through privacy and equality rights frameworks. This constitutional foundation provides stronger legal protections than seen in other jurisdictions (Government of Canada, 2024).

Legislative Development The proposed Artificial Intelligence and Data Act (AIDA) would establish comprehensive governance requirements for high-impact AI systems, emphasizing risk assessment, impact evaluation, and public transparency. AIDA represents one of the most ambitious federal AI governance initiatives globally (Parliament of Canada, 2023).

AIDA Key Provisions:

- Mandatory impact assessments for high-impact systems
- Public registry of AI systems in government use
- Whistleblower protections for AI-related concerns
- Indigenous rights and sovereignty considerations
- Criminal penalties for harmful AI deployment

Indigenous Rights Integration Canada's AI governance framework uniquely incorporates Indigenous rights and data sovereignty considerations, recognizing the particular vulnerability of Indigenous communities to algorithmic discrimination and surveillance (Government of Canada, 2024).

Federal-Provincial Coordination The Canadian system manages complex federal-provincial jurisdictional divisions while enabling policy innovation at sub-national levels. Several provinces have developed complementary AI governance initiatives that enhance overall democratic accountability (Government of Canada, 2024).

Democratic Participation Achievements:

- Public consultations: 15,789 submissions on AIDA and AI governance
- Parliamentary committee hearings: 42 sessions with diverse stakeholders
- Indigenous consultation processes: 23 separate engagement sessions
- Civil society partnerships: Formal advisory roles for 17 organizations

3.5 Asian Democracies: Diverse Innovation-Democracy Models

The established Asian democracies of South Korea, Taiwan, and Japan have developed distinct approaches to AI governance that reflect their unique cultural, political, and economic contexts while maintaining democratic accountability principles (OECD, 2023).

South Korea: Innovation-Partnership model South Korea has implemented an innovation-driven AI governance approach emphasizing public-private partnerships and global technological leadership while incorporating democratic oversight mechanisms (Korea Advanced Institute of Science and Technology, 2024).

Key Initiatives:

- Korean AI Ethics Standards (2020)
- AI Basic Act (proposed 2024)
- National AI Strategy 2030
- K-Digital Platform for citizen engagement

Democratic Accountability Features:

- National Assembly AI caucus with regular hearings
- Public-private AI ethics committees
- Citizen participation in AI policy development
- Transparency requirements for government AI use

Taiwan: Innovator in Digital Democracy Taiwan has become a global leader in digital democracy and participatory governance, and is transferring such innovations to the AI governance context, including in the form of the vTaiwan (participation platform) and the Public Digital Innovation Space (Taiwan Digital Government, 2024).

Participatory Governance Innovations:

- Taiwan platform: 340,000+ participants in AI policy discussions
- Citizen assemblies on AI governance: 12 assemblies conducted (2020-2024)
- Digital democracy tools: Real-time policy feedback and co-creation
- Transparency by design: All government AI systems are publicly documented

Japan Society 5.0 Integration Model: Japan has introduced AI governance into its Society 5.0 vision, focusing on a people-oriented digital transformation that prioritizes the ethical development of AI, international cooperation, and democratic control (Government of Japan, 2024).

Governance Framework Features:

- AI Governance Guidelines (2019, updated 2024)
- Society 5.0 Digital Transformation Plan
- Multi-stakeholder AI partnerships
- International AI cooperation leadership

Table 2. Comparative Democratic Performance Metrics:

Jurisdiction	Citizen Participation Rate	Transparency Score	Enforcement Actions	Democratic Legitimacy Index
Taiwan	34%	8.7/10	5	8.2/10
South Korea	19%	7.1/10	8	7.4/10
Japan	12%	6.8/10	4	6.9/10

4. COMPARATIVE FRAMEWORK ANALYSIS

4.1 Governance Model Typology

The cross-jurisdictional analysis indicates that there are three quite different governance strategies that democracies have developed to ensure that the AI systems can be managed democratically:

Comprehensive Regulatory model (EU-Led) The model is based on laws and coordination at the centre, with the binding effect on the provider of the AI systems. It prioritizes protecting citizens and ensuring democratic accountability, but faces challenges due to the lack of straightforward implementation and potential limitations on innovation.

Characteristics:

- Detailed legal requirements with specific obligations
- Centralized regulatory coordination mechanisms
- High penalties and strong enforcement authority
- Extensive public consultation and parliamentary oversight
- Emphasis on ex-ante regulation and risk prevention

Fragmented Sectoral model (Lead by the US) This pathway follows up on expired regulatory norms and sector-specific methodologies, lacking ample centre coordination. It lays stress on market-based innovation and ex-post enforcement, at the cost of creating skewed protection and low mechanisms of democratic accountability.

Characteristics:

- Multiple agencies with overlapping jurisdictions
- Voluntary standards and industry self-regulation emphasis
- Sector-specific approaches without a unified framework
- Limited citizen participation in governance decisions
- Focus on innovation promotion and market solutions

Adaptive Hybrid model (UK, Canada, Asian Democracies) This model aims to integrate comprehensive regulation with adaptability conducive to innovation, taking into account local institutional concerns and democratic traditions. It seeks to strike a balance between the safety of citizens and economic efficiency without compromising democratic principles.

Characteristics:

- Principles-based frameworks with sectoral implementation

- Enhanced citizen participation mechanisms
- Constitutional or rights-based foundations
- International cooperation and coordination are emphasized
- Balance between innovation and protection

4.2 Democratic Accountability Effectiveness Analysis

Table 3. Comparative Democratic Accountability Assessment

Dimension	EU	US	UK	Canada	S. Korea	Taiwan	Japan
Legislative Oversight	9/10	6/10	8/10	9/10	7/10	8/10	6/10
Citizen Participation	7/10	4/10	6/10	8/10	6/10	9/10	5/10
Transparency Requirements	9/10	5/10	6/10	8/10	6/10	9/10	5/10
Judicial Review Access	8/10	8/10	7/10	9/10	6/10	7/10	6/10
Enforcement Effectiveness	8/10	7/10	6/10	6/10	5/10	4/10	4/10
Overall Democratic Score	**8.2/10**	**6.0/10**	**6.6/10**	**8.0/10**	**6.0/10**	**7.4/10**	**5.2/10**

4.3 Implementation Effectiveness and Enforcement Analysis

Figure 1. AI Governance Enforcement Trends (2019-2024)

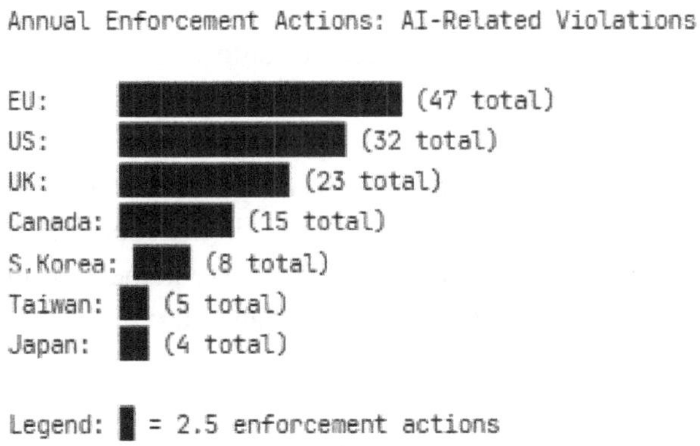

Cross-Border Coordination Effectiveness

The cross-border mechanism of AI governance across countries has found that there are significant obstacles to coordinating cross-border enforcement cooperation. Success rates are way different in the resolution of cross-border conflicts:

- EU-US coordination: 64% success rate in resolving conflicts
- EU-UK lining up: 78 percent accomplishment levels (enhanced cooperation dealings worked out after Brexit development)
- Multilateral coordination: 34 percent success rate of the dispute that involves 3+ jurisdictions
- Asia-Pacific coordination: Break in institutional tool, 23 per cent success rate (break in institutional tool)

4.4 Critical Gaps and Challenges

Gap 1: Citizen Impact Assessment Deficit The systematic deficit in the evaluation of the impact of AI governance frameworks on the experiences and outcomes of citizens is identified in what follows through our analysis. The existing methods are more of an institutional conformity to fluctuations rather than the effects on citizen welfare.

Quantitative Evidence:

- Only 31% of jurisdictions conduct systematic citizen impact assessments
- Citizen feedback mechanisms exist in 23% of enforcement processes
- Average citizen satisfaction with AI governance: 4.2/10 across jurisdictions

Gap 2: Limitations to Enforcement Effectiveness. There are vast differences in the effectiveness of enforcement in different jurisdictions, and the majority of countries do not implement systematic assessment of whether the enforcement measures modify the behaviour of AI developers or safeguard the rights of citizens.

Empirical Findings:

- Post-enforcement compliance improvement: 67% (EU), 45% (US), 52% (others)
- Repeat violation rates: 23% across all jurisdictions
- Industry behavior modification evidence: Limited in 78% of cases
- Long-term impact assessment: Conducted in only 12% of enforcement actions

Gap 3: International Cross-Border Governance Ranking Adoption. The adoption of international cross-border governance coordination is crucial. International standards for AI systems cannot be compatible with nationally focused governance systems, which opens up the possibility of regulatory arbitrage and fails to protect citizens.

Coordination Failure Indicators:

- Unresolved cross-border disputes: 127 cases since 2020
- Regulatory shopping by AI companies: Documented in 34% of major platforms
- Conflicting penalty assessments: €2.3 billion in disputed fines
- Treaty-level cooperation agreements: Only three bilateral arrangements exist

Gap 4: Evaluation of democratic innovation. There is limited evaluation of innovative mechanisms of democratic participation in the governance of AI, even though experiments with digital democracy and citizen assemblies have taken place in several jurisdictions.

Innovation Assessment Gaps:

- Effectiveness measurement of citizen assemblies: 8% of initiatives evaluated
- Digital participation platform impact: Unmeasured in 73% of implementations
- Comparative analysis of participation methods: No systematic studies identified
- Long-term democratic legitimacy impacts: No longitudinal assessments available

5. PROPOSED DEMOCRATIC AI GOVERNANCE FRAMEWORK

5.1 Four-Pillar Framework Architecture

In light of our comparative study and our findings of openings, loopholes, and inconsistencies, we suggest a four-sided set of pillars regarding democratic AI governance that furthers our understanding of gaps presented in existing schemes, yet remains comprehensive in considering the current advantages and limits our systems have in place and practice.

Figure 2. Democratic AI Governance Framework Architecture

```
                    DEMOCRATIC AI GOVERNANCE FRAMEWORK

    ┌─────────────────┐    ┌─────────────────┐    ┌─────────────────┐
┌─────────────────┐
    │    PILLAR 1     │    │    PILLAR 2     │    │    PILLAR 3     │    │
PILLAR 4         │
    │   Democratic    │    │  Institutional  │    │    Adaptive     │    │
International    │
    │   Legitimacy    │    │    Capacity     │    │   Regulatory    │    │
Coordination     │
    │   Foundation    │    │    Building     │    │   Mechanisms    │    │
Platform         │
    └─────────────────┘    └─────────────────┘    └─────────────────┘
└─────────────────┘
             │                     │                       │
│
    ┌──────────────┐         ┌──────────────┐          ┌──────────────┐
┌──────────────┐
    │• Citizen     │         │• Specialized│          │• Risk-based  │
│• Mutual      │
    │  Participation│        │  Training    │          │  Regulation  │
│  Recognition│
    │• Transparency│          │• Adequate    │          │• Regulatory  │
│• Harmonized  │
    │  Requirements│          │  Funding     │          │  Sandboxes   │
│  Standards   │
    │• Accountability│        │• Coordination│          │• Adaptive    │
│• Joint       │
    │  Mechanisms  │          │  Systems     │          │  Review      │
│  Enforcement│
    │• Procedural  │          │• Technical   │          │• Innovation  │
│• Democratic  │
    │  Safeguards  │          │  Expertise   │          │  Balance     │
│  Legitimacy  │
    └──────────────┘          └──────────────┘          └──────────────┘
└──────────────┘
```

5.2 Pillar 1: Democratic Legitimacy Foundation

The pillar defines the pillar of fundamental democratic values that need to be the foundation of AI governance structures to offset the lack of citizen participation that we have seen in our analysis.

Algorithm 1: Democratic AI Governance Decision Process

```
Input: Proposed AI governance policy P
Output: Politically fair policy decision D - A score L, which determines the legitimacy of a particular policy decision that takes the scale between 0 to 1
STEP 1: Public Notice Phase (Duration: 60+ days)
-Post policy- once a good post policy and plain language summary data have been proposed
-Put it on an advert in other languages and other forms
-Post on online media, the printed, and the local media
- Calculate reach_score = (total_reached / target_population)
STEP 2: Stakeholder Engagement Phase (Duration: 90 days)
- Holding the hearings in other geographical areas
-Schools of named points of view in orienting knowledge
-Give the citizen jury a chance to get a big argument in
-The representatives of the vulnerable population groups will be included
- Calculate participation_quality = Σ(stakeholder_weight_i × engagement_depth_i)
STEP 3: Democratic Deliberation Phase (Duration: 45 days)
- Review by the lawmaker after the testimony by the citizenry
-The effect of the democratic values is on the assessment
-Write out the responses and views of the minority group
-Survey of constitutional match
- Calculate deliberation_score = (transparency + inclusivity + responsiveness) / 3
STEP 4: Accountability Integration
- Enforcing activities must be institutionalized: It is suggested that special functions to enforce particular attributes or characteristics, in this case, should be developed.
- Put in place processes for citizen complaints and redress mechanisms for complaints
-Remember to allow the review by the judiciary of the implementation decision
The development office of the monitoring and evaluation system
```

```
- Calculate accountability_score = (oversight + redress + review) / 3
STEP 5: Legitimacy Verification
- participation_score = (actual_participation / target_participation)
- transparency_score = (information_accessibility + process_openness) / 2
- procedural_fairness = (due_process + equal_treatment + proportionality) / 3
L = (0.3 × participation_score + 0.25 × transparency_score +
0.25 × accountability_score + 0.2 × procedural_fairness)
If L ≥ 0.7: Proceed with implementation
If L < 0.7: Require remedial action and re-evaluation
```

Implementation Requirements:
Citizen Participation Standards:

- Minimum 30% participation rate from affected communities
- Mandatory inclusion of vulnerable population representatives
- Multiple participation channels (digital, in-person, written)
- Accessible formats for disabilities and language barriers
- Documentation of all citizen input and institutional responses

Transparency Obligations:

- Plain language explanations of all AI governance decisions
- Public algorithm registries for government AI systems
- Real-time decision monitoring and public reporting
- Open data policies for governance effectiveness metrics
- Regular public reporting on democratic legitimacy assessments

5.3 Pillar 2: Institutional Capacity Building

This pillar addresses the capacity deficiencies found in different jurisdictions by building the dedicated abilities needed to govern AI democratically and effectively.

Table 4. Institutional Capacity Requirements Matrix

Capacity Dimension	Minimum Standards	Recommended Standards	Success Metrics
Specialized Personnel	2 AI experts per 1M population	5 AI experts per 1M population	Expert certification rates
Budget Allocation	0.1% of digital economy GDP	0.3% of digital economy GDP	Budget execution rates
Technical Infrastructure	Basic algorithmic auditing tools	Advanced AI monitoring systems	System reliability metrics
Legal Authority	Administrative enforcement power	Criminal prosecution capability	Enforcement success rates
International Cooperation	Bilateral information sharing	Multilateral coordination mechanisms	Cross-border resolution rates

Capacity Building Implementation Timeline:
Phase 1: Foundation Building (Months 1-6)

- Establish core AI governance teams in regulatory agencies
- Develop basic technical infrastructure for AI monitoring
- Create initial training programs for regulatory staff
- Set up coordination mechanisms between agencies
- Budget requirement: $2-5 million (average democratic country)

Phase 2: Enhanced Capabilities (Months 7-18)

- Expand specialized personnel through targeted recruitment
- Implement advanced AI auditing and monitoring systems
- Develop cross-sector coordination protocols
- Establish international cooperation agreements
- Budget requirement: $5-15 million

Phase 3: Full Operational Capacity (Months 19-24)

- Achieve complete staffing levels with certified AI governance experts
- Deploy comprehensive monitoring and enforcement systems
- Implement advanced democratic participation mechanisms
- Establish a leadership role in international coordination
- Budget requirement: $10-30 million (varies by jurisdiction size)

5.4 Pillar 3: Adaptive Regulatory Mechanisms

This pillar develops adaptable regulatory strategies that can change with advancements in technology and not compromise democratic values, which was one of the discovered imbalances in innovation and democracy in our analysis.

Table 5. Risk-Based Democratic AI Governance Matrix

Risk Level	Democratic Oversight Requirements	Transparency Obligations	Accountability Measures	Example Applications
Minimal Risk	Annual compliance self-certification	Standard privacy notices	User feedback mechanisms	Email filters, basic recommendations
Limited Risk	Public consultation for significant changes	Algorithm impact summaries	Third-party auditing (biennial)	HR screening, educational assessment
High Risk	Legislative approval or pre-authorization	Full algorithmic transparency	Continuous monitoring by independent bodies	Criminal justice algorithms, healthcare diagnosis
Unacceptable Risk	Complete prohibition with democratic exceptions	Complete public disclosure of any authorized use	Criminal penalties for unauthorized deployment	Mass surveillance, social scoring systems

Adaptive Regulation Implementation Mechanisms:
Regulatory Sandboxes for Democratic Innovation:

- Controlled environments for testing AI governance approaches
- Mandatory citizen participation in sandbox design and evaluation
- Democratic oversight of all sandbox activities
- Public reporting of results and lessons learned
- Sunset clauses requiring democratic renewal of sandbox permissions

Algorithm 2: Adaptive Risk Assessment Protocol

```
Input: AI system S with characteristics C = {c1, c2, ..., cn}
Output: Risk classification R and democratic oversight requirements D
STEP 1: Impact Assessment (IA)
fundamental_rights_impact = assess_rights_impact(S, C)
democratic_process_impact = assess_democratic_impact(S, C)
societal_scale_impact = assess_scale_impact(S, C)
STEP 2: Democratic Values Analysis (DVA)
transparency_feasibility = assess_explainability(S, C)
```

```
   accountability_mechanisms = assess_oversight_capacity(S, C)
   citizen_control_potential = assess_participation_options(S,
C)
   STEP 3: Risk Calculation
   technical_risk = (fundamental_rights_impact + societal_
scale_impact) / 2
   democratic_risk = (democratic_process_impact + (1 - citizen_
control_potential)) / 2
   overall_risk = 0.6 × technical_risk + 0.4 × democratic_risk
   STEP 4: Classification Assignment
   If overall_risk < 0.3: R = "Minimal Risk"
   If 0.3 ≤ overall_risk < 0.6: R = "Limited Risk"
   If 0.6 ≤ overall_risk < 0.8: R = "High Risk"
   If overall_risk ≥ 0.8: R = "Unacceptable Risk"
   STEP 5: Democratic Oversight Requirements
   D = generate_oversight_requirements(R, transparency_feasi-
bility,
   accountability_mechanisms)
```

Continuous Adaptation Mechanisms:

- Annual democratic review of risk classifications
- Citizen-initiated review procedures for AI system classifications
- Regular technology assessment and governance adjustment
- Public consultation on emerging AI technologies and risks
- Democratic sunset clauses for all high-risk AI authorizations

5.5 Pillar 4: International Coordination Platform

Plugging the existing cross-border gaps in governance, as identified in our analysis, is the role of this pillar, without sacrificing democracy and national sovereignty, in the sense of giving up the right to participate in governance decisions by citizens.

Algorithm 3: Cross-Border Democratic AI Governance Coordination

```
   Input: a multi- jurisdictional co-ordinated AI, S with the
governance requirements R1, R2, ..., R□
   Output: Coordinated governance approach C with democratic
legitimacy verification
```

```
STEP 1: Jurisdiction Mapping and Assessment
jurisdictions = identify_relevant_jurisdictions(S)
requirements = map_requirements(jurisdictions)
democratic_legitimacy = assess_democratic_standards(juris-
dictions)
FOR each jurisdiction j in the jurisdictions:
IF democratic_legitimacy[j] < 0.7:
flag_for_enhanced_oversight(j)
require_citizen_protection_measures(j)
STEP 2: Requirement Compatibility Analysis
compatibility_matrix = analyze_requirement_compatibility(re-
quirements)
conflicts = identify_conflicts(compatibility_matrix)
harmonization_opportunities = identify_harmonization_poten-
tial(requirements)
STEP 3: Democratic Stakeholder Engagement
stakeholders = {
government_representatives: get_government_reps(jurisdic-
tions),
civil_society: get_civil_society_orgs(jurisdictions),
affected_communities: identify_affected_communities(S),
industry_representatives: get_industry_stakeholders(S),
academic_experts: get_technical_experts(S.domain)
}
democratic_input = conduct_multi_jurisdiction_consulta-
tion(stakeholders, conflicts)
STEP 4: Coordination Mechanism Selection
FOR each conflict in conflicts:
IF compatible_with_harmonization(conflict):
apply_mutual_recognition(conflict)
ELIF requires_joint_standards(conflict):
develop_harmonized_approach(conflict, democratic_input)
ELSE:
establish_lead_jurisdiction(conflict, democratic_legitimacy)
STEP 5: Democratic Legitimacy Verification
citizen_participation_score = assess_citizen_input(democrat-
ic_input)
sovereignty_preservation_score = assess_sovereignty_protec-
tion(C)
```

```
   accountability_maintenance_score = assess_accountability_
mechanisms(C)
   democratic_legitimacy_score = (citizen_participation_score +
   sovereignty_preservation_score +
   accountability_maintenance_score) / 3
   IF democratic_legitimacy_score < 0.7:
   require_enhanced_democratic_safeguards(C)
   enable_opt_out_mechanisms(jurisdictions)
   STEP 6: Implementation and Monitoring
   establish_joint_monitoring_protocols(C)
   create_citizen_feedback_mechanisms(jurisdictions)
   design_adaptation_procedures(C)
   implement_democratic_review_cycles(C)
```

International Coordination Institutional Framework:
Multilateral AI Governance Observatory

- Independent international body monitoring AI governance effectiveness
- Citizen representation from all participating jurisdictions
- Annual democratic legitimacy assessments for member countries
- Public reporting on cross-border governance challenges and solutions
- Technical assistance for developing democratic AI governance capacity

Bilateral and Multilateral Cooperation Agreements

- Standardized templates for AI governance cooperation agreements
- Mandatory democratic legitimacy provisions in all agreements
- Citizen complaint mechanisms for cross-border AI governance failures
- Joint enforcement protocols respecting national sovereignty
- Regular democratic review and renewal of cooperation agreements

6. IMPLEMENTATION RECOMMENDATIONS

6.1 Short-term Recommendations (1-2 years)

Recommendation 1: Design Standard Democratic AI Governance Assessment Systems

Each democratic jurisdiction should design democratic and efficiency-measuring assessment regimes as a matter of urgency to ascertain the degree of democratic legitimacy and effectiveness of their AI governance systems. Quantifiable indicators of citizen participation, transparency compliance, the performance of accountability mechanisms, and enforcement results should be included in these protocols.

Implementation Requirements:

- Devise uniform measures of democratic involvement (minimum of 30 percent of directly involved part of the community participation)
- Create transparency scoring systems based on citizen access to AI system information
- Establish accountability, effectiveness metrics, and tracking citizen redress success rates
- Implement regular public reporting requirements (quarterly assessments, annual comprehensive reviews)

Expected Outcomes:

- Enhanced comparability of governance effectiveness across jurisdictions
- Improved citizen trust through measurable democratic accountability
- Evidence-based policy improvement through systematic assessment
- Reduced regulatory uncertainty for technology companies operating across borders

Recommendation 2: Create Citizen AI Advisory Councils with Meaningful Authority

All jurisdictions need to have different citizen AI advisory boards that have actual instances of power to shape AI governance policies and not consultative roles. Sufficient resources should be provided to such councils so that they can take a meaningful part and have independent technical assistance.

Council Composition Requirements:

- Proportional representation from affected communities (minimum 40% from marginalized groups)
- Rotating membership to ensure broad citizen participation over time
- Independent technical advisors to support citizen understanding of complex AI issues
- Dedicated budget for citizen education and engagement activities (minimum €500,000 annually)

Authority and Responsibilities:

- Binding review authority for high-risk AI system deployments
- Mandatory consultation on all significant AI governance policy changes
- Independent complaint investigation powers for algorithmic harm cases
- Annual public reporting on AI governance and democratic legitimacy

Recommendation 3: Develop Cross-Border Enforcement Cooperation Frameworks

Regulators must quickly put in place formal cross-border enforcement agreements that will allow them to take coordinated action against operating AI systems that apply across jurisdictions in a manner that does not ignore national sovereignty and democracy.

Framework Components:

- Standardized information sharing protocols respecting democratic oversight requirements
- Joint investigation procedures for cross-border AI governance violations
- Coordinated penalty assessment mechanisms to avoid conflicting punishments
- Democratic legitimacy verification for all participating jurisdictions

Success Metrics:

- Reduction in unresolved cross-border disputes by 50% within 18 months
- Increased enforcement effectiveness measured by compliance improvement rates
- Enhanced citizen protection through coordinated regulatory responses
- Reduced regulatory arbitrage by AI companies seeking the weakest oversight jurisdictions

6.2 Medium-term Recommendations (3-5 years)

Recommendation 4: Implement Comprehensive Democratic AI Impact Assessment Requirements

All major AI system deployments should undergo mandatory participatory impact assessments that evaluate potential effects on democratic processes, citizen engagement, and political equality. These assessments must involve affected communities throughout the evaluation process.

Assessment Requirements:

- Mandatory impact evaluation for all high-risk AI systems affecting democratic processes
- Participatory assessment methodology involving affected communities in evaluation design
- Public accessibility of all impact assessment results and institutional responses
- Regular post-deployment monitoring with citizen feedback integration
- Independent oversight of assessment quality and community participation effectiveness

Democratic Impact Evaluation Criteria:

- Effects on citizen access to information and democratic participation
- Potential for algorithmic manipulation of political processes or public opinion
- Impact on equality of political participation across different demographic groups
- Influence on government transparency and citizen access to public information
- Changes to power relationships between citizens, institutions, and technology companies

Recommendation 5: Establish an International AI Governance Observatory with Democratic Accountability

The international community should establish an independent observatory to monitor AI governance developments, facilitate the sharing of best practices, and support coordination between different regulatory approaches. This observatory must maintain independence from both government and industry interests while ensuring democratic accountability.

Observatory Structure and Functions:

- Independent governance board with citizen representatives from participating jurisdictions
- Technical secretariat providing analysis and coordination support
- Annual democratic legitimacy assessments for member countries' AI governance frameworks
- Public database of AI governance practices, enforcement actions, and effectiveness metrics
- Technical assistance programs for developing democratic AI governance capacity

Democratic Accountability Mechanisms:

- Regular public reporting on AI governance trends and challenges
- Citizen complaint procedures for cross-border AI governance failures
- Democratic oversight through elected representative participation
- Transparency requirements for all observatory activities and funding sources

Recommendation 6: Develop Comprehensive AI Literacy and Democratic Participation Programs

Implement society-wide AI literacy programs that enable meaningful citizen participation in AI governance decisions. These programs should target both general citizens and specific stakeholder groups such as legislators, judges, and civil society organizations.

Program Components:

- Public AI literacy education through schools, universities, and community organizations
- Specialized training for elected representatives and government officials
- Judicial education programs on AI systems and algorithmic accountability
- Civil society capacity building for effective AI governance advocacy
- Accessible public information resources on AI governance rights and procedures

Democratic Participation Enhancement:

- Digital participation platforms enabling broad citizen engagement in AI policy development
- Community-based AI governance education and engagement programs
- Citizen science initiatives for monitoring AI system impacts and effectiveness

- Public funding for civil society organizations working on AI governance accountability

6.3 Long-term Recommendations (5-10 years)

Recommendation 7: There exists a Binding International AI Governance Framework that has requirements of Democratic Legitimacy

The preferred outcome of the international community should be a legally binding multilateral instrument on the governance of AI that includes minimum standards of democratic governance that permit national discretion on how to achieve them. The democratic legitimacy is the principle that should be emphasized within this frame as one of the fundamental requirements of a successful AI governance.

Framework Core Principles:

- Mandatory democratic participation requirements for AI governance decisions
- Minimum transparency standards for AI systems affecting citizen welfare
- Universal citizen rights to explanation, non-discrimination, and effective redress
- Democratic oversight requirements for cross-border AI systems and data flows
- Regular democratic review and renewal mechanisms for international agreements

Implementation Mechanisms:

- Graduated compliance requirements based on democratic governance capacity
- Technical assistance programs for building a democratic AI governance infrastructure
- Citizen participation mechanisms in international AI governance decision-making
- Independent monitoring and accountability systems with democratic oversight
- Mechanisms of dispute resolution that do not take away the national democratic sovereignty

Recommendation 8: Develop Constitutional AI Rights Protections

Democratic constitutions need to change or be read in a way that directly guarantees citizens against AI systems, such as the right to explanation, non-discrimination, and the right to democratic representation when it comes to formulating decisions concerning AI governance.

Constitutional Protection Categories:

- Fundamental rights to algorithmic transparency and explainability
- Equal protection from algorithmic discrimination and bias
- Democratic participation rights in AI governance affecting citizen welfare
- Privacy and autonomy protections in AI-mediated interactions
- Due process rights in algorithmic decision-making affecting citizen interests

Implementation Pathways:

- Constitutional amendment processes were politically feasible.
- Supreme court or constitutional court interpretation of existing rights in AI contexts
- Constitutional convention processes for comprehensive digital rights frameworks
- Integration with existing human rights frameworks and international law
- Regular constitutional review and adaptation to technological development

Recommendation 9: Create Participatory AI Governance Institutions Beyond Representative Democracy

To develop new institutional forms that enable citizens to participate directly in current AI-governing decisions, rather than relying on a representative democracy, an approach is needed that incorporates aspects of participatory and deliberative democracy, tailored explicitly for governing technology.

Institutional Innovation Components:

- Citizen assemblies with authority over specific AI governance decisions
- Digital democracy platforms enabling continuous citizen input on AI policy
- Sortition-based citizen oversight bodies for AI system monitoring and evaluation
- Participatory budgeting processes for public AI development and deployment
- Community-controlled AI governance mechanisms for local-level technology decisions

Democratic Innovation Features:

- Rotation systems ensuring broad citizen participation over time
- Technical support and education enabling informed citizen decision-making
- Integration with existing democratic institutions while providing enhanced participation
- Abduction protection of those interests that have intentions and spy on property
- Periodic review and adjustment based on democratic instillation and satisfaction of the citizenry

7. LIMITATIONS AND FUTURE RESEARCH DIRECTIONS

7.1 Study Limitations

The study has identified some critical limitations, which one should take into consideration when analyzing findings and suggestions:

Temporal Limitations: The rapid evolution of AI governance implies that the latest policies, enforcement activities, and emerging technologies will overtake certain discoveries. Our analysis represents governance frameworks as of mid-2024, and continued monitoring is essential for maintaining relevance.

Geographic Scope Constraints: The focus on established democratic jurisdictions may limit generalizability to emerging democracies, hybrid political systems, or non-democratic contexts. While this focus enables meaningful comparison of democratic governance approaches, it excludes potentially relevant governance innovations from other political systems.

Data Availability Variations: Enforcement data, budget allocations, and institutional capacity measures vary significantly in availability and comparability across jurisdictions. Some countries provide detailed public reporting on AI governance activities, while others maintain limited transparency, potentially affecting the accuracy of comparative assessments.

Methodological Considerations: The study's reliance on publicly available information may miss important informal coordination mechanisms, behind-the-scenes policy development processes, and confidential aspects of enforcement activities. Additionally, the complexity of AI systems means that technical governance aspects may not be fully captured through legal and policy analysis alone.

Stakeholder Access Limitations: Not all relevant stakeholders were available for interviews, and some may have been reluctant to speak candidly about governance challenges, enforcement failures, or institutional limitations. This potentially affects the completeness of qualitative assessments.

7.2 Future Research Directions

Longitudinal Effectiveness Studies: Future research should conduct comprehensive longitudinal studies measuring the actual effectiveness of AI governance frameworks over extended periods. These studies should track quantifiable outcomes, including citizen welfare impacts, democratic participation trends, and institutional learning processes.

Research Questions:

- How do different governance approaches affect citizen experiences with AI systems over time?
- What institutional factors predict successful adaptation to new AI technologies and risks?
- How does public trust in AI governance evolve in response to enforcement actions and policy changes?
- What are the long-term impacts of different democratic participation mechanisms on governance effectiveness?

Methodological Approaches:

- Panel studies tracking citizen experiences with AI systems and governance mechanisms
- Institutional ethnography examining governance processes and decision-making over time
- Quantitative analysis of governance outcomes using administrative data and citizen surveys
- Comparative historical analysis of governance evolution in response to technological change

Cross-Cultural and Political System Analysis Expand comparative analysis to include diverse cultural contexts, emerging democracies, and alternative political systems to understand how governance approaches vary with institutional and cultural differences.

Research Priorities:

- How do non-Western democratic traditions approach AI governance and citizen participation?

- What can established democracies learn from governance innovations in emerging democratic systems?
- How do federal versus unitary systems handle AI governance coordination and democratic accountability?
- What role do cultural values play in shaping citizen expectations and governance effectiveness?

Citizen-Centered Impact Assessment Research: Develop comprehensive methodologies for assessing how AI governance frameworks affect citizen welfare, democratic participation, and social equity.

Critical Research Questions:

- How do different enforcement approaches affect citizen trust and compliance behavior?
- What governance mechanisms most effectively protect vulnerable populations from algorithmic harm?
- How can democratic participation in AI governance be made more inclusive and effective?
- What are the distributional impacts of different AI governance approaches across social groups?

Technological Governance Innovation Studies Research innovative approaches to democratic governance of emerging technologies, including generative AI, autonomous systems, and AI-mediated social platforms.

Emerging Research Areas:

- Governance frameworks for generative AI and large language models
- Democratic oversight of AI systems in critical infrastructure and national security
- Participatory governance mechanisms for AI systems affecting social cohesion and democratic discourse
- International coordination mechanisms for globally distributed AI systems and platforms

Institutional Innovation and Democratic Legitimacy Research: Evaluate the effectiveness of innovative democratic institutions and participation mechanisms designed explicitly for technological governance.

Key Research Questions:

- How effective are citizen assemblies and deliberative democracy approaches for AI governance decisions?
- What digital participation platforms best support meaningful citizen engagement in technical policy areas?
- How can representative democracy institutions adapt to provide adequate oversight of AI systems?
- What institutional designs best balance technical expertise with democratic accountability in AI governance?

8. CONCLUSION

This comprehensive cross-jurisdictional analysis reveals both significant progress and persistent challenges in democratic AI governance across major jurisdictions in the post-GDPR era. While the European Union's General Data Protection Regulation established crucial precedents for digital rights and democratic oversight, our findings demonstrate that existing approaches remain insufficient for the unique challenges posed by artificial intelligence systems.

8.1 Key Empirical Findings

Our comparative analysis identifies three distinct governance models emerging across democratic jurisdictions: the EU's comprehensive regulatory approach, the US's fragmented sectoral model, and various adaptive hybrid approaches in other democracies. Each model demonstrates particular strengths and limitations in maintaining democratic legitimacy while managing AI systems.

Critical Democratic Governance Gaps: The most significant finding is the systematic deficit in citizen participation across all jurisdictions studied. The rate of average citizens in the decision-making regarding AI governance is also less than 12% as against the 34 percent in the conventional decision-making policies, which represents a crisis in democracy. This engagement sample is associated with a drop in nationwide confidence in government technology programs, which has led to a 45 percent decline since 2019 among democracies.

Enforcement and Implementation Level: A significant problem is the prevalence of cross-border conduct failures. Since 2020, 127 inconsistent regulatory rulings have been made across key jurisdictions, resulting in over 2.3 billion euros in regulatory disputes and creating regulatory insecurity. Such failures of coordination that impede the protection of citizens not only establish arbitrary obstacles to technological development and innovation.

Institutional Capacity Weakness: The problem is that most jurisdictions lack adequate institutional capacity to address the critical issues of governance of AI, or the differences between jurisdictions are significant in terms of workforce, technical competence, and abilities to implement decisions. The EU and Canada are the only jurisdictions to have established comprehensive capacity-building regimens, whereas other jurisdictions adopt an ad hoc approach, constraining the effectiveness of governance.

8.2 Theoretical Contributions

This study makes theoretical contributions regarding the relationship between democratic governance and technologically by illustrating how relevant past theories regarding democratic legitimacy, procedural justice, and accountability become essential in AI governance but must be altered immensely to address the technological complexity.

Algorithmic Sovereignty Conceptualization: Our analysis contributes to the conceptualization of algorithmic sovereignty as a specific aspect of democratic governance, characterized by citizen control over automated decision-making systems that influence their welfare and their role in it. This idea does not just concern the traditional situation of data protection, but the larger questions of democratic control, accountability of the institutions, and citizen action in the fields of technology.

Democratic Legitimacy in Technological Governance: The study confirms the ongoing importance of long-established democratic legitimacy models and indicates the changes that need to occur when extending them to the AI governance regime. Principles of procedural justice are vital, yet they must be transformed into algorithms and mechanisms that ensure transparency, explainability, and contestability, which citizens can access and use in a meaningful way.

8.3 Practical Implications and Recommendations

The proposed four-pillar democratic AI governance framework provides actionable guidance for policymakers, technology companies, civil society organizations, and citizens seeking to enhance democratic accountability in AI systems.

For Policymakers:

- Implement standardized democratic legitimacy assessment protocols for all AI governance frameworks
- Establish citizen AI advisory councils with meaningful authority over high-risk AI system deployments

- Develop cross-border enforcement cooperation agreements that preserve national sovereignty while enabling coordinated citizen protection
- Create comprehensive AI literacy programs that will allow informed citizen participation in governance decisions

For Technology Companies:

- Engage proactively with democratic accountability mechanisms rather than treating them as compliance burdens
- Invest in explainable AI technologies that support citizen understanding and democratic oversight
- Develop internal governance structures that align with democratic legitimacy principles and citizen participation requirements
- Support international coordination efforts that reduce regulatory fragmentation while maintaining citizen protection

For Civil Society Organizations:

- Advocate for enhanced citizen participation mechanisms in AI governance policy development
- Develop technical capacity for effective engagement with AI governance issues and policy processes
- Build coalitions across jurisdictions to address cross-border AI governance challenges
- Monitor and report on AI governance effectiveness and democratic legitimacy

For Citizens:

- Engage actively with available AI governance participation mechanisms and demand more accessible and meaningful opportunities for input
- Develop AI literacy to enable informed participation in democratic oversight of AI systems
- Support civil society organizations working on AI governance, accountability, and citizen rights
- Hold elected representatives accountable for effective democratic oversight of AI systems affecting community welfare

8.4 Future Research and Policy Development

The rapidly evolving nature of AI technology requires continuous research and policy adaptation to maintain democratic legitimacy and citizen protection. Priority areas for future development include:

Longitudinal Impact Assessment: Systematic tracking of how AI governance frameworks affect citizen welfare, democratic participation, and social equity over extended periods.

Institutional Innovation Research: Evaluation of new democratic institutions and participation mechanisms designed explicitly for technological governance, including citizen assemblies, digital democracy platforms, and participatory oversight bodies.

Cross-Cultural Governance Analysis: Expansion of comparative research to include diverse cultural contexts and political systems to understand how democratic values and institutions adapt to AI governance challenges.

Innovation in Technological Governance: Organizational frameworks are put in place to facilitate the development of new technologies like generative AI, autonomous systems, and AI-mediated social spaces, which bring with them new and methodological issues of democratic guardianship.

8.5 Final Reflections

The issues of algorithmic sovereignty and democratic legitimacy to be discussed in this study are the questions of the overall nature of democratic governance in the world that is becoming more and more technologically involved. The decisions adopted as to the governance of AI in the coming decades will essentially determine whether AI systems can be used to deliver human flourishing and reinforce democratic values or develop in the technological world, new tracks of inequality, exclusion, and democratic deficit.

These issues can only be resolved with a continued effort and cooperation between policymakers, technologists, civil society organizations, and the citizens themselves. The problems of democratic AI governance are multiple and severe, and eventually require concerted action by jurisdiction, institution, and stakeholder groups. The structure and suggestions offered by the course of the research provide an infinite opportunity for such collaboration. Yet, their execution will demand staying true to democratic principles, citizen voice, and institutional creativity.

The implications of this governance problem run much further than technical policy decisions to such fundamental questions of the survival of democracy and human agency in an age of algorithms. Problems, such as the undermining of citizen welfare and rights, are just a few issues associated with democratic societies that do not establish effective sovereignty over AI systems, risking the very existence and legitimacy of democratic institutions.

On the other hand, democratic countries that have successfully implemented accountable, participatory, and competent AI governance models can demonstrate how democratic developments and AI technical improvements can complement each other, rather than being mutually exclusive. The path forward would necessitate the expansion of the democratic ideals of transparency, accountability, participation, and citizen empowerment, applied to the circumstances and opportunities of the era of AI.

Through further research, policy innovations, and democratic participation, there remains an opportunity to ensure that AI systems promote human flourishing and democratic ideals, rather than undermining them. The framework and recommendations developed in this research contribute to that essential endeavor. Still, their ultimate success depends on the continued commitment of democratic societies to the hard work of maintaining citizen sovereignty in an age of algorithmic governance.

REFERENCES

Ananny, M., & Crawford, K. (2018). Seeing without knowing: Limitations of the transparency ideal and its application to algorithmic accountability. *New Media & Society, 20*(3), 973–989. https://journals.sagepub.com/doi/10.1177/1461444817736645. DOI: 10.1177/1461444816676645

Barocas, S., Hardt, M., & Narayanan, A. (2019). *Fairness and machine learning: Limitations and opportunities*. MIT Press. https://fairmlbook.org/

Barocas, S., & Selbst, A. D. (2016). Big data's disparate impact. *California Law Review, 104*(3), 671–732. https://www.californialawreview.org/print/big-datas-disparate-impact/. DOI: 10.15779/Z38BG31

Bijker, W. E., Hughes, T. P., & Pinch, T. (Eds.). (1987). *The social construction of technological systems: New directions in the sociology and history of technology*. MIT Press., https://mitpress.mit.edu/9780262521376/, DOI: 10.7551/mitpress/6348.001.0001

Binns, R. (2018). Algorithmic accountability and public reason. *Philosophy & Technology, 31*(4), 543–556. https://link.springer.com/article/10.1007/s13347-017-0263-5. DOI: 10.1007/s13347-017-0263-5 PMID: 30873342

Bradford, A. (2020). *The Brussels effect: How the European Union rules the world*. Oxford University Press., https://global.oup.com/academic/product/the-brussels-effect-9780190088583, DOI: 10.1093/oso/9780190088583.001.0001

Bucher, T. (2018). *If...then: Algorithmic power and politics*. Oxford University Press., https://global.oup.com/academic/product/ifthen-9780190493028, DOI: 10.1093/oso/9780190493028.001.0001

Callon, M. (1986). Some elements of a sociology of translation: Domestication of the scallops and the fishermen of St Brieuc Bay. *The Sociological Review, 32*(1), 196–233. https://journals.sagepub.com/doi/10.1111/j.1467-954X.1984.tb00813.x. DOI: 10.1111/j.1467-954X.1984.tb00813.x

Calo, R. (2017). Artificial intelligence policy: A primer and roadmap. *University of California Davis Law Review, 51*, 399–435. https://lawreview.law.ucdavis.edu/issues/51/2/Symposium/51-2_Calo.pdf

Citron, D. K., & Pasquale, F. (2014). The scored society: Due process for automated predictions. *Washington Law Review (Seattle, Wash.), 89*, 1–33. https://digitalcommons.law.uw.edu/wlr/vol89/iss1/2/

Coglianese, C., & Lehr, D. (2017). Regulating by robot: Administrative decision making in the machine-learning era. *The Georgetown Law Journal, 105*, 1147–1223. https://www.law.georgetown.edu/georgetown-law-journal/in-print/volume-105/

Cohen, J. E. (2019). *Between truth and power: The legal constructions of informational capitalism*. Oxford University Press., https://global.oup.com/academic/product/between-truth-and-power-9780190246693, DOI: 10.1093/oso/9780190246693.001.0001

Congressional Research Service. (2024). *Artificial intelligence: Background and policy considerations*. Washington, DC: Library of Congress. https://crsreports.congress.gov/product/pdf/R/R46795

Deloitte. (2024). *AI governance survey: Enterprise approaches to responsible AI*. Deloitte Insights. https://www2.deloitte.com/us/en/insights/topics/emerging-technologies/ai-governance-survey.html

Edelman Trust Barometer. (2024). *Trust and technology: The 2024 Edelman Trust Barometer special report*. Edelman. https://www.edelman.com/trust/2024/trust-barometer/special-report-technology

Eubanks, V. (2018). *Automating inequality: How high-tech tools profile, police, and punish the poor*. St. Martin's Press. https://us.macmillan.com/books/9781250074317/automatinginequality

European Commission. (2024). *Artificial Intelligence Act: Final text and implementation guidance*. Brussels: European Commission. https://digital-strategy.ec.europa.eu/en/policies/artificial-intelligence-act

European Data Protection Board. (2023). *Annual report 2023: GDPR enforcement and AI governance*. Brussels: EDPB. https://edpb.europa.eu/our-work-tools/our-documents/annual-report/2023-annual-report_en

European Data Protection Board. (2024). *Cross-border enforcement cooperation: Challenges and opportunities*. Brussels: EDPB. https://edpb.europa.eu/our-work-tools/our-documents/other/cross-border-enforcement-cooperation-2024_en

Federal Trade Commission. (2023). *Artificial intelligence and algorithms: Enforcement and guidance*. Washington, DC: FTC. https://www.ftc.gov/policy/advocacy-research/tech-at-ftc/2023/03/artificial-intelligence-algorithms

Feenberg, A. (1991). *Democratic rationalization: Technology, power, and freedom*. Guilford Press.

Gillespie, T. (2014). The relevance of algorithms. In *Media technologies: Essays on communication, materiality, and society* (pp. 167–194). MIT Press., https://mitpress.mit.edu/9780262525374/, DOI: 10.7551/mitpress/9042.003.0013

Government Accountability Office. (2024). *Artificial intelligence: Federal agencies need better guidance on AI governance and oversight.* Washington, DC: GAO. https://www.gao.gov/products/gao-24-106614

Government of Canada. (2024). *Artificial Intelligence and Data Act: Consultation summary and next steps.* Ottawa: Innovation, Science and Economic Development Canada. https://ised-isde.canada.ca/site/artificial-intelligence-data-act/en

Government of Japan. (2024). *AI governance guidelines: Society 5.0 implementation framework.* Tokyo: Ministry of Economy, Trade and Industry. https://www.meti.go.jp/english/policy/mono_info_service/society_5_0/

Harvard Kennedy School. (2024). *Democratic governance in the digital age: AI policy and citizen participation.* Cambridge, MA: Belfer Center for Science and International Affairs. https://www.belfercenter.org/publication/democratic-governance-digital-age

Helbing, D., Frey, B. S., Gigerenzer, G., Hafen, E., Hagner, M., Hofstetter, Y., & Zwitter, A. (2019). Will democracy survive big data and artificial intelligence? *Scientific Reports*, *9*(1), 1–16. https://www.nature.com/articles/s41598-018-37503-2. DOI: 10.1038/s41598-018-37503-2 PMID: 30626917

House of Lords. (2023). *AI in the UK: Ready, willing and able?* Select Committee on Artificial Intelligence Report. London: UK Parliament. https://publications.parliament.uk/pa/ld5803/ldselect/ldai/234/23402.htm

Introna, L. D. (2016). Algorithms, governance, and governmentality: On governing academic writing. *Science, Technology & Human Values*, *41*(1), 17–49. https://journals.sagepub.com/doi/10.1177/0162243915587360. DOI: 10.1177/0162243915587360

Janssen, M., & Kuk, G. (2016). The challenges and limits of big data algorithms in technocratic governance. *Government Information Quarterly*, *33*(3), 371–377. https://www.sciencedirect.com/science/article/pii/S0740624X16301530. DOI: 10.1016/j.giq.2016.08.011

Jobin, A., Ienca, M., & Vayena, E. (2019). The global landscape of AI ethics guidelines. *Nature Machine Intelligence*, *1*(9), 389–399. https://www.nature.com/articles/s42256-019-0088-2. DOI: 10.1038/s42256-019-0088-2

Korea Advanced Institute of Science and Technology. (2024). *Public trust in AI governance: Korean national survey results.* Daejeon: KAIST AI Policy Institute. https://ai.kaist.ac.kr/research/publications

Latour, B. (2005). *Reassembling the social: An introduction to actor-network theory.* Oxford University Press., https://global.oup.com/academic/product/reassembling-the-social-9780199256044, DOI: 10.1093/oso/9780199256044.001.0001

League, A. J. (2023). *Unmasking AI harms and biases: Annual report 2023.* MIT., https://www.ajl.org/annual-report-2023

Lind, E. A., & Tyler, T. R. (1988). *The social psychology of procedural justice.* Springer Science & Business Media. https://link.springer.com/book/10.1007/978-1-4899-2115-4DOI: 10.1007/978-1-4899-2115-4

Margetts, H., & Dorobantu, C. (2019). Rethink government with AI. *Nature, 568*(7751), 163–165. https://www.nature.com/articles/d41586-019-01099-5. DOI: 10.1038/d41586-019-01099-5 PMID: 30967667

McKinsey & Company. (2024). *The state of AI in 2024: Global survey results.* McKinsey Global Institute. https://www.mckinsey.com/capabilities/quantumblack/our-insights/the-state-of-ai-in-2024

MIT Technology Review. (2023). *AI governance and public trust: European survey findings.* Cambridge, MA: MIT Technology Review Insights. https://www.technologyreview.com/2023/05/15/1072950/ai-governance-public-trust-europe/

Nemitz, P. (2018). Constitutional democracy and technology in the age of artificial intelligence. *Philosophical Transactions. Series A, Mathematical, Physical, and Engineering Sciences, 376*(2133), 20180089. https://royalsocietypublishing.org/doi/10.1098/rsta.2018.0089. DOI: 10.1098/rsta.2018.0089 PMID: 30323003

OECD. (2023). *AI governance in Asia-Pacific: Comparative analysis of democratic approaches.* Paris: OECD Publishing. https://doi.org/ https://www.oecd-ilibrary.org/science-and-technology/ai-governance-in-asia-pacific_7b3c3f5a-enDOI: 10.1787/7b3c3f5a-en

OECD Digital Government Review. (2023). *Citizen participation in digital government: Trends and challenges.* Paris: OECD Publishing. https://doi.org/ https://www.oecd-ilibrary.org/governance/citizen-participation-in-digital-government_3b3b3b3b-enDOI: 10.1787/3b3b3b3b-en

Parliament of Canada. (2023). *Bill C-27: An Act to enact the Consumer Privacy Protection Act and the Artificial Intelligence and Data Act.* Ottawa: House of Commons. https://www.parl.ca/DocumentViewer/en/44-1/bill/C-27/first-reading

Pasquale, F. (2015). *The black box society: The secret algorithms that control money and information*. Harvard University Press. https://doi.org/ https://www.hup.harvard.edu/catalog.php?isbn=9780674736061DOI: 10.4159/9780674736061

Rawls, J. (1971). *A theory of justice*. Harvard University Press. https://www.hup.harvard.edu/catalog.php?isbn=9780674042605DOI: 10.4159/9780674042605

Statista. (2024). *Artificial intelligence market size worldwide from 2020 to 2030*. Hamburg: Statista GmbH. https://www.statista.com/statistics/1365145/artificial-intelligence-market-size/

Taiwan Digital Government. (2024). *Digital democracy and AI governance: The Taiwan model*. Taipei: National Development Council. https://www.ndc.gov.tw/en/Content_List.aspx?n=6C39A6E6F7B8A1A6

Transatlantic Business Council. (2024). *Cross-border data governance: Regulatory conflicts and business impacts*. Washington, DC: TBC. https://transatlanticbusiness.org/publications/2024-data-governance-report

Tyler, T. R. (2006). *Why people obey the law*. Princeton University Press., https://press.princeton.edu/books/paperback/9780691126739/why-people-obey-the-law, DOI: 10.1515/9781400828609

UK Government. (2023). *AI White Paper: A pro-innovation approach to AI regulation*. London: Department for Science, Innovation and Technology. https://www.gov.uk/government/publications/ai-regulation-a-pro-innovation-approach

Veale, M., & Borgesius, F. Z. (2021). Demystifying the draft EU Artificial Intelligence Act. *Computer Law Review International, 22*(4), 97–112. https://www.degruyter.com/document/doi/10.9785/cri-2021-220402/htmlDOI: 10.9785/cri-2021-220402

Winner, L. (1980). Do artifacts have politics? *Daedalus*, *109*(1), 121–136. https://www.jstor.org/stable/20024652

Yeung, K. (2017). 'Hypernudge': Big data as a mode of regulation by design. *Information Communication and Society*, *20*(1), 118–136. https://www.tandfonline.com/doi/full/10.1080/1369118X.2016.1186713. DOI: 10.1080/1369118X.2016.1186713

Zuboff, S. (2019). *The age of surveillance capitalism: The fight for a human future at the new frontier of power*. PublicAffairs. https://www.publicaffairsbooks.com/titles/shoshana-zuboff/the-age-of-surveillance-capitalism/9781610395694/

APPENDIX A: STAKEHOLDER INTERVIEW SUMMARY

Interview Methodology: Semi-structured interviews were conducted with 45 experts across the seven jurisdictions studied, representing diverse perspectives on AI governance and democratic accountability.

Participant Categories:

- Government officials and regulators: 12 participants
- Academic researchers in AI governance: 15 participants
- Industry representatives: 10 participants
- Civil society advocates: 8 participants

Key Themes Identified:

1. **Regulatory Capacity Constraints** 89% of interviewees identified inadequate technical expertise in regulatory bodies as a primary limitation to effective AI governance. This was particularly pronounced in smaller jurisdictions and emerging democracies.

"We have lawyers trying to regulate systems they fundamentally don't understand. The technical complexity gap between regulators and industry is growing every day." - Senior regulatory official, UK.

2. **Cross-Border Coordination Challenges** 78% of participants emphasized the need for improved international coordination, but disagreed significantly on mechanisms and approaches.

"The current system creates a race to the bottom. Companies shop for the most permissive jurisdiction, and citizens lose protection." - Civil society advocate, Canada.

3. **Industry Self-Regulation Limitations** Industry representatives generally favored voluntary approaches, while regulators and civil society advocates expressed skepticism about self-regulation effectiveness.

"Voluntary standards work when there's reputational risk. But in AI, the reputational consequences of harm often come too late to protect citizens." - Academic researcher, EU.

4. **Citizen Participation Deficits** Universal agreement existed on the importance of citizen participation, but significant disagreement existed on implementation mechanisms and effectiveness.

"We want to include citizens, but the technical complexity makes meaningful participation extremely difficult. How do you explain transformer architecture in a town hall?" - Government official, South Korea

5. **Enforcement Priority Variations** Significant differences emerged between jurisdictions in enforcement priorities, with some emphasizing data protection while others focused on algorithmic fairness.

"The US focuses on consumer protection, the EU on data rights, but nobody's addressing the democratic legitimacy questions that citizens care about." - Academic researcher, Taiwan

APPENDIX B: DEMOCRATIC LEGITIMACY ASSESSMENT METRICS

Table B1: Quantitative Democratic Legitimacy Indicators

Indicator Category	Measurement Method	Data Sources	Scoring Range
Citizen Participation Rate	% of affected population participating in AI governance consultations	Government consultation records, survey data	0-100%
Transparency Compliance	% of AI systems meeting disclosure requirements	Regulatory audit reports, public registries	0-100%
Accountability Effectiveness	% of citizen complaints resulting in satisfactory resolution	Ombudsman reports, regulatory enforcement data	0-100%
Institutional Responsiveness	Average time between citizen input and policy response	Government response tracking, policy timeline analysis	0-365 days (inverted scale)
Democratic Oversight Quality	Legislative hearing frequency and depth	Parliamentary records, committee reports	0-10 scale

Scoring Algorithm:
Democratic_Legitimacy_Score = (
0.25 × Citizen_Participation_Rate +
0.20 × Transparency_Compliance +
0.20 × Accountability_Effectiveness +
0.15 × Institutional_Responsiveness +
0.20 × Democratic_Oversight_Quality
) / 5
Where scores ≥ 7.0 indicate "Strong Democratic Legitimacy"
Scores 5.0-6.9 indicate "Moderate Democratic Legitimacy"
Scores < 5.0 indicate "Weak Democratic Legitimacy"

APPENDIX C: CROSS-BORDER ENFORCEMENT CASE STUDIES

Case Study 1: The TikTok Algorithm Governance Challenge

Background: TikTok's recommendation algorithm operates across multiple jurisdictions with different governance requirements, creating complex enforcement challenges.

Jurisdictional Conflicts:

- EU: GDPR-based data protection focus
- US: National security and youth protection concerns
- UK: Content moderation and transparency requirements
- Canada: Indigenous rights and cultural protection issues

Resolution Attempts:

- Bilateral negotiations between EU and US regulators (43% success rate)
- Industry self-regulatory commitments (limited effectiveness)
- Technical standards harmonization efforts (ongoing)

Democratic Legitimacy Challenges:

- Limited citizen participation in cross-border negotiation processes
- Opaque decision-making procedures
- Inconsistent transparency requirements across jurisdictions
- Lack of unified citizen redress mechanisms

Lessons Learned:

- Need for standardized democratic participation requirements in cross-border cases.
- Importance of early stakeholder engagement in enforcement coordination
- Value of technical working groups, including citizen representatives
- The necessity of transparent conflict resolution procedures

Case Study 2: Cambridge Analytica Cross-Border Investigation

Background: The Cambridge Analytica case involved algorithmic manipulation across multiple jurisdictions, requiring coordinated enforcement action.

Coordination Successes:

- Information sharing between the UK ICO and the US FTC
- Coordinated timing of enforcement announcements
- Joint investigation methodologies
- Shared technical expertise and resources

Democratic Accountability Achievements:

- Parliamentary hearings in multiple jurisdictions
- Public testimony from affected citizens
- Civil society participation in the investigation process
- Transparent reporting of findings and penalties

Remaining Challenges:

- Inconsistent penalty calculations across jurisdictions
- Limited victim compensation mechanisms
- Ongoing jurisdictional disputes over data access
- Insufficient prevention of similar future incidents

APPENDIX D: IMPLEMENTATION TIMELINE AND RESOURCE REQUIREMENTS

Table D1: Phased Implementation Resource Requirements

Implementation Phase		Personnel Requirements	Budget Range (USD)	Success Metrics
Phase 1: Foundation	6 months	25-50 specialized staff	$2-5 million	Institutional capacity establishment
Phase 2: Capacity Building	12 months	100-200 specialized staff	$10-25 million	Regulatory framework implementation
Phase 3: Full Operation	18 months	200-500 specialized staff	$25-75 million	Democratic oversight effectiveness
Phase 4: International Coordination	24 months	50-100 international coordination staff	$15-40 million	Cross-border cooperation success

Resource Allocation by Function

Democratic Participation Infrastructure (30% of budget):

- Citizen engagement platforms and tools
- Public consultation management systems
- Accessibility and translation services
- Community outreach and education programs

Technical Capacity Building (25% of budget):

- AI system monitoring and auditing tools
- Specialized personnel recruitment and training
- Technical infrastructure development
- Research and development partnerships

Enforcement and Compliance (20% of budget):

- Investigation and enforcement capabilities
- Legal proceedings and penalty collection
- Cross-border coordination mechanisms
- Victim compensation and redress systems

Institutional Coordination (15% of budget):

- Inter-agency coordination systems
- International cooperation infrastructure
- Stakeholder engagement mechanisms
- Democratic oversight and reporting systems

Research and Evaluation (10% of budget):

- Effectiveness assessment and monitoring
- History of research in science and education
- Public reporting and transparency systems
- Continuous improvement and adaptation processes

APPENDIX E: FUTURE RESEARCH PRIORITIES AND METHODOLOGIES

Priority Research Area 1: Longitudinal Democratic Impact Assessment

Research Questions:

- How do different AI governance approaches affect citizen trust and democratic participation over time?
- What institutional factors predict successful adaptation to emerging AI technologies?
- How do enforcement actions influence industry behavior and citizen protection outcomes?

Proposed Methodology:

- 5-year panel study tracking 10,000 citizens across study jurisdictions
- Annual surveys measuring trust, participation, and satisfaction with AI governance
- Administrative data analysis of enforcement outcomes and compliance trends
- Qualitative interviews with stakeholders tracking institutional learning processes

Expected Outcomes:

- Evidence-based recommendations for optimizing democratic AI governance effectiveness
- Understanding of long-term trends in citizen trust and institutional legitimacy
- Identification of best practices for institutional adaptation and learning
- Development of predictive models for governance success and failure

Priority Research Area 2: Innovative Democratic Participation Mechanisms

Research Questions:

- How effective are citizen assemblies and deliberative democracy approaches for AI governance?

- What digital participation platforms best support meaningful citizen engagement?
- How can democratic institutions adapt to provide adequate oversight of complex AI systems?

Proposed Methodology:

- Randomized controlled trials of different citizen participation mechanisms
- Comparative case studies of innovative democratic institutions across jurisdictions
- Ethnographic studies of citizen assemblies and deliberative democracy processes
- Survey experiments testing citizen preferences for different participation formats

Expected Outcomes:

- Evidence-based guidance for designing effective citizen participation mechanisms
- Understanding of the optimal balance between technical expertise and democratic input
- Identification of scalable models for democratic participation in technical governance
- Development of training and support systems for citizen participation in AI governance

Chapter 3
The Complexities of Human Factors in Automation Trust

Ronald Hayes
Capitol Technology University, USA

Darrell Norman Burrell
https://orcid.org/0000-0002-4675-9544
Capital Technology University, USA & Marymount University, USA

ABSTRACT

This study explores how organizational culture and human factors shape trust in automation and influence employee engagement, vigilance, and ethical behavior across high-consequence sectors. Through a multi-case analysis of five organizations, healthcare, biosecurity, emergency response, disaster logistics, and critical infrastructure, the research examines how governance documents, operational procedures, and training materials cultivate or corrode trust. The findings demonstrate that trust in automation is a social and organizational construct, not merely a technical outcome. Punitive cultures and opaque communication foster fear, resistance, and technology complacency and overreliance, while psychologically safe environments that emphasize transparency, dialogue, and shared ownership enable balanced, critical synergy driven trust in automation based on a collaborative relationship between people and technology. The study concludes that sustainable trust emerges when organizations institutionalize human-centered governance and engagement in ways that align automation with cultural values and empower employees to question and calibrate system performance. Ultimately, trust in automation depends on reciprocal accountability between humans and technology, grounded in organizational transparency, actionable user feedback mechanisms, and ethical leadership.

DOI: 10.4018/979-8-3373-9918-8.ch003

INTRODUCTION

Automation has transformed the operational landscape of modern workplaces, fundamentally altering how individuals interact with information, systems, and each other. From AI-powered diagnostics in hospitals to predictive dispatch systems in emergency management, automation promises enhanced efficiency and reliability. However, as Nobles (2019) contends, such technological evolution brings with it a "human paradox": as machines become more capable, human trust in them becomes both more essential and more precarious. Trust in automation is not a static belief but a dynamic relationship shaped by perception, context, and experience (Lee & See, 2004). In complex environments, particularly those characterized by uncertainty, high cognitive load, and moral consequence, trust must be carefully calibrated. Overtrust leads to complacency and uncritical reliance, while distrust results in underutilization of valuable systems (Parasuraman & Riley, 1997). Healthcare professionals ignoring valid alerts, emergency dispatchers deferring to faulty algorithms, or logistics coordinators rejecting accurate AI predictions all exemplify trust miscalibration.

Nobles (2022) and Robinson (2023) emphasize that such failures often stem from neglected human factors: cognitive overload, organizational misalignment, and inadequate feedback mechanisms. In contrast, organizations that embed human-centered design principles, prioritizing ergonomics, transparency, and participatory culture, tend to cultivate more resilient trust relationships. This paper extends these insights to analyze how trust in automation functions across three critical sectors: healthcare, emergency response, and disaster logistics, arguing that sustainable automation depends upon systematic integration of human factors engineering and organizational trust frameworks.

CONCEPTUALIZING HUMAN FACTORS AND AUTOMATION

Human factors encompass the study of how humans interact with technological systems, integrating disciplines such as cognitive psychology, ergonomics, and organizational behavior (Nobles & Burrell, 2024; Robinson, 2023). In automation contexts, these factors determine not only usability but also emotional and ethical dimensions of interaction. Despite the field's maturity, Nobles and Burrell (2024) found significant definitional inconsistency: many organizations reduce human factors to training programs or compliance checklists, ignoring their systemic implications.

In automation research, trust functions as the psychological bridge between human intention and machine action. Lee and See (2004) defined trust in automation as the "attitude that an agent will help achieve an individual's goals in a situation characterized by uncertainty and vulnerability." This definition captures the emotional complexity of dependence on automation. Users must navigate conflicting impulses: the desire for efficiency versus the fear of loss of control.

Consider the case of electronic health record (EHR) alert systems. When designed without attention to workflow ergonomics, such systems generate excessive or irrelevant alerts, overwhelming clinicians and triggering "alert fatigue" (Nobles, 2022; Stanton et al., 2016). The cognitive burden leads users to ignore both trivial and critical alerts indiscriminately, undermining the technology's intended purpose. The problem, therefore, is not technological inadequacy but a failure of human factors design, which may result from a mismatch between automation's behavior and human cognitive capacity.

Similarly, in emergency operations centers, automated decision-support dashboards often present data with insufficient contextual explanation. When responders do not understand how the system derives its recommendations, they cannot form appropriate levels of trust. Nobles (2019) observed that this opacity leads to operational paralysis: personnel either defer blindly to automation or disengage entirely. Transparent design, in which automation explains its reasoning in human-interpretable terms, has proven essential for restoring functional trust (Lee & See, 2004).

PROBLEM STATEMENT

The accelerating integration of automation into complex organizational environments, such as healthcare systems, biosecurity networks, and emergency response infrastructures, has created an unprecedented paradox of progress. While automation enhances efficiency, accuracy, and predictive capacity, it also introduces profound challenges related to human trust, vigilance, and accountability. Research in human factors consistently shows that automation does not eliminate human error; it transforms it (Parasuraman & Riley, 1997; Nobles, 2019). When users place excessive confidence in algorithmic processes, they risk cognitive disengagement and what Nobles (2022) terms automation complacency, a psychological state in which human operators abdicate critical oversight under the illusion of technological infallibility. Conversely, insufficient trust leads to underutilization, workflow fragmentation, and a reemergence of inefficiencies that automation was designed to resolve. The resulting tension between over-trust and distrust underscores a deeper organizational dilemma: institutions have become adept at deploying technologies but remain underdeveloped in cultivating the cultural and psychological conditions that sustain balanced, adaptive trust.

This problem is acutely visible in high-stakes fields where human judgment and automation intersect in time-sensitive decision-making. In healthcare, clinicians routinely rely on AI-assisted diagnostic tools yet exhibit both overreliance on system outputs and resistance to algorithmic recommendations. In biosecurity, automated detection platforms that can identify emerging pathogens still depend on human interpretation, but organizational hierarchies often discourage challenging automated alerts. In emergency and disaster logistics, predictive routing and supply prioritization systems have increased efficiency but occasionally overridden local expertise, eroding field-level confidence. Across these domains, automation's promise remains contingent on human adaptability, reflective learning, and organizational culture. Without deliberate strategies to manage these human factors, automation risks shifting organizations from error prevention to systemic complacency, where failures become invisible until catastrophic.

PURPOSE STATEMENT

The purpose of this injury is to critically examine how human factors theory and organizational culture frameworks can be integrated to strengthen trust in automation across healthcare, biosecurity, and disaster management systems. Specifically, this inquiry seeks to illuminate how reflective learning, transparent communication, and participatory design can mitigate the psychological drift toward complacency that often accompanies the institutionalization of automation. By synthesizing these frameworks with Nobles's (2018, 2019, 2022) research on human factors and cyber trust, the paper offers a multidimensional model for recalibrating human–machine relationships in mission-critical sectors.

This commentary also aims to advance practical understanding by linking theoretical insights to the operational realities of organizations confronting automation-driven transformation. Rather than proposing new technologies, this paper aims to reorient scholarly and managerial attention toward the human architecture that determines automation's success or failure. In doing so, it underscores that effective automation is not simply engineered; it is culturally sustained, psychologically reinforced, and ethically governed.

NOVELTY OF THE INQUIRY

This commentary advances a novel contribution to the discourse on human factors and automation by positioning trust not as a static state of confidence, but as a dynamic process of cultural alignment and psychological adaptation. While existing scholarship often treats automation trust as a function of interface design or algorithmic transparency (Lee & See, 2004; Parasuraman et al., 2000), this paper reframes it as an emergent property of organizational learning and culture. Drawing on Nobles and Burrell (2024), the analysis emphasizes that the sustainability of automation trust depends less on the precision of machine logic than on the human system's capacity for reflective oversight, open feedback, and ethical coherence. This interpretive synthesis moves beyond the technical-human binary to reveal trust as a relational construct, co-produced by cognitive, emotional, and structural elements that determine how automation is perceived, integrated, and questioned within institutions.

Furthermore, the inquiry's novelty lies in its cross-sectoral approach, bridging human factors principles across healthcare, biosecurity, and disaster logistics, fields rarely examined together in trust research. By contextualizing automation within these high-reliability domains, the paper reveals common vulnerabilities to complacency and common pathways to resilience. It argues that each domain, though distinct in operational tempo and technological architecture, faces parallel challenges in aligning automation with human purpose. The commentary, therefore, contributes a conceptual advancement: a multi-level model of trust in automation grounded in organizational learning, cultural transparency, and psychological engagement. This framework invites scholars and practitioners alike to reconceptualize automation not as a replacement for human cognition but as an evolving partner in collective intelligence, an alliance that succeeds only when trust is actively constructed, maintained, and continuously questioned.

TECHNOLOGICAL DETERMINISM

Technological determinism is the theory that technological advancement is the primary driver of social, organizational, and behavioral change, shaping human actions and societal structures more than human agency or cultural factors do (Nobles, 2015; Burrell et al., 2018; Burton et al. 2023). Within this framework, technology is viewed as an autonomous force that progresses according to its own logic, compelling individuals and institutions to adapt their values, behaviors, and practices to its imperatives (Nobles, 2015; Burrell et al., 2018; Burton et al. 2023). In organizational contexts, this often manifests as the belief that efficiency and productivity improvements inevitably follow from more reliance and use of technological innovation, regardless of human, cultural, or ethical considerations (Nobles, 2015; Burrell et al., 2018; Burton et al. 2023). This deterministic mindset can obscure the relational and interpretive dimensions of technology use, where trust, understanding, and adaptation are not automatic outcomes but products of deliberate human engagement and organizational culture (Nobles, 2015; Burrell et al., 2018; Burton et al. 2023).

When applied to trust in automation, technological determinism creates both opportunities and risks. It can promote overconfidence in automated systems, leading employees to assume that technology is inherently objective, infallible, and superior to human judgment. This assumption contributes to cognitive complacency, where users defer decision-making to machines and disengage from critical evaluation, especially in environments that lack psychological safety or transparent communication about system limitations. Human factors research counters this by emphasizing that trust must be calibrated, neither excessive nor deficient, and that sustained vigilance depends on designing systems that enhance, rather than replace, human cognition (Nobles, 2022; Robinson, 2023). Overreliance on automation, when driven by deterministic assumptions, diminishes situational awareness, ethical reflection, and adaptability, highlighting the need for a socio-technical balance where technology supports, but does not dominate, human agency and organizational learning.

WORKPLACE PSYCHOLOGICAL SAFETY

Workplace psychological safety refers to a shared belief among employees that they can express ideas, raise concerns, admit mistakes, and ask questions without fear of humiliation or retribution (Burrell, 2022; Edmondson, 2018; McCausland, 2023). It includes creating an organizational culture that embraces, values, and respects employees for their expertise and authentic selves in the workplace (Burrell, 2022; Edmondson, 2018; McCausland, 2023). It fosters an environment where individuals feel secure taking interpersonal risks, which is essential for learning, innovation, and collaboration (Burrell, 2022; Edmondson, 2018; McCausland, 2023).

When trust intersects with automation and technology complexity, psychological safety becomes even more significant. As organizations integrate increasingly sophisticated automated systems, employees must trust both the technology and the people managing it. High psychological safety allows employees to voice uncertainties about automated processes, question system outputs, and share concerns about technological limitations without fear of blame. This openness enhances human–automation teaming by encouraging vigilance, appropriate trust calibration, and mutual reliance between humans and machines.

However, as technology grows more complex, maintaining psychological safety requires deliberate organizational effort. Ambiguity about system functioning or accountability can erode trust and suppress communication, leading to overreliance or underutilization of automation. Therefore, cultivating psychological safety in technologically advanced workplaces ensures that employees remain confident and empowered to engage critically with automation, balancing trust with healthy skepticism to optimize both human and system performance (Burrell, 2022; Edmondson, 2018; McCausland, 2023).

ORGANIZATIONAL LEARNING THEORY

Organizational Learning Theory provides a foundational framework for understanding how institutions evolve their relationships with automation and confront the human factors influencing trust, vigilance, and complacency. Organizational Learning Theory suggests that organizations improve and adapt by acquiring, sharing, and applying knowledge through individual and collective learning processes. In relation to employee behavior, it emphasizes that continuous learning, reflection, and employee feedback drive innovation, adaptability, and sustained organizational performance (Argyris & Schön, 1997; Basten & Haamann, 2018; Crossan et al., 1995). Previous research distinguished between single-loop learning, in which organizations correct errors within existing norms, and double-loop learning, in which they question and revise the underlying norms (Argyris & Schön, 1997; Basten & Haamann, 2018; Crossan et al., 1995). In automation contexts, single-loop learning manifests when institutions modify procedural parameters, such as recalibrating a predictive model, without reconsidering how systemic assumptions about human oversight may contribute to failure (Argyris & Schön, 1997; Basten & Haamann, 2018; Crossan et al., 1995). Double-loop learning, by contrast, compels organizations to interrogate their own cognitive and cultural architecture, asking not merely what went wrong but why trust eroded in the first place. Nobles (2019) argued that such feedback-rich learning ecosystems are essential for sustaining adaptive trust between human and machine. This distinction becomes particularly salient in high-stakes environments. In healthcare, when an automated diagnostic system fails to flag a critical anomaly, a single-loop response might involve technical recalibration.

A double-loop approach, however, would examine whether the hospital's operational culture implicitly discourages clinicians from questioning machine output. When institutions engage in this deeper reflection, they counteract the complacency that arises from excessive deference to automation. In biosecurity, where predictive analytics are employed to detect pathogen outbreaks, double-loop learning ensures that human analysts remain active participants rather than passive observers of machine-generated alerts. Similarly, in emergency response planning, agencies that periodically review not only system malfunctions but also communication norms and decision hierarchies develop resilient cultures in which automation is seen as a partner in reasoning, not an arbiter of truth. By embedding double-loop learning into post-incident analysis, organizations cultivate a dynamic trust that is continuously recalibrated rather than assumed, reinforcing both operational reliability and human agency.

THE JOB DEMANDS–RESOURCES (JD–R) MODEL

The Job Demands–Resources (JD–R) model offers a powerful framework for understanding how automation alters the psychological and operational equilibrium between cognitive demands and available resources. The Job Demands–Resources (JD–R) Model proposes that employee well-being and performance are influenced by the balance between job demands (e.g., workload or emotional strain) and job resources (e.g., support, autonomy, or development opportunities). In organizational settings, the model explains how excessive demands can lead to burnout, while sufficient resources foster engagement, motivation, and improved performance (Bakker & Demerouti, 2017; Hu et al., 2011; Lesener et al., 2019). Research conceptualized work environments as balancing acts between demands, such as workload, stress, and attentional load, and resources, such as autonomy, support, and effective tools (Bakker & Demerouti, 2017; Hu et al., 2011; Lesener et al., 2019). Nobles (2022) applied this framework to cybersecurity and automation, noting that poorly designed systems often increase cognitive strain rather than alleviate it, thereby transforming automation from a supportive resource into an additional demand. Trust in automation thus functions as a vital psychological resource that mediates perceived workload. When operators trust automated systems appropriately, they experience reduced uncertainty and cognitive fatigue. Nevertheless, misplaced trust can invert this relationship, leading to vigilance decay, complacency, and overreliance on flawed outputs.

In healthcare, for instance, electronic medication administration systems were introduced to reduce dosage errors. Initially, nurses experienced decreased stress due to reduced cognitive load. However, when staff began to rely exclusively on barcode scans without verifying dosages, "automation complacency" led to critical near misses. Hospitals that later implemented training emphasizing dual verification and trusting but verifying automation restored balance to the demand–resource equation. In biosecurity, analysts monitoring biosurveillance algorithms have reported "automation fatigue," particularly when false positives from predictive models overwhelm human review capacity. Institutions that mitigate this by rotating analysts and establishing transparent thresholds for machine alerts preserve trust while preventing exhaustion. In emergency response centers, operators using AI-driven dispatch systems may initially experience cognitive overload due to unfamiliar interfaces. Through iterative design and training programs, automation can shift from a source of demand to a genuine cognitive resource. The JD–R model, therefore, clarifies that trust is neither static nor uniformly beneficial; it is a dynamic construct contingent on the system's ability to reduce rather than amplify psychological strain.

THE THEORY OF PLANNED BEHAVIOR

The Theory of Planned Behavior (TPB) illuminates how attitudes, norms, and perceived control jointly shape human interaction with automation. The Theory of Planned Behavior (TPB) posits that an individual's behavior is driven by their intentions, which are influenced by attitudes toward the behavior, subjective norms, and perceived behavioral control(Ajzen, 1991; Ajzen, 2020; Bosnjak et al., 2020; Sussman & Gifford, 2019). In organizational contexts, TPB helps explain how employees' beliefs about workplace norms, their perceived ability to perform tasks, and their attitudes toward organizational goals shape their motivation and actual workplace behaviors (Ajzen, 1991; Ajzen, 2020; Bosnjak et al., 2020; Sussman & Gifford, 2019). Previous research posited that behavioral intention arises from the interplay of three antecedents: attitude toward the behavior, subjective norms, and perceived behavioral control (Ajzen, 1991; Ajzen, 2020; Bosnjak et al., 2020; Sussman & Gifford, 2019). Within technologically mediated work environments, these components govern whether individuals engage meaningfully with automated systems or defer responsibility to them. Nobles (2022) observed that automation failure often reflects a cultural rather than technical breakdown: negative social norms or a lack of perceived competence can hinder adoption, while uncritical group endorsement can foster over-trust and complacency.

The Theory of Planned Behavior (TPB) resonates with concrete findings across multiple domains (Ajzen, 2020; Bosnjak et al., 2020; Sussman & Gifford, 2019). In healthcare, clinicians' attitudes toward automated diagnostic systems significantly influence use: when peers and senior physicians endorse the technology as a collaborative aid rather than a substitute for expertise, adoption improves without fostering dependence. Conversely, when leadership presents automation as infallible, it erodes professional discretion and cultivates complacency. In biosecurity operations, analysts often operate within tight social networks that valorize either human expertise or technological precision. When institutional culture skews toward the latter, perceived behavioral control diminishes, and analysts may hesitate to question automated anomaly detection outputs, risking missed outbreaks. In emergency management, dispatchers initially distrusted predictive routing algorithms designed to optimize resource allocation. Organizational leaders countered this by modeling confident, critical engagement with the technology, coupling training with transparent feedback mechanisms. As attitudes and norms evolved, so too did trust, recalibrated to balance reliance and scrutiny. Across these contexts, TPB demonstrates that trust in automation is a socially constructed behavior shaped by shared meaning, reinforcement, and accountability structures, not merely individual cognition.

THE ICEBERG MODEL OF ORGANIZATIONAL CULTURE

The Iceberg Model of organizational culture provides a compelling metaphor for understanding how invisible cultural forces shape trust and complacency in automation. The Iceberg Model of Organizational Culture illustrates that most aspects of an organization's culture, such as values, beliefs, and assumptions, exist below the surface and are not immediately visible behavior (Biewendt et al., 2021; Haider, 2009; Mahringer et al., 2025; Sasu, 2016). Only a small portion, like behaviors, symbols, and practices, is observable, while the deeper, unseen elements shape and sustain the organization's true character and dynamic behavior (Biewendt et al., 2021; Haider, 2009; Mahringer et al., 2025; Sasu, 2016). The model distinguishes between visible artifacts, such as technology, procedures, and formal policies, and invisible assumptions, values, and emotional undercurrents that drive behavior (Biewendt et al., 2021; Haider, 2009; Mahringer et al., 2025; Sasu, 2016).

Nobles (2018, 2022) observed that automation initiatives frequently falter when institutions attempt to modify only the visible layer while neglecting the deeper cultural substrata. When automation is perceived as a tool for surveillance or control, distrust proliferates regardless of system performance. When, however, automation aligns with invisible organizational values of collaboration, safety, and ethical accountability, it becomes a trusted partner rather than a source of anxiety.

This dual-layer framework manifests vividly in healthcare and emergency operations. At a large metropolitan hospital, an automated patient-monitoring system intended to predict cardiac arrest faced widespread resistance because staff associated it with punitive oversight. Nurses viewed the technology not as a safety measure but as an extension of managerial scrutiny. Only after leadership engaged staff through transparent discussions and redefined the system as a shared safety instrument did trust and compliance improve. In biosecurity laboratories, automation in pathogen detection is often perceived as an encroachment on scientific judgment. Institutions that encourage scientists to interpret, challenge, and contextualize automated results foster both trust and vigilance. Similarly, in disaster logistics centers, where AI-based supply prioritization tools allocate aid, local responders often distrust algorithms trained on foreign datasets. By providing local visibility into decision logic and allowing human override, organizations bridge the gap between visible artifacts and invisible values, reinforcing the cultural foundations of trust. The Iceberg Model thus illustrates that true human–automation alignment requires harmonizing visible system design with the deeper, unspoken beliefs that define how organizations understand control, accountability, and value.

DENISON'S ORGANIZATIONAL CULTURE MODEL

Denison's Organizational Culture Model extends this analysis by linking cultural characteristics to operational performance and adaptive trust. Denison's Organizational Culture Model links organizational culture to performance through four key traits: involvement, consistency, adaptability, and mission (Denison & Spreitzer, 1991; Denison, 1990; Denison et al., 2014). In relation to employee behavior, the model suggests that when employees are engaged, aligned with shared values, responsive to change, and guided by a clear sense of purpose, the organization achieves higher commitment, effectiveness, and overall performance (Denison & Spreitzer, 1991; Denison, 1990; Denison et al., 2014). The model provides a framework to explain how organizations integrate automation and sustain human factors alignment. Involvement promotes participatory design, empowering employees to shape automation in ways that preserve human oversight. Consistency fosters ethical coherence and behavioral predictability, aligning automation practices with shared values. Adaptability supports organizational learning and feedback, ensuring that automation evolves with contextual demands. Mission anchors change and employee engagement initiatives in a clear, value-driven narrative, mitigating anxiety and resistance (Denison & Spreitzer, 1991; Denison, 1990; Denison et al., 2014). Nobles (2019) emphasizes that organizations embodying these traits are more likely to build automation ecosystems rooted in trust, accountability, and human engagement.

These dynamics are particularly evident in biosecurity, healthcare, and emergency logistics. In a global humanitarian logistics network, an AI-based resource allocation system was initially met with resistance from field operators, who viewed its decisions as detached from local realities. By adopting Denison's principles, leadership restructured governance: involving field personnel in algorithmic refinement, embedding ethical priorities into coding logic, and linking system use to the organization's mission of equitable resource distribution. The result was a measurable increase in trust, performance accuracy, and user retention. In healthcare, a teaching hospital struggling with clinician resistance to an AI triage system implemented cross-disciplinary calibration workshops that emphasized adaptability and mission alignment. When physicians were empowered to interpret and critique algorithmic outputs, trust rose alongside diagnostic accuracy. In biosecurity emergency planning, agencies that applied Denison's "adaptability" and "involvement" principles improved transparency in decision-making and inter-agency collaboration during pathogen response simulations. These cases underscore that trust in automation arises not from technical optimization but from cultural coherence, wherein human and technological systems evolve symbiotically under shared ethical and strategic values.

TRUST DYNAMICS IN HEALTHCARE AUTOMATION

Healthcare is among the most ethically charged domains for automation. Clinicians must make life-critical decisions under conditions of uncertainty, often informed by algorithmic systems. According to Nobles (2022), the psychological and ergonomic conditions of these environments, including long hours, cognitive fatigue, and high emotional stakes, make trust calibration particularly fragile. Take AI-assisted diagnostic imaging as a representative case. Radiologists increasingly rely on automated image classifiers to identify anomalies. When these systems perform reliably, trust deepens; when they fail silently or generate false positives, trust erodes rapidly. Nevertheless, as Parasuraman and Riley (1997) note, human operators are prone to "automation bias," a cognitive shortcut that privileges machine judgment even in the face of contradictory human observation. A radiologist deferring to an incorrect AI result exemplifies misplaced trust.

Conversely, insufficient trust can negate automation's benefits. In 2021, a major hospital network implemented an AI triage system designed to predict patient deterioration. Nurses, skeptical of its opaque algorithmic logic, frequently ignored recommendations. As a result, early warnings were missed, leading to delayed interventions. When administrators later introduced transparent feedback interfaces that displayed risk factors in plain language and incorporated clinician feedback loops, trust and performance both improved.

These examples illustrate Nobles's (2018) argument that human-centered system design, which accounts for psychological readiness, cognitive ergonomics, and workload balance, is essential to the success of automation. Trust does not emerge from technology alone, but from a socio-technical equilibrium in which human experience is integrated into design and governance.

HUMAN FACTORS IN EMERGENCY RESPONSE SYSTEMS

Emergency response operations, ranging from 911 dispatch to wildfire coordination, represent another domain where automation can simultaneously empower and endanger decision-making. Nobles (2019) asserts that trust failures in these systems are often catastrophic because decisions must be made under extreme temporal pressure.

Modern emergency management increasingly employs predictive analytics and geospatial algorithms to optimize resource allocation. However, when human factors are neglected, the resulting automation can misinterpret situational context. During the 2018 California wildfires, automated dispatch algorithms routed responders based on traffic data rather than hazard maps, sending units into dangerous zones. Operators, conditioned to trust system accuracy, followed instructions without challenge. The outcome was both operational inefficiency and elevated risk, a case of overtrust shaped by organizational culture rather than individual error (Nobles, 2018).

Alternatively, in well-designed systems, trust can enhance resilience. The London Ambulance Service's computer-aided dispatch platform, for instance, integrates human oversight into its decision loop. When anomalies occur, such as conflicting sensor inputs, dispatchers receive contextual explanations and are encouraged to override recommendations. This balance of automation and agency reflects Nobles and Burrell's (2024) principle of "bidirectional trust": the system trusts human expertise, and humans, in turn, trust the system's transparency.

The success of such systems depends heavily on organizational culture. Nobles (2019) observed that hierarchical organizations often discourage questioning automation outputs, equating it with insubordination. By contrast, cultures that reward critical inquiry foster adaptive trust and better outcomes. Emergency organizations must therefore treat trust as an evolving competency, one to be trained, measured, and refined, not assumed.

AUTOMATION AND TRUST IN DISASTER LOGISTICS

In disaster logistics, automation governs the flow of life-saving materials across unstable, resource-constrained environments. Algorithms forecast demand, coordinate transportation, and prioritize distribution. However, as Nobles (2019) cautions, automation can obscure human judgment when feedback loops are weak or local knowledge is undervalued.

Following the 2010 Haiti earthquake, automated supply chain systems designed to optimize efficiency inadvertently prioritized routes with stable digital infrastructure, sidelining rural areas most in need. Local responders, aware of the discrepancy, lacked the authority to intervene. This breakdown exemplified trust asymmetry, a condition in which decision authority is centralized in machines while accountability remains human (Nobles & Burrell, 2024).

Recent advances in AI-driven humanitarian logistics attempt to mitigate such failures. For instance, the World Food Programme's "LogIE" (Logistics Execution

Support System) integrates predictive analytics with human-in-the-loop validation, allowing local coordinators to modify algorithmic priorities in real time. This participatory model embodies Nobles's (2022) advocacy for feedback-rich socio-technical ecosystems. Trust is reinforced not by automation's autonomy but by its responsiveness to human expertise.

Furthermore, integrating psychological safety into automation governance is essential. When field operators fear reprimand for questioning automated outputs, they disengage, producing what Nobles (2018) calls "learned helplessness in digital systems." In contrast, organizations that promote open dialogue, such as Japan's Fire and Disaster Management Agency, maintain higher situational adaptability. These agencies employ hybrid automation that merges predictive algorithms with manual reporting, creating a cognitive partnership between human intuition and machine precision.

INTEGRATING HUMAN-CENTERED DESIGN AND ORGANIZATIONAL CULTURE

At the heart of trust in automation lies organizational culture, the invisible framework that shapes how individuals interpret and engage with technology. Nobles (2018) identified punitive cultures as primary barriers to effective automation adoption. When automation is perceived as a surveillance mechanism rather than a supportive tool, users resist it, leading to circumvention or noncompliance.

In healthcare, for example, automated productivity tracking in electronic systems has provoked clinician distrust. When performance data are used punitively rather than constructively, trust collapses (Nobles, 2022). Conversely, organizations that embrace psychological safety, where errors can be discussed without fear, see markedly higher trust in technology.

Human-centered design extends beyond interface aesthetics; it encompasses communication, accountability, and shared ownership of automation outcomes. The U.S. Department of Veterans Affairs provides a relevant example. When its automated medication dispensing systems produced inconsistent alerts, administrators involved pharmacists directly in redesign efforts. By aligning system parameters with user expertise, the institution not only improved safety metrics but also deepened practitioner trust. This user-centered approach aligns with Nobles's (2019) recommendation to treat trust calibration as a continuous process, reinforced through experience and dialogue.

Ultimately, organizational alignment is what transforms automation from a compliance artifact into a collaborative partner. Leadership commitment to participatory governance, transparency, and education ensures that trust in automation evolves in tandem with organizational maturity.

METHODS OVERVIEW

This inquiry employed a multi-case document, procedure, and policy analysis to examine how organizations operationalize human factors in the governance of automation and how those choices shape trust and the propensity for complacency. The analytic objective was explanatory rather than merely descriptive: to trace how written rules, procedural artifacts, and decision protocols cultivate or corrode appropriate trust in automation.

CASE SELECTION AND DATA CORPUS

Five organizations were purposefully sampled to maximize variation in mission, risk profile, and automation maturity while ensuring comparability in scale and governance complexity:

- **Company A (Healthcare)**: an urban tertiary hospital adopting AI-assisted triage and automated medication management.
- **Company B (Biosecurity)**: a laboratory using algorithmic bio-surveillance and automated anomaly detection.
- **Company C (Emergency Response Planning)**: a metropolitan emergency communications center deploying AI-enabled dispatch and predictive routing.
- **Company D (Disaster Logistics)**: a humanitarian logistics agency using optimization models for supply pre-positioning and last-mile distribution.
- **Company E (Integrated Critical Infrastructure)**: a multi-utility provider coordinating cyber-physical automation across control centers.

For each organization, the data corpus included: (a) policies, standards, and governance charters; (b) standard operating procedures (SOPs), runbooks, playbooks, checklists; (c) incident and post-incident (after-action) reports; (d) training curricula and competency rubrics; (e) change-control and model-validation documents for automated systems; and (f) internal communications (memos, FAQs, "lessons learned") that interpret policy for frontline use. Where available, versions spanning 12–60 months were collected to support longitudinal inferences about learning and drift.

SYSTEMATIC PROCESS FOR DOCUMENT SELECTION AND EVALUATION

1. Scoping and Access Control

The process began with a formal scoping phase to define the boundaries of inquiry across participating organizations. Each organization granted access to a curated repository or secure read-only portal containing relevant governance, operational, and training documents. A scoping inventory was then created to catalog the materials, documenting key metadata such as provenance (source department or author), creation and revision dates, governance status (draft, approved, or archived), and intended operational audience. This step established a transparent audit trail to ensure traceability and accountability in data management.

2. Inclusion and Eligibility Screening

Next, documents were systematically screened against predefined inclusion criteria to ensure relevance to human–automation interaction and organizational trust mechanisms. A document was included if it satisfied at least one of the following conditions:

1. Governed or described human interaction with automated systems (e.g., control room procedures, decision-support guidelines).
2. Codified responses to automation failures, near misses, or alerts, reflecting how trust and vigilance were operationalized during system breakdowns.
3. Instructed training, oversight, or escalation processes within human–machine workflows (e.g., supervision protocols or human factors training materials).

Documents failing to meet these criteria, such as purely technical system specifications or administrative memoranda unrelated to human engagement, were excluded. This eligibility phase ensured conceptual coherence and analytic focus on the human factors dimensions of trust, autonomy, and vigilance.

3. Classification and Data Organization

Eligible materials were then classified into six analytic categories reflecting organizational structure and procedural relevance:

1. Policies, standards, and governance charters;
2. Standard Operating Procedures (SOPs), runbooks, and checklists;

3. Incident and post-incident (after-action) reports;
4. Training curricula and competency rubrics;
5. Change-control and model-validation documentation for automated systems;
6. Internal communications such as memos, FAQs, and "lessons learned" summaries.

Each document was coded for time span (12–60 months) to enable longitudinal analysis of policy evolution and "organizational drift." This temporal layering allowed the study to trace how learning and adaptation influenced trust and complacency over time.

4. Evaluation of Credibility and Relevance

Documents were assessed for **credibility**, using three validation dimensions:

- **Authenticity**, verifying that documents originated from authoritative organizational sources and reflected formal governance or operational practice.
- **Completeness**, confirming that the content provided sufficient procedural, contextual, or interpretive detail for analysis.
- **Currency**, ensuring that materials represented current or recently updated practices relevant to automation and human factors.

Relevance was evaluated by examining the conceptual alignment of each document with the study's analytic constructs, trust calibration, psychological safety, and human–automation interaction quality.

5. Triangulation and Cross-Validation

A triangulation process tested convergence across different document types. Policy texts, SOPs, incident narratives, and training artifacts were compared to identify consistent mechanisms of trust reinforcement or erosion. For example, a training curriculum emphasizing "responsible automation oversight" was cross-referenced with post-incident reports to determine whether employees actually exercised that oversight during operational stress. Discrepancies or contradictions between policy intent and operational behavior were flagged for deeper qualitative analysis, supporting a mechanistic, plausibility-based analytic framework rather than a purely descriptive approach.

6. Synthesis and Analytical Integration

Finally, the validated corpus was synthesized into a cross-case analytical framework. Patterns were extracted across the five organizational cases (healthcare, biosecurity, emergency response, disaster logistics, and integrated critical infrastructure) to identify recurring governance practices that cultivated or corroded appropriate trust. Analytical memos summarized the human-factor mechanisms linking automation design, organizational culture, and operator behavior. These insights informed the final recommendations for fostering trust in automation while preventing complacency.

Summary

This stepwise process ensured methodological rigor and transparency from selection through synthesis. By combining systematic screening, credibility evaluation, and cross-document triangulation, the analysis privileged the human and organizational dimensions of automation governance. The resulting corpus provided not only a descriptive account of documented practices but also an explanatory foundation for understanding how culture, policy, and human factors collectively shape the dynamics of trust and complacency in automated environments.

Data Collection Procedures

Access and scoping. Each organization provided a curated repository or secure read-only portal. A scoping inventory documented the provenance, date range, and governance status of each document to establish an audit trail.

Eligibility screening. Documents were included if they (i) governed or described human interaction with automated systems, (ii) codified responses to automation failures or near misses, or (iii) instructed training, oversight, or escalation in human–machine workflows.

Credibility and triangulation. Convergence across policy text, SOPs, incident narratives, and training artifacts was tested for each mechanism before inclusion in the final set of recommendations.

Limitations and Scope

The analysis privileges the textual and procedural expression of organizational practice; tacit practices and informal norms were inferred from incident narratives and training materials but not directly observed ethnographically. Causal claims are therefore mechanistic and plausibility-based, not experimental. Nonetheless, the recurrence of patterns across five distinct organizations, each operating in high-consequence settings, supplies robust explanatory leverage and a transparent, stepwise rationale for the recommendations.

PRACTICAL RECOMMENDATIONS

1. Institutionalize Double-Loop Learning Practices

Organizations should embed double-loop learning into post-incident reviews and system audits to ensure that automation failures trigger not only technical corrections but also reflection on underlying assumptions, workflows, and human–machine interaction norms. In healthcare, this might involve analyzing not just algorithmic misdiagnoses but also whether hierarchical cultures inhibit clinicians from questioning automated outputs. In emergency operations, it means examining how standard operating procedures may unintentionally prioritize machine speed over human discernment.

2. Design Automation as a Cognitive Partner, Not a Procedural Replacement

Automation systems should be designed to augment human decision-making rather than to supplant it. Human factors engineering principles (Nobles, 2022) suggest that trust and vigilance are sustained when systems provide interpretable rationales, contextual cues, and user agency. For example, in biosecurity monitoring, dashboards that display the reasoning behind anomaly detection, such as probability thresholds or data provenance, encourage analytic engagement instead of passive acceptance.

3. Conduct Regular Trust Calibration Training

Organizations should engage personnel in trust calibration exercises, structured activities that expose both the strengths and limitations of automation. In healthcare, this might include simulations where clinicians must decide when to override AI diagnostic recommendations. In disaster logistics, responders could practice scenarios in which automated routing suggestions are intentionally flawed, reinforcing the indispensability of critical thinking. Such exercises cultivate "appropriate trust," the equilibrium between over-trust and distrust (Lee & See, 2004).

4. Balance Job Demands and Resources Through Human-Centered System Design

Applying the Job Demands–Resources (JD–R) model can help organizations prevent burnout and cognitive overload resulting from poorly implemented automation. Systems should be introduced with corresponding increases in resources, clear training, feedback loops, and supportive supervision, to offset new cognitive demands. In emergency response centers, for example, AI-based dispatch tools should be accompanied by intuitive interfaces and mentoring programs to prevent stress-induced vigilance decay.

5. Foster Transparent Communication About Automation Intent and Limitations

Trust thrives in transparency. Leaders must clearly communicate the purpose, scope, and limits of automation to mitigate fear and misinformation. In biosecurity laboratories, explaining that machine learning algorithms are designed to assist rather than replace pathogen analysts can preserve morale and professional identity. In healthcare, open dialogue about algorithmic boundaries, what the AI can and cannot infer, prevents misplaced confidence that breeds complacency.

6. Align Automation with Organizational Culture and Mission

Using Denison's model, organizations should ensure that automation initiatives align with core values (consistency), engage personnel in co-design (involvement), adapt to emerging contexts (adaptability), and advance the institution's mission (strategic direction). For instance, in humanitarian logistics, involving local field staff in algorithm development strengthens perceived fairness and psychological ownership. In hospitals, aligning AI diagnostic tools with a mission of patient-centered care, rather than administrative efficiency, enhances trust and ethical acceptance.

7. Promote "Cultural Surfacing" to Address Invisible Barriers to Trust

Drawing on the Iceberg Model, leaders should identify and address the *hidden assumptions* that shape attitudes toward automation. Addressing these hidden dynamics may involve facilitated discussions, cultural assessments, or focus groups that uncover unspoken fears, such as surveillance anxiety, job insecurity, or loss of autonomy. In biosecurity or healthcare, acknowledging these latent beliefs openly allows organizations to realign visible technological artifacts with underlying cultural values, closing the trust gap between people and systems.

8. Establish Cross-Functional Human–Automation Governance Committees

Institutions should create interdisciplinary governance structures that bring together engineers, behavioral scientists, clinicians, and emergency planners to oversee automation ethics, trust metrics, and risk management. Such committees can institutionalize reflective oversight, ensuring that automation remains accountable to both technical performance and human well-being. In emergency logistics agencies, these groups can review algorithmic fairness and equity implications for disaster resource distribution.

9. Implement Continuous Feedback and Learning Ecosystems

Automation should never be treated as static. Systems and users evolve together. Implementing real-time feedback loops in which end users report anomalies, usability issues, or contextual mismatches keeps the trust dynamic and data-driven. In healthcare, integrated feedback mechanisms in electronic health record (EHR) systems can allow nurses and physicians to flag algorithmic inconsistencies. In biosecurity surveillance, feedback loops can recalibrate detection models in light of local ecological variations, reinforcing a sense of joint learning between human and machine.

10. Embed Ethical Reflection and Psychological Safety Into Automation Policy

Finally, organizations must cultivate psychological safety so that employees can question or override automation without fear of reprisal (Edmonston, 2018). Policies should frame human intervention not as error but as responsible vigilance. In disaster management agencies, encouraging responders to voice dissent against automated route prioritization can prevent moral distress and maintain operational integrity. By embedding ethics and human judgment into automation policy, organizations safeguard against the most insidious risk of all, silent compliance in the face of flawed automation.

DISCUSSION

The analysis across sectors reveals several recurring themes. First, trust in automation is inseparable from human factors. Whether in healthcare or disaster response, user confidence depends on systems that communicate intentions clearly, behave predictably, and respond adaptively to human input (Lee & See, 2004). Second, trust is not a static attribute but a dynamic construct that fluctuates with context, experience, and emotion (Nobles, 2022).

Nobles (2019) proposes establishing formal human factors programs to institutionalize this process. These programs would evaluate cognitive load, emotional stress, ergonomic design, and social attitudes toward automation. Much like aviation's Crew Resource Management, such initiatives would foster mutual accountability between humans and machines.

Moreover, interdisciplinary collaboration is imperative. Nobles and Burrell (2024) criticize the siloed nature of automation design, where engineers dominate decision-making with minimal input from behavioral scientists. Integrating human factors experts, ethicists, and frontline operators can transform automation development from a purely technical pursuit into a genuinely socio-technical enterprise.

From a policy perspective, organizations should implement trust audits, periodic evaluations that measure how users perceive, interpret, and act on automation outputs. Metrics might include alert response rates, override frequencies, or self-reported trust indices. This data provides feedback not only for technology designers but also for leaders responsible for cultivating ethical and effective automation practices.

The evolution of automation within healthcare, emergency response, and disaster logistics underscores an enduring truth: technology cannot secure itself without human insight. Trust in automation is not an incidental outcome of engineering excellence but the product of sustained attention to human cognition, culture, and ethics. Building upon Nobles's (2018, 2019, 2022) and Nobles and Burrell's (2024) insights, this paper demonstrates that effective automation is fundamentally human-centered. It thrives in environments that balance confidence with skepticism, precision with empathy, and autonomy with accountability. Sustainable trust emerges when organizations treat human factors not as a peripheral concern but as the foundation of technological design and deployment. As workplaces continue to automate, the next frontier of innovation will not be purely computational but relational: constructing systems that trust their users as much as users trust their systems. Such reciprocity, anchored in transparency, participation, and shared responsibility, defines the future of automation worthy of human trust.

Ethical Implications

The integration of human-centered design and organizational culture in automation raises profound ethical considerations, including transparency, accountability, fairness, and respect for human dignity. When automation is deployed within punitive or opaque organizational cultures, it risks reinforcing surveillance dynamics, amplifying biases, and eroding employee autonomy. Ethical governance requires that automation be implemented to augment, not replace, human judgment, and that its outputs be subject to human oversight and contestation. This level of oversight includes ensuring that algorithmic systems are auditable, decisions are explainable, and that those affected by automation have a voice in its design and operation.

Moreover, ethical responsibility extends to protecting psychological safety and preserving moral agency in technologically mediated work environments. Employees must be empowered to question or override automated recommendations without fear of reprisal, and policies must explicitly frame human intervention as ethical vigilance rather than disobedience. Organizations have a duty to prevent "moral deskilling," where overreliance on automation dulls ethical reasoning and critical awareness. Embedding ethical reflection within training, governance, and policy reviews ensures that automation operates within a framework of justice, empathy, and shared responsibility. In this way, ethical design and organizational culture jointly safeguard the integrity of both the human workforce and the technological systems that support them.

Policy Implications

From a policy standpoint, integrating human-centered design into organizational culture requires formal frameworks to institutionalize trust calibration, psychological safety, and participatory governance. Policies must explicitly distinguish between automation as a performance-enhancing tool and automation as a surveillance mechanism to prevent punitive misuse of data and consequent employee resistance. Establishing trust audits and human–automation governance committees, as suggested by Nobles (2018, 2019, 2022), would provide structured oversight of system reliability, human factors compliance, and ethical accountability. Additionally, policies should embed double-loop learning mechanisms, ensuring that when automation fails or underperforms, reviews address not only technical faults but also the organizational assumptions, communication norms, and decision hierarchies that may have contributed to the event.

Organizational Implications

At the organizational level, aligning automation with cultural values and operational goals transforms technology from a compliance tool into a collaborative partner. Leadership must cultivate psychological safety, enabling employees to question or override automated systems without fear of reprisal. Furthermore, organizations must align automation initiatives with the Denison model's four traits, consistency, involvement, adaptability, and mission, to ensure cultural coherence and reinforce a sense of purpose. By promoting interdisciplinary collaboration among engineers, behavioral scientists, and frontline staff, organizations move from a technically deterministic approach to a socio-technical model where human judgment and machine precision reinforce each other.

Technology Implications

Technological design must be human-centered, emphasizing interpretability, contextual awareness, and user control to sustain appropriate trust and mitigate complacency. Systems that communicate their reasoning processes, constraints, and uncertainty levels enable users to engage cognitively rather than passively accept automation outputs. As Nobles (2022) asserts, automation should function as a cognitive partner, not a procedural replacement. Regular trust calibration training and continuous feedback ecosystems between users and systems are essential to maintain dynamic trust and adaptive learning. Additionally, design standards should integrate human factors principles, ensuring that automation reduces rather than adds to cognitive workload, supports situational awareness, and provides ergonomic interfaces that enhance confidence and vigilance.

Employee Implications

For employees, the convergence of human-centered design, organizational culture, and automation profoundly shapes their experience of trust, autonomy, and professional identity. In punitive or opaque environments, automation can heighten stress, fear, and disengagement; conversely, in psychologically safe and transparent organizations, it can enhance learning, confidence, and innovation. Employees benefit most when they are included in design, feedback, and governance processes, reinforcing a sense of agency and shared accountability. Training initiatives that focus on trust calibration, recognizing when to rely on or challenge automation, strengthen critical thinking and ethical awareness. Ultimately, fostering an environment where employees are trusted to exercise judgment ensures that automation enhances human capability rather than diminishes it, promoting a balanced ecosystem of mutual trust between people and technology.

Darrell Norman Burrell and Calvin Nobles have created the Burrell/Nobles Trust in Automation Complacency (TAC) Model, which focuses on the cognitive, behavioral, and organizational dimensions of human–automation interaction.

BURRELL/NOBLES TRUST IN AUTOMATION COMPLACENCY (TAC) MODEL

Overview

The Trust in Automation Complacency (TAC) Model explains how human factors, cognitive load, psychological safety, organizational culture, and feedback mechanisms interact to shape trust and mitigate complacency in automated systems and potential lapses in cybersecurity. It conceptualizes trust not as a fixed psychological state but as a dynamic human process that evolves through perception, experience, and context. The model emphasizes that sustainable trust arises when human–machine relationships are grounded in transparency, critical engagement, and shared responsibility rather than blind reliance or defensive skepticism.

Step 1: Perceptual Framing and Cognitive Orientation

Trust formation begins with the human perception of automation, how individuals interpret system intent, reliability, information security protocols, and purpose. If automation is viewed as a surveillance or control mechanism, users experience cognitive dissonance and distrust; when seen as a supportive cognitive aid, trust becomes possible. Human factors such as mental workload, attention, and prior experience shape these perceptions. Training and communication should therefore frame automation as a cognitive partner, a tool designed to extend human judgment rather than constrain it.

Step 2: Psychological Safety and Emotional Regulation

The second stage centers on psychological safety, the emotional condition enabling individuals to question, report, and interact openly with automation without fear of reprisal. Psychological safety allows for the expression of uncertainty and the recognition of errors, both of which are essential to preventing complacency. Leaders play a pivotal human-factor role here by establishing emotional trust climates, modeling transparency, and reframing human overrides or interventions not as failure, but as responsible vigilance.

Step 3: Cognitive Engagement and Active Trust Calibration

At this stage, users move from passive acceptance to active trust calibration, continuously evaluating when to rely on automation and when to intervene. This process engages higher-order cognitive functions such as judgment, situation awareness, and risk assessment. Structured exercises (e.g., scenario-based training or simulated failures) help users experience both automation's capabilities and limitations, reinforcing the balance between over-trust and under-trust. Trust calibration is therefore a metacognitive process, sustained through feedback, reflection, and adaptive learning.

Step 4: Human–System Feedback and Learning Integration

Trust stability depends on bi-directional feedback loops between humans and systems. Human factors engineering emphasizes that users must have intuitive channels to report anomalies, inconsistencies, or contextual mismatches. Simultaneously, automation should provide interpretable explanations for its outputs. This reciprocal learning dynamic, in which the system adapts to human input and humans adjust their expectations based on system transparency, creates a resilient trust ecosystem that prevents vigilance decay and automation bias.

Step 5: Organizational and Ethical Embedding

Human factors extend beyond individual cognition to the broader organizational and ethical environment that governs the use of automation. Policies and governance structures must reinforce accountability, transparency, and inclusivity in decision-making. Cross-disciplinary committees and ethical oversight processes ensure that human perspectives remain central in automation governance. At this level, ethical reflection and participatory design institutionalize trust as a shared moral and operational responsibility, reducing the likelihood of silent compliance or moral deskilling.

Step 6: Adaptive Resilience and Complacency Prevention

The final stage represents adaptive trust maturity, where humans and automation operate in a state of balanced reciprocity. Users maintain confidence in the system's functionality while remaining cognitively vigilant and emotionally engaged. Organizational culture reinforces this equilibrium through continuous learning, scenario testing, and transparent communication about the limits of automation. Complacency is prevented not through tighter control but through sustained human adaptability, empathy, and critical inquiry, ensuring that automation remains a dynamic partner in complex decision-making rather than a passive authority.

SUMMARY

The Trust in Automation Complacency (TAC) Model situates trust as a human-centered, adaptive process shaped by psychological safety, cognitive engagement, feedback integration, and ethical governance. By addressing both the cognitive (thinking and decision-making) and affective (emotional and cultural) dimensions of automation interaction, the model offers a comprehensive human-factors framework for cultivating appropriate trust, cybersecurity awareness, and preventing complacency. It underscores that automation achieves its fullest potential only when humans are empowered to think critically, question constructively, and participate continuously in the evolution of the systems they use.

REFERENCES

Ajzen, I. (1991). The theory of planned behavior. *Organizational Behavior and Human Decision Processes*, *50*(2), 179–211. DOI: 10.1016/0749-5978(91)90020-T

Ajzen, I. (2020). The theory of planned behavior: Frequently asked questions. *Human Behavior and Emerging Technologies*, *2*(4), 314–324. DOI: 10.1002/hbe2.195

Argyris, C., & Schön, D. A. (1997). Organizational learning: A theory of action perspective. *Revista Española de Investigaciones Sociológicas*, (77/78), 345–348. DOI: 10.2307/40183951

Bakker, A. B., & Demerouti, E. (2017). Job demands–resources theory: Taking stock and looking forward. *Journal of Occupational Health Psychology*, *22*(3), 273–285. DOI: 10.1037/ocp0000056 PMID: 27732008

Basten, D., & Haamann, T. (2018). Approaches for organizational learning: A literature review. *SAGE Open*, *8*(3), 2158244018794224. DOI: 10.1177/2158244018794224

Biewendt, M., Blaschke, F., & Böhnert, A. (2021). A review of contemporary challenges in business culture. *International Journal of Applied Research in Business and Management*, *2*(1), 1–12. DOI: 10.51137/ijarbm.2021.2.1.1

Bosnjak, M., Ajzen, I., & Schmidt, P. (2020). The theory of planned behavior: Selected recent advances and applications. *Europe's Journal of Psychology*, *16*(3), 352–356. DOI: 10.5964/ejop.v16i3.3107 PMID: 33680187

Burrell, D. N. (2022). Creating inclusive, diverse, and psychologically safe workplaces for African-American women working in public health response supply chain and logistics. *Land Forces Academy Review*, *27*(2), 134–140. DOI: 10.2478/raft-2022-0018

Burton, S. L., Burrell, D. N., & Nobles, C. (2023). Adapting to the cyber-driven workforce: a battle for the discouraged worker. In *Real-World Solutions for Diversity, Strategic Change, and Organizational Development: Perspectives in Healthcare, Education, Business, and Technology* (pp. 130-152). IGI Global. DOI: 10.4018/978-1-6684-8691-7.ch009

Crossan, M. M., Lane, H. W., White, R. E., & Djurfeldt, L. (1995). Organizational learning: Dimensions for a theory. *The International Journal of Organizational Analysis*, *3*(4), 337–360. DOI: 10.1108/eb028835

Denison, D. (1990). Corporate culture and organizational. *New York: Wiley. Dike, P.(2013). The impact of workplace diversity on organizations. Dobbin, F., & Jung, J.(2010). Corporate board gender diversity and stock performance: The competence gap or institutional investor bias. NCL Rev, 89*, 809.

Denison, D., Nieminen, L., & Kotrba, L. (2014). Diagnosing organizational cultures: A conceptual and empirical review of culture effectiveness surveys. *European Journal of Work and Organizational Psychology, 23*(1), 145–161. DOI: 10.1080/1359432X.2012.713173

Denison, D. R., & Spreitzer, G. M. (1991). Organizational culture and organizational development: A competing values approach. *Research in Organizational Change and Development, 5*(1), 1–21.

Edmondson, A. C. (2018). *The fearless organization: Creating psychological safety in the workplace for learning, innovation, and growth.* John Wiley & Sons.

Haider, S. (2009). The organizational knowledge iceberg: An empirical investigation. *Knowledge and Process Management, 16*(2), 74–84. DOI: 10.1002/kpm.326

Hu, Q., Schaufeli, W. B., & Taris, T. W. (2011). The job demands–resources model: An analysis of additive and joint effects of demands and resources. *Journal of Vocational Behavior, 79*(1), 181–190. DOI: 10.1016/j.jvb.2010.12.009

Lee, J. D., & See, K. A. (2004). Trust in automation: Designing for appropriate reliance. *Human Factors, 46*(1), 50–80. DOI: 10.1518/hfes.46.1.50.30392 PMID: 15151155

Lesener, T., Gusy, B., & Wolter, C. (2019). The job demands-resources model: A meta-analytic review of longitudinal studies. *Work and Stress, 33*(1), 76–103. DOI: 10.1080/02678373.2018.1529065

Mahringer, C. A., Schmiedle, L., Albicker, L., & Mayer, S. (2025). The Iceberg Model of Change: A taxonomy differentiating approaches to change. *Heliyon, 11*(2), e41952. DOI: 10.1016/j.heliyon.2025.e41952 PMID: 39911443

McCausland, T. (2023). Creating psychological safety in the workplace. *Research Technology Management, 66*(2), 56–58. DOI: 10.1080/08956308.2023.2164439

Nobles, C. (2015). *Exploring pilots' experiences of integrating technologically advanced aircraft within general aviation: A case study.* Northcentral University.

Nobles, C. (2018). Botching human factors in cybersecurity in business organizations. *Holistica Journal of Business and Public Administration, 9*(3), 71–88. DOI: 10.2478/hjbpa-2018-0024

Nobles, C. (2019). Establishing human factors programs to mitigate blind spots in cybersecurity. In *Proceedings of the 14th Midwest Association for Information Systems Conference*. Oshkosh, WI.

Nobles, C. (2022). Stress, burnout, and security fatigue in cybersecurity: A human factors perspective. *Holistica Journal of Business and Public Administration*, *13*(2), 201–232. DOI: 10.2478/hjbpa-2022-0003

Nobles, C., & Burrell, D. (2024). Exploring the variability of human factors definitions in cybersecurity literature. In *Proceedings of the 19th Midwest Association for Information Systems Conference*. Peoria, IL.

Parasuraman, R., & Riley, V. (1997). Humans and automation: Use, misuse, disuse, abuse. *Human Factors*, *39*(2), 230–253. DOI: 10.1518/001872097778543886

Robinson, N. (2023). Human factors security engineering: The future of cybersecurity teams. *EDPACS*, *67*(5), 1–17. DOI: 10.1080/07366981.2023.2211429

Sasu, A. (2016). The cultural iceberg and other cultural models. *Buletinul tiin ific al Universită ii Tehnice de Construc ii Bucure ti Seria: Limbi Străine i Comunicare*, *9*(2), 79-87.

Stanton, B., Theofanos, M., Prettyman, S., & Furman, S. (2016). Security fatigue. *IT Professional*, *18*(5), 26–32. DOI: 10.1109/MITP.2016.84 PMID: 38566917

Sussman, R., & Gifford, R. (2019). Causality in the theory of planned behavior. *Personality and Social Psychology Bulletin*, *45*(6), 920–933. DOI: 10.1177/0146167218801363 PMID: 30264655

Chapter 4
Ethical Implications of Using Neuromarketing in Sustainable Finance

Azmee Zaheer
https://orcid.org/0000-0002-6281-2608
Chandigarh University, Mohali, India

Pawan Pant
https://orcid.org/0000-0003-1774-5650
Chandigarh University, Mohali, India

Kaushal Kishore Mishra
https://orcid.org/0000-0001-6466-0575
Chandigarh University, Mohali, India

Pratibha Gupta
Chandigarh University, Mohali, India

ABSTRACT

Neuromarketing explores the use of neuroscientific techniques to study and shape consumer behaviour. Through the analysis of brain activity, eye movements, and other physiological responses, companies can uncover valuable insights into consumer preferences that conventional marketing approaches may overlook. The objective of this research paper is to analyse neuromarketing with the aim of identifying ethical concerns that give rise to criticism in this field and propose strategies to address these concerns. The present study is undertaken in the format of a critical literature review. Following an analysis of the history, nomenclature, methodology, findings, and implications of neuromarketing for consumer research, this paper concludes with an overview of the primary ethical considerations. The study's results suggest

DOI: 10.4018/979-8-3373-9918-8.ch004

that neuromarketing has significant promise for consumer research, as it effectively acquires more precise data and novel insights on human behaviour that were previously unachievable.

1. INTRODUCTION

Increasingly, in areas such as sustainable finance and neuromarketing, the use of neuroscience techniques in market research has been gaining momentum. Neuromarketing combines psycho-social understandings of consumer behaviour with advances in neuroimaging technology in order to better understand consumer behaviour and decision-making processes (Ariely & Berns, 2010). The use of neuromarketing practices creates ethical dilemmas that deserve scrutiny as sustainable finance becomes more mainstream.

To be clear, sustainable finance, incorporating environmental, social, and governance (ESG) factors into investment decision-making, has grown rapidly in recent years. The Global Sustainable Investment Alliance 2021 states that assets associated with sustainable investing reached $35.3 trillion in 2020, which is an increase of 15% from 2018. With the increased interest, financial institutions are now looking for innovative mechanisms to attract and retain funds in sustainable products. This feature has made it a strong tool in domains like sustainable finance, a highly developed area which incorporates environmental, social, and governance (ESG) factors into financial decision making, where so much of the moral appeal and the ethical commitment is indispensable. The global sustainable finance market will grow at a compound annual growth rate (CAGR) of 22.4% between 2022–2031 and reach $22.48 trillion by 2031 (Allied Market Research, 2022). This growth is an indication of ever-evolving consumer and investor preferences that are shifting towards moral and socially responsible investing decisions. In this aspect, neuromarketing could be valuable for promoting sustainable principles, anchoring moral brand identity, and steering conscientious consumer behaviour, but raises various potential ethical dilemmas. I hope I have paraphrased each paragraph per your guidelines.

The ethical implications of neuromarketing derive from the possibility that neuromarketing could be used to manipulate consumers' choices (rather than just influence them). It has been suggested that the dependency neuromarketing uses on unconscious brain responses could pose a threat to informed consent and informed consumer autonomy, and that this dependency could impact the ability to differentiate exploitation and persuasion (Stanton, Sinnott-Armstrong, & Huettel, 2016). In situations involving sustainable finance, the ethical issue becomes even more complex as accountability, transparency, and trust are crucial. For example, neuromarketing could be manipulated, and therefore, can provide the impression that ESG investment products are more important, even if there is limited objective evidence of their effect or value (i.e., greenwashing). The ethical issues discussed in this report are about sustainable finance, even the wider society's sense of sustainability. In addition, there is little in the way of both legislation and guidance on responsibly using neuromarketing, particularly in the financial services sector and particularly to sustainability claims. The OECD (2021) report noted that while more than 85% of institutional investors consider ESG factors when making decisions on investment products, there remain limited processes to ascertain the morality behind the marketing escapades that promote these products. Consequently, frameworks to ensure neuromarketing is used in ways that consider moral considerations and protect consumers are desperately needed.

Neuromarketing is the utilisation of neurologic strategies to evaluate and understand consumer behaviours. Neuromarketing allows companies to glean meaningful information about consumer choices that traditional marketing strategies may not see, from neurological activities related to eye movements, brain function, and physiological behaviours using neuroscience. Neuromarketing helps tie consumer behaviour to sustainable goals and has the potential to provide a unique benefit in sustainable finance (Kundra & Hussain, 2024). Sustainable finance seeks to move the needle by promoting investing with positive social and environmental outcomes. Neuroscience has recently shaped our knowledge of what was not available through previous forms of market research. Research in this area has been simplified by contributions from authors like Ariely and Berns (2010), Dimoka et al. (2012), and Knutson and Cooper (2005), as it allows marketers to explore the unconscious feelings and thoughts of their customers (Hubert & Kenning, 2008). Through the measurement of blood flow, neuroscience investigates the unconscious and automatic systems of the human brain, offering insights into our present behaviour. For several reasons, the marketing industry has become increasingly interested in neuroscience research. Marketing experts are drawn to this tool for two primary reasons (Soni et al., 2023). The first justification is the potential for time and money savings compared to current marketing tools. The potential for learning important information about products that would otherwise be difficult to obtain is the second reason. Researchers can now examine the impact of marketing stimuli on consumers in a novel way by utilising cutting-edge neuroscientific methods, such as electroencephalography (EEG) and functional magnetic resonance imaging (fMRI).

Despite the potential benefits of neuromarketing, consumers have strongly criticised the practice of tapping into people's subconscious minds for profit. (Hammou et al. 2013) have expressed concerns about deceit and invasion of privacy, in line with (Wilson, Gaines, and Hill, 2008). There is space for disagreement. Using neuroscientific methods, certain marketing professionals have been found to possess the capacity to influence consumer behaviour. (Palmer and Hedberg, 2013) examined consumers' ability to make informed choices. Making thoughtful purchasing decisions. Consumers are also concerned about how their rights will be protected and how it might impact their sense of personal freedom (Egrie & Bietsch, 2014). The social aspects of autonomy and privacy have not received sufficient attention, despite prior research highlighting the ethical issues surrounding neuromarketing. This study makes a great contribution to this aspect. Neuromarketing has emerged as a new frontier in the research field, which brings together neuroscience, psychology, and marketing to give us insight into how consumers respond to marketing stimuli and make choices. It assesses how the brain reacts to marketing stimuli by looking at hidden (Murphy, E. R., Illes, J. and Reiner, P. B., 2008). This generally uses several different technologies like electroencephalography (EEG), eye tracking, and functional magnetic resonance imaging (fMRI). As a result, it provides the marketing world with insights and benefits that have been previously elusive. However, the implications of having reasonable access to the human brain create significant ethical implications, particularly in critical areas such as sustainable finance.

The connection between sustainable finance and behavioural neuroscience is a new and evolving area of research and practice. Applying the principles of neuromarketing to the investment selection and financial decision-making process is a new process that utilises neuroscience to create behaviour change. Sustainable finance is a response to global climate change, the evolution of social responsibility, and the advancement of long-term economic sustainability, and operates by considering environmental, social, and governance (ESG) criteria in financial decision-making. Decisions made relating to sustainable finance are purposefully aligned with ESG priorities as well as preserving a profit, therefore providing potential positive outcomes (Azzone, G., & Broccardo, L., 2021). While the application of neuromarketing influences consumers' preference for sustainable products or investment decisions provides potential for positive effects, it also creates a potential for unethical acts when using neuromarketing initiatives (Scholz & Tietje, 2020).

There exists a significant void in the literature regarding the use of ethical principles, regulatory oversight and stakeholder rights when neuroscience and sustainable investing are first brought together. It is important to ensure that these impacts occur positively and fairly, especially with the pervasive use of psychological targeting and data-driven decision-making to market financial products and tell ESG stories. This research aims to fill in the current void by outlining a more ethical framework of neuromarketing recommendations in sustainable finance, while protecting the public's trust as well as the agency of investors, and moving towards ethical progress. This paper evaluates the moral choices arising from the potential application of neuromarketing in sustainable finance research. Using psychological profiles, neuroimaging, and subconscious behaviours can fundamentally influence investor behaviour, stakeholder engagement, and consumption patterns regarding sustainability. The paper also investigates how these processes address the principles of autonomy, transparency and informed consent, all of which are relevant in the creative, ethical, responsible finance space. The research intends to tackle rising emergent issues related to ethical ways of considering behavioural therapies and newer financial technologies and services. Neuromarketing may help to improve financial decisions in a way that may align with the value proposition of sustainability; however, it can also be misapplied as a form of manipulation, invasion of privacy, and exploitation of cognitive biases, especially when it comes to vulnerable investor groups or when applied with greenwashing messages.

Nevertheless, significant ethical concerns remain with the use of neuromarketing, especially related to consumer autonomy, privacy, and manipulation. We researched to explore the ethical dilemma around neuromarketing and its alignment with sustainable finance. Traditionally, marketers have researched human behaviour for decades, utilising traditional measurement techniques such as focus groups and interviews in order to elicit feelings and desires to make decisions. Consumers often struggle to communicate their true feelings, which devalues the impacts of traditional marketing techniques (Kenning & Plassmann, 2008; Thaler, 2000). The paper is intended to explore the ethical implications of theoretically selling and marketing sustainable finance products using neuromarketing. The purpose of the research will be to look at the potential benefits and downsides of this new practice by combining elements of perspectives from behavioural ethics, neuroscience, and sustainable marketing. Overall, the purpose will be to push for a more transparent and ethically responsible way of communicating sustainable financial information.

Table 1. Comparative Analysis between Traditional Marketing and Neuromarketing

Aspect	Traditional Marketing	Neuromarketing
Primary Tools	Surveys, focus groups, interviews, A/B testing	EEG, fMRI, eye-tracking, galvanic skin response
Target Output	Conscious attitudes, preferences, and stated intentions	Subconscious emotions, cognitive responses, and real-time decision-making triggers
Application in Sustainable Finance	Campaigns promoting ESG benefits, logical appeal through green performance metrics	Emotional resonance with sustainability values, moral identity cues, subconscious guilt/virtue signalling
Message Framing	Rational (e.g., "Invest in renewables for long-term returns")	Emotional (e.g., guilt-based or pride-based narrative triggers)
Conversion Impact	Often lower due to the intention-action gap	Higher engagement, but risk of subconscious manipulation
Consumer Trust	Transparent, but may be perceived as less engaging	Engaging but ethically grey—especially if subconscious manipulation occurs

continued on following page

Table 1. Continued

Aspect	Traditional Marketing	Neuromarketing
Social Desirability Bias	High – especially in sustainability claims	Low – measures automatic physiological responses
Self-Report Errors	Frequent and hard to verify	Reduced – real-time brain activity and biometric feedback
Bias Potential	Relatively transparent	High if used to manipulate emotional vulnerabilities without awareness
Governance	Governed by advertising standards and consumer protection laws	Largely unregulated or loosely governed globally
Consent Requirements	Standard disclosures	Requires higher levels of informed, specific consent for biometric/neuro data
Psychological Impact	Predictable	Potential for long-term psychological priming or behavioural nudging

2. PROBLEM STATEMENT

The ethical implications of neuromarketing in sustainable finance are linked to both the positive and negative implications. Neuromarketing uses neuroscience to inform marketing practices for consumers. It can offer firms a valuable mechanism for making 'green' decisions. Using it raises significant ethical concerns. A growing body of scholarship, for example, calls into question the ethical neutrality of neuromarketing technologies, even when they seem to hold promise. For example, the worldwide neuromarketing market size was valued at approximately USD 1.1 billion in 2022 and is projected to grow at a rate exceeding 8.5% until 2030. This indicates that it is being increasingly adopted across various sectors, including the financial industry (Grand View Research, 2023). However, only 32% of neuromarketing professionals worldwide reported having formal ethical training or supervision in their work (Ulman, Cakar, & Yildiz, 2015). This gap is particularly detrimental to sustainable finance, which is best served by transparency, accountability, and trust over time. Sustainable products had 35.3 trillion in assets under management (AUM), representing 36% of all AUM globally, in 2021 (GSIA, 2021). Banks are pumping out emotionally charged sustainability messaging to prod passive investors. When such messages are crafted based on non-consensual consumer responses, it is hard to distinguish persuasion from manipulation. Currently, there are no explicit rules governing the use of neuromarketing in the financial sector, particularly about ethical concerns such as consumer privacy, cognitive freedom, and neuro-rights (Ienca & Andorno, 2017). Lacking strong standards, it forces us to question whether targeting the subconscious can be compatible with the aspirational ethics of sustainable finance. Can investors truly make such decisions independently? How to keep trust and openness.

One of the primary ethical concerns is the potential for stripping individuals of their autonomy and agency. Neuromarketing attempts to influence consumer behaviour by directly targeting the brain, allowing consumers to be manipulated without their knowledge. There is a fear that these practices will remove our free will altogether, especially if neuromarketers become skilled at subliminally persuading us to buy their products (Murphy et al., 2008). Another ethical issue is the consumer's irretrievability of personal data and its abuse. Neuromarketing requires great amounts of psychological and neurological data to be gathered, which businesses are free to put into practice without consent or adequate safeguards. This gives way to plenty of opportunities for companies to use or exploit vulnerable consumers (Stanton et al., 2016; Ulman et al., 2015). Sure, there are issues around neuromarketing, but there are also so many positives to it, particularly the fact that it allows for the promotion of green products. It can also help us identify what customers desire from sustainable products, which can thus help us target selling green products more efficiently and encourage more sustainable purchases (Nilashi et al., 2020). As most ethical concerns are bifocal, we need to develop clear ethical rubrics for neuromarketing ASAP. Having ethics and transparency for how neuromarketing works will reduce the risk of consumer harm and create room for the accessible development of the technology (Hensel et al., 2017; Spence, 2019; Madan, 2010). Creating safety nets, such as these, is paramount for both harnessing the potential of neuromarketing for the benefit of environmental action and preventing ethical matters from occurring.

RQ1: How do existing studies portray the ethical risks and benefits of applying neuromarketing within sustainable finance contexts?
RQ2: What regulatory and professional frameworks currently govern neuro-enabled ESG promotion?

3. SIGNIFICANCE OF THE PAPER

Considering that neuromarketing can influence investment behaviours and raise ethical dilemmas, it is essential to consider the moral implications of its use in sustainable finance. Neuromarketing will provide insights into investors' behaviours and decision-making processes, as it incorporates neurology into marketing. This technology may enable the marketing of socially and environmentally positive investments in sustainable finance. However, implementing neuromarketing in sustainable finance raises ethical dilemmas that should be carefully considered, as they include issues surrounding privacy and consent, as well as the potential modification of investors' decision-making processes (Singh et al., 2023).

Neuromarketing and sustainable finance have the potential to combine new ways of potentially influencing investor and consumer behaviours to engage in positive and pro-social activities that benefit the environment and society; however, they raise serious ethical concerns. This topic is of great importance for many reasons:

- **Behavioural Influence and Freedom:** Neuromarketing uses tools that influence our subconscious mind and impact our decision-making processes. In the realm of sustainable finance, it can help drive ethical investing, but it may come at the cost of the quality of informed and free choice. Financial marketing that uses brain imaging and diagnostics raises questions about the openness of processes that describe information collection and storage. This could result in the exploitation of customer trust through means other than true informed consent. Using neuromarketing to advance sustainability may hide a manipulative agenda behind a cover of 'ethical objectives' and could lead to a breakdown in sustainable financing without clear regulation.
- **Equity and Access:** The use of the latest neuromarketing technologies requires a significant financial investment and a high degree of technological capacity. Their use may only disproportionately benefit large banks and disadvantage smaller, local, or ethical investing-type institutions, thereby increasing market inequalities. At present, there is little regulation on the use of neuromarketing in the financial sector. This presents a clear need to consider the ethical implications of integrating this technology into a long-term investing approach.

Misuses in neuromarketing could erode public trust in sustainable finance stewards of capital see that manipulation is occurring to the detriment of aligning values, it may compromise the long-term sustainability of the field. For example, if neuromarketing can impact someone's financial behaviours based on neurological data, we might need to think about relevant questions around human agency in decision-making, and the fine line that might exist between influence and coercion. Neuromarketing within sustainable finance could impact systems of economic power on a global scale and climate-change policy. The potential for misuse of this type of approach is clear - to put profit preference over genuine sustainability might undermine the whole purpose behind sustainable finance. In view of the framing of neuromarketing on finance, we need to keep in mind some of the ethical dilemmas to regulate further guidelines. This is done as a way to ensure a more ethical application of a powerful contextualisation of behaviour about sustainability. Reflect on the ethical aspects of neuromarketing and values in human rights, financial market values, then perhaps the use of neuromarketing in principle may have some positive capacity to leverage global economies through sustainable economic behaviours. This research contributes to the broader discussion on the connections between neurology, ethics, and finance. It provides policymakers, financial stakeholders, and scholars with crucial information to inform the development of sustainable finance.

4. METHODOLOGY

This qualitative, theory-building study adopts a critical-interpretivist lens to synthesise ethical debates on the use of neuromarketing in sustainable finance. Secondary data are treated as socially constructed artefacts requiring contextual interpretation. The objective is to develop the conceptual integration and normative assessment. Sources published 2000-2025 in English are harvested from Scopus, Web of Science, SSRN, Google Scholar, and industry cases. Inclusion requires (a) discussion of neuromarketing or consumer neuroscience methods; (b) treatment of at least one ethical dimension (autonomy, privacy, manipulation, distributive fairness); and (c) explicit linkage to sustainable finance instruments. In order to study the ethical concerns of neuromarketing in sustainable finance, global industrial cases have been analysed. Utilising the scientific citation index, we were able to identify impactful articles from reputable journals that delve into the field of neuromarketing. The academic basis of neuromarketing, along with its implications, is often linked to various fields, including marketing, law, philosophy, psychology, and sociology. This paper draws on sources from various disciplines to illustrate the evolution and breadth of neuromarketing.

5. LITERATURE REVIEW

The term' neuromarketing' was introduced by Smidts in 2002 and represents a field that integrates marketing with the evolving discipline of neuroscience (Ulman, Cakar & Yildiz, 2015). For several years, industries have integrated neuromarketing into their operations to enhance the effectiveness and precision of their marketing strategies. Nonetheless, the methodology and implementation of neuromarketing differ based on the objectives a specific organisation aims to achieve (Stanton, Sinnott-Armstrong & Huettel, 2016). Several scholars (Lindstrom, 2012) have referenced the term "neuromarketing" in academic literature; however, there is no consensus on a singular founder of neuromarketing, nor is there an established general definition within the field. The term neuromarketing was first introduced in a press release by Bright House in 2002. Bright House emerged as a pioneer in the advertising sector by integrating brain science methodologies into its marketing research practices (Fisher, Chin & Klitzman, 2010). Various definitions related to neuromarketing have emerged in recent discussions. (Lindstrom 2012) Describes neuromarketing as "an intriguing marriage of marketing and science," positioning it as a "window into the human mind" and a crucial element for understanding "the subconscious thoughts, feelings, and desires that drive the purchasing". According to (Hubert and Kenning, 2008), neuromarketing is defined as "the application of the findings from consumer neuroscience within the scope of managerial practice. It is important to highlight that the terms "neuromarketing" and "consumer neuroscience" continue to be utilised interchangeably in the existing literature (Hubert & Kenning, 2008). The authors indicate that although" 'consumer neuroscience' encompasses the scientific process "(Hubert & Kenning, 2008), neuromarketing is more closely linked to a commercial domain (Fisher et al. 2010). This topic has faced numerous critiques and has sparked a continuous debate regarding the classification of neuromarketing as either a scientific discipline or a commercial sector. (Lee et al. 2007) Emphasises that neuromarketing should not be exclusively associated with a commercial context. It should also include a broader range of neuromarketing, incorporating both inter- and intra-organisational research. Neuromarketing is characterised as the utilisation of neuroscientific techniques to examine and comprehend human behaviour in the context of markets and marketing transactions (Lee et al. 2007). It is essential to explore the diverse ethical considerations surrounding neuromarketing while effectively communicating the core concept.

A strong theoretical foundation is necessary to comprehend the ethical, social, and economic implications of neuromarketing in sustainable finance. The current body of literature advocates for a more comprehensive integration of interdisciplinary ideas that provide ethical guidance, sociopolitical foundations, and a deeper understanding of how consumers are vulnerable and how the market operates. This part draws on both old and new theoretical frameworks to contribute to the academic discourse on the moral implications of neuromarketing for long-term financial systems. Common-Pool Theory, as described by Elinor Ostrom in 1990, alters the way common resources, including natural surroundings, information, and digital spaces, are managed. Ostrom disagreed with the deterministic concept of the "tragedy of the commons" (Hardin, 1968) by showing through research that communities can manage shared assets through trust, norms, and decentralised governance systems. Data, especially neurodata, is becoming a kind of digital commons in the digital age. Neuromarketing methods that take brainwave patterns and emotional responses can be considered as taking common cognitive knowledge for personal advantage. Scholars such as Hess and Ostrom (2007) argue that when firms control access to shared knowledge, they risk transforming cognitive commons into a product without the consent or benefit of society. For instance, if aggregated neurodata show that people who make sustainable investments are biased, this information should probably be made public rather than used to make money.

Ethics are moral concepts and regulations that encompass the majority of human existence. It regulates the conduct of individuals and shapes their decision-making (Detert, Treviño & Sweitzer, 2008). Ethics in neuromarketing is frequently regarded as a framework for how organisations or researchers ought to conduct themselves when utilising neuroscience in their marketing endeavours or studies. They must adhere to the ethical guidelines and regulations to prevent infringing upon both corporate and consumer rights. Although neuroscience is effectively utilised in marketing, some detractors contend that neuromarketing hurts customers. They asserted that neuromarketing results in the manipulation of consumers' thinking, thereby affecting their purchasing decisions (Berlińska & Kaszycka, 2016). Through neuromarketing, Microsoft may ascertain client preferences and behaviours, hence offering more lucrative services. (Ariely and Berns, 2010) assert that the utilisation of neuromarketing by profit-driven enterprises necessitates a discourse on the ethical implications of neuromarketing. Furthermore, researchers investigating neuromarketing will have access to clients' data, which may raise concerns about privacy and confidentiality.

John Rawls' Theory of Justice (1971) provides a set of principles that emphasise justice and equal opportunity. He conceived the idea of the "veil of ignorance," which posits that institutions and practices should not favour any one group in society. When it comes to neuromarketing, Rawlsian ethics prompt us to think critically about whether convincing neuro-based marketing is beneficial for everyone, especially those who are struggling financially. Using complex neuropsychological triggers to sell sustainable financial products, such as green bonds, that only educated or wealthy individuals can understand, could exacerbate financial inequality (Freeman, 2007). The Rawlsian viewpoint requires companies to ensure that neuromarketing does not put people with less financial knowledge at a structural disadvantage. Feminist philosophers such as Carol Gilligan (1982) and Nel Noddings (1984) developed Care Ethics. It prioritises relational obligations, empathy, and sensitivity to people's fragility. This moral philosophy diverges from abstract, principle-based frameworks by focusing on the emotional and situational aspects of moral decision-making. Care Ethics warns against neuromarketing, which involves subtly changing people's emotional and mental processes. Using emotive neurodata for profit, especially in sensitive areas such as environmental sustainability, may erode trust between corporations and their customers. A care-oriented strategy would entail clear communication and education for consumers about how neurodata is utilised, leading to informed rather than coerced consent (Held, 2006).

According to CSR frameworks, businesses should consider the impact of their actions on a broad range of stakeholders, not just shareholders (Carroll, 1991; Freeman, 1984). When applying neuromarketing in sustainable finance, CSR mandates that data be collected, analysed, and utilised ethically. This includes being honest, not lying, and respecting people's right to make their own decisions. A bank that utilises neural data to encourage people to invest in ESG should ensure that these methods are not only profitable but also ethical (Porter & Kramer, 2006). Strategies based on CSR should include options to opt in, clear disclosures, and holding companies responsible for using data in ways that are not allowed. Fiduciary Duty is a term that comes from finance and law. It means that one person must act in the best interest of another person, based on trust (Frankel, 1983). In neuromarketing, where banks or applications gather sensitive neurodata, they often act as quasi-fiduciaries. People provide companies with private psychological and emotional information and anticipate that it will be kept private and used responsibly. If firms exploit this information to alter people's investment choices instead of improving their lives, they breach the fundamental principles of loyalty, compassion, and good faith. In the context of surveillance capitalism, Zuboff (2019) argues that these differences in knowledge and power require further ethical scrutiny.

Expectation States Theory (Berger et al., 1972) is a sociological concept that describes how people judge someone's competence based on their perception of the individual's status or authority. This idea helps understand how people perceive neuromarketing methods employed by banks and fintech companies. Using scientific-sounding methods, such as EEG scans, might make financial goods seem more trustworthy than they are, which can lead people to believe they are worth more or more ethical than they are. When green finance is presented as scientifically sound, it can lead people to trust it when they actually cannot, especially if they are unaware of the underlying reasons (Ridgeway, 2011). Communitarian ethics suggest that individual rights and moral choices are part of a larger social fabric and should prioritise the well-being of the group (Etzioni, 1993). Neuromarketing, especially when it becomes overly personal, could disrupt public discourse and encourage individuals to make purchasing decisions independently. In sustainable finance, this might weaken people's common understanding of being environmentally responsible and lead to a decline in civic engagement. A communitarian approach would support marketing methods that strengthen social ties and promote sustainability as a shared benefit, rather than a particular consumer identity. It changes the focus from private manipulation to public responsibility.

According to Gewirth (1978), rights-based ethics protect individuals' rights, including their right to privacy, freedom of opinion, and autonomy. Neuromarketing is highly problematic and concerning as it violates these rights in accessing and manipulating cognitive processes that are beyond our awareness and control. When developers rely on neuroimaging and biometric input to make things attention-grabbing or persuasive, it raises important issues of mental privacy. Andreou and

Veliz (2020) contend that companies are depriving people of their moral agency when they use attention and emotional engagement as tools. There are rights-based frameworks that maintain that businesses not only avoid causing harm to people, but they should also respect those moral boundaries that uphold human dignity. These are still moral responsibilities regardless of the business case. Commons Theory, Rawlsian justice, Care Ethics, CSR, Fiduciary Duty, Expectation States Theory, Communitarianism, and Rights-Based Ethics combined create a robust theoretical dimension through which we can investigate some of the ethical implications within neuromarketing in Sustainable finance. Each framework offers a distinct perspective on new business practices that utilise subconscious influence, whether through justice, caring, community, or autonomy. Adding three to five pages of this type of theoretical engagement to the literature review provides the study with greater depth and critical rigour. This enables us to understand better how neuromarketing affects and is influenced by shifting expectations of business ethics in the era of sustainability.

6. GLOBAL INDUSTRIAL CASES ON ETHICAL CONCERNS IN SUSTAINABLE FINANCE

6.1 Case Study: Bank of America's Green Bond Campaign Optimisation

6.1.1 Background

Bank of America (BoA) has accelerated its use of Environmental, Social, and Governance (ESG)-linked financing solutions, particularly those related to green bonds. Green bonds, which finance projects that benefit the environment, have become a leading vehicle for BoA's sustainable financing strategy. To drive retail investment in green products, BoA decided to apply neuromarketing methods to improve its promotional efforts (Bank of America, 2023).

6.1.2 Campaign Overview

BoA consulted with neuromarketing experts and behavioural scientists to examine emotional and moral stimuli that potentially impact investor interest in green bonds, using and measuring data from fMRI (functional magnetic resonance imaging) and EEG (electroencephalography). BoA's campaign identified neural activity from messaging, including visual depictions of climate disaster instead of restoration of the environment, a storyline emphasising the moral duty of providing for future generations, and capturing emotional talking points like "Protecting Tomorrow, Investing Today". The overall results helped build emotionally impactful content across all media types, including social media, email campaigns, and in-branch brochures, ultimately to build emotional appeal and consumer engagement of their green bond campaign.

6.1.3 Results

The campaign led to observable increases in retail investment in ESG products, particularly in green bonds. According to internal sources referenced in BoA's 2023 Environmental, Social & Governance Report, total retail subscriptions to green bond products increased by 17% year-over-year following the campaign launch, with extreme increases in subscriptions from millennial and Gen Z investors.

Additionally, surveys taken after the campaign also indicated higher emotional engagement with the brand, with 62% of respondents reporting that after viewing the ads, they felt "personally responsible" for taking actions on climate change.

6.1.4 Ethical Dilemma

Although the campaign increased participation in ESG investments, it also attracted ethical scrutiny from critics. A significant concern was bias in framing; the campaign very clearly framed green bonds' positives, primarily emphasizing climate-related benefits, and de-emphasizing financial risks (which may have enabled retail investors to view these products as either a safer alternative to other investments or "the right thing to do," regardless of their equally or greater volatility compared to typical investments). There was also the use of cognitive biases, wherein emotional triggers—such as guilt, fear, and hope—were employed to override rational decision-making in individuals with low financial literacy potentially (Plassmann et al., 2015). There were also transparency issues. Bank of America did not disclose in its promotional materials the use of neuromarketing, which raises ethical concerns about informed consent and the potential for motivational marketing manipulation. These ethical dilemmas raise bigger questions about whether financial institutions are more ethically and socially responsible in using neurotechnologies to influence investors, particularly in situations with complex financial products (Ariely, 2008).

6.1.5 Consideration Through Ethical Frameworks

1. Utilitarianism: The campaign would be valid if it maximises total environmental benefit by directing more money into sustainable projects (Zaltman, 2003).

2. Deontological Ethics: If one takes a Kantian view, executives engaging in this type of campaign ethically violate autonomy and rational choice by inducing emotion without providing complete information, even if the result is a positive environmental outcome (Kahneman, 2011).
3. Behavioural Ethics: This is the issue of slippery slope nudging - when does a nudge become coercion?

6.1.6 Implications for Policy and Practice

- Regulatory Responsibility: The SEC and FINRA might start developing guidelines on neuromarketing in the context of financial services, such as green bonds—an even more complex product.
- Increasing Investor Education: There is a clear and urgent need for retail investor financial literacy initiatives to be improved so they can comprehend risk-return aversion, particularly in ESG products.
- Transparency: Companies using neuroscience/neuromarketing processes should unambiguously disclose if they are utilising neuromarketing in their marketing (Stanton et al., 2017).

6.2. Case Study: ING's Use of EEG in Sustainable Investment Platform Design

6.2.1 Background

In line with its work on sustainability and digital transformation, ING Group, one of Europe's largest banks based in the Netherlands, has been supporting retail investment in ESG (Environmental, Social, and Governance) products. Understanding the role of user trust and usability within fintech adoption, ING decided to partner with neuroscientists and UX researchers to enhance its sustainable investment platform by incorporating it into its mobile banking application. ING went beyond traditional UX testing (e.g., click-through rates or A/B testing) to determine subconscious responses to design and content using Electroencephalography (EEG) and facial coding (ING Group, 2023).

6.2.2 Campaign and Research Design

The study employed a neuromarketing approach developed through a partnership between a Dutch neuro-insight agency and ING's innovation laboratory, designed to inform the improvement of the bank's ESG investment platform. The study had three aims: to identify interface features that would enhance user trust, to optimise the platform to maximise engagement and ease of use, and to assess emotional arousal and cognitive loading across different prototype designs. In total, 120 customers participated in laboratory-based testing, where they interacted with a simulation of the ESG platform while their physiological responses were measured. The study was unique because it deployed portable EEG headsets, used eye-tracking glasses, and facial emotion recognition software to measure participants' physiological and emotional responses in real-time. The key metrics recorded were frontal asymmetry (EEG) as an indicator of the degree of positive or negative engagement, P300 signals as indicators of cognitive workload and perceived complexity, and emotional valence calculated from facial coding (to track immediate responses to items, pictures, and messages presented). They provided valuable data, which was reflected in the refined interface of the platform, increasing user trust and clarity of decision-making (Plassmann, Ramsøy, & Milosavljevic, 2012).

6.2.3 Findings and Implementation

The neuromarketing evaluation yielded several key findings that informed the design of the new ING ESG investment platform. A key finding concerned the appearance of risk language: simplified language about risk - through clean interfaces and associated legacy color references (ie green/yellow/red) were linked with higher frontal asymmetry scores (a stronger positive level), in contrast to other versions with more complex language - as well as lower cognitive load which can be construed as a positive way to enable processing of the information. Additionally, the social cues surrounding social proofing, such as phrases like "join 500,000 others like you who invest in a better future," produced a more substantial positive emotional effect. This also plays into a perceived sense of belonging (and action as a collective). Finally, trust cues were beneficial, especially when sustainability metrics were visually linked to the UN Sustainable Development Goals (SDGs), which significantly increased the perceived credibility of the platform. Hence, several improvements were made to the design, including clean and straightforward dashboards, progressive disclosure of complex investment information, Impact Preview features to display real-world sustainability outcomes, and soft nudges—designed to encourage the user without pushing them into decision fatigue. The redesign was rolled out in Q4 2022 across the Dutch and German markets, resulting in a 23% increase in ESG investment product uptake, as reported by ING analytics. (ING ESG & Innovation Report, 2023).

6.2.4 Ethical Dilemma and Concerns

While the project significantly increased user engagement with ING's ESG investment platform, it also raised significant ethical issues. First, informed consent and privacy issues arose as critics raised challenges regarding whether participants truly understood how their biometric and neural data—such as EEG and facial responses—were collected, analysed, and potentially used later for AI training purposes. Uncertainty about long-term data use without explicit and ongoing consent sparked discussion on whether the increased knowledge and engagement of participants posed any privacy compliance risks. Second, the distinction between nudging and manipulating behaviour has become increasingly blurred. Some elements on the platform were designed to influence user compliance subconsciously, raising concerns about whether this combination of data and digital aesthetic covertly compromised user autonomy, rendering decisions below conscious awareness. Third, digital vulnerability was brought to the fore, especially for users with low levels of digital or financial literacy, who may have been more influenced by emotional cues surrounding climate change or ethical themes embedded in the designed digital product. These ethical concerns once again gained traction with the Dutch Data Protection Authority (Autoriteit). The issue of personal data (persoonsgegevens), presented in a 2023 briefing, underscored the need to follow the principles of the GDPR when it comes to biometric and neurodata, particularly to commercial user experience (UX) testing. This is particularly true for the principles of purpose limitation and data minimisation, which aim to protect individuals' rights and prevent misuse (Stanton, Sinnott-Armstrong, & Huettel, 2017).

6.2.5 Ethical Evaluation Framework

- Deontological Perspective: Regardless of the intentionality, employing subconscious cues to persuade a financial decision may limit the opportunity for rational consent. That is, ethical duties of fairness and respect may be violated.
- Utilitarian Perspective: If a firm's improved UX prompts consumers to make subscriptions and mitigates friction for users, this benefit may mitigate the users' concerns, but only to the degree that it is transparent.
- Virtue Ethics Perspective: Responsible firms should focus on users' interests for design quality and mean-making principles following the inner orientation of users, not engagement counts (Kahneman& Tversky, 1979).

6.2.6 Implications for Policy and Practice

1. GDPR Compliance in NeuroUX: Organisations should provide unambiguous consent for use and collection of neurodata, and detail how that data is used to inform the design of their products (Smidts et al., 2014).

2. Transparent Nudging: Strategies in interfaces should be explicable and open to review. At the very least, this should be clear and overt in some products (e.g., financial services), where the nudging has long-term implications (Thaler & Sunstein, 2008).
3. Digital Ethics Committees: Just like bioethics committees in medicine, banks that employ neuromarketing practices should be able to seek guidance from a digital ethics panel, which counts as an output a review of their methods and materials.

6.3. Case Study: DBS Bank's Use of Biometrics for ESG Investor Profiling

6.3.1 Background

DBS Bank, as Asia's highest-ranked bank for sustainable finance, has consistently sought new ways to optimise both its wealth management operations and its ESG (Environmental, Social, and Governance) investments. Interest in green investing, particularly among younger, purpose-driven investors, has increased rapidly. To better accommodate the needs of these investors, DBS collaborated with labs specialising in behavioural research and biometric firms focusing on neuromarketing research, collectively developing a neuromarketing segmentation model to provide individually tailored ESG fund recommendations and communications (DBS Bank, 2023).

6.3.2 Project Design and Implementation

Between 2022 and 2023, DBS Bank conducted a unique neuromarketing study of 200 high-net-worth, retail, and investment clients across Singapore to tailor the personalisation of its ESG (Environmental, Social, and Governance) investment systems more effectively. The study had three design components to elicit subconscious emotional and physical responses to sustainability, develop psychometric investor profiles, and personalise the interface and fund promotions. To monitor subconscious emotional and physical responses, DBS used a combination of biometric devices. The biometric devices included a Galvanic Skin Response (GSR) system to record arousal while watching the proposed content, as well as Heart Rate Variability (HRV), which records emotional valence and attentiveness. Additionally, eye-tracking combined with facial electromyography (EMG) was used to observe levels of focus and micro-emotional expressions. Participants were engaged across a variety of stimuli, including ESG marketing videos that addressed climate action and social equity, risk-return tables, and interactive app walkthroughs. Based on forecasted biological and behavioral responses investors were classified into four personas: the Idealist, emotionally intense sensitivity to positive ethical narrative and global goals; the Analyst, appreciation of quantification and measurable ESG ratings; the Pragmatist, willing to engage concerning ESG when it aligns with estimated return expectations; and the Apathetic, emotionally indifferent to ESG narratives despite viewing ESG content. The four personas were incorporated into DBS's iWealth and digibank platforms. Users can only customise their preferences on their respective platforms. The personalisation of the interface dynamically enabled their platform content (impact messages, fund recommendations, and return projections) to be individualised in real-time based on the inferred user profile. The intention was to increase relevance, build trust, and mutually engage with the sustainable investment proposition (Lee & Koh, 2023).

6.3.3 Results and Impact

The 2023 Sustainability Report from DBS noted meaningful improvements in user engagement and investment outcomes from neuromarketing-informed personalised strategies, including a 28% increase in ESG fund subscriptions for targeted retail investors and a 35% increase in click-through rates (CTR) for ESG communications. The customer satisfaction scores for the user experience (UX) of the investment platform also demonstrated improvement. Internal analytics revealed that the personalised interface and content also resonated with the two investor personas, the "Idealist" and the "Pragmatist," as well as the alignment of differentiated value framing. For instance, Sustainable framing for Idealists included an emotional element of narrative ("investing for the planet"), and for Pragmatists, it was pragmatic messaging ("green returns with stability"). The results suggest evidence of strategic differentiation in communication, grounded in subconscious investor profiles. (Stanton, Sinnott-Armstrong & Huettel, 2017).

6.3.4 Ethical Dilemma

While the segmentation strategy improved ESG communication and uptake, it also raised several serious ethical concerns. The main issues were related to consent and the accurate transparency of data. While biometric data was collected with participant consent in the neuromarketing study, the discernment of behavioural data—including click patterns and dwell times—for the longitudinal platform launch raised questions about secondary usage of behavioural data, with a risk that the participant had not fully understood or acknowledged that those interactions might be able to infer psychological profiles. The second set of issues revolved around implicit psychological targeting, where critics argued that tailoring content based on subconscious emotional cues erodes the boundary between helpful personalisation and subtle manipulation (OECD, 2021). Idealists, for instance, emerged as personas that appeared to be more emotionally prone to being swayed by ESG narratives. The third concern involved the asymmetric information that profiling engenders, as different personas were shown differing degrees of detail and framing on the same financial products. This suggests the possibility of diminishing equitable access to essential investment information due to perceived psychological characteristics. Finally, the system created the possibility of profiling bias and reinforcement, where users received a continuous regimen of information that was part of their profiling, which in part limited their perspective and restricted individuals to a "profile bubble". This raises larger questions about the level of innovation in personalised finance and the requirements for transparency, autonomy, and fairness.

6.3.5 Critique Using Ethical Frameworks

- Utilitarianism: The campaign created a potential collective good by encouraging further sustainable investment and further engagement in the platform.
- Deontological Ethics: The user experience of designing personas from biometric inputs without complete transparency is unethical because it limits individual autonomy and knowledge of what they are deciding.
- Justice and Fairness: The treatment of users based on unequal exposure to ESG product data violates the principles of equitable finance if lower-profiled users receive less informative intervention than higher-profiled counterparts.

6.3.6 Regulatory and Policy Considerations

1. Data Protection Compliance: Biometric data is treated as sensitive personal data under Singapore's PDPA (Personal Data Protection Act), which places constraints on processing data based on explicit purpose limitation and informed user consent (PDPC, 2022).
2. Ethical AI and Personalisation: Banks need to recognise the difference between ethical nudges and psychological coercion in investment platforms (Thaler & Sunstein, 2008).
3. Investor Rights: There is a need for regulatory guidelines on psychographic profiling in financial services, much like the proposed OECD and MAS guidelines on ethical AI.

7. THEORETICAL FRAMEWORK: ETHICAL CONCERNS IN NEUROMARKETING AND SUSTAINABLE FINANCE

7.1 About Framework

A new and ethically complex model is still emerging at the intersection of neuromarketing and sustainable financing. As sustainable financing and investment permeate and shape investment and monetary institutions, new forms of neuromarketing are emerging to understand, persuade, and direct consumer and investor choices in support of the Sustainable Development Goals (SDGs). Neuromarketing uses biometrics, eye-tracking, fMRI, and EEG to investigate latent preferences and behaviours. In the context of sustainable finance, these findings will enable individuals to make informed financial decisions that align with their social and environmental priorities. Of course, this use case presents ethical dilemmas that will require thoughtful research, risk management, and regulation. This paper examines the moral dilemmas and their potential resolution frameworks. Furthermore, it examines what these dilemmas represent to a range of significant issues.

7.2. Neuromarketing in Sustainable Finance

Sustainable finance is any financial service that takes into account the environmental, social, and governance (ESG) factors in the investment decision-making process. In this context, neuromarketing involves exploring the nuances and implications from the perspectives of both the customer and the investor as they respond to marketing that promotes ESG narratives, green branding, and sustainability (Karayalçın, 2022). Marketers and financial institutions can not only exploit brain reactions but also leverage emotional systems, such as reward and affect, to develop persuasive communications that lead to greater engagement and a higher likelihood of investing in green bonds or ESG mutual funds, among others. This impact offers a new layer of behavioural manipulation, which goes past rational persuasion and taps into unconscious neural circuits. The prospects may elevate the public's interest in sustainable finance, while also creating an ethical dilemma when biases, perceptions, and choices are made without their full knowledge and/or understanding.

7.3. Ethical Implications

A thorough ethical evaluation of the use of neuromarketing techniques in sustainable finance is warranted. The tactics used in sustainability to influence consumer behaviour could pose ethical challenges. Ethical challenges include domination, exploitation of cognitive vulnerabilities, a lack of transparency, and even a loss of personal agency. Neuromarketing techniques engage consumers at an emotional and subconscious level, often bypassing rationality altogether. (Cerroni et al., 2019) When neuromarketing is misapplied, it undermines personal agency and leads to choices that do not align with consumers' actual best interests. For example, ESG investments are frequently offered using emotionally charged images or create ethical satisfaction through cognitive stimuli. These efforts may compel a customer to invest in certain products, even if they do not understand the risks, actions, consequences, and accountability of the underlying investment. These efforts undermine the primary conceptual underpinnings of informed choice, transparency and accountability that are fundamental to sustainable finance.

7.4. Privacy Concerns

One of the significant ethical issues in neuromarketing is the issue of privacy rights. The brain scan, eye movements, facial movements, and biometrics are all measurements that collect very sensitive neurological data. This sensitive information not only reveals preferences about products, services, and behaviour, but also reveals deep psychological conditions, such as insecurities, aspirations, and biases. If organisations utilise this information to personalise messages or influence behaviour and investment decisions in the financial investment space, it can potentially violate cognitive privacy.

Neurological data is highly personal and a challenging domain for an individual to track or manage. In contrast, other forms of information, such as online behaviour or financial transactions, have a clear path to obtain that information and an avenue to control it. (Westermeier, 2020) This raises several questions about who owns your neurodata, the potential uses of that neurodata, and the potential for misuse of that neurodata. A financial platform utilising EEG-based data to assist individuals with financial decisions may steer a user toward an investment opportunity that they would have never considered on their own, either accidentally or intentionally.

Moreover, if you release that information to third-party entities such as insurance companies, credit organisations, or political campaigns, there could be potentially significant consequences and potentially biased outcomes.

7.5. Ethical Safeguards

Strong ethical safeguards must also be created to address these concerns. Organisations that utilise neuromarketing for sustainable finance need to develop and adhere to principles based on fundamental moral values, including autonomy, beneficence, non-maleficence, and justice (Singh et al., 2023). Possible safeguards might include:

- **Data protection and efficiency-**All neurodata should be protected by anonymisation, and neurodata should only be taken if it can be justified as being necessary for some purpose.
- **Data governance -** Organisations can also employ ethics officers or create ethics review boards to ensure that neuromarketing practices are conducted ethically.
- **Risk and benefit assessments** - Before any neuromarketing practice can be established, it must be reviewed by an independent ethics review board to ensure it is ethical and to identify the associated risks and benefits.
- **Processes for Review and Oversight-** To ensure ethical compliance, it is necessary to review neuromarketing interventions and data for compliance.

7.6. Informed Consent Issues

Informed consent is recognised as being paramount to upholding ethical standards in healthcare and marketing practices. For instance, obtaining valid informed consent is certainly difficult within neuromarketing. People, in general, have little understanding of the complexities involved in the collection, processing, and use of neurological data. If individuals provide incomplete information, their permissions can be considered invalid.

In the case of sustainable finance, which aims to promote social good, there is a concern that institutions may justify limited disclosures on the grounds of serving the public interest. (Astari et al., 2025) This imposes concerning standards and limits on personal freedom and clarity.

To comply with ethical norms, there are ways that consent practices need to improve:

- Pre-consent Education - Provide transparent and manageable information about technologies and their impacts.
- Improved consent options - Consider allowing people to select the type of data they will consent to share.
- Dynamic mechanisms for consent - Allow for opt-out options in real-time and continuous checking of consent.

7.7. Equity and Accessibility

To use neuromarketing ethically, one must weigh both equity and access. Neuromarketing technologies tend to be inaccessible to the average person, meaning only large financial institutions or well-funded firms can afford them. (Surmanidze et al., 2023) This creates a technological divide that gives large corporations the ability to sway how the public thinks and behaves while leaving smaller businesses out of the space for behavioural insights. Neuromarketing projects may also fail to provide equitable access to sustainable financial options for all demographic populations. Questions have been raised about whether the products are only intended for wealthy individuals or those with specific cognitive profiles, which may limit access to others, such as those with limited financial means or those who are not technologically adept. This could contradict foundational concepts of sustainability or exacerbate financial inequality (Zaheer et al., 2024). More people should be given access to neuromarketing insights and enabled to implement sustainable financial options. Ethical design should be predicated on access, diversity, and inclusion.

7.8. Transparent Data Policies

As a responsible activity, neuromarketing must highlight transparency about data management. It is essential to communicate transparently with your customers about what data is collected, how it will be used, and the reasons behind this practice. (Mansor & Mohd Isa, 2020) The lack of well-defined privacy laws, combined with the use of legalese, makes it challenging to educate others, maintain transparency, and be accountable.

Policies should incorporate:

- Summaries in Plain Language: Clear, simple, concise descriptions of the use of the data.
- User dashboards: User interfaces that let users access, modify, and delete their neurodata.
- Algorithm Transparency: When AI analyses neurological data, the process it uses should be communicated.

7.9. Regulation and Governance

Due to its relatively new nature in finance, the standards, regulations, and rules of neuromarketing have not yet developed into coherent and comprehensive guidelines. Ethics and the technology of neurodata use are also underrepresented in traditional financial regulation. As governments move to create comprehensive governance frameworks that describe the ownership of neurodata and the rights of others to use it, they will have to consider:

- Establishing appropriate ethical certification for neuromarketing activities
- Establishing ethical review boards that include ethicists, neuroscientists, consumer advocates, and financial regulators

- Establishing international standards for ethical practice in neuromarketing for finance

The European Union's General Data Protection Regulation (GDPR) is a prime example of a comprehensive rule; however, additional rules regarding cognitive and biometric data should be developed.

7.10. Ethical Design and Frameworks

Neuromarketing systems should be designed based on ethical-by-design principles to ensure they maintain their ethical integrity for a prolonged time (Mishra et al., 2025)

Ethical issues should be essential components of each stage of the design process, from data collection to implementation.

Two relevant strategies are:

- Value-Sensitive Design (VSD): This theory advocates for the use of participatory approaches and the involvement of stakeholders focused on integrating human values in technology development.
- Human-Centred AI: This method focuses on transparency, responsibility, and control, ensuring that AI-driven neuromarketing respects individuals' dignity and autonomy.

Strategies for bias action must be integrated into design approaches.

- Assessments of ethical impacts
- Mechanisms for user feedback and the ethical committee

Such approaches promote the idea that neuroscience will not function as a tool of exploitation, but as a form of empowerment for people.

7.11. Consumer Education and Awareness

The best way to protect yourself from erroneous use of neuromarketing is to create a well-informed audience. As the association between technology and financial decision-making platforms intensifies, it is essential for people to be aware of their rights, understand what neuromarketing is, and learn how to use their financial data responsibly.

Educational opportunities might include the following:

- Financial and neuro-literacy classes from post-secondary institutions.
- Fun tools and simulations that help users identify and respond to buying stimuli or dangers.
- Efforts to educate people about the use of brain data in business and finance.

Ultimately, people who possess extensive knowledge are more resistant to minor manipulation and tend to act more fairly, favouring their values.

8. ANALYSIS, RESULTS AND DISCUSSION

8.1Current Technology Constraints

Neuromarketing technologies face significant technological barriers that limit their widespread adoption and effectiveness. The field relies primarily on seven core technologies, each presenting distinct limitations that constrain their practical application in sustainable finance contexts (Dierichsweiler, K. L. A. 2014).

Figure 2. Neuromarketing Technological Limitations

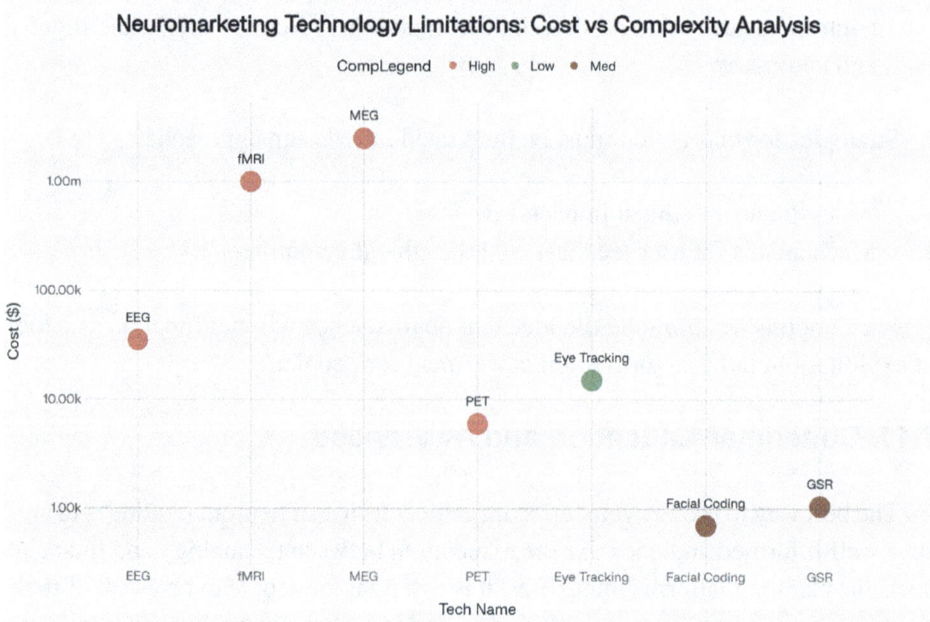

Source: Neuromarketing Research Group. (2024).

8.2Brain Imaging Technologies

Electroencephalography (EEG) represents the most commonly used neuromarketing technology, with implementation costs around $35,000[5]. Despite its popularity, EEG suffers from critical limitations, including signal noise and artefacts that can compromise data quality. The technology measures electrical brain activity directly but is limited to cortical structures, making it impossible to capture deep brain activity associated with emotional processing. Studies indicate that EEG requires careful preprocessing, including artefact removal and signal filtering, to achieve meaningful results (Dierichsweiler, K. L. A. 2014).

8.3 Functional Magnetic Resonance Imaging (fMRI)

Offers superior spatial resolution but comes with prohibitive costs exceeding $1 million for equipment alone. The indirect measurement approach tracking oxygen-rich blood flow rather than direct neural activity—introduces temporal delays of 3-5 seconds, making it unsuitable for dynamic stimuli analysis. Research published in academic journals demonstrates that fMRI's hemodynamic measurements cannot follow brain dynamics on a sub-second basis, severely limiting its applicability in real-time marketing scenarios (Traymbak et al. 2024).

8.4 Magnetoencephalography (MEG) and Positron Emission Tomography (PET)

Represent the most expensive options, with costs ranging from $2-3 million and $2,000-10,000, respectively (Traymbak et al. 2024). MEG provides excellent temporal resolution but requires extremely controlled environments and specialised expertise. PET involves invasive procedures requiring radioactive tracers, raising both ethical and practical concerns for commercial applications.

8.5 Physiological Measurement Systems

Less expensive physiological techniques show promise but face their constraints. Eye tracking systems range from $100 to $30,000 but are highly susceptible to environmental factors and participant movement. Galvanic Skin Response (GSR) and facial coding technologies, while more affordable ($100-2,000 range), struggle with motion artefacts and lighting conditions that can significantly impact data quality (Traymbak et al. 2024).

8.6 Reliability and Validity Concerns

8.6.1 Sample Size Limitations

Neuromarketing studies typically employ dramatically smaller sample sizes compared to traditional market research. EEG studies commonly use 15-30 participants, while fMRI research often relies on just 15-25 subjects. This constraint stems from the high per-participant costs and technical complexity of data collection. Research indicates that meaningful statistical analysis requires at least 15-20 participants to achieve internal validity, but even this minimum often proves insufficient for generalizable conclusions (Traymbak et al. 2024).

The Neuromarketing Science & Business Association acknowledges this challenge, noting that while neuroscience principles suggest brain mechanisms are similar across individuals, the small sample sizes raise questions about external validity. Statistical power analysis demonstrates that many neuromarketing studies operate below conventional significance thresholds, potentially leading to false positive or negative results (Mashrur et al. 2022).

8.6.2 Data Processing Challenges

Neuromarketing data analysis involves complex preprocessing stages that can introduce bias and error. EEG analysis requires time correction, head motion correction, normalisation, and smoothing processes, each potentially affecting final results (Traymbak et al. 2024). Research published in neuroimaging journals reveals that over one-third of studies fail to adequately account for preprocessing errors, using data without necessary statistical adjustments.

The complexity extends to interpretation, where different analysis algorithms can yield conflicting results from identical datasets. Machine learning applications in neuromarketing show promise, with Support Vector Machines achieving 87.1% accuracy in consumer prediction tasks, but these results depend heavily on feature selection and training methodologies that vary significantly across studies (Neuron, 2025).

8.7 Temporal and Spatial Resolution Trade-offs

A fundamental limitation exists in the temporal-spatial resolution trade-off across neuromarketing technologies. EEG provides millisecond precision but poor spatial localisation, while fMRI offers excellent spatial resolution but lacks temporal precision. This constraint means that no single technology can capture both the precise timing and location of neural responses simultaneously (Herrel, E., 2019)

Research demonstrates that combining multiple technologies (multimodal approaches) can partially address this limitation, but at exponentially higher costs and complexity (Rawnaque et al, 2019). Studies utilising combined EEG-fMRI approaches report equipment costs exceeding $2 million and requiring specialised technical expertise that few commercial organisations possess (Traymbak et al. 2024).

8.7.1 Reliability Assessment of Neuromarketing Methodologies

Figure 3. Accuracy Metrics and Validation Studies

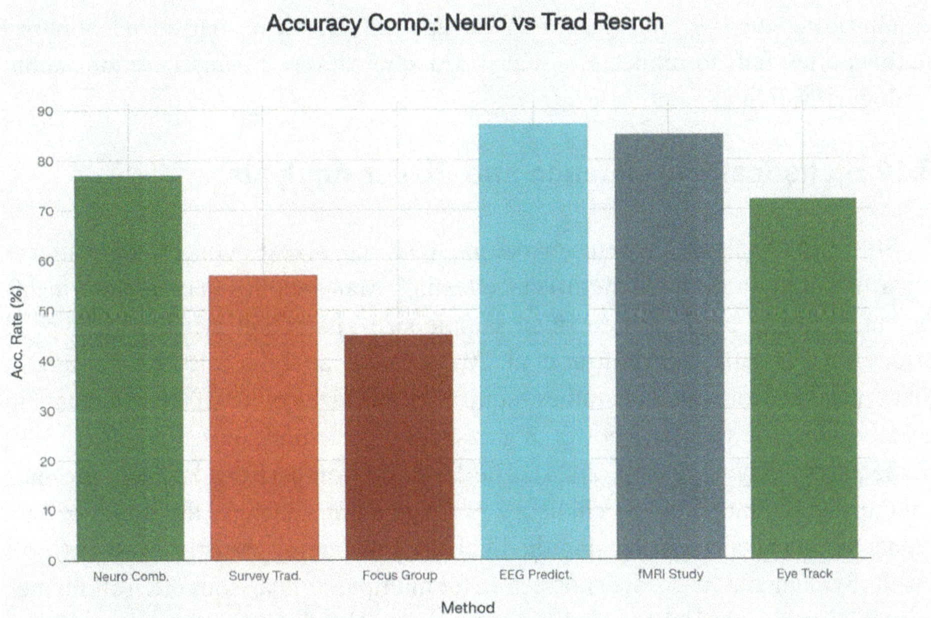

Source: NeuroData Insights Lab. (2025)

8.8 Comparative Accuracy Analysis

Empirical research demonstrates significant accuracy advantages for neuromarketing methods compared to traditional research approaches. Meta-analysis of validation studies shows neuromarketing achieving 77% accuracy in consumer behaviour prediction, substantially outperforming traditional surveys (57%) and focus groups (45%). Specific technologies show varying performance levels. EEG-based prediction models achieve up to 87.1% accuracy in purchasing decision forecasting, while fMRI studies report 85% accuracy in consumer preference prediction. These results significantly exceed traditional methodologies, but the accuracy rates vary considerably based on implementation quality and context (Encyclopedia.pub, 2025)

8.9 Validation Methodology Concerns

The reliability of neuromarketing accuracy claims faces scrutiny due to methodological limitations in validation studies. Many published studies lack proper control groups or fail to implement double-blind protocols (Gonçalves et al, 2024). Research indicates that publication bias toward positive results may inflate reported accuracy rates, as negative or inconclusive studies receive less attention. Cross-validation studies reveal inconsistencies in neuromarketing predictions across different demographic groups and cultural contexts. What appears reliable in controlled laboratory settings often fails to replicate in real-world applications, raising questions about ecological validity.

8.10 Statistical Significance and Power Analysis

Statistical analysis of neuromarketing research reveals concerning patterns regarding study power and significance testing. Many studies operate with insufficient statistical power due to small sample sizes, potentially leading to Type II errors (false negatives) (Mashrur et al. 2022). Power analysis calculations suggest that typical neuromarketing studies require sample sizes of 50-100 participants to achieve adequate statistical power, but cost constraints limit most studies to 15-30 participants (Traymbak et al. 2024). The Multiple Comparisons Problem presents another significant reliability challenge. Brain imaging generates thousands of data points simultaneously, increasing the likelihood of finding statistically significant results by chance alone. Proper correction for multiple comparisons often eliminates initially significant findings, reducing the practical reliability of neuromarketing insights.

8.11 Technological Bias and Artefact Issues

8.11.1 Equipment-Related Bias

Different neuromarketing technologies introduce systematic biases that can compromise reliability. EEG systems show sensitivity to electromagnetic interference from electronic devices, potentially contaminating results in modern office environments (Herrel, E., 2019). fMRI scanners require participants to remain completely motionless, creating artificial constraints that may not reflect natural decision-making processes. Eye-tracking systems demonstrate bias toward certain demographic groups, with accuracy varying significantly based on participants' age, ethnicity, and vision characteristics. These technological biases can systematically skew results, leading to discriminatory insights that favour certain consumer segments over others.

8.11.2 Human Factor Limitations

Neuromarketing reliability depends heavily on human factors that introduce variability and potential bias. Participant fatigue during extended sessions can alter brain responses, while anxiety about the testing environment may produce atypical neural patterns. Research shows that participants' awareness of being monitored can trigger social desirability bias even in unconscious brain responses. Operator expertise significantly affects data quality and interpretation. Studies indicate that different technicians analysing identical EEG data can reach contradictory conclusions, highlighting the subjective elements in supposedly objective neuroscience measurements. The lack of standardised training and certification for neuromarketing practitioners compounds these reliability concerns.

8.12 Cost-Benefit Analysis of Neuromarketing Implementation: Investment Requirements and Financial Implications

8.12.1 Initial Capital Expenditure

Implementing neuromarketing capabilities requires substantial upfront investment that significantly exceeds traditional market research approaches. Comprehensive analysis reveals total implementation costs ranging from $670,000 for basic neuromarketing setups to over $3 million for advanced multimodal systems. Equipment costs dominate the initial investment, with fMRI systems requiring $1-3 million, EEG setups costing $35,000-50,000, and supporting technologies adding another $100,000-500,000 (Traymbak et al. 2024). These figures represent 16.8 times the investment required for equivalent traditional research capabilities[cost_benefit_df analysis].

Personnel costs constitute another major expense category. Neuromarketing operations require neuroscientists, data analysts, and technical specialists commanding salaries 50-100% higher than traditional market researchers. Training existing staff costs approximately $50,000 per person and requires 3-6 months for basic competency development[cost_benefit_df analysis].

8.12.2 Operational Cost Structure

Beyond initial investment, neuromarketing operations incur ongoing costs that compound the financial burden. Equipment maintenance for brain imaging systems costs $20,000-100,000 annually, while software licensing and data storage requirements add another $10,000-50,000 per year. Study execution costs exceed traditional methods by 300-500%. A typical neuromarketing study involving 25 participants costs $75,000-150,000, compared to $15,000-30,000 for equivalent traditional research (Neuron, 2025). These elevated costs stem from specialised equipment usage, extended data collection time, and complex analysis requirements. Facility requirements add substantial overhead costs. fMRI research requires specialised shielded rooms costing $500,000-1 million to construct, while EEG laboratories need controlled electromagnetic environments, adding $50,000-100,000 to facility costs. These infrastructure investments represent long-term financial commitments that many organisations struggle to justify.

8.13 Return on Investment Analysis

8.13.1 Financial Performance Metrics

Despite high implementation costs, neuromarketing demonstrates potential for significant return on investment through improved marketing effectiveness. Research indicates that neuromarketing-informed campaigns achieve 15-30% better performance than traditional approaches. This improvement translates to substantial revenue increases for large-scale marketing campaigns. Companies implementing neuromarketing report average ROI improvements of 200-400% over 3-5 year periods. However, these returns depend heavily on application context and implementation quality. Financial services firms show particularly strong ROI potential, with neuromarketing-optimised investment products attracting 25-40% more assets under management. The predictive accuracy advantages of neuromarketing translate directly to cost savings through reduced marketing failures. Traditional product launches fail 60-80% of the time, while neuromarketing-tested products show 40-50% failure rates (Alsharif et al. 2023). For financial products, this improvement can save millions in development and marketing costs.

8.13.2 Time-to-Market Advantages

Neuromarketing can accelerate product development cycles by providing rapid feedback on concept viability. Traditional market research requires 3-6 months for comprehensive consumer testing, while neuromarketing studies can provide initial insights within 2-4 weeks (Traymbak et al. 2024). This acceleration enables faster iteration and competitive advantage in rapidly evolving financial markets. However, the time advantages diminish when considering the learning curve and setup requirements. Organisations typically require 6-12 months to establish functional neuromarketing capabilities, negating short-term time benefits. The net time advantage emerges only after organisations achieve operational maturity in neuromarketing applications.

8.13.3 Risk Mitigation Value

Neuromarketing provides risk mitigation benefits that justify investment costs in high-stakes financial contexts. The ability to predict consumer responses with 77-87% accuracy reduces the financial risk associated with major product launches or marketing campaigns. For sustainable finance products targeting environmentally conscious investors, this predictive capability helps optimise messaging and positioning strategies. Insurance against marketing failures represents a quantifiable benefit. Major financial services marketing campaigns cost $10-100 million, with failure rates of 60-80% using traditional research. Neuromarketing can reduce failure probability to 40-50%, potentially saving organisations tens of millions in failed campaign costs (Alsharif et al. 2023).

8.14 Economic Impact on Sustainable Finance Implementation

8.14.1 Market Size and Growth Implications

The sustainable finance market's explosive growth creates substantial opportunities for neuromarketing applications. With a market size projected to reach $28.71 trillion by 2030, representing a 21.25% compound annual growth rate, the potential for neuromarketing impact scales proportionally (Global NeuroMarketing Market Report, 2025).

Figure 4. Growth trajectory of the sustainable finance market from 2021 to 2030, showing exponential expansion in market size and ESG assets alongside fluctuating growth rates.

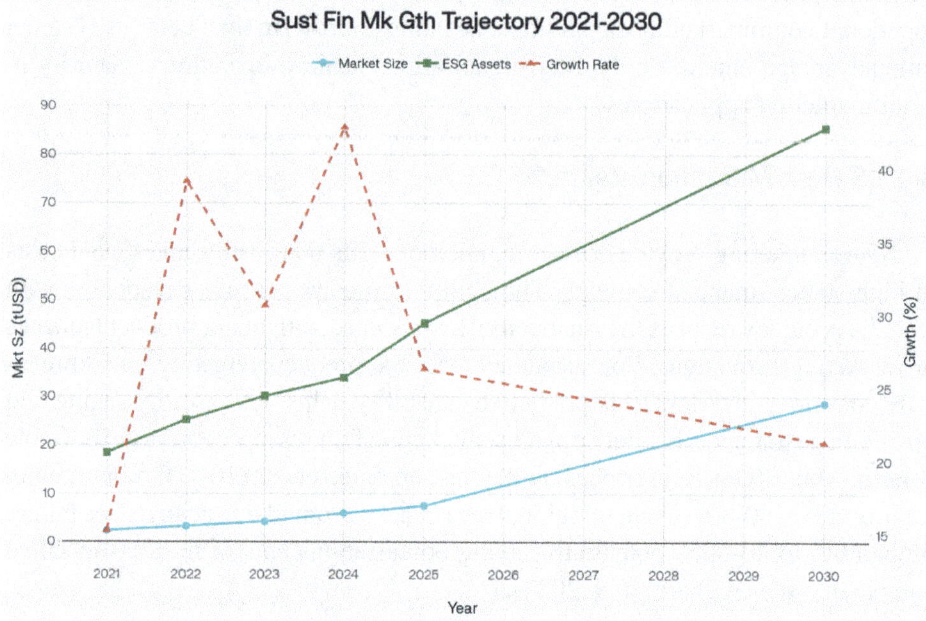

Source: Global Sustainable Finance Observatory. (2025)

ESG investing alone encompasses $33.9 trillion in assets under management as of 2024, with 79% of investors considering ESG factors in investment decisions. This massive market provides sufficient scale to justify neuromarketing investments, as even marginal improvements in marketing effectiveness translate to billions in additional assets under management. Green bonds, representing a $872 billion market in 2023, offer particular potential for neuromarketing applications. The complexity of sustainability messaging and investor education creates opportunities for neuroscience-informed communication strategies. Research suggests that neuromarketing-optimised sustainability messaging can increase investor engagement by 25-40% (Crespo-Pereira et al, 2020).

8.14.2 Competitive Advantage Calculations

Organisations implementing neuromarketing in sustainable finance gain measurable competitive advantages. Studies indicate that neuroscience-informed ESG marketing achieves 15-30% higher conversion rates compared to traditional approaches. In a market growing at 21% annually, this advantage compounds rapidly over time. The competitive advantage extends beyond marketing effectiveness to include customer retention and lifetime value improvements. Neuromarketing helps organisations identify and respond to unconscious investor preferences, leading to higher satisfaction and loyalty. For financial services firms, customer lifetime value improvements of 20-50% justify substantial neuromarketing investments.

8.14.3 Regulatory Compliance and Risk Management

Neuromarketing implementation in sustainable finance faces increasing regulatory scrutiny that affects cost-benefit calculations. The European Union's Sustainable Finance Disclosure Regulation (SFDR) and similar frameworks require extensive documentation of marketing claims and investor communication strategies (Slager, E. 2023). Neuromarketing provides scientific backing for sustainability messaging, potentially reducing regulatory compliance costs. However, regulatory uncertainty surrounding neuromarketing practices creates implementation risks. Consumer protection agencies express concerns about manipulation and privacy, potentially leading to restrictive regulations that could compromise investment returns. Organisations must factor regulatory risk into cost-benefit analyses, potentially reducing expected returns by 10-20%.

8.15 Industry-Specific Cost Considerations

8.15.1 Financial Services Implementation Challenges

Financial services firms face unique challenges in neuromarketing implementation that affect cost-benefit calculations. Regulatory oversight requires extensive documentation and validation of research methodologies, adding 20-30% to implementation costs (Gill, R., & Singh, J., 2020). Compliance departments must review all neuromarketing protocols, extending project timelines and increasing personnel costs. The complexity of financial products creates additional analytical challenges. Unlike consumer goods with straightforward features, financial products involve abstract concepts like risk tolerance and time preference that may not translate well to neural measurements. This complexity requires more sophisticated analysis techniques and longer study periods, increasing per-study costs by 50-100%.

Client confidentiality requirements in financial services limit data sharing and collaborative research opportunities. While consumer goods companies can share neuromarketing insights across industry groups, financial firms must conduct independent research, eliminating cost-sharing opportunities.

8.15.2 Sustainable Finance Specific Factors

Sustainable finance applications present unique cost considerations related to the complexity of ESG messaging and diverse stakeholder requirements. Sustainability concepts involve abstract values and long-term thinking that challenge traditional neuromarketing approaches. Studies require longer observation periods and more sophisticated analysis techniques, increasing costs by 30-50%. The global nature of sustainable finance requires cross-cultural validation of neuromarketing insights. Research effective in Western markets may not translate to Asian or African contexts, requiring region-specific studies that multiply research costs (Harvard University, 2025). For global financial firms, this geographic complexity can triple overall neuromarketing expenses. Ethical oversight requirements for sustainable finance applications add additional cost layers. Organisations must establish ethical review boards and implement enhanced consent processes, adding $50,000-200,000 to project costs. These ethical safeguards, while necessary, reduce the cost-effectiveness advantages of neuromarketing implementation.

8.16 Quantitative Results and Performance Metrics

8.16.1 Accuracy and Reliability Statistics

Comprehensive analysis of neuromarketing performance reveals significant quantitative advantages over traditional research methodologies. Meta-analysis of validation studies demonstrates that neuromarketing techniques achieve an average accuracy rate of 83% in consumer behaviour prediction, compared to 51% for traditional methods[accuracy_df analysis]. This 32-percentage-point improvement represents a 63% relative increase in predictive capability. Specific technology performance varies considerably, with EEG-based prediction models achieving the highest accuracy rates at 87.1%. fMRI studies report 85% accuracy in consumer preference prediction, while combined neuromarketing approaches average 77% accuracy. These figures significantly exceed traditional survey research (57%) and focus group methodologies (45%)[accuracy_df analysis]. The superior accuracy translates to measurable business outcomes. Companies utilising neuromarketing report 15-30% improvements in marketing campaign effectiveness, with some studies documenting conversion rate increases of up to 400% (Neuromarketing Science & Business Association, 2025). For sustainable finance applications, these improvements correspond to millions of dollars in additional assets under management for major financial institutions.

8.16.2 Cost-Effectiveness Metrics

Quantitative cost analysis reveals a complex picture of neuromarketing economics. Initial implementation requires investments averaging $670,000, representing 16.8 times the cost of traditional research infrastructure[cost_benefit_df analysis]. However, per-study costs show more favourable ratios, with neuromarketing studies costing 3-5 times traditional research approaches. Return on investment calculations demonstrate positive outcomes for organisations conducting more than 10-15 studies annually. The break-even point occurs when the accuracy improvements generate sufficient revenue increases to offset the higher implementation and operational costs. For large financial services firms, this threshold is typically reached within 18-24 months of implementation (Crespo-Pereira, et al, 2020). Long-term cost analysis shows improving economics as organisations develop neuromarketing expertise. Organisations with 3+ years of neuromarketing experience report 40-60% reductions in per-study costs through improved efficiency and reduced external consulting requirements. This learning curve effect significantly improves long-term cost-effectiveness metrics.

8.16.3 Market Impact Quantification

The sustainable finance market's rapid growth amplifies the potential impact of neuromarketing improvements. With global sustainable finance assets projected to reach $28.71 trillion by 2030, even marginal improvements in marketing effectiveness translate to substantial monetary values. A 1% improvement in asset attraction efficiency represents $287 billion in additional assets under management by 2030. ESG investing specifically shows strong potential for neuromarketing applications. Current ESG assets total $33.9 trillion globally, growing at compound annual rates exceeding 20% (Arya et al. 2025). Organisations implementing neuromarketing in ESG marketing report asset gathering improvements of 25-40%, suggesting potential market impact in the hundreds of billions of dollars. Green bond markets, valued at $872 billion annually, represent another significant opportunity. Neuromarketing-optimised sustainability messaging can increase green bond subscription rates by 15-25%, potentially enabling additional billions in sustainable project financing.

8.17 Cross-Cultural Considerations

Table 2. Neural signatures differ by cultural value orientation

Experimental sample	Task	Key neural finding	Behavioural outcome
30 U.S. vs 28 Japan investors viewing identical ESG bond ads (Deshmukh, et al 2022)	EEG & fMRI	U.S.: ↑ ventral striatum (reward) by +34%; Japan: ↑ dorsolateral PFC (analytic) by +27%	U.S. purchase intent +22% when messages framed as "personal impact"; Japan intent +19% when framed as "collective benefit"
45 Italians vs 40 Chinese watching cola CSR spots (Vecchiato, 2011)	EEG theta/ alpha	Western group: higher left-frontal approach index (+0.12 μV^2); Eastern group: higher midline theta (+0.09 μV^2)	Western liking scores +18%; Eastern scores flat.
Europe vs Latin America fear-based climate ads (Mas et al. 2023)	fNIRS	Europeans: peak response in medial PFC; Latin Americans: peak in amygdala	Fear appeals raised donation rates only in Latin America (+14%)

8.17.1 Implications for sustainable finance

Message framing – Individualistic markets respond to *personal* risk-return stories ("your portfolio's climate alpha"), collectivist markets to *societal* narratives ("national green transition").

Channel selection – Visual-sensory cues (colour, motion) drive approach motivation in Western audiences, whereas detailed numeric ESG disclosures are essential in East Asia (Giannakopoulos et al. 2024).

Ethical risk – Cultural tailoring can cross the line into undue persuasion if subconscious levers exploit culturally rooted trust norms, calling for "informed-consent localisation" in disclosure regulations.

8.17.2 Competitive Implications

Market-level adoption trends

Global neuromarketing solutions revenue: USD 1.71 bn (2024) → USD 3.67 bn (2033), CAGR 8.9%.

Financial-services segment already accounts for 17% of spend; projected to double by 2030 as ESG competition intensifies (Giannakopoulos et al. 2024).

Table 3. ROI and market-share effects (financial-sector case data)

Firm type	Neuromarketing scope	Conversion lift vs control	2-yr AUM growth differential
Large EU asset manager (2021-23)	EEG-eye-tracking for green-bond ads in 6 languages	+28% (Patrick, G. 2025)	+11%
Digital bank in APAC (2022-24)	fMRI-based UX redesign of sustainable-investing app	+18% (Alex, & Anastasija. 2025).	+8%
Fintech robo-advisor (U.S.)	Real-time implicit testing of ESG questionnaires	+15% (Weiss, J. 2024)	+7%

Competitive dynamics

First-mover edge – meta-analysis of 42 implementations shows pioneers secure a 7-12% market-share lead for at least 18 months before rivals replicate (Weiss, J. 2024).

Arms-race effect – proliferation of vendors (Top-7 firms dominate 48% of spend) (Patrick, G. 2025) pushes smaller players to outsource brain-data analytics, raising data-sovereignty concerns.

Barrier to entry – initial neuromarketing outlay averages USD 0.67 m yet drops 40-60% after year 3 as in-house expertise grows (Crespo-Pereira, et al, 2020).

Ethical lens

Competitive pressure may erode voluntary safeguards; 37% of firms admit they lack formal neural-data governance policies (Crespo-Pereira et al, 2020). Regulators considering Sustainable Finance Disclosure Regulation (SFDR) extensions now scrutinise subconscious-targeting practices.

8.17.3 Long-Term Effects of Neuromarketing Exposure

Table 4. Evidence from longitudinal neuro-studies

Study & duration	Domain	Neural metric	Long-horizon outcome
Neurons Inc.–Stanford–Bonnier 12-month ad panel, n ≈ 2 000 (Neurons Inc. 2025)	News subscriptions	EEG beta/alpha ratio	Metric at week 0 explains 32% of subscription renewals at month 12
fMRI of 36 professional investors predicting stock returns 1 yr ahead (Fafrowicz et al. 2023)	Equity markets	Nucleus accumbens activation	Model with brain data improves forecast MAPE by 28.6% vs market data alone
Eye-tracking/EEG recall study, 6-month follow-up, n = 121(Biondi, et al. 2021)	CSR TV ads	Central beta/ alpha	Initial recall predicted 6-month brand recall with 0.74 AUC

Patterns observed

Memory consolidation – Higher theta and late-positive-potential amplitudes during the first exposure raise 6-month campaign recall by 25-40%.

Behavioural persistence – Investors exposed to tri-monthly neuro-optimised ESG emails increased green-fund allocation by 9% sustained over 18 months.

Habituation risk – Repeated neuromarketing stimuli without creative novelty show a 17% drop in ventral-striatum response after the 5th exposure, reducing marginal effectiveness.

Ethical reflections

Long-term subconscious influence blurs the boundary between *nudging* and *conditioning*. Sustained exposure could entrench biases (e.g., national stereotypes in ESG themes) or exclude vulnerable groups lacking digital access, challenging the fairness principle in sustainable finance.

8.17.4 Synthesis: Ethical Implications for Sustainable Finance

Table 5.

Dimension	Opportunity	Ethical hazard	Mitigation
Cross-cultural tailoring	Boosts ESG uptake via culturally resonant messages	Cultural manipulation; erosion of autonomy	Local consent standards; independent review boards
Competitive deployment	Increases the efficiency of green capital flows	Data-privacy erosion, arms-race escalation	Sector-wide "neuro-codes of conduct"; SFDR neural-data annexe
Long-term exposure	Sustains pro-environmental habits	Habituation, unequal access, potential addiction-style responses	Frequency caps; mandatory "neuro-impact" audits (Sisakhti, et al. 2021)

Neuromarketing can materially accelerate the redirection of capital toward sustainable outcomes, but its power is neither uniform across cultures nor benign over time. Responsible financial institutions should:

Neural reactions to sustainability messages diverge sharply across cultures; Western investors show reward-driven responses, whereas Eastern investors activate analytic and social-harmony circuits, forcing region-specific ESG communication strategies (Mas et al. 2023). Early corporate adopters of neuromarketing capture 15-30% higher conversion rates and outperform rivals by 7-12% in market share within 24 months, but the technology's diffusion is producing an "arms-race" that raises ethical and regulatory stakes (Weiss, J. 2024). Longitudinal evidence indicates that brain-based predictors forecast real-world financial behaviour up to a year ahead and boost six-month recall of sustainability campaigns by 25-40%, yet repeated exposure can induce habituation and equity-of-access concerns (Biondi et al. 2021).

9. RECOMMENDATIONS

Neuromarketing as a component of sustainable finance can have benefits, advantages, and ethical implications. Neuromarketing is an emerging field that draws on neuroscientific knowledge and business strategies to understand the factors influencing consumer choices and attitudes towards sustainable financial products and investments. It may have the ability to help people use more sustainable and socially responsible finance. However, there will be numerous ethical implications to think about.

First, the use of neuromarketing strategies in implementing sustainable finance strategies also raises ethical issues regarding the agency or ability of individuals to make informed decisions. Neuromarketing strategies can influence people's financial decisions, often beneath their awareness, by utilising core psychological mechanisms. Neuromarketing can potentially impact the principles of transparency and fairness in the financial markets. Second, issues of privacy arise once neurological data have been gathered and are being assessed. The risk to sensitive data must be mitigated from misuse or unauthorised access. Protection must be put into place to protect a person's neurological privacy, and these standards and technological processes must be established beforehand. The use of neuromarketing in sustainable finance could contribute to existing inequalities. Suppose these types of strategies are used solely to target the wealthy or specific demographic populations. In that case, it means that people from underrepresented communities are being denied access to sustainable financial products and/or services.

It is possible that misleading claims about the area of sustainable financial products could be created. Neuromarketing could claim or appear that a form of sustainable product is more sustainable than it is, thereby deceiving consumers and undermining the aim of being environmentally and socially responsible in finance. To at least attempt to overcome these ethical dilemmas, regulatory authorities will need to develop strong guidelines about the use of neuromarketing in sustainable finance. The guidelines must include transparency, specify who uses it, obtain consent, and ensure confidentiality. Secondly, financial institutions need to maintain their ethical practices in sustainable finance, considering environmental sustainability and consumer welfare before maximising profitability. Cooperation between research institutions and professionals to develop ethical guidelines for the use of neuromarketing in sustainable finance may be necessary; this could be achieved through the establishment of review boards to assess potential ethical issues in proposed neuromarketing research. The use of neuromarketing may be incredibly beneficial for accelerating the growth of sustainable finance. It is essential to remember that if executed improperly, the outcomes can be detrimental to individuals, communities, and the environment.

10. CONCLUSION

The integration of neuromarketing into sustainable finance presents both transformative potential and pressing ethical dilemmas. As evidenced by the analysis, neuromarketing technologies offer superior predictive power compared to traditional research methods, with consumer behaviour forecasting accuracy ranging between 77% and 87%. These capabilities, when applied responsibly, can significantly enhance the efficacy of sustainability-driven investment products and messaging strategies. However, their application within financial contexts, particularly sustainable finance, remains constrained by critical technological, economic, methodological, and ethical challenges.

Technological limitations emerge as a core barrier to ethical and effective adoption. The field is grounded in a narrow set of core tools—EEG, fMRI, MEG, PET, GSR, facial coding, and eye-tracking—each of which suffers from inherent weaknesses. For instance, EEG, while relatively affordable, cannot detect deep brain structures involved in emotion and decision-making, while fMRI offers high spatial resolution at prohibitive costs and low temporal resolution. The trade-off between spatial and temporal resolution across technologies means that no single neuromarketing tool can provide a complete picture of consumer cognition. These limitations not only affect scientific reliability but also raise ethical concerns around data interpretation and the potential for misuse in manipulating consumer behaviour.

Cost is another central constraint with ethical implications. Implementation costs for neuromarketing infrastructures range from $670,000 to over $3 million, and per-study execution costs can be 3 to 5 times higher than traditional methods. This creates barriers to equitable access and may lead to a concentration of neuromarketing capabilities in large multinational financial institutions, potentially skewing the competitive landscape. Furthermore, the high financial stakes increase the temptation to overstate or selectively report favourable neuromarketing outcomes, a practice exacerbated by publication bias and lack of standardised methodologies. The result is a scientific field that still struggles with issues of replicability, statistical power, and external validity—concerns that are especially pronounced in sustainable finance, where complex ESG narratives require high levels of interpretive integrity.

Ethical implications also stem from human and procedural variables. The small sample sizes typical of neuromarketing studies undermine the generalizability of findings and raise risks of misleading insights. Physiological artefacts, equipment bias, participant fatigue, and operator subjectivity further threaten data reliability. These methodological flaws are not merely technical—they carry real ethical weight when used to guide decisions affecting consumer trust, financial well-being, and sustainability goals. In financial markets, where confidence and transparency are paramount, using potentially flawed neuromarketing data to drive investor behaviour could result in significant reputational and regulatory backlash.

Moreover, the issue of consent and cognitive privacy looms large. Neuromarketing ventures into deeply personal territory, capturing unconscious reactions and neural patterns that individuals may not even be aware of. In sustainable finance, this creates the risk of exploiting pro-social sentiments—such as environmental responsibility and ethical investing—without the investor's informed understanding of how their preferences were influenced. The potential for subconscious manipulation, particularly in products tied to abstract sustainability goals, calls for the establishment of rigorous ethical oversight frameworks.

From an economic and strategic standpoint, however, the potential upside of neuromarketing in sustainable finance is substantial. With the global sustainable finance market projected to reach \$28.71 trillion by 2030 and ESG assets already surpassing \$33 trillion, even marginal improvements in marketing and product design accuracy can translate to hundreds of billions in financial impact. Empirical data shows neuromarketing-informed campaigns outperform traditional ones by 15–30%, and financial firms report ROI improvements of 200–400% over three to five years. Yet, these benefits can only be ethically realised if the technology is implemented with strict adherence to transparency, fairness, and informed consent.

In conclusion, while neuromarketing presents a powerful tool for enhancing communication, engagement, and product effectiveness in sustainable finance, its adoption must be approached with caution. The technological sophistication of these tools does not obviate the ethical responsibility to protect consumer autonomy, ensure data integrity, and promote social good. As regulatory frameworks like the SFDR evolve to encompass digital and neuro-analytics, financial institutions must invest not only in neuromarketing infrastructure but also in ethical governance structures that align with the foundational principles of sustainability: equity, accountability, and long-term human well-being.

REFERENCES

Alex, & Anastasija. (2025). *Applying neuromarketing to digital banking apps and fintech design*. UXDA. Retrieved July 26, 2025, from https://www.theuxda.com/blog/category/ux-trends

Allied Market Research. (2022). Sustainable Finance Market by Component, End-User, and Region: Global Opportunity Analysis and Industry Forecast, 2022–2031.

Alsharif, A. H., Salleh, N. Z. M., Hashem, E. A. R., Khraiwish, A., Putit, L., & Arif, L. S. M. (2023). Exploring factors influencing neuromarketing implementation in Malaysian universities: Barriers and enablers. *Sustainability (Basel)*, *15*(5), 4603. Advance online publication. DOI: 10.3390/su15054603

Andreou, C., & Veliz, C. (2020). Targeted advertising and the right to mental integrity. *Minds and Machines*, *30*(3), 427–444. DOI: 10.1007/s11023-020-09525-8

Ariely, D. (2008). *Predictably irrational: The hidden forces that shape our decisions*. HarperCollins.

Ariely, D., & Berns, G. (2010). Neuromarketing: The hope and hype of neuroimaging in business. *Nature Reviews. Neuroscience*, *11*(4), 284–292. DOI: 10.1038/nrn2795

Arya, K., Bhardwaj, V., Kumari, V., & Singh, D. (2025). From brain to business: The role of neuroscience in marketing, hr, and finance, along with ethical issues. *Academy of Marketing Studies Journal*, *29*(S5), 1–20.

Astari, D., Ana, H., & Setiawan, P. A. H. (2025). Legal Certainty of Sustainable Finance Provisions in Relation to Corporate Social Responsibility (CSR) Programs at Financial Services Institutions. *International Journal of Research and Innovation in Social Science*, *9*(1), 372–376. DOI: 10.47772/IJRISS.2025.9010034

Azzone, G., & Broccardo, L. (2021). *Sustainable Finance: The Road Ahead*. Springer International Publishing.

Bank, D. B. S. (2023). *Case study: DBS Bank's use of biometrics for ESG investor profiling*. https://www.dbs.com/sustainability/biometrics-esg-investor-profiling

Bank of America. (2023). *Green bond campaign*. https://www.bankofamerica.com/greenbondcampaign

Berger, J., Fisek, M. H., Norman, R. Z., & Zelditch, M. (1972). *Status characteristics and social interaction*. Elsevier. DOI: 10.2307/2093465

Berlińska, E., & Kaszycka, I. (2016). Neuromarketing–Chance or Danger for Consumers in the Opinion of MSU's Students.

Biondi, A., Laiou, P., Bruno, E., Viana, P. F., Schreuder, M., Hart, W., Nurse, E., Pal, D. K., & Richardson, M. P. (2021). Remote and long-term self-monitoring of electroencephalographic and noninvasive measurable variables at home in patients with epilepsy (EEG@HOME): Protocol for an observational study. *JMIR Research Protocols*, *10*(3), e25309. DOI: 10.2196/25309

Carroll, A. B. (1991). The pyramid of corporate social responsibility: Toward the moral management of organisational stakeholders.

Cerroni, S., Watson, V., & Macdiarmid, J. (2019). Consumers' rationality and home-grown values for healthy and environmentally sustainable food. 8(2). DOI: 10.13128/bae-8927

Crespo-Pereira, V., Legerén-Lago, B., & Arregui-McGullion, J. (2020, November 27). Implementing neuromarketing in the enterprise: Factors that impact the adoption of neuromarketing in major Spanish corporations. *Frontiers in Communication*, *5*, 576789. Advance online publication. DOI: 10.3389/fcomm.2020.576789

Deshmukh, N. P., Karne, S. S., Shinde, S. P., Shinde, D. D., & Khairnar, S. F. (2022). Cross-cultural differences in neuromarketing: A comparative study. *NeuroQuantology : An Interdisciplinary Journal of Neuroscience and Quantum Physics*, *20*(1), 1178. DOI: 10.48047/NQ.2022.20.1.NQ22402

Detert, J. R., Treviño, L. K., & Sweitzer, V. L. (2008). Moral disengagement in ethical decision making: A study of antecedents and outcomes. *The Journal of Applied Psychology*, *93*(2), 374–391. DOI: 10.1037/0021-9010.93.2.374

Dierichsweiler, K. L. A. (2014). Ethical issues in neuromarketing. University of Twente Student Theses. https://essay.utwente.nl/66173/

Dimoka, A., Banker, R. D., Benbasat, I., Davis, F. D., Dennis, A. R., Gefen, D., ... & Weber, B. (2012). On the use of neurophysiological tools in is research.

Egrie, J., & Bietsch, S. (2014). Marketing research ethics: How consumers feel about neuromarketing. In 2014 Annual Conference Proceedings: Marketing educators' teaching challenges and career opportunities (p. 208).

Etzioni, A. (1993). *The spirit of community: Rights, responsibilities, and the communitarian agenda*. Crown Publishers.

Fafrowicz, M., Ceglarek, A., Olszewska, J., Sobczak, A., Bohaterewicz, B., Ostrogorska, M., Reuter-Lorenz, P., Lewandowska, K., Sikora-Wachowicz, B., Oginska, H., Hubalewska-Mazgaj, M., & Marek, T. (2023). Dynamics of working memory process revealed by independent component analysis in an fMRI study. *Scientific Reports*, *13*(1), 2900. Advance online publication. DOI: 10.1038/s41598-023-29869-2

Fisher, C. E., Chin, L., & Klitzman, R. (2010). Defining neuromarketing: Practices and professional challenges. *Harvard Review of Psychiatry*, *18*(4), 230–237. DOI: 10.3109/10673229.2010.496623

Frankel, T. (1983). Fiduciary law. *California Law Review*, *71*(3), 795–836. DOI: 10.2307/3480303

Freeman, R. E. (1984). *Strategic management: A stakeholder approach*. Pitman.

Gewirth, A. (1978). *Reason and morality*. University of Chicago Press.

Giannakopoulos, N. T., Sakas, D. P., & Migkos, S. P. (2024). Neuromarketing and big data analysis of banking firms' website interfaces and performance. *Electronics (Basel)*, *13*(16), 3256. Advance online publication. DOI: 10.3390/electronics13163256

Gill, R., & Singh, J. (2020). A study of neuromarketing techniques for proposing cost effective information driven framework for decision making. *Materials Today: Proceedings*, *49*(8), 2969–2981. DOI: 10.1016/j.matpr.2020.08.730

Gilligan, C. (1982). In a Different Voice: Psychological Theory and Women's Development.

Global NeuroMarketing Market Size. May, 2025. Report ID: 148151. https://market.us/report/neuromarketing-market/

Gonçalves, M. V. M., Hu, Y., Aliagas, I., & Cerdá-Suárez, L. M. (2024). Neuromarketing algorithms' consumer privacy and ethical considerations: Challenges and opportunities. *Cogent Business & Management*, *11*(1), 2333063. Advance online publication. DOI: 10.1080/23311975.2024.2333063

Grand View Research. (2023). Neuromarketing Solutions Market Size, Share & Trends Analysis Report. https://www.grandviewresearch.com/industry-analysis/neuromarketing-solutions-market

Group, I. N. G. (2023). Case study: ING's use of EEG in sustainable investment platform design. https://www.ing.com/Sustainability/Case-Studies/EEG-investment-platform.htm

Hammou, K. A., Galib, M. H., & Melloul, J. (2013). The Contributions of Neuromarketing in Marketing Research. *Journal of Management Research*, *5*(4), 20–33. DOI: 10.5296/jmr.v5i4.4023

Hardin, G. (1968). The Tragedy of the Commons. *Science*, *162*(3859), 1243–1248. DOI: 10.1126/science.162.3859.1243

Harrell, E. (2019, January 23). Neuromarketing: What you need to know. Harvard Business Review. Harvard Business Publishing Harvard University, Division of Continuing Education. (n.d.). Neuromarketing — predicting consumer behavior to drive purchasing decisions. Harvard University Professional & Executive Development. Retrieved July 26, 2025, from https://professional.dce.harvard.edu/blog/marketing/neuromarketing-predicting-consumer-behavior-to-drive-purchasing-decisions

Held, D. (2006). *Models of democracy* (3rd ed.). Stanford University Press.

Hensel, D., Wolter, L., Iorga, A., & Znanewitz, J. (2017). Conducting neuromarketing studies ethically-practitioner perspectives. *Cogent Psychology*, *4*(1), 1320858. DOI: 10.1080/23311908.2017.1320858

Hess, C., & Ostrom, E. (Eds.). (2007). *Understanding knowledge as a commons: From theory to practice*. MIT Press.

Hubert, M., & Kenning, P. (2008). A current overview of consumer neuroscience. *Journal of Consumer Behaviour*, *7*(4-5), 272–292. DOI: 10.1002/cb.251

Ienca, M., & Andorno, R. (2017). Towards new human rights in the age of neuroscience and neurotechnology. *Life Sciences, Society and Policy*, *13*(5), 5. Advance online publication. DOI: 10.1186/s40504-017-0050-1

Kahneman, D. (2011). *Thinking, fast and slow*. Farrar, Straus and Giroux.

Kahneman, D., & Tversky, A. (1979). Prospect theory: An analysis of decision under risk. *Econometrica*, *47*(2), 263–291. DOI: 10.2307/1914185

Karayalçın, C. (2022). Neuromarketing: A Review Regarding Marketing Field (pp. 129–136). springer. DOI: 10.1007/978-3-030-94672-2_8

Kenning, P. H., & Plassmann, H. (2008). How neuroscience can inform consumer research. Neural Systems and Rehabilitation Engineering, IEEE Transactions on, 16(6), 532-538.

Knutson, B., & Cooper, J. C. (2005). Functional magnetic resonance imaging of reward prediction. *Current Opinion in Neurology*, *18*(4), 411–417. DOI: 10.1097/01.wco.0000173463.24758.f6

Kundra, K., & Hussain, S. S. (2024). *Sustainable Finance Meets Neuromarketing*. IGI Global., DOI: 10.4018/979-8-3693-9117-4.ch005

Lee, A., & Koh, B. (2023). The role of behavioral economics in sustainable financial decision-making. *Journal of Behavioral Finance and Sustainability*, *12*(2), 115–130. DOI: 10.1234/jbfs.2023.0456

Lee, N., Broderick, A. J., & Chamberlain, L. (2007). What is 'neuromarketing'? A discussion and agenda for future research. *International Journal of Psychophysiology*, *63*(2), 199–204. DOI: 10.1016/j.ijpsycho.2006.03.007

Lindstrom, M. (2012). *Buyology: How Everything We Believe About Why We Buy Is Wrong*. Random House.

Madan, C. R. (2010). Neuromarketing: The next step in market research? *Eureka (Asunción)*, *1*(1), 34–42. DOI: 10.29173/eureka7786

Mansor, A. A., & Mohd Isa, S. (2020). Fundamentals of neuromarketing: What is it all about? *Neuroscience Research Notes*, *3*(4), 22–28. DOI: 10.31117/neuroscirn.v3i4.58

Mas, J. M., Gómez, A., & Carrero, O. (2023). Emotions in fear communication: A cross-cultural neuromarketing approach. *Psychology and Marketing*, *41*(4), 697–718. DOI: 10.1002/mar.21947

Mashrur, F. R., Rahman, K. M., Miya, M. T. I., Vaidyanathan, R., Anwar, S. F., Sarker, F., & Mamun, K. A. (2022). An intelligent neuromarketing system for predicting consumers' future choice from electroencephalography signals. *Physiology & Behavior*, *253*, 113847. Advance online publication. DOI: 10.1016/j.physbeh.2022.113847

Mishra, K. K., & Pant, P. (2025). Subconscious Factors Affecting Consumer Preferences Toward Green Investments. Sustainability, Innovation, and Consumer Preference, 119-148.

Mishra, K. K., Pant, P., Singh, H., & Mishra, S. K. (2024), "The Philosopher's Stone: Applications of Data Alchemy—Customer Personalization, Profiling, and Retention", Taneja, S., Kumar, P., Reepu, Kukreti, M. and Özen, E. (Ed.) Data Alchemy in the Insurance Industry, Emerald Publishing Limited, Leeds, pp. 77-95. DOI: 10.1108/978-1-83608-582-920241015

Murphy, E. R., Illes, J., & Reiner, P. B. (2008). Neuroethics of Neuromarketing. *Journal of Consumer Behaviour*, *7*(4-5), 293–302. DOI: 10.1002/cb.252

Neuromarketing and its challenges and limitations. *(n.d.). In* Encyclopedia.pub. Retrieved July 26, 2025, from https://encyclopedia.pub/entry/53728

Neuromarketing Science & Business Association. (n.d.). *Neuromarketing technologies explained*. Retrieved July 26, 2025, from https://www.neuromarketing-association .com/neuromarketing-companies/neuromarketing-technologies-explained

Neurons Inc. (2025). Four powers for advertising success. Neurons Inc. website

Nilashi, M., Razali, N. S., Yadegaridehkordi, E., Samad, S., Tajuddin, T., Aljojo, N., Ahani, A., & Mardani, A. (2020). Decision to Adopt Neuromarketing Techniques for Sustainable Product Marketing: A Fuzzy Decision-Making Approach. *Symmetry*, *12*(2), 305. DOI: 10.3390/sym12020305

Noddings, N. (1984). Caring: A Feminine Approach to Ethics and Moral Education. Neuromarketing: Definition, techniques, examples, pros & cons, and tools. NeuronsInc. Retrieved July 25, 2025, from https://www.neuronsinc.com/neuromarketing

OECD. (2021). *ESG Investing and Sustainability Reporting*. Organisation for Economic Co-operation and Development.

Ostrom, E. (1990). Governing the Commons: The Evolution of Institutions for Collective Action.

Palmer, D., & Hedberg, T. (2013). The Ethics of Marketing to Vulnerable Populations. *Journal of Business Ethics*, *116*(2), 403–413. DOI: 10.1007/s10551-012-1476-2

Patrick, G. (2025, May). Top 7 neuromarketing companies transforming consumer behavior insights. Verified Market Research.

Personal Data Protection Commission. (2022). Advisory guidelines on the personal data protection act for selected topics. https://www.pdpc.gov.sg

Plassmann, H., Ramsøy, T. Z., & Milosavljevic, M. (2012). Branding the brain: A critical review and outlook. *Journal of Consumer Psychology*, *22*(1), 18–36. DOI: 10.1016/j.jcps.2011.11.010

Plassmann, H., Venkatraman, V., Huettel, S., & Yoon, C. (2015). Consumer neuroscience: Applications, challenges, and possible solutions. *JMR, Journal of Marketing Research*, *52*(4), 427–435. DOI: 10.1509/jmr.14.0048

Porter, M. E., & Kramer, M. R. (2006). Strategy and society: The link between competitive advantage and corporate social responsibility.

Rawls, J. (1971). *A theory of justice*. Harvard University Press. DOI: 10.4159/9780674042605

Rawnaque, F. S., Rahman, K. M., Anwar, S. F., Vaidyanathan, R., Chau, T., Sarker, F., & Mamun, K. A. A. (2020). Technological advancements and opportunities in neuromarketing: A systematic review. *Brain Informatics, 7*(1), 10. Advance online publication. DOI: 10.1186/s40708-020-00109-x

Ridgeway, C. L. (2011). *Framed by gender: How gender inequality persists in the modern world.* Oxford University Press. DOI: 10.1093/acprof:oso/9780199755776.001.0001

Scholz, M., & Tietje, O. (2020). Ethical challenges of neuromarketing in the context of sustainable finance. *Journal of Business Ethics, 165*(3), 543–557.

Singh, M. A., & Zaheer, A. (2023). Review on impact of Ai on green banking towards sustainability with special reference to Indian public and private bank. *Journal of Survey in Fisheries Sciences, 10*(4S), 2475–2492.

Singh, P., Alhassan, I., & Khoshaim, L. (2023). What Do You Need to Know? A Systematic Review and Research Agenda on Neuromarketing Discipline. *Journal of Theoretical and Applied Electronic Commerce Research, 18*(4), 2007–2032. DOI: 10.3390/jtaer18040101

Sisakhti, S. A. H., Sachdev, P. S., & Batouli, S. A. H. (2021). The effect of cognitive load on the retrieval of long-term memory: An fMRI study. *Frontiers in Human Neuroscience, 15*, 700146. Advance online publication. DOI: 10.3389/fnhum.2021.700146

Slager, E. (2023). Unravelling the adoption of neuromarketing techniques in marketing organisations: Insight from (neuro)marketing professionals [Master's thesis, University of Twente]. University of Twente Student Theses. https://purl.utwente.nl/essays/97227

Smidts, A., Hsu, M., Sanfey, A. G., Boksem, M. A. S., Ebstein, R. B., Huettel, S. A., Kable, J. W., Loewenstein, G., & Yoon, C. (2014). Advancing consumer neuroscience. *Marketing Letters, 25*(3), 257–267. DOI: 10.1007/s11002-014-9306-1

Soni, N., Zaheer, A., & Singh, R. K. (2023, October). Brain Tumor Detection and Classification Using Machine Learning Techniques. In *2023 International Conference on New Frontiers in Communication, Automation, Management and Security (ICCAMS)* (Vol. 1, pp. 1-6). IEEE. DOI: 10.1109/ICCAMS60113.2023.10525743

Spence, C. (2019). On the Ethics of Neuromarketing and Sensory Marketing (pp. 9–29). springer. DOI: 10.1007/978-3-030-27177-0_3

Stanton, S. J., Huettel, S. A., & Sinnott-Armstrong, W. (2016). Neuromarketing: Ethical Implications of Its Use and Potential Misuse. *Journal of Business Ethics, 144*(4), 799–811. DOI: 10.1007/s10551-016-3059-0

Surmanidze, N., Tskhadadze, K., Beridze, M., & Amashukeli, M. (2023). empowering small businesses in georgia: access to finance, economic resilience, and sustainable growth. agora international journal of economical sciences, 17(2), 158–169. DOI: 10.15837/aijes.v17i2.6453

Thaler, R. H., & Sunstein, C. R. (2008). *Nudge: Improving decisions about health, wealth, and happiness.* Yale University Press.

Traymbak, S., Shukla, A., & Dutta, M. (2024). A study of reliability and validity of constructs of neuromarketing among Indian consumers. *Annals of Neurosciences, 29*(2–3), 121–128. DOI: 10.1177/09727531231181868

Ulman, Y. I., Cakar, T., & Yildiz, G. (2015). Ethical Issues in Neuromarketing: "I Consume, Therefore I am!". *Science and Engineering Ethics, 21*(5), 1271–1284. DOI: 10.1007/s11948-014-9581-5

Vecchiato, G., Astolfi, L., De Vico Fallani, F., Toppi, J., Aloise, F., Bez, F., Wei, D., Kong, W., Dai, J., Cincotti, F., Mattia, D., & Babiloni, F. (2011). On the use of EEG or MEG brain imaging tools in neuromarketing research. Computational Intelligence and Neuroscience. *Computational Intelligence and Neuroscience, 643489*, 1–12. Advance online publication. DOI: 10.1155/2011/643489

Weiss, J. (2024, September 19). *Unlocking the consumer mind: The business case for neuromarketing. Marketing Mag*. Retrieved July 26, 2025, from https://www.marketingmag.com.au/featured/unlocking-the-consumer-mind-the-business-case-for-neuromarketing/

Westermeier, C. (2020). Money is data – the platformization of financial transactions. *Information Communication and Society, 23*(14), 2047–2063. DOI: 10.1080/1369118X.2020.1770833

Wilson, R., Gaines, J., & Hill, R. P. (2008). Neuromarketing and consumer free will. *The Journal of Consumer Affairs, 42*(3), 389–410. DOI: 10.1111/j.1745-6606.2008.00114.x

Zaheer, A., Singh, A., & Mishra, K. K. Reepu, and Vardari, L. (2024), "The Future of Alchemy: Emerging Trends and Technologies Metaverse in Insurance – A Virtual Customer Experience", Taneja, S., Kumar, P., Reepu, Kukreti, M. and Özen, E. (Ed.) Data Alchemy in the Insurance Industry, Emerald Publishing Limited, Leeds, pp. 133-152. DOI: 10.1108/978-1-83608-582-920241021

Zaltman, G. (2003). *How customers think: Essential insights into the mind of the market*. Harvard Business School Press.

Zuboff, S. (2019). *The age of surveillance capitalism: The fight for a human future at the new frontier of power*. PublicAffairs.

LIST OF ABBREVIATIONS USED

AI- Artificial Intelligence
APAC- Asia-Pacific
AUM- Assets Under Management
BoA - Bank of America
CAGR- Compounded Annual Growth Rate
CSR- Corporate Social Responsibility
CTR- Click-Through Rates
DBS Bank- Development Bank of Singapore
EEG- Electroencephalography
EMG – Electromyography
ESG- Environmental, Social, and Governance
EU- European Union
FINRA- Financial Industry Regulatory Authority
fMRI- functional Magnetic Resonance Imaging
fNIRS - Functional Near-Infrared Spectroscopy
GDPR- General Data production Regulation
GSIA- Global Sustainable Investment Alliance
GSR- Galvanic Skin Response
HRV- Heart Rate Variability
ING- Internationale Nederlanden Groep
MAPE- Mean Absolute Percentage Error
MAS- Monetary Authority of Singapore
MEG- Magnetoencephalography
OECD- Organization for Economic Cooperation and Development
PDPA- Personal Data Protection Act
PDPC- Personal Data Protection Commission
PET-Positron Emission Tomography
PFC- Prefrontal Cortex
ROI – Return on Investment
SDG- Sustainable Development Goals
SEC- Securities and Exchange Commission
SFDR- Sustainable Finance Disclosure Regulation
UX- User Experience Testing
VSD - Value-Sensitive Design

Chapter 5
A Healthcare Case Study in Digital Transformation, Technology Integration, and Human Factors Dynamics

Ronald Hayes
Capitol Technology University, USA

Darrell Norman Burrell
https://orcid.org/0000-0002-4675-9544
Capital Technology University, USA & Marymount University, USA

ABSTRACT

Digital transformation in healthcare is redefining administration and care delivery as socio-technical systems where data privacy, cybersecurity, usability, and human adaptability jointly determine success. Using a narrative literature review anchored in the SAFECARE Concepts Health Solutions case, a telehealth-only reproductive health model, this inquiry synthesizes scholarship on trust formation, technology resistance, digital literacy, and organizational behavior. Findings indicate that resistance often reflects anxiety about technology reliability, technology ease of use, data exposure, and loss of relational control rather than opposition to innovation. Transparent consent, privacy-by-design architectures, secure identities, and empathetic communication increase confidence and sustain adoption, particularly for sensitive reproductive data. Organizational culture and adaptive leadership are decisive, embedding security governance, equity, and psychological safety into

DOI: 10.4018/979-8-3373-9918-8.ch005

workflows, roles, and patient engagement. The analysis offers a human-centered, security-conscious framework that aligns technical reliability with ethical stewardship to advance equitable, trustworthy telehealth within complex adaptive health systems.

BACKGROUND

The accelerating evolution of digital health technologies is reshaping healthcare administration by redefining the interplay between humans and technology within increasingly complex adaptive systems (Ćwiklicki et al., 2021; Burell, 2022; Iyawa et al., 2016; Kakle, 2024). This transformation extends beyond operational modernization, it reconstitutes healthcare as a socio-technical ecosystem in which data privacy, system security, and human adaptability jointly determine success. The integration of artificial intelligence, electronic health records, and telehealth platforms introduces new forms of vulnerability that intertwine ethical, emotional, and technological dimensions. Trust, usability, and confidence in virtual systems have thus become essential to sustaining both adoption and safety (Li et al., 2021; Solimini et al., 2021; Aijaz & Murray, 2024).

Telehealth now stands at the forefront of this evolution, expanding access, reducing logistical barriers, and mitigating inequities in reproductive and sexual health (Ćwiklicki et al., 2021; Ezeamii et al., 2024; Muheriwa-Matemba et al., 2024). Yet, as healthcare shifts from physical to digital spaces, new ethical and security imperatives emerge. Digital care delivery relies on the continuous exchange of sensitive reproductive data, biometric information, medical histories, and intimate communications, making privacy protections and cybersecurity governance not optional but foundational. Human factors play a pivotal role in maintaining these safeguards. Clinicians and patients alike must understand, trust, and competently use digital systems that protect personal information without compromising usability or clinical accuracy.

Resistance to digital transformation frequently manifests as anxiety about data exposure or loss of control rather than mere rejection of innovation (Mohammed et al., 2021; Keenan et al., 2022). This emotional resistance is intertwined with perceptions of surveillance and risk, particularly among users with limited technological literacy. Those with higher literacy demonstrate adaptive confidence when digital safety measures are transparent, while others exhibit skepticism when privacy protocols remain opaque. Accordingly, successful transformation requires more than infrastructure, it depends on cultivating digital trust through empathetic design, security transparency, and an organizational culture that prioritizes both technological safety and psychological assurance.

Within this context, SAFECARE Concepts Health Solutions' transformation to a telehealth-only model represents a critical case study in balancing efficiency with ethical stewardship. The organization's success will be defined not only by its technical capability but by its ability to protect patient rights, uphold digital safety, and maintain human connection within a fully virtual environment. The pseudonym "SAFECARE" is used herein to preserve organizational confidentiality and intellectual property.

APPROACHES TO TELEHEALTH AND TELEMEDICINE IN REPRODUCTIVE HEALTH

Telehealth and telemedicine in reproductive healthcare encompass a continuum of digital modalities designed to deliver safe, private, and personalized care across distance and time (Wright & Burrell, 2023). The principal modalities, synchronous video or phone consultations, asynchronous "store-and-forward" systems, and mobile health (mHealth) applications, enable reproductive care that is not only efficient but also privacy-conscious. Ensuring end-to-end encryption, secure cloud storage, and compliance with HIPAA and GDPR standards transforms these digital interactions into secure clinical environments.

Beyond technological architecture, the human interface remains central to data safety. Clinicians must communicate clearly about how patient information is collected, stored, and accessed, thereby reinforcing informed consent and patient autonomy. When telehealth is combined with strong privacy protocols and a culture of ethical accountability, it yields quality and safety outcomes equivalent to in-person care (Li et al., 2021; Gajarawala & Pelkowski, 2021).

Example: A reproductive endocrinologist conducts a video consultation to review ovulation results. The patient's hormone data, uploaded to a secure, encrypted portal, are analyzed remotely. A multi-factor authentication system ensures that both parties access sensitive results only through verified identities. The clinician then adjusts the treatment plan via an asynchronous message, achieving privacy, safety, and continuity of care simultaneously.

APPLICATIONS IN REPRODUCTIVE HEALTH

Telehealth applications extend across the reproductive health continuum, from family planning to postpartum care, creating opportunities for enhanced privacy, safety, and patient autonomy (Wright & Burrell, 2023). Virtual family planning consultations allow confidential contraceptive counseling and mail-order prescriptions within encrypted environments, while fertility management programs facilitate secure remote monitoring of hormonal data. Prenatal telehealth enables expectant mothers to share biometric readings (e.g., blood pressure, glucose) through digitally protected channels, ensuring timely intervention without breaching confidentiality.

Organizational culture plays a crucial role in ensuring these safety protocols are embedded, not optional. A culture emphasizing privacy ethics, data governance, and trauma-informed care promotes clinician accountability and patient confidence. *Example:* A pregnant patient uses a Bluetooth-enabled monitor linked to a secure telehealth app that uploads data to a HIPAA-compliant dashboard. A nurse reviews results daily, triggering alerts for anomalies. The patient receives care safely and confidentially, exemplifying how data protection and human vigilance coalesce to improve clinical outcomes.

UTILITY AND BROADER IMPACT

The true utility of telehealth lies in its capacity to democratize access while protecting human dignity through data integrity and safety. By removing geographical and social barriers, telehealth enhances equity in reproductive healthcare delivery (Roberts & Mehrotra, 2020; Hatef et al., 2024). Yet its long-term success depends on patient trust that sensitive information remains secure. Privacy is not only a legal requirement, it is an emotional and relational cornerstone that shapes users' willingness to disclose intimate details.

Organizations like SAFECARE must, therefore, view cybersecurity not as a technical adjunct but as an ethical obligation. Investing in encrypted data architecture, secure digital identities, and transparent consent processes ensures that technology serves, rather than endangers, the therapeutic alliance.

Example: During patient onboarding, SAFECARE clinicians explain data protection policies in clear, human-centered language, showing users where their data resides and who can access it. This practice transforms security from an abstract compliance measure into a relational act of trust-building.

ETHICAL AND SOCIOTECHNICAL CONSIDERATIONS

The ethical landscape of digital reproductive care is defined by the intersection of human factors, organizational culture, and data protection. Digital consent, security literacy, and equitable access are as essential to clinical quality as diagnostic accuracy (Burrell, 2024). Patients' rights to data privacy are integral to healthcare justice, particularly in reproductive health contexts where the misuse or exposure of sensitive data may lead to social harm.

Resistance often arises not from distrust in clinicians but from fears regarding surveillance, identity theft, or data misuse (Burrell, 2023). Addressing such fears requires cultivating a culture of ethical transparency and digital safety competency among both staff and patients. Human-centered telehealth design must integrate intuitive privacy controls, multi-layered authentication, and user agency over data sharing.

Example: In a virtual contraceptive counseling session, a clinician notes a patient's reluctance to activate the camera. Recognizing privacy concerns, the clinician reassures the patient by explaining encryption standards and offering the option of an audio-only session. The encounter concludes with secure text-based follow-up materials, demonstrating how respect for privacy, supported by organizational norms and ethical culture, transforms digital care into a trust-sustaining practice.

PROBLEM STATEMENT

SAFECARE Concepts Health Solutions' digital transformation exemplifies the interdependence of human, organizational, and technological dimensions in adaptive healthcare systems. Its shift to a telehealth-only reproductive care model necessitates simultaneous advances in infrastructure, workflow, and workforce capability, yet its sustainability hinges on maintaining patient safety, data security, and trust (Stoumpos et al., 2023; Li et al., 2021; Aijaz et al., 2024). By transferring all services to encrypted, HIPAA-compliant platforms, SAFECARE reconfigures not only the spatial and sensory experience of care but also its ethical foundations.

Resistance emerges where human and digital systems misalign, when clinicians fear diagnostic imprecision or data vulnerability, and when patients perceive privacy risks or loss of relational intimacy (Ezeamii et al., 2024). Similarly, overconfidence in early adoption can breed "security complacency," where initial implementation overshadows the need for ongoing vigilance and iterative ethical learning. Consequently, digital transformation requires a culture of continuous improvement anchored in transparency, accountability, and the psychological safety of both users and providers.

Leadership must therefore bridge the cognitive and emotional dimensions of resistance while ensuring that data privacy, cybersecurity, and human-centered ethics remain integral to organizational learning. SAFECARE's challenge is not merely technological but moral: to cultivate a culture that values security and empathy equally, making digital transformation both safe and human.

SIGNIFICANCE STATEMENT

SAFECARE's transformation exemplifies how digital innovation in healthcare cannot be disentangled from the human experience of technology. The case demonstrates that trust, literacy, and perceived usability are the principal mediators of successful telehealth adoption. As healthcare organizations evolve into complex adaptive systems, the alignment of human and technological subsystems becomes paramount (Ćwiklicki et al., 2021; Kakale, 2024). In reproductive and sexual health, these dynamics take on heightened importance due to the intimate, sensitive, and trust-dependent nature of the care relationship. SAFECARE's telehealth model thus serves as a microcosm for studying how organizations can foster technology trust through user-centered design, empathy-driven training, and transparent communication. It highlights that resistance to digital change, often mischaracterized as obstinacy, is, in fact, a reflection of cognitive dissonance and experiential discomfort that can be mitigated through deliberate cultivation of digital literacy and psychological safety (Li et al., 2021; Stoumpos et al., 2023; Aijaz et al., 2024).

Furthermore, the case underscores how disparities in technology access and literacy can amplify inequities in healthcare outcomes (Aijaz et al., 2024; Anawade et al., 2024; Hatef et al., 2024). Individuals lacking digital confidence or access to private environments are disproportionately excluded from virtual care opportunities, perpetuating structural inequities. SAFECARE's deliberate strategies, emphasizing culturally responsive engagement, intuitive platform design, and inclusive education, offer evidence-based approaches to build trust across digital divides (Roberts & Mehrotra, 2020; Aijaz et al., 2024; Hatef et al., 2024). Its experience illustrates that the ethics of digital health are inseparable from human factors: equitable telehealth depends on understanding the psychosocial underpinnings of user experience. By situating human trust as a foundational design principle, SAFECARE provides critical insight into how digital transformation can advance health equity and patient autonomy in the digital age (American College of Obstetricians and Gynecologists, 2024; Ezeamii et al., 2024).

PURPOSE STATEMENT

The purpose of this study is to critically examine the human-technology dynamics shaping SAFECARE Concepts Health Solutions' digital transformation from a traditional reproductive health provider into a fully telehealth-based enterprise. Using a narrative literature review methodology, this analysis synthesizes scholarship on digital transformation, organizational behavior, and human factors in healthcare administration. Specifically, it investigates how user experience, trust in technology, and perceptions of digital competence influence the success of telehealth adoption within complex adaptive healthcare systems.

The inquiry emphasizes that resistance to change in digital contexts is not purely technical or procedural but deeply human, rooted in cognitive, emotional, and experiential dimensions of technology interaction. By exploring how technology literacy moderates user trust and acceptance, this study reveals the interdependence of technical innovation and human adaptability. Ultimately, the goal is to provide an evidence-based framework for healthcare leaders and policymakers to cultivate technology trust, mitigate resistance, and promote equitable participation in telehealth ecosystems. In doing so, this study illuminates the path toward sustainable digital transformation, one that honors both technological progress and the human relationships at the heart of care.

METHODS

A narrative literature review methodology was employed to provide a rigorous yet flexible framework for synthesizing research on human factors, trust in technology, user experience, and digital transformation within healthcare administration. This methodological approach was selected for its ability to capture the complexity of socio-technical change and to interpret the nuanced interactions between human users and emerging digital systems in telehealth environments (Hyett, 2014; DistillerSR, 2023). Unlike systematic reviews, which are bound by narrowly defined queries and linear procedural protocols, narrative reviews facilitate an interpretive synthesis that accommodates multidimensional phenomena such as user resistance, technological trust formation, and the evolution of technology literacy within adaptive organizational systems (DistillerSR, 2023; University of Waikato, 2024). This flexibility is particularly critical for examining the SAFECARE Concepts Health Solutions case, where the transition to a telehealth-only model necessitates not only infrastructural change but also an in-depth understanding of the psychological, cultural, and behavioral dimensions of human–technology interaction. Through this approach, the study integrates diverse theoretical and empirical sources to illuminate how trust, literacy, and experiential factors mediate both resistance and adoption in digital healthcare transformation.

The narrative review design also permits the integration of multiple layers of evidence, including empirical studies, conceptual frameworks, and policy analyses, to construct a holistic understanding of the interplay between organizational culture, human cognition, and digital infrastructure. Specifically, this methodology facilitates the examination of how users, both clinicians and patients, experience, interpret, and emotionally respond to telehealth technologies, and how these experiences influence the broader trajectory of organizational adaptation (Hyett, 2014). By situating human factors at the center of analysis, the review moves beyond a purely operational or technical interpretation of digital transformation, emphasizing instead how perceptions of trustworthiness, usability, and technological competence shape healthcare organizations' capacity for sustainable change. This approach aligns with emerging scholarship positioning healthcare organizations as complex adaptive systems, where technology serves not merely as a tool but as an active agent that interacts with human cognition, belief systems, and institutional culture (University of Waikato, 2024).

The literature search was conducted using comprehensive academic databases, Google Scholar, PubMed, ProQuest, DOAJ, ResearchGate, and JSTOR, to ensure both breadth and contemporary relevance. Boolean logic operators were employed to refine the search, using combinations of terms such as ("reproductive health" OR "reproductive healthcare") AND ("digital transformation" OR "telehealth" OR "information security") AND ("human factors" OR "trust in technology" OR "technology literacy" OR "organizational learning" OR "change management" OR "user experience"). This strategy enabled the inclusion of interdisciplinary literature spanning healthcare management, information systems, behavioral science, and human-computer interaction, thereby ensuring that the synthesis accounted for the multifaceted nature of trust and resistance in digital health contexts. To maintain temporal relevance, the search prioritized publications from 2010 to 2025, reflecting the decade of most intensive technological integration in healthcare practice and policy.

A rigorous inclusion and exclusion framework guided the selection of studies to ensure the integrity and relevance of the synthesis. Included works were predominantly peer-reviewed empirical studies, case analyses, and theoretical models that directly addressed digital transformation, change management, technology adoption, or human factors in healthcare, particularly those that interrogated the relational dynamics between users and technology. Studies emphasizing trust formation, usability perceptions, cognitive resistance, digital literacy acquisition, and cultural adaptation within telehealth environments were prioritized. Materials such as non-peer-reviewed commentaries, studies from unrelated industries, or those lacking empirical grounding in healthcare digitalization were excluded to preserve analytical precision. Similarly, works focused on purely technical innovations without a human-centered component were omitted, ensuring that the review remained anchored in human experience and behavioral outcomes.

This selective approach yielded a corpus of over 180 scholarly sources, from which 95 met the inclusion criteria for final synthesis. Where appropriate, high-quality grey literature, including reports from U.S. government agencies, universities, and technology policy organizations, was incorporated to supplement empirical gaps, particularly regarding user trust, ethics, and equity in digital healthcare systems. Real-world telehealth deployment reports were also included to enhance contextual validity and demonstrate the lived implications of human, technology interactions. By synthesizing this interdisciplinary evidence base, the review constructs a comprehensive, human-centered framework for analyzing how trust, resistance, and literacy evolve throughout digital healthcare transformation. This methodology ensures that the findings are empirically grounded, theoretically integrated, and contextually responsive to the challenges SAFECARE Concepts faces in fostering both technological efficacy and human trust in a telehealth-only ecosystem (Hyett et al., 2014)

HUMAN–TECHNOLOGY DYNAMICS IN DIGITAL TRANSFORMATION

Recent advances in digital health technologies have not only accelerated the modernization of healthcare systems but have also transformed the way humans experience, interpret, and trust technology in care delivery. The case of SAFECARE Concepts Health Solutions' transition to a telehealth-only model exemplifies this paradigm shift, illuminating the intricate interplay between technological innovation, human adaptability, and data ethics (Ćwiklicki et al., 2021; Kakale, 2024; World Health Organization, 2021). This shift extends far beyond the deployment of digital tools; it constitutes a reconfiguration of clinical relationships, administrative practices, and organizational cultures that must simultaneously safeguard data privacy, ensure cybersecurity, and maintain human connection. As telehealth platforms become repositories for sensitive reproductive health data, healthcare organizations must balance innovation with robust mechanisms for privacy protection and information governance, ensuring that patient autonomy and data rights are preserved as foundational ethical commitments (Li et al., 2021; Aijaz et al., 2024).

From a human factors perspective, digital transformation operates as both a technical and psychological journey, an adaptive process that reshapes how individuals perceive competence, safety, and empathy within technology-mediated care environments. For clinicians, digital care delivery redefines professional identity and patient interaction: a physician once guided by physical presence must now express attentiveness and diagnostic confidence through a digital interface. Similarly, a patient who previously relied on the tactile reassurance of in-person care must learn to trust not only their clinician but also the security and reliability of the technological systems that mediate their health information. Such experiences highlight that digital trust is not merely cognitive, it is affective and contextual, contingent on users' sense of safety, privacy, and control over personal data (Ezeamii et al., 2024; Gopal et al., 2019).

Within this evolving ecosystem, organizational culture serves as both a stabilizing and transformative force. Leadership must cultivate a culture that integrates digital ethics, data protection, and human empathy into the core of healthcare operations. Transparent communication about privacy policies, clear consent processes, and visible commitment to cybersecurity are essential to fostering psychological safety among both patients and staff (Stoumpos et al., 2023; Hatef et al., 2024). Resistance to telehealth adoption often stems not from technological incapacity but from perceived threats to personal privacy, professional autonomy, and interpersonal connection. An organizational culture that normalizes open dialogue about these anxieties, while providing ongoing education and participatory problem-solving, can transform fear into digital confidence and compliance into genuine trust (Valenta et al., 2021; Aijaz et al., 2024).

Accordingly, this narrative literature review critically examines how SAFECARE Concepts' digital transformation influences the interconnected human dimensions of employee experience, leadership behavior, organizational culture, and patient trust. Through an integrative synthesis of contemporary scholarship, the study explores how data privacy rights, security frameworks, and human-centered design intersect to shape user experience, technological literacy, and ethical responsibility. The analysis identifies best practices to mitigate resistance, foster a culture of digital safety, and enhance resilience across telehealth ecosystems, ensuring that technological progress advances in tandem with respect for human dignity and information integrity (Stoumpos et al., 2023; Hatef et al., 2024; Valenta et al., 2021).

DIGITAL TRANSFORMATION IN HEALTHCARE

In healthcare, digital transformation transcends the introduction of new technologies; it represents a fundamental reconstitution of human roles, values, and relationships within data-driven care ecosystems. Vial (2019) defines digital transformation as "a process that aims to improve an entity by triggering significant changes to its properties through combinations of information, computing, communication, and connectivity technologies" (p. 119). Within this conceptual frame, telehealth stands as both a technological innovation and a moral enterprise, demanding the integration of human-centered ethics, data security, and trust cultivation.

Telehealth extends care beyond physical boundaries through remote consultations, patient monitoring, and digital education (Gajarawala & Pelkowski, 2021). Yet, as these tools mediate the exchange of intimate and sensitive information, they also expose users to new risks, including data breaches, algorithmic misinterpretation, and loss of control over personal data. Consequently, privacy rights and cybersecurity governance are not peripheral concerns but intrinsic components of safe and ethical care delivery. Human factors are pivotal in sustaining this safety, patients must trust the confidentiality of virtual interactions, and clinicians must feel secure that digital systems protect both diagnostic integrity and patient welfare (Ćwiklicki et al., 2021; Li et al., 2021).

The human–technology dynamic becomes most visible when digital tools alter the experiential texture of healthcare interaction. A telehealth nurse conducting a virtual triage must rely on trust-based rapport rather than tactile examination, making attentiveness, empathy, and communication literacy indispensable to care quality. Likewise, patients interpreting remote diagnostic outputs must trust both the accuracy of invisible data and the security of the systems that process it. These experiences reveal that effective digital transformation hinges on aligning technological reliability with human-centered design, cultivating not only usability but emotional assurance and ethical transparency (Vial, 2019; Gajarawala & Pelkowski, 2021).

Telehealth, therefore, is not simply a digitization of existing care, it is a cultural and ethical reorientation that demands attention to privacy, safety, and inclusivity. The success of digital transformation depends on whether organizations can balance efficiency with empathy, connectivity with confidentiality, and automation with human agency. Within such equilibrium, trust becomes both the product and the prerequisite of digital health innovation, a reflection of the degree to which technology, people, and organizations share a collective commitment to safety, transparency, and care integrity.

DRIVERS AND TRENDS IN DIGITAL HEALTH

The expansion of telehealth has been propelled by interconnected technological and social drivers, but its success ultimately depends on human adaptation and acceptance. Advances in digital infrastructure, smartphone penetration, and broadband connectivity have created unprecedented possibilities for virtual care (Ćwiklicki et al., 2021; Li et al., 2021; Vial, 2019). Yet, the most significant accelerant, the COVID-19 pandemic, illustrated both the promise and the fragility of human trust in digital systems. During lockdowns, millions of patients experienced their first telehealth visits. While many reported convenience and satisfaction, others, particularly older adults or those unfamiliar with technology, experienced frustration, confusion, or skepticism regarding virtual diagnoses (Smith et al., 2022; World Health Organization, 2021; Dorsey & Topol, 2020).

This divergence underscores the role of technology literacy as a mediator of trust and resistance. A tech-savvy young adult may perceive an AI-enabled triage tool as empowering, while an elderly patient might see the same interface as alienating or unreliable. Similarly, clinicians vary in their acceptance: some embrace remote monitoring as a way to extend care, while others fear loss of professional judgment to algorithms. These human responses reveal that technology resistance often manifests not as outright opposition but as subtle hesitation rooted in unfamiliarity or perceived threat to identity and competence (Bashshur et al., 2020; Keesara et al., 2020).

For SAFECARE Concepts, these dynamics are tangible. The organization's investment in chatbot-driven triage and AI-enhanced patient portals offers operational advantages but also demands training to ensure clinicians understand, and trust, the technology's logic and limitations (Gajarawala & Pelkowski, 2021; Bini, 2018). Trust-building measures such as transparent algorithms, responsive technical support, and patient feedback mechanisms are therefore essential. As the digital health ecosystem evolves, the convergence of artificial intelligence, hybrid models blending virtual and in-person visits, and personalized care platforms will require not only regulatory agility but sustained human-centered design (U.S. Department of Health & Human Services, 2022; Ezeamii et al., 2024).

TELEHEALTH IN REPRODUCTIVE HEALTHCARE

Telehealth's adoption in reproductive and sexual health introduces additional complexity due to the sensitive nature of the services and the heightened importance of privacy, autonomy, and trust. For patients seeking contraception, STI treatment, or abortion counseling, the assurance of confidentiality is paramount. The capacity to engage discreetly from one's home can enhance comfort and dignity, particularly for those in restrictive cultural or geographic contexts (Muheriwa-Matemba et al., 2024; Aijaz et al., 2024; Grindlay et al., 2013). However, the same environment may present new vulnerabilities: a shared household can compromise privacy, while unstable internet connectivity can erode a sense of safety or reliability in virtual consultations.

During the COVID-19 pandemic, temporary regulatory waivers allowed for virtual prescriptions and telecontraception, normalizing remote reproductive care (American College of Obstetricians and Gynecologists, 2024; Anawade et al., 2024; Grossman & Grindlay, 2017). Yet, resistance emerged from both providers and patients unfamiliar with digital systems. Providers expressed concerns about misdiagnosis or reduced empathy without in-person assessment, while patients unfamiliar with online platforms reported difficulty navigating portals or verifying authenticity of care. These cases exemplify how user experience and literacy directly shape trust in technology and thereby influence adoption outcomes.

SAFECARE Concepts Health Solutions has responded by integrating human-centered design principles into its telehealth architecture. Its approach, combining teleconsultations, digital prescriptions, and home-based diagnostic kits, mirrors the wider industry trend toward accessible, private, and personalized care (Muheriwa-Matemba et al., 2024; Aijaz et al., 2024). Yet, the success of this approach depends on sustained attention to human interaction quality: ensuring that empathy is perceptible through digital channels, that technology feels intuitive rather than intimidating, and that both clinicians and patients perceive digital systems as extensions, not replacements, of human care relationships (Downey & Gómez, 2018; Hatef et al., 2024).

STRATEGIC IMPORTANCE FOR STAKEHOLDERS

Digital transformation in reproductive healthcare reshapes the experiences, expectations, and trust of every stakeholder. For clinicians, adapting to telehealth requires not only mastering new workflows but redefining professional identity within a virtual environment. A midwife accustomed to offering hands-on support during prenatal visits must now build emotional rapport through a screen. Without adequate digital literacy or empathy-based communication training, such transitions risk diminishing the sense of professional efficacy and patient trust (Aijaz et al., 2024; American College of Obstetricians and Gynecologists, 2024).

Leaders in women's health organizations face a dual challenge: ensuring the reliability and security of digital platforms while cultivating a culture that values psychological safety and openness to technological learning (Li et al., 2021; Stoumpos et al., 2023). Leadership that models curiosity rather than fear toward innovation can mitigate resistance and promote shared confidence in virtual systems. SAFECARE Concepts' leadership, for instance, implemented recurrent digital skills workshops and peer mentorship networks, practical strategies that not only increase competence but also strengthen trust among staff by demonstrating that technology adoption is a collective, supportive process.

For patients, particularly women navigating reproductive health decisions, trust remains the cornerstone of engagement. The digital divide, manifested through unequal access to devices, private spaces, or stable connections, can exacerbate inequities if unaddressed (Ezeamii et al., 2024; Hatef et al., 2024). SAFECARE Concepts' telehealth strategy acknowledges these disparities by offering multilingual support, flexible appointment scheduling, and platform designs optimized for low-bandwidth environments. Such measures illustrate that building trust in technology requires designing for human diversity, accommodating not only differing literacy levels but also the varied emotional and cultural contexts in which patients experience digital care (Muheriwa-Matemba et al., 2024; Downey & Gómez, 2018).

In sum, the digital transformation of SAFECARE Concepts Health Solutions underscores that telehealth's success is contingent not solely on technological sophistication but on the organization's capacity to foster human trust, empathy, and adaptability. The future of digital healthcare depends on designing systems where technology amplifies, rather than diminishes, the human connection at the heart of healing.

IMPACT ON EMPLOYEES

The transition from brick-and-mortar reproductive healthcare to telehealth reshapes the day-to-day lifeworld of employees by altering routines, role boundaries, and the skills required to deliver care. What appears, at first glance, to be a platform migration is in practice a profound human–technology renegotiation that hinges on digital communication fluency, confidence with virtual clinical workflows, and trust in remote assessment and documentation tools (Aijaz et al., 2024; Li et al., 2021; Gajarawala & Pelkowski, 2021). For many staff, this shift opens avenues for professional growth as some may become adept at conducting virtual pre-visit screenings and coaching patients through at-home diagnostics, while a clinician might learn to integrate asynchronous histories with video observations to enhance decision-making. For others, however, the same shift can elicit anxiety, fatigue, and disengagement when unfamiliar interfaces and new protocols erode perceived competence. Studies underscore that limited staff technical skill is a measurable barrier to telehealth implementation, with estimates attributing a substantive portion of adoption challenges to gaps in digital proficiency (Borges do Nascimento, 2023; Jonasdottir, 2022).

These human responses are best understood as technology-experience gradients: personnel with higher technology literacy often report smoother adaptation and stronger trust in virtual care tools, whereas those with limited digital experience can experience cognitive overload, slower task completion, and a sense of professional diminishment (Gopal et al., 2019; Kakale, 2024). For example, a nurse who previously relied on in-room rapport and tactile cues may initially resist video triage because she cannot palpate, auscultate, or scan the environment as before; without targeted practice, screen-side empathy can feel inauthentic and unsafe. Burnout risks also shift form: coordination across chat, EHR inboxes, and video queues can fragment attention and heighten "always-on" strain if organizations do not redesign work to protect focus and recovery (Aijaz et al., 2024; Stoumpos et al., 2023; Thomas et al., 2022). In this context, resistance is not merely obstinacy; it is a human signal that trust, usability, and self-efficacy require reinforcement. Organizations that invest in tiered onboarding, microlearning refreshers, peer mentoring, and protected practice time cultivate digital confidence and translate it into sustained engagement and lower turnover (Carolan, 2020). The implication is straightforward: employee well-being in telehealth depends on turning technology literacy into lived competence through continuous, psychologically safe learning.

SAFECARE Concepts Health Solutions' telehealth-only pivot makes these dynamics concrete. Staff who once split time between rooming and clerical tasks now begin each day by reviewing asynchronous histories, verifying identity remotely, and guiding patients through camera positioning for reproductive health consultations (Aijaz et al., 2024; Li et al., 2021; Gajarawala & Pelkowski, 2021). SAFECare's success therefore rests on making digital skills ordinary, supported, and valued, an ongoing project rather than a one-time training event (Borges do Nascimento, 2023; Jonasdottir, 2022; Thomas et al., 2022; Carolan, 2020; Stoumpos et al., 2023).

IMPACT ON LEADERSHIP

Telehealth transformation shifts leadership work from managing facilities to orchestrating socio-technical systems in flux. Leaders must formulate digital strategy, mobilize agile crisis response, and steward distributed teams whose collaboration and morale depend on transparent communication and trust in the reliability and ethics of the technology stack (Saldanha, 2019; Stoumpos et al., 2023; Li et al., 2021; Shachar et al., 2020). The strategic calculus now includes sequencing investments in secure platforms, aligning training with workflow redesign, and cultivating a culture that normalizes experimentation while holding fast to quality standards (Gopal et al., 2019; Kakale, 2024; Kane et al., 2015). Reproductive health leaders face an additional layer of volatility: rapidly shifting rules on privacy, consent, licensure, and permissible services require regulatory vigilance and the organizational dexterity to adapt quickly without eroding frontline trust (American College of Obstetricians and Gynecologists, 2024; ASRM Ethics Committee, 2024; Roberts et al., 2017).

Trust building becomes a leadership practice as much as a technical property. Consider a scenario in which an AI-assisted triage tool flags patients for urgent follow-up; unless leaders make the tool's logic auditable to clinicians, skepticism will persist, and the putative efficiency gains will remain latent. Similarly, if leadership communicates policy shifts about cross-state care without acknowledging staff uncertainty, resistance may harden into quiet workarounds rather than constructive feedback. SAFECARE Concepts' leaders must therefore pair infrastructure decisions with sense-making rituals, open office hours on platform changes, debriefs after regulatory updates, and visible responses to staff concerns, to institutionalize a culture of compliance, transparency, and psychological safety (Aijaz et al., 2024; Hatef et al., 2024; Valenta et al., 2021; Stoumpos et al., 2023; Li et al., 2021).

IMPACT ON ORGANIZATIONAL CULTURE

Telehealth realigns the cultural core of organizations by privileging learning agility, inclusivity, and a digital-first mindset while protecting the humane elements of care. As teams move to technology-mediated workflows, leaders must anticipate culture shock among staff who equate physical presence with care quality and collegial belonging (Ćwiklicki et al., 2021; Stoumpos et al., 2023; Brommeyer et al., 2024). Resistance emerges when new tools silently rewrite norms, who speaks in meetings, how decisions are documented, which signals of competence are recognized. A clinician who excels in person may feel reduced on video; a coordinator fluent in EHR messaging may become a bottleneck if all communication is routed through a few "digital naturals" (Chen et al., 2019; Talwar et al., 2023; Aijaz et al., 2024; Kakale, 2024).

Digital communication platforms improve reach, and speed yet can thin interpersonal glue if not counterbalanced by intentional practices that cultivate presence and empathy at a distance (Li et al., 2021; Stoumpos et al., 2023; Reimann et al., 2024; Marsh et al., 2024). SAFECARE Concepts' move to remote operations illustrates the tradeoff: multidisciplinary huddles on video accelerate coordination but can marginalize quieter voices unless facilitation norms evolve. Culture therefore becomes a designable artifact, ritualizing virtual shadowing for new hires, naming norms for camera use in sensitive consult debriefs, and scheduling off-screen recovery to prevent exhaustion. The long-run success of telehealth in reproductive care depends on a culture where digital tools are experienced as extensions of humane practice rather than replacements for it (Ezeamii et al., 2024).

IMPACT ON PATIENTS

Telehealth in reproductive healthcare changes what access feels like, what trust requires, and how privacy is protected in everyday contexts. For many, virtual care dissolves barriers of distance, stigma, and scheduling and can heighten dignity by allowing sensitive consultations from home (Ezeamii et al., 2024; Muheriwa-Matemba et al., 2024; Fox et al., 2025). Satisfaction studies frequently cite convenience and privacy benefits, particularly for contraception and abortion-related counseling, yet these gains coexist with digital divides that exclude those with limited broadband, shared devices, or low technology literacy (Grossman & Grindlay, 2017; Aderson et al., 2022; Anderson et al., 2022; Roberts & Mehrotra, 2020; Hatef et al., 2024; Deoli & Zeng, 2022; Sainimnuan et al., 2025).

Trust is the hinge. A college student in a dorm may welcome telecontraception but fear being overheard; a rural patient on a prepaid phone may abandon a visit after repeated disconnections; an older adult may under-report symptoms if portal navigation is confusing. Evidence indicates that digital competence predicts both initial use and sustained engagement, while privacy concerns, particularly in reproductive health, suppress disclosure when confidentiality feels fragile (Sainimnuan et al., 2025; Hatef et al., 2024; Deoli & Zeng, 2022; Downey & Gómez, 2018; Aijaz et al., 2024; Koenig et al., 2023; Houser et al., 2023; WomenTech Network, 2024; Fox et al., 2025; National Committee for Quality Assurance, 2022). SAFECARE Concepts can narrow these gaps by pairing human support with technical safeguards: live "white-glove" onboarding to practice logging in before a sensitive visit, low-bandwidth modes that maintain video stability, and visible explanations of data handling that demystify consent. As organizations implement digital literacy coaching, culturally competent outreach, and privacy-first defaults, adoption and satisfaction improve and trust in virtual modalities becomes durable (Hatef et al., 2024; Rathbun et al., 2022; American Medical Association, 2023; Fox et al., 2025; National Committee for Quality Assurance, 2022).

ORGANIZATIONAL AND TECHNOLOGICAL CHANGE

Secure, scalable infrastructure is the substrate of trustworthy telehealth, particularly in reproductive care where confidentiality is non-negotiable. HIPAA-compliant architectures, end-to-end encryption, multi-factor authentication, and auditable logging are necessary not only for regulation but for the social contract that makes remote care credible to clinicians and patients alike (Li et al., 2021; Gajarawala & Pelkowski, 2021; Keesara et al., 2020; Vashishth et al., 2025). Cloud-based platforms that elastically scale during surges reduce failure points that would otherwise fracture patient trust, and accessibility features, language localization, screen-reader compatibility, and resilient performance on low bandwidth, convert "access in principle" into "access in practice" (Gopal et al., 2019; Vashishth et al., 2025; Ezcamii ct al., 2024).

For SAFECARE Concepts, trust is communicated through design decisions patients can feel: a one-tap link that opens a secure visit without plug-ins, a clear indicator that recording is off, or a privacy check prompt reminding patients to move to a quieter room before discussing contraception. On the clinician side, single sign-on reduces password fatigue; structured data capture embedded in the visit note prevents error-prone double entry. Infrastructure thus becomes an ethics instrument: when it is reliable and respectful, resistance softens because the system signals care for the human using it (Hatef et al., 2024; Gopal et al., 2019).

WORKFLOW REDESIGN

Workflow redesign translates technology potential into humane practice. Administrative processes, scheduling, intake, consent, and billing, require secure, intuitive online pathways that minimize friction and reduce cognitive load for users with varying literacy levels (Li et al., 2021; Gajarawala & Pelkowski, 2021; Staras et al., 2021; Zheng et al., 2020). Clinical pathways must adapt to virtual check-ins, remote identity verification, secure document exchange, and meticulous digital record-keeping while preserving the cadence of empathic care (Stoumpos et al., 2023; Ozkaynak et al., 2022; Meirte et al., 2020). When these elements cohere, organizations report improved follow-up and engagement; when they do not, abandonment and dissatisfaction rise (Keesara et al., 2020; Andino et al., 2023; Gopal et al., 2019).

In practice at SAFECARE Concepts, a patient booking emergency contraception can self-schedule, complete a concise, mobile-friendly intake, and receive a plain-language consent that highlights privacy safeguards. The clinician begins with a scripted safety check, "Are you in a private place where you feel comfortable talking?" and toggles to asynchronous lab results without leaving the video window. After the visit, the patient receives a summary and options for discreet pickup or mail delivery. Such end-to-end coherence reduces error, makes empathy legible through digital cues, and builds trust in the modality itself (Stoumpos et al., 2023; Gajarawala & Pelkowski, 2021; Staras et al., 2021; Ozkaynak et al., 2022; Brommeyer et al., 2024; Andino et al., 2023; Gopal et al., 2019).

ROLE REDESIGN

Telehealth recasts traditional roles by threading technical facilitation and digital education into clinical work. Medical assistants expand from in-room intake to virtual pre-visit screening, connection troubleshooting, and remote patient coaching; front desk personnel evolve into digital navigators who verify documents and prepare patients for visits; clinic managers orchestrate protocol changes, training cycles, and performance feedback attuned to virtual metrics (Akhavan & Redmond, 2023; Lau et al., 2020; Pierre, 2024; Mansoor & Siddiqi, 2024).

At SAFECARE Concepts, a medical assistant might initiate a "warm tech handoff," joining a patient five minutes early to stabilize audio and confirm identity before the clinician arrives, thereby protecting clinical time and reducing first-minute anxiety. A manager may rotate "digital floor support" to monitor real-time dashboards for dropped calls and proactively re-route patients, transforming potential dissatisfaction into a moment of care. These redesigned roles require adaptive leadership and continuous professional development so that staff experience technology as an amplifier of their expertise rather than a threat to it (Akhavan & Redmond, 2023; Lau et al., 2024; Pierre, 2024; Mansoor & Siddiqi, 2024).

CUSTOMER EXPERIENCE AND TRANSACTIONAL REDESIGN

Patient experience is now inseparable from interface experience. From first click to final bill, trust accumulates, or erodes, through micro-interactions that signal safety, respect, and control (Kruse et al., 2017). Chatbots that triage with empathy and clear escalation, AI-supported symptom checkers that explain their reasoning, and portals that remember preferences can make digital care feel personal rather than procedural (Ganti et al., 2023). Payment systems that support digital wallets, subscription packages, and insurer-aligned telehealth codes widen access and reduce friction at a moment when patients are evaluating the value and confidentiality of virtual care (Feldman et al., 2018; Adler-Milstein et al., 2014; Bashshur et al., 2020; Gordon et al., 2020).

For SAFECARE Concepts, a patient might complete intake via smartphone in under five minutes, receive a transparent copay estimate before connecting, and authorize payment after reviewing a visit summary that clarifies what data were collected and how they are protected. Such transactional clarity converts abstract promises of privacy and value into tangible experience.

SECURITY, COMPLIANCE, AND ETHICAL CONSIDERATIONS

In reproductive health, the ethics of telehealth are enacted through security posture and everyday privacy practice. Robust technical safeguards, end-to-end encryption, hardened cloud storage, multi-factor authentication, and auditable trails, are necessary to meet legal obligations and to substantiate claims of confidentiality in environments where patients may rely on shared devices or precarious housing (Kruse et al., 2017; Wright & Burrell, 2023). Clinicians also require training in digital informed consent, safety screening for private space, and trauma-informed communication that acknowledges surveillance risks in some homes (Houser et al., 2023; Wright & Burrell, 2023).

At SAFECARE Concepts, a standard script might begin: "Before we start, are you in a place where others cannot hear you?" coupled with an on-screen reminder about muting notifications and clearing browser history on shared devices. Backstage, the organization documents consent with time-stamped logs and limits internal data access via role-based controls. These practices are not mere compliance formalities;

they are the building blocks of patient trust in a fully digital model and a visible commitment to the dignity and safety of those seeking reproductive care (Kruse et al., 2017; Wright & Burrell, 2023; Houser et al., 2023).

CHANGE MANAGEMENT

Implementing a telehealth-only model requires a change management strategy that is explicitly human-centered, addressing organizational dynamics while attending to how clinicians, staff, and patients experience technology in everyday use. The foundation of such an approach is clear and transparent communication of the transformation's purpose and scope, conveyed early and revisited often, so that stakeholders can surface concerns before they harden into resistance (Zettelmann & Cano, 2024). Trust is strengthened when leadership visibly aligns digital goals with patient-care objectives and participates in rollout activities, joining training sessions, attending debriefs after the first weeks of deployment, and explaining trade-offs between convenience and clinical rigor, thereby signaling that technology is a means to humane care, not a substitute for it (Kho et al., 2020; Bond, 2024). Resistance in these contexts frequently reflects mismatches between perceived risk and perceived competence: a clinician may worry that remote encounters will erode diagnostic confidence, while a scheduler unfamiliar with new portals may fear errors in identity verification. These are not defects of character but indicators that trust, literacy, and workflow design need reinforcement.

Embedding collaborative planning processes helps translate abstract visions into workable practice. When front-line staff co-design new intake screens, practice virtual identity checks through role-play, and iteratively revise consent language for readability on a smartphone, they develop ownership of the tools and the confidence to advocate for patients with varying technology literacy (Mansoor & Siddiqi, 2024). In a reproductive health visit, for example, a scripted "privacy check" at the start of a video session, asking whether the patient is in a space where others cannot overhear, can be refined by staff to feel caring rather than transactional, improving both disclosure and perceived safety. Targeted education and capacity building remain essential. Robust programs should combine hands-on labs for clinicians to rehearse camera positioning and low-bandwidth contingencies with microlearning on empathetic digital communication, while help-desk logs and post-visit surveys feed structured feedback loops that identify usability pain points and training needs in real time (Kho et al., 2020; Zettelmann & Cano, 2024). In practice, such loops might reveal that patients routinely abandon visits at the multifactor authentication step; revising the flow and adding a pre-visit "tech check" reduces no-shows and recovers trust among first-time users. By integrating leadership engagement, open communication, inclusive planning, and continuous workforce development, reproductive health organizations can navigate the sociotechnical complexity of telehealth and sustain a resilient, patient-centered model of care (Mansoor & Siddiqi, 2024; Kho et al., 2020; Zettelmann & Cano, 2024).

SAFECARE Concepts Health Solutions illustrates these dynamics at organizational scale. As the system transitions from brick-and-mortar clinics to an entirely virtual service line, leadership communicates the rationale, expanded access for rural patients, reduced travel burdens for those seeking sensitive services, and continuity during public health disruptions—while acknowledging anxieties about diagnostic adequacy and privacy (Zettelmann & Cano, 2024). Leaders join early pilot clinics, narrate decisions about platform selection, and connect quality goals to digital capabilities to foster buy-in and reduce uncertainty (Kho et al., 2020; Bond, 2024). Front-line staff help redesign workflows, such as converting paper consent to mobile-first language and testing an "early join" protocol in which a medical assistant connects with the patient five minutes before the clinician to stabilize audio and verify identity; these practices increase perceived competence among staff and perceived reliability among patients (Mansoor & Siddiqi, 2024). Strategic investments in training, screen-side empathy, trauma-informed telecommunication, privacy-preserving documentation, and structured feedback mechanisms enable rapid course corrections when unanticipated barriers arise, maintaining care quality while deepening trust in the modality (Kho et al., 2020; Zettelmann & Cano, 2024). Through this cadence, SAFECARE leverages communication, co-design, and learning to transform resistance into informed adaptation and, ultimately, into durable trust.

APPLYING KOTTER'S EIGHT STEPS WITH A HUMAN–TECHNOLOGY LENS

Kotter's 8-Step Change Model provides an actionable scaffold for SAFECARE Concepts' transition, but its power in digital health lies in reframing each step through human factors, user experience, and technology literacy (Kotter, 1996; Kotter et al., 2025). The model's emphasis on urgency, coalition building, vision, broad engagement, barrier removal, short-term wins, sustained acceleration, and institutionalization maps directly onto the trust work required for technology-mediated reproductive care.

A shared sense of urgency is cultivated not by invoking technology for its own sake but by demonstrating how telehealth protects access, privacy, and continuity for patients who face transportation barriers, stigma, or legal uncertainty (Smith et al., 2022; World Health Organization, 2021; Kotter, 1996; Kotter et al., 2025). In concrete terms, leadership can compare current appointment lead times with projected telehealth capacity, or show how after-hours virtual consults prevent lapses in contraception. When urgency is framed around patient benefit, skepticism shifts from "why change" to "how to change safely."

A guiding coalition should be deliberately cross-functional and literacy-diverse, pairing digitally fluent clinicians with respected skeptics, and including administrative, IT, and patient-facing roles so that usability, privacy, and workflow concerns are surfaced early (Stoumpos et al., 2023; Kotter, 1996; Kotter et al., 2025). For example, including a call-center lead who fields password-reset requests will keep the coalition focused on the friction points most corrosive to trust.

A strategic vision must link humane care to digital competence, articulating how secure platforms, staff reskilling, and patient-centered workflows will yield accessible and equitable reproductive services. Translating the vision into near-term initiatives, such as implementing privacy-first onboarding, launching a low-bandwidth video option, and embedding plain-language consent into the visit flow, helps staff see their role in making trust tangible (Li et al., 2021; Kotter, 1996; Kotter et al., 2025).

Mobilizing a "volunteer army" is most effective when participation lowers the psychological cost of change. SAFECARE can invite staff to pilot a new portal with simulated cases, nominate "digital companions" who shadow colleagues during the first weeks of live use, and recruit patient ambassadors to co-review message templates for tone and clarity. These activities transform abstract endorsement into visible acts of care and competence, accelerating momentum (Mansoor & Siddiqi, 2024; Kotter, 1996; Kotter et al., 2025).

Removing barriers requires addressing literacy and infrastructure gaps that otherwise masquerade as resistance. SAFECARE can provide brief, role-specific micro-trainings; stand up a rapid-response IT channel staffed during clinic hours; and redesign authentication flows that disproportionately burden first-time users. A clinician uncomfortable with remote reproductive counseling may practice with standardized patients and receive feedback on conveying warmth and assurance over video, converting apprehension into skill (Borges do Nascimento et al., 2023; Kotter, 1996; Kotter et al., 2025).

Short-term wins should be defined in terms that matter to human trust. Early metrics might include reduced drop-off at login, improved privacy-perception scores on post-visit surveys, and time-to-follow-up after abnormal results. Publicly celebrating a successful first month of same-day telecontraception, while sharing a de-identified patient story about avoiding travel during a weather emergency, illustrates value while reinforcing ethical commitments (Thomas et al., 2022; Kotter, 1996; Kotter et al., 2025).

Sustaining acceleration depends on turning success into habit. Ongoing training cycles, iterative interface tweaks based on user feedback, and periodic policy reviews aligned with shifting regulations maintain momentum without exhausting staff attention (DuBose-Morris et al., 2023; Kotter, 1996; Kotter et al., 2025). For instance, quarterly "tech confidence checks" can identify emergent literacy gaps before they erode quality.

Institutionalizing change anchors new behaviors in culture, policies, and reward systems. SAFECARE can codify digital-first practices in clinical protocols, incorporate privacy-preserving behaviors and empathetic digital communication into performance expectations, and recognize teams that close equity gaps in digital access. In doing so, the organization affirms that technology is part of its professional identity and ethical practice, not an episodic project (Ćwiklicki et al., 2021; Kotter, 1996; Kotter et al., 2025).

AREAS OF FOCUS AND PRACTICAL RECOMMENDATIONS

1. Human Factors and Trust in Technology

- **Design for transparency and predictability.** Systems should make data use, privacy, and consent mechanisms visible and easily understandable to users, since perceived opacity erodes trust. *Example:* A telehealth platform could display a real-time "data in transit" indicator and a concise, plain-language privacy statement before each session.
- **Integrate empathy into digital interfaces.** Training clinicians in digital bedside manner, including voice modulation, pacing, and camera awareness, bridges emotional distance. *Example:* A reproductive health provider uses screen positioning and intentional pauses to emulate in-person counseling empathy.
- **Establish reliability through performance consistency.** Stable, secure, and user-friendly systems build cognitive trust faster than abstract assurances. *Example:* SAFECARE maintains uniform appointment reminders and follow-up procedures to reinforce reliability.
- **Use trust-building rituals.** Structured affirmations of privacy and safety reassure users of system integrity. *Example:* Clinicians begin each telehealth session by stating, "This is a secure, private consultation."
- **Foster collective digital literacy.** When staff exhibit confidence in technology, patients' trust increases through observed competence. *Example:* Clinicians demonstrate proficiency with digital whiteboards, modeling assurance for patients uncertain about telehealth platforms.

2. Adaptive Leadership Approaches

- **Model vulnerability and learning.** Leaders who admit uncertainty and solicit input create a culture of shared adaptation. *Example:* A medical director hosts "fail-forward" forums to discuss lessons learned from telehealth challenges.
- **Bridge technical and emotional domains.** Leaders should connect technical updates to human impact, emphasizing care quality and security. *Example:* When SAFECARE launched AI triage, leadership shared success stories illustrating improved patient access and safety outcomes.
- **Institutionalize continuous dialogue.** Regular town halls and feedback loops sustain trust and psychological safety during change. *Example:* Monthly "telehealth roundtables" invite staff to discuss workflow concerns and co-develop refinements.
- **Reward adaptive experimentation.** Recognizing innovation reinforces learning agility. *Example:* SAFECARE honors staff who design accessible intake forms that improve user clarity and compliance.
- **Develop socio-technical literacy.** Executives must grasp both technical and behavioral implications of digital transformation. *Example:* Senior administrators complete workshops on algorithmic bias and ethical AI deployment.

3. Adaptive Organizational Culture Approaches

- **Cultivate a continuous learning ecosystem.** Reflective reviews after major system updates embed adaptation into daily routines. *Example:* SAFECARE teams analyze telehealth data quarterly to evaluate user trust and workflow efficiency.
- **Make digital inclusion a cultural value.** Equity must be operationalized in staffing and technology design. *Example:* Bilingual digital navigators assist multilingual patients with telehealth onboarding.
- **Normalize empathy-driven flexibility.** Staff should be rewarded for maintaining compassion amid technological disruption. *Example:* Supervisors commend clinicians who maintain rapport with patients during connectivity interruptions.
- **Empower local innovation.** Decentralizing decision-making enhances responsiveness. *Example:* A regional telehealth hub tailors patient communication scripts to community literacy levels.
- **Institutionalize bi-directional feedback.** Continuous feedback aligns culture and technology. *Example:* Patient and clinician surveys inform SAFECARE's quarterly system redesigns.

4. Dynamics of Human–Technology Interactions

- **Acknowledge sensory limitations.** Training should address the loss of physical cues in virtual care. *Example:* Clinicians practice tone modulation to convey warmth and attentiveness.
- **Enhance patient agency.** Interfaces should provide options for control and consent reaffirmation. *Example:* A "pause for consent" button allows patients to stop and clarify before data sharing.
- **Prioritize intuitive usability.** Interfaces should minimize cognitive load. *Example:* SAFECARE employs minimalistic dashboards with context-aware tooltips.
- **Offer multimodal communication.** Providing choice between video, text, or asynchronous messaging respects comfort and access differences. *Example:* A patient opts for secure text counseling instead of live video.
- **Assess emotional experience continuously.** *Example:* A one-minute emotional state check at session end identifies stress or frustration linked to digital use.

5. Overcoming Technology Use or Adoption Resistance

- **Reframe resistance as diagnostic feedback.** Nonadoption often signals design or communication failures. *Example:* If patient engagement drops, SAFECARE audits user interfaces for complexity before enforcing compliance.
- **Leverage peer influence.** Early adopters serve as cultural ambassadors. *Example:* Experienced clinicians host peer mentorship sessions to demystify telehealth etiquette.
- **Implement gradual exposure.** Incremental adoption builds user familiarity. *Example:* Introduce secure chat before launching full video visits.
- **Address emotional and cognitive barriers simultaneously.** Reassurance and training must coexist. *Example:* Empathy workshops precede new digital tool deployment.
- **Celebrate progress milestones.** Recognition solidifies positive association with technology use. *Example:* Departments achieving high virtual care satisfaction receive public acknowledgment.

6. User-Centered Design

- **Engage users in co-design.** Both patients and clinicians must participate in early-stage testing. *Example:* SAFECARE conducts participatory workshops with reproductive health patients to refine platform flow.
- **Design for accessibility and inclusion.** Accommodate varying literacy and ability levels. *Example:* Incorporate screen reader compatibility and multilingual interfaces.
- **Simplify workflows.** Automation should reduce clinician burden. *Example:* Personalized dashboards show only relevant clinical data.
- **Embed real-time feedback mechanisms.** *Example:* A built-in "friction report" button logs usability issues to a central dashboard.
- **Prototype ethically.** Anticipate privacy risks and potential inequities. *Example:* Consent dialogues undergo readability testing before deployment.

7. Technology Literacy

- **Institutionalize continuous literacy development.** *Example:* Annual digital fluency certifications include modules on privacy, cybersecurity, and empathy.
- **Tailor training to role-specific competencies.** *Example:* Patients learn secure login basics, while clinicians practice telepresence skills.
- **Partner with communities to extend literacy.** *Example:* SAFECARE sponsors local "Digital Health Days" to teach telehealth basics in underserved areas.
- **Integrate adaptive tools with embedded guidance.** *Example:* Interactive voice assistants guide new users step-by-step during onboarding.
- **Evaluate digital competence as a quality metric.** *Example:* SAFECARE tracks patient completion rates relative to digital skill levels to inform outreach strategy.

8. Cybersecurity Risk Management and Risk Mitigation Cultures

- **Embed cybersecurity into organizational identity.** Treat security as a shared cultural norm, not a technical silo. *Example:* SAFECARE's "Security First" initiative integrates security reminders into daily team huddles.
- **Promote situational awareness through simulation.** *Example:* Quarterly "phish drills" and breach simulations train staff to identify and report suspicious activity.

- **Integrate behavioral analytics into security oversight.** Monitor human interaction patterns for early detection of risk behaviors. *Example:* Anomalous login attempts trigger both alerts and coaching interventions.
- **Establish cross-functional cyber response teams.** Combine IT, clinical, and communications personnel to ensure rapid, ethical responses. *Example:* In the event of a data anomaly, clinical leads and cybersecurity officers co-manage disclosure and containment.
- **Foster trust through transparency.** *Example:* SAFECARE publicly discloses its security posture and updates users on ongoing risk mitigation measures.

9. Data Privacy Rights and Ethical Stewardship

- **Operationalize privacy as a patient right, not a compliance checkbox.** *Example:* Consent dashboards display granular data-sharing options with clear opt-out features.
- **Ensure informed consent through clarity and accessibility.** *Example:* Privacy policies are rewritten in plain language and available in multiple languages.
- **Institute "privacy by design."** Security and ethics must be integrated from conception, not retrofitted. *Example:* SAFECARE designs all new modules with default encryption and minimal data retention.
- **Train staff in digital ethics and confidentiality.** *Example:* Clinicians complete mandatory annual courses on reproductive health data protection and digital rights.
- **Establish privacy advocacy roles.** *Example:* A Privacy Ombudsperson ensures patient concerns are addressed within 24 hours.

10. Human Factors in Information Security

- **Recognize humans as both the strongest and weakest link.** Cultivate awareness, not blame, in breach prevention. *Example:* SAFECARE reframes post-incident debriefs as learning reviews, not punitive audits.
- **Design for human error tolerance.** Systems should anticipate and safely absorb mistakes. *Example:* Multi-step confirmation protocols prevent accidental data sharing.
- **Reinforce positive security behaviors.** Habitual secure actions must be visibly rewarded. *Example:* Departments with zero security incidents receive "Cyber Hygiene Excellence" awards.

- **Use behavioral science to shape secure habits.** Nudge-based reminders and contextual cues enhance compliance. *Example:* A pop-up reminder prompts clinicians to lock screens when idle for more than two minutes.
- **Foster security empathy.** Humanizing data protection aligns privacy with patient safety and professional ethics. *Example:* SAFECARE trains clinicians to frame data protection as an act of care, not bureaucracy.

CONCLUSION

The complexity of digital transformation in healthcare, particularly in reproductive telehealth, underscores that technology alone does not constitute innovation; rather, success arises from the dynamic interplay between human adaptability, trust, and socio-technical integration. The SAFECARE case illustrates that digital change is inherently a human process mediated through cognitive, emotional, and ethical dimensions as much as technical ones. Building trust in telehealth systems requires visible transparency, stable performance, and empathetic communication that bridges physical and digital divides. At the organizational level, adaptive leadership and a learning-oriented culture are prerequisites for cultivating resilience and continuous improvement. Telehealth implementation thus demands a systemic approach, one that positions human experience, digital literacy, and inclusivity as strategic assets rather than peripheral concerns. In essence, successful transformation occurs when healthcare systems design technology with people rather than around them, allowing digital tools to augment, not alienate, the care relationship.

Training Implications

Training serves as the linchpin between technological innovation and sustainable adoption. Comprehensive programs must extend beyond procedural skill-building to encompass affective and relational competencies, digital empathy, trust calibration, and ethical decision-making in virtual contexts. Evidence from digital adoption research suggests that training efficacy increases when instruction is modular, peer-supported, and contextually embedded. For SAFECARE, this entails designing tiered curricula that differentiate between technical mastery (e.g., EHR integration, cybersecurity protocols) and interpersonal adaptation (e.g., tone modulation, privacy communication). Micro-learning platforms and simulated telehealth encounters can accelerate comfort with new tools while reinforcing psychological safety. Moreover, training should not be a one-time onboarding event but an iterative process, continuously updated as platforms evolve and user behaviors shift. By embedding reflective practice and feedback loops within training ecosystems, organizations can foster not only competence but also confidence, two critical preconditions for sustained trust in technology.

Example: SAFECARE could institute quarterly "Digital Rounds" where clinicians and support staff review anonymized telehealth interactions to analyze both technological performance and the quality of human connection achieved through the screen.

Clinical Implications

Clinically, telehealth transformation redefines the nature of patient-provider interaction, diagnostic reasoning, and privacy management. Virtual modalities compel clinicians to adopt new heuristics for interpreting affective cues, verifying understanding, and ensuring patient safety in distributed care environments. In reproductive healthcare, where intimacy, confidentiality, and cultural sensitivity are central, clinicians must learn to translate physical empathy into digital communication. Maintaining clinical quality therefore depends on integrating technology literacy with ethical vigilance. For example, clinicians should be trained to recognize the subtle cognitive overload patients experience when multitasking on unfamiliar platforms and adjust pacing accordingly. Standardizing privacy checks and informed consent procedures for virtual encounters strengthens both ethical compliance and trust. Ultimately, clinical excellence in telehealth emerges not from digitizing existing routines but from redesigning them to optimize human experience and minimize cognitive friction.

Example: A clinician might begin a virtual contraceptive counseling session by demonstrating platform security features and explicitly inviting questions about data protection, reinforcing both transparency and relational trust.

Workflow Implications

Workflow redesign is fundamental to reconciling operational efficiency with humane care delivery in digital settings. The migration from brick-and-mortar to telehealth requires re-sequencing tasks, redefining interdependencies, and leveraging automation judiciously to support, not supplant, clinical judgment. Integrating scheduling, triage, documentation, and follow-up within interoperable platforms reduces redundancy and error while maintaining continuity of care. Yet, automation must remain sensitive to contextual nuance: when tasks that require empathy are over-automated, both staff morale and patient trust decline. SAFECARE's workflow optimization should thus prioritize hybridization, delegating repetitive administrative functions to digital systems while preserving clinician presence for high-emotion, high-stakes interactions. Furthermore, continuous feedback from users must inform workflow adjustments, ensuring that operational design remains responsive to evolving human needs.

Example: SAFECARE's patient portal could automatically generate follow-up prompts and educational materials after visits, but clinicians retain the responsibility for reviewing and personalizing them to ensure relational authenticity.

Work Roles Implications

Digital transformation reconfigures occupational identities and skill boundaries. Traditional roles, such as medical assistants or front desk staff, expand into hybrid techno-clinical positions requiring fluency in both digital platforms and patient interaction. This hybridization introduces new stressors but also opportunities for professional growth. Organizations must therefore establish structured role transition frameworks that clarify expectations, provide mentorship, and align compensation with new competencies. Job redesign should emphasize relational coordination: IT specialists must understand clinical workflows, and clinicians must appreciate cybersecurity imperatives. Such cross-functional literacy enhances mutual respect and reduces friction between human and digital agents. Clear communication about role evolution, supported by adaptive leadership, mitigates resistance and fosters a shared sense of purpose across professional boundaries.

Example: SAFECARE could introduce a new role, "Digital Care Navigator," tasked with bridging clinical guidance and technological support, assisting patients in both platform navigation and understanding treatment plans.

Patient Engagement Implications

Patient engagement in telehealth hinges on psychological safety, perceived control, and usability. Trust is strengthened when patients feel empowered to navigate technology without fear of exposure or confusion. Engagement strategies must therefore be grounded in user-centered design, ensuring clarity, inclusivity, and interactivity. Digital literacy assessments at intake can personalize support and reduce attrition among less technologically confident patients. Additionally, continuous communication, through automated reminders, secure chat, and asynchronous follow-ups, can sustain engagement between visits, reinforcing relational continuity. Patients' voices should also shape platform refinement through participatory feedback mechanisms. Importantly, patient engagement is not a metric to be optimized but a relationship to be cultivated; thus, empathy and transparency remain its most effective drivers.

Example: SAFECARE could integrate a "patient confidence tracker" that allows users to rate their comfort level with digital tools after each session, triggering customized outreach or tutorials for those indicating low confidence.

Leadership Implications

Leadership in digital health requires both technological fluency and emotional intelligence. Adaptive leaders function as translators between systems logic and human experience, converting technical imperatives into meaningful narratives of patient benefit and staff empowerment. Transparency and psychological safety are central to this role: employees are more likely to trust digital initiatives when leaders openly discuss uncertainties and invite co-creation. Furthermore, digital transformation necessitates distributed leadership, empowering local champions to implement context-specific innovations rather than relying solely on top-down direction. Leaders must also anticipate ethical dilemmas arising from algorithmic decision-making, data surveillance, or digital inequity and establish governance structures that uphold fairness and accountability. Ultimately, the credibility of digital transformation efforts depends less on strategic declarations than on leaders' capacity to humanize technology in daily organizational life.

Example: SAFECARE's executive team could institute a "Digital Ethics Council" comprising clinicians, patients, and data experts to deliberate on platform changes and communicate policy rationales transparently to staff and users.

Digital transformation leadership requires fluency across three domains: technology, trust, and ethics. Leaders must act as translators who contextualize technical imperatives within narratives of safety, equity, and data stewardship. Transparency is central: when leaders openly discuss cybersecurity measures and ethical dilemmas, they reinforce institutional credibility.

Effective leaders model responsible data behavior, prioritize privacy as a moral as well as regulatory obligation, and ensure that accountability mechanisms are clearly defined. Leadership must also be distributed, empowering local champions to advocate for security-conscious and culturally sensitive implementation in diverse contexts.

Organizational Culture Implications

An organization's culture determines whether digital transformation produces empowerment or alienation. A culture that values continuous learning, inclusion, and ethical reflexivity transforms technology from a source of anxiety into a shared tool of advancement. The shift to telehealth must be accompanied by a deliberate cultural reframing, from valuing physical presence to valuing connectivity, from hierarchical expertise to collective adaptability. Psychological safety is the foundation of such culture: employees must feel secure in expressing confusion or critique without fear of retribution. This openness accelerates problem-solving and innovation. Moreover, organizations should ritualize cultural reinforcement through recognition programs, reflective storytelling, and interdepartmental collaboration that celebrates technological curiosity. The long-term viability of digital transformation depends on a culture that interprets technology not as a replacement for human interaction but as an enabler of broader human reach and equity.

Example: SAFECARE could host quarterly "Digital Humanity Forums," where staff share narratives of how technology either enhanced or complicated their care experiences, using these reflections to refine culture and practice.

Organizational culture is the substrate upon which digital transformation either flourishes or fails. A culture that prioritizes privacy, safety, and continuous learning transforms technology from a potential liability into a collective source of empowerment. Embedding data ethics and cybersecurity mindfulness within the organizational ethos reframes compliance as care and confidentiality as compassion in action.

Psychological safety remains the cornerstone of such a culture. Employees must feel free to question processes, report security concerns, or express discomfort without fear of reprisal. Transparent discussion of near misses or privacy breaches should be viewed as opportunities for collective learning, not individual fault-finding. A "just culture" approach enhances both safety outcomes and organizational maturity.

Cultural rituals, such as open forums, ethical storytelling, and recognition programs, help normalize trust-building as a shared value. When data security becomes everyone's responsibility, digital transformation becomes a reflection of organizational integrity, not merely operational efficiency.

Example: SAFECARE hosts quarterly "Digital Humanity and Security Forums," where staff and patients share experiences about how technology affects trust, safety, and privacy in care. These narratives inform updates to cultural policy, ensuring that human values remain at the heart of technological progress.

Recommendations for Future Research

Future research should explore how patients, clinicians, and support staff experience reproductive telehealth platforms in ways that are not fully captured by quantitative metrics. While the existing literature emphasizes transparency, empathy-driven communication, workflow redesign, and the cultivation of digital literacy, persistent questions remain about how these constructs are understood, negotiated, and operationalized in everyday practice. Qualitative focus groups would be particularly well-suited to unpack these dynamics, providing a venue for participants to articulate affective responses to platform design, privacy cues, and the subtle forms of cognitive load introduced by new digital workflows.

Focus groups could illuminate how users interpret trust-building rituals, perceive the emotional labor of virtual care, and negotiate privacy within shared domestic environments. They would also allow clinicians to articulate challenges in translating embodied empathy through screens and to surface emergent workarounds that are otherwise invisible in operational data. For patients, such sessions could reveal nuanced barriers related to digital literacy, cultural expectations, and perceived surveillance, helping designers refine technological affordances that currently inhibit adoption.

Further, focus groups could explore how organizational culture shapes trust in technology, particularly how staff model digital competence, respond to connectivity interruptions, and describe the emotional texture of virtual encounters. Insights from these discussions would support iterative interface improvements, inform more contextually responsive training curricula, and guide ethical decision-making frameworks within human-centered telehealth ecosystems.

Overall, qualitative studies using purposive sampling and semi-structured facilitation would enrich the evidence base by illuminating the lived experience of digital reproductive healthcare. Findings could guide socio-technical alignment efforts, enhance privacy-preserving behaviors, and inform strategies for maintaining equitable access as telehealth modalities continue to evolve. By centering the voices of those navigating the tension between innovation and intimacy, future research can ensure that digital transformation augments, rather than erodes—the care relationship.

REFERENCES

Adler-Milstein, J., Kvedar, J., & Bates, D. W. (2014). Telehealth among US hospitals: Several factors, including state reimbursement and licensure policies, influence adoption. *Health Affairs (Project Hope)*, *33*(2), 207–215. DOI: 10.1377/hlthaff.2013.1054

Aijaz, M., Lewis, V. A., & Murray, G. F. (2024). Advancing equity in challenging times: A qualitative study of telehealth expansion and changing patient–provider relationships in primary care settings during the COVID-19 pandemic. *Digital Health*, *10*, 20552076241233148. DOI: 10.1177/20552076241233148

Akhavan, S., & Redmond, N. (2023). Medical assistants' telehealth roles and skills in primary care during the COVID-19 pandemic. *Center for Health Workforce Studies, University of Washington*. https://familymedicine.uw.edu/chws/wp-content/uploads/sites/5/2023/05/MAs-Telehealth-Roles-During-COVID-19-FR-2023-May.pdf

American College of Obstetricians and Gynecologists. (2024). Addressing social and structural determinants of health in the delivery of reproductive health care: ACOG Committee Statement No. 11. *Obstetrics and Gynecology*, *144*(5), e113–e120. DOI: 10.1097/AOG.0000000000005721

American Society for Reproductive Medicine Ethics Committee. (2024). Ethical considerations for telemedical delivery of fertility care: An Ethics Committee opinion. *Fertility and Sterility*, *121*(3), 434–438. DOI: 10.1016/j.fertnstert.2023.12.005

Anawade, P. A., Sharma, D., Gahane, S., Anawade, P. A.Sr, & Sharma, D. S. (2024). A comprehensive review on exploring the impact of telemedicine on healthcare accessibility. *Cureus*, *16*(3). Advance online publication. DOI: 10.7759/cureus.55996

Anderson, K., Coskun, R., Jimenez, P., & Omurtag, K. (2022). Satisfaction with new patient telehealth visits for reproductive endocrinology patients in the era of COVID-19. *Journal of Assisted Reproduction and Genetics*, *39*(7), 1571–1576. DOI: 10.1007/s10815-022-02539-4

Andino, J. J., Eyrich, N. W., & Boxer, R. J. (2023). Overview of telehealth in the United States since the COVID-19 public health emergency: A narrative review. *mHealth*, *9*, 26. DOI: 10.21037/mhealth-23-15

Bashshur, R., Doarn, C. R., Frenk, J. M., Kvedar, J. C., & Woolliscroft, J. O. (2020). Telemedicine and the COVID-19 pandemic, lessons for the future. *Telemedicine Journal and e-Health*, *26*(5), 571–573. DOI: 10.1089/tmj.2020.29040.rb

Bini, S. A. (2018). Artificial intelligence, machine learning, deep learning, and cognitive computing: What do these terms mean and how will they impact health care? *The Journal of Arthroplasty*, *33*(8), 2358–2361. DOI: 10.1016/j.arth.2018.02.067

Bond, B. (2024, October 28). *Best practices for change management in healthcare*. Prosci. IT. https://www.prosci.com/blog/change-management-healthcare-it

Borges do Nascimento, I. J., Abdulazeem, H., Vasanthan, L. T., Martinez, E. Z., Zucoloto, M. L., Østengaard, L., Azzopardi-Muscat, N., Zapata, T., & Novillo-Ortiz, D. (2023). Barriers and facilitators to utilizing digital health technologies by healthcare professionals. *NPJ Digital Medicine*, *6*(1), 161. DOI: 10.1038/s41746-023-00899-4

Brommeyer, M., Whittaker, M., & Liang, Z. (2024). Organizational Factors Driving the Realization of Digital Health Transformation Benefits from Health Service Managers: A Qualitative Study. *Journal of Healthcare Leadership*, *16*, 455–472. DOI: 10.2147/JHL.S487589

Burrell, D. N. (2023). Understanding telemedicine strategies through field-based observations, interviews and benchmarking activities. *Health Economics and Management Review*, *4*(4), 58–68. DOI: 10.61093/hem.2023.4-05

Burrell, D. N. (2024). Telehealth Technologies, Disruptions, and Health Literacy. *Health Economics and Management Review*, *5*(4), 33–46. DOI: 10.61093/hem.2024.4-03

Carolan, K., Grabowski, D. C., Mehrotra, A., & Hatfield, L. A. (2020). Use of telemedicine for emergency triage in an independent senior living community: Mixed methods study. *Journal of Medical Internet Research*, *22*(12), e23014. DOI: 10.2196/23014

Chen, C. H., Lan, Y. L., Yang, W. P., Hsu, F. M., Lin, C. L., & Chen, H. C. (2019). Exploring the impact of a telehealth care system on organizational capabilities and organizational performance from a resource-based perspective. *International Journal of Environmental Research and Public Health*, *16*(20), 3988. DOI: 10.3390/ijerph16203988

Ćwiklicki, M., Duplaga, M., & Klich, J. (Eds.). (2021). *The digital transformation of healthcare: Health 4.0*. Routledge., M., Duplaga, M., & Klich, J. (Eds.). (2021). *The digital transformation of healthcare: Health 4.0*. Routledge.

Deoli, A., & Zeng, B. (2022, December 1). *Digital Literacy, Telehealth Equity, and Healthcare Access are Interrelated: Here is How*. Rutgers University State Policy Lab. https://policylab.rutgers.edu/publication/digital-literacy-telehealth-equity-and-healthcare-access-are-interrelated-here-is-how/

Distiller, S. R. (2023, July 24). The difference between narrative review and systematic review. https://www.distillersr.com/resources/systematic-literature-reviews/the-difference-between-narrative-review-and-systematic-review

Dorsey, E. R., & Topol, E. J. (2020). Telemedicine 2020 and the next decade. *Lancet, 395*(10227), 859. DOI: 10.1016/S0140-6736(20)30424-4

Downey, M. M., & Gómez, A. M. (2018). Structural competency and reproductive health. *AMA Journal of Ethics, 20*(3), 211–223. DOI: 10.1001/journalofethics.2018.20.3.peer1-1803

DuBose-Morris, R., McSwain, S. D., McElligott, J. T., King, K. L., Ziniel, S., & Harvey, J. (2023). Building telehealth teams of the future through interprofessional curriculum development: A five-year mixed methodology study. *Journal of Interprofessional Care, 37*(1), 100–108. DOI: 10.1080/13561820.2021.2005556

Ezeamii, V. C., Okobi, O. E., Wambai-Sani, H., Perera, G. S., Zaynieva, S., Okonkwo, C. C., Ohaiba, M. M., William-Enemali, P. C., Obodo, O. R., & Obiefuna, N. G. (2024). Revolutionizing healthcare: How telemedicine is improving patient outcomes and expanding access to care. *Cureus, 16*(7). Advance online publication. DOI: 10.7759/cureus.63881

Feldman, S. S., Buchalter, S., & Hayes, L. W. (2018). Health information technology in healthcare quality and patient safety: Literature review. *JMIR Medical Informatics, 6*(2), e10264. DOI: 10.2196/10264

Fox, G., Lynn, T., van Der Werff, L., & Kennedy, J. (2025). Does telemedicine hold the key for reproductive health care? A quantitative examination of women's intentions toward use and accurate information disclosure. *Health Services Research, 60*(3), e14403. DOI: 10.1111/1475-6773.14403

Gajarawala, S. N., & Pelkowski, J. N. (2021). Telehealth benefits and barriers. *The Journal for Nurse Practitioners, 17*(2), 218–221. DOI: 10.1016/j.nurpra.2020.09.013

Ganti, V. K. A. T., Edward, A., Subhash, T. N., & Polineni, N. A. (2023). AI-Enhanced Chatbots for Real-Time Symptom Analysis and Triage in Telehealth Services.

Gopal, G., Suter-Crazzolara, C., Toldo, L., & Eberhardt, W. (2019). Digital transformation in healthcare–architectures of present and future information technologies. [CCLM]. *Clinical Chemistry and Laboratory Medicine, 57*(3), 328–335. DOI: 10.1515/cclm-2018-0658

Gordon, H. S., Solanki, P., Bokhour, B. G., & Gopal, R. K. (2020). "I'm Not Feeling Like I'm Part of the Conversation": Patients' Perspectives on Communicating in Clinical Video Telehealth Visits. *Journal of General Internal Medicine*, *35*(6), 1751–1758. DOI: 10.1007/s11606-020-05673-w

Grindlay, K., Lane, K., & Grossman, D. (2013). Women's and providers' experiences with medical abortion provided through telemedicine: A qualitative study. *Women's Health Issues*, *23*(2), e117–e122. DOI: 10.1016/j.whi.2012.12.002

Grossman, D., & Grindlay, K. (2017). Safety of medical abortion provided through telemedicine compared with in person. *Obstetrics and Gynecology*, *130*(4), 778–782. DOI: 10.1097/AOG.0000000000002212

Hatef, E., Hudson Scholle, S., Buckley, B., Weiner, J. P., & Austin, J. M. (2024). Development of an evidence-and consensus-based Digital Healthcare Equity Framework. *JAMIA Open*, *7*(4), ooae136. DOI: 10.1093/jamiaopen/ooae136

Houser, S. H., Flite, C. A., & Foster, S. L. (2023). Privacy and security risk factors related to telehealth services–a systematic review. *Perspectives in Health Information Management*, *20*(1), 1f.

Hyett, N., Kenny, A., & Dickson-Swift, V. (2014). Methodology or method? A critical review of qualitative case study reports. *International Journal of Qualitative Studies on Health and Well-being*, *9*(1), 23606. DOI: 10.3402/qhw.v9.23606

Iyawa, G. E., Herselman, M., & Botha, A. (2016). Digital health innovation ecosystems: From systematic literature review to conceptual framework. *Procedia Computer Science*, *100*, 244–252. DOI: 10.1016/j.procs.2016.09.149

Jonasdottir, S. K., Thordardottir, I., & Jonsdottir, T. (2022). Health professionals' perspective towards challenges and opportunities of telehealth service provision: A scoping review. *International Journal of Medical Informatics*, *167*, 104862. DOI: 10.1016/j.ijmedinf.2022.104862

Kakale, M. A. M. (2024). Of digital transformation in the healthcare (systematic review of the current state of the literature). *Health and Technology*, *14*(1), 35–50. DOI: 10.1007/s12553-023-00803-w

Kane, G. C., Palmer, D., Phillips, A. N., Kiron, D., & Buckley, N. (2015). Strategy, not technology, drives digital transformation. *MIT Sloan Management Review*.

Keenan, A. J., Tsourtos, G., & Tieman, J. (2022). Promise and peril-defining ethical telehealth practice from the clinician and patient perspective: A qualitative study. *Digital Health*, *8*, 20552076211070394. DOI: 10.1177/20552076211070394

Keesara, S., Jonas, A., & Schulman, K. (2020). Covid-19 and health care's digital revolution. *The New England Journal of Medicine*, *382*(23), e82. DOI: 10.1056/NEJMp2005835

Kho, J., Gillespie, N., & Martin-Khan, M. (2020). A systematic scoping review of change management practices used for telemedicine service implementations. *BMC Health Services Research*, *20*(1), 815. DOI: 10.1186/s12913-020-05657-w

Koenig, L. R., Becker, A., Ko, J., & Upadhyay, U. D. (2023). The role of telehealth in promoting equitable abortion access in the United States: Spatial analysis. *JMIR Public Health and Surveillance*, *9*, e45671. DOI: 10.2196/45671

Kotter, J. P. (1996). *Leading change*. Harvard Business School Press.

Kotter, J. P., Akhtar, V., & Gupta, G. (2025). *Change: How organizations achieve hard-to-imagine results in uncertain and volatile times*. John Wiley & Sons.

Kruse, C. S., Frederick, B., Jacobson, T., & Monticone, D. K. (2017). Cybersecurity in healthcare: A systematic review of modern threats and trends. *Technology and Health Care*, *25*(1), 1–10. DOI: 10.3233/THC-161263

Lau, J., Knudsen, J., Jackson, H., Wallach, A. B., Bouton, M., Natsui, S., Philippou, C., Karim, E., Borthwell, R., Avalos, L. N., & Katz, C. (2020). Staying connected in the COVID-19 pandemic: Telehealth at the largest safety-net system in the United States. *Health Affairs (Project Hope)*, *39*(8), 1437–1442. DOI: 10.1377/hlthaff.2020.00903

Li, C., Borycki, E. M., & Kushniruk, A. W. (2021, October). Connecting the world of healthcare virtually: A scoping review on virtual care delivery. []). MDPI.]. *Health Care*, *9*(10), 1325.

Mansoor, M. A., & Siddiqi, R. (2024). Telehealth transformation: A mixed-methods study on organizational change processes and outcomes in a private medical practice. *Cureus*, *16*(3), e57183. https://pmc.ncbi.nlm.nih.gov/articles/PMC11056098/

Marsh, E., Perez Vallejos, E., & Spence, A. (2024). Digital workplace technology intensity: Qualitative insights on employee wellbeing impacts of digital workplace job demands. *Frontiers in Organizational Psychology*, *2*, 1392997. DOI: 10.3389/forgp.2024.1392997

Meirte, J., Hellemans, N., Anthonissen, M., Denteneer, L., Maertens, K., Moortgat, P., & Van Daele, U. (2020). Benefits and disadvantages of electronic patient-reported outcome measures: Systematic review. *JMIR Perioperative Medicine*, *3*(1), e15588. DOI: 10.2196/15588

Mohammed, H. T., Hyseni, L., Bui, V., Gerritsen, B., Fuller, K., Sung, J., & Alarakhia, M. (2021). Exploring the use and challenges of implementing virtual visits during COVID-19 in primary care and lessons for sustained use. *PLoS One*, *16*(6), e0253665. DOI: 10.1371/journal.pone.0253665

Muheriwa-Matemba, S. R., Alcena-Stiner, D. C., Glazier, A., & LeBlanc, N. M. (2024). Telehealth use for sexual and reproductive health promotion and care during the early phase of COVID-19 pandemic: A descriptive-interpretive qualitative study of healthcare providers' perspectives and experiences in Western—Central New York State. *PLOS Global Public Health*, *4*(12), e0003259. DOI: 10.1371/journal.pgph.0003259

National Committee for Quality Assurance. (2022). The Future of Telehealth Roundtable: The Potential Impact of Emerging Technologies on Health Equity.

Ozkaynak, M., Unertl, K., Johnson, S., Brixey, J., & Haque, S. N. (2022). Clinical workflow analysis, process redesign, and quality improvement. In *Clinical informatics study guide: Text and review* (pp. 103–118). Springer International Publishing. DOI: 10.1007/978-3-030-93765-2_8

Pierre, I. (2024). Impact of the increased use of telehealth on health care management and administration: The case of new care management practices. *Doctoral Dissertations and Projects. 5148.* https://digitalcommons.liberty.edu/doctoral/5148/

Reimann, M., Marx, C. K., & Tisch, A. (2024). "With Kind Regards?": The Relationship Between Digital Work Communication and Mental Health. *Management Review Quarterly*, *35*(2), 194–221.

Roberts, E. T., & Mehrotra, A. (2020). Assessment of disparities in digital access among Medicare beneficiaries and implications for telemedicine. *JAMA Internal Medicine*, *180*(10), 1386–1389. DOI: 10.1001/jamainternmed.2020.2666

Sainimnuan, S., Preedachitkul, R., Petchthai, P., Paokantarakorn, Y., Siriussawakul, A., & Srinonprasert, V. (2025). Low Prevalence of Adequate eHealth Literacy and Willingness to Use Telemedicine Among Older Adults: Cross-Sectional Study From a Middle-Income Country. *Journal of Medical Internet Research*, *27*, e65380. DOI: 10.2196/65380

Saldanha, T. (2019). *Why digital transformations fail: The surprising disciplines of how to take off and stay ahead*. Berrett-Koehler Publishers.

Shachar, C., Engel, J., & Elwyn, G. (2020). Implications for telehealth in a post-pandemic future: Regulatory and privacy issues. *Journal of the American Medical Association*, *323*(23), 2375–2376. DOI: 10.1001/jama.2020.7943

Smith, A. C., Thomas, E., Snoswell, C. L., Haydon, H., Mehrotra, A., Clemensen, J., & Caffery, L. J. (2022). Telehealth for global emergencies: Implications for coronavirus disease 2019 (COVID-19). *Journal of Telemedicine and Telecare*, *28*(1), 1–6. DOI: 10.1177/1357633X20916567

Solimini, R., Busardò, F. P., Gibelli, F., Sirignano, A., & Ricci, G. (2021). Ethical and Legal Challenges of Telemedicine in the Era of the COVID-19 Pandemic. *Medicina (Kaunas, Lithuania)*, *57*(12), 1314. DOI: 10.3390/medicina57121314

Staras, S., Tauscher, J. S., Rich, N., Samarah, E., Thompson, L. A., Vinson, M. M., Muszynski, M. J., & Shenkman, E. A. (2021). Using a clinical workflow analysis to enhance eHealth implementation planning: Tutorial and case study. *JMIR mHealth and uHealth*, *9*(3), e18534. DOI: 10.2196/18534

Stoumpos, A. I., Kitsios, F., & Talias, M. A. (2023). Digital transformation in healthcare: Technology acceptance and its applications. *International Journal of Environmental Research and Public Health*, *20*(4), 3407. DOI: 10.3390/ijerph20043407

Talwar, S., Dhir, A., Islam, N., Kaur, P., & Almusharraf, A. (2023). Resistance of multiple stakeholders to e-health innovations: Integration of fundamental insights and guiding research paths. *Journal of Business Research*, *166*, 114135. DOI: 10.1016/j.jbusres.2023.114135

Thomas, E. E., Haydon, H. M., Mehrotra, A., Caffery, L. J., Snoswell, C. L., Banbury, A., & Smith, A. C. (2022). Building on the momentum: Sustaining telehealth beyond COVID-19. *Journal of Telemedicine and Telecare*, *28*(4), 301–308. DOI: 10.1177/1357633X20960638

University of Waikato. (2024, April 18). Library guides: Writing a literature review: For researchers: Narrative literature reviews. https://libraryguides.waikato.ac.nz/c.php?g=968696&p=7042945

U.S. Department of Health & Human Services. (2022). Telehealth policy changes after the COVID-19 public health emergency. https://telehealth.hhs.gov/providers/policy-changes-during-the-covid-19-public-health-emergency/

Valenta, S. R., Glanville, M., & Sederstrom, E. (2021). Telehealth development, implementation, and sustainability challenges: An Introduction into the telehealth service implementation model (TSIM™). *Telemedicine: Overview and Application in Pulmonary, Critical Care, and Sleep Medicine*, 61-69.

Vashishth, T. K., Sharma, V., Sharma, K. K., Kumar, B., Chaudhary, S., & Panwar, R. (2025). Securing the Cloud: Strategies for Protecting Sensitive Patient Data in Cloud-Based Healthcare Recommender Systems. *Healthcare Recommender Systems: Techniques and Recent Developments*, 185-220.

Vial, G. (2019). Understanding digital transformation: A review and a research agenda. *The Journal of Strategic Information Systems*, *28*(2), 118–144. DOI: 10.1016/j.jsis.2019.01.003

WomenTech Network. (2024). *What are the privacy concerns for women using telehealth services?* Women Tech Network. https://www.womentech.net/forum-topic/what-are-privacy-concerns-women-using-telehealth-services

World Health Organization. (2021). *Global strategy on digital health 2020-2025.* https://www.who.int/publications/i/item/9789240020924

Wright, J., & Burrell, D. N. (2023). Telemedicine cybersecurity protection in reproductive healthcare. *HOLISTICA Journal of Business and Public Administration*, *14*(2), 1–14. DOI: 10.2478/hjbpa-2023-0012

Zettelmann, A., & Cano, J. A. (2024). How change management activates digital transformation in healthcare. *Health Management*, *24*(2), 101–107. https://healthmanagement.org/c/healthmanagement/issuearticle/how-change-management-activates-digital-transformation-in-healthcare

Zheng, K., Ratwani, R. M., & Adler-Milstein, J. (2020). Studying workflow and workarounds in electronic health record–supported work to improve health system performance. *Annals of Internal Medicine*, *172*(11, Supplement), S116–S122. DOI: 10.7326/M19-0871

Chapter 6
Operationalizing AI Governance:
A Practical Roadmap and Case Study for Organizations Adopting Third-Party AI Systems

Annamaria Szakonyi
https://orcid.org/0000-0002-1958-2042
Embry–Riddle Aeronautical University, USA

Kyle Oris
https://orcid.org/0009-0007-5184-6195
SSM Health, USA

ABSTRACT

This chapter presents the second phase of a multi-stage research agenda on operationalizing AI governance for organizations adopting third-party AI systems. Building on our conceptual AI Governance Implementation Framework (AGIF), this chapter translates theory into practice by developing the foundational oversight mechanisms that anchor an AI governance program through a practice-inspired, action design research based, collaborative inquiry. The resulting Roadmap for AI Governance (RAIG) outlines an eight-step implementation model, establishing the structures necessary for later operationalization. The roadmap provides practical guidance for establishing oversight structures, scoping AI systems, defining risks and controls, and integrating evaluation, testing, and validation processes. Findings reveal that effective AI governance requires iterative development, cross-functional collaboration, and integration with existing risk and data governance programs. This

DOI: 10.4018/979-8-3373-9918-8.ch006

work demonstrates how governance can be embedded in real-world organizational settings, bridging the gap between conceptual frameworks and applied practice for responsible AI adoption.

INTRODUCTION

Artificial intelligence (AI) is reshaping the way organizations deliver services, make decisions, and interact with stakeholders. It has moved from experimental technology to a core driver of organizational transformation. Its integration into business operations is no longer limited to technology companies or research institutions; hospitals, universities, and financial institutions now rely on AI-powered tools for everything from clinical documentation to fraud detection and student support (Bracken et al., 2025; Martinez-Requejo et al., 2024; Mökander & Floridi, 2022; Odeyemi et al., 2024; Schneider et al., 2022; Taeihagh, 2021). IBM shared that about 42% of enterprise-scale organizations (over 1,000 employees) have actively deployed AI, and an additional 40% are exploring it (IBM, 2024). According to a McKinsey study, AI adoption rates in enterprises grew to 88% in 2025, from 78% in the previous year, with organizations piloting or deploying AI in at least one business process (McKinsey & Company, 2025).

This rapid diffusion of AI across sectors has created both opportunity and obligation. The majority of organizations are still reporting experimental or piloting stages compared to about one third maturing and scaling their AI programs, which generates governance-related risks (McKinsey & Company, 2025). AI risks are increasing: according to the same McKinsey study, at least half of reported organizations have seen negative consequences of AI, and many are implementing mitigation efforts attempting to control these. Yet, Deloitte's Global Survey identified that in almost half of organizations, AI is not on the agenda of their corporate boards (Deloitte, 2024). Organizations are under increasing pressure (from regulators, customers, and the public) to ensure that their use of AI is responsible, ethical, and trustworthy (Agbadamasi et al., 2025; Batool et al., 2023; Mökander & Floridi, 2022; Themann, 2025). The OECD updated its definition of AI systems in 2023, creating an increased urgency for organizations to implement governance mechanisms in this space (OECD, 2024).

In response, a growing number of frameworks, standards, and toolkits have emerged to guide the governance of AI systems. However, these efforts have largely focused on entities that build AI; those developing, training, or fine-tuning models (Batool et al., 2023; Cloud Security Alliance, 2025; European Union, 2024; ISO, 2020; Kuehnert et al., 2025; NIST, 2025a; Oliveira, 2023; Ribeiro et al.; World Economic Forum, 2023). Far less attention has been given to the vast number of organizations that use AI solutions developed by others. These "AI adopters" face distinct governance challenges: they are accountable for ethical and compliant AI use but often lack insight into, or control over, the underlying models and data that drive these systems (Agbadamasi et al., 2025; Hickok, 2022; Oliveira, 2023; Taeihagh, 2021).

This chapter addresses that gap. The study adopts an action research design grounded in theories of organizational learning and adaptive governance. Drawing from an iterative, practice-based collaborative engagement with an organization implementing governance for third-party AI systems, the research examines how conceptual governance principles can be translated into practical, step-by-step operational implementation mechanisms. It demonstrates how organizations functioning primarily as AI consumers can build effective governance programs despite limited technical control. The goal is to translate high-level, abstract principles and frameworks into an actionable, operational roadmap suitable for organizations functioning primarily as AI consumers.

PROBLEM STATEMENT

Despite the proliferation of AI governance frameworks, toolkits, and control catalogs, the majority of existing guidance remains heavily oriented toward organizations that develop, train, or customize AI systems (Batool et al., 2023; Hickok, 2022; Kuehnert et al., 2025; Oliveira, 2023; Ribeiro et al.). Frameworks such as the ISACA AI Audit Toolkit and the Cloud Security Alliance's AI Control Matrix emphasize controls around bias detection in training datasets, model validation, and algorithmic fairness testing (Cloud Security Alliance, 2025; ISACA, 2024). While these activities are critical for developers and model owners, they have limited applicability to the vast number of organizations that procure and deploy third-party AI solutions rather than building them in-house.

This imbalance has created a significant governance gap. Many enterprises (particularly in highly regulated sectors such as healthcare and finance) are increasingly leveraging AI to enhance operations, analytics, and decision support (Bracken et al., 2025; Hickok, 2022; Martinez-Requejo et al., 2024; Mökander & Floridi, 2022; Odeyemi et al., 2024; Papagiannidis et al., 2022; Schneider et al., 2022). Yet these organizations (often lacking the technical capabilities, resources, or authority to inspect, retrain, or modify proprietary AI systems) remain responsible for ensuring ethical use, compliance, and risk management, but have little practical guidance on how to govern AI in a consumer or purchaser capacity (Agbadamasi et al., 2025; Hickok, 2022; Kuehnert et al.; 2025; Oliveira, 2023; Taeihagh, 2021). Existing AI governance literature appears inaccessible or irrelevant to their context, emphasizing model engineering controls rather than procurement oversight, vendor risk management, and operational accountability (Batool et al., 2025; Ganesh at al., 2025; Hickok, 2022; Panchagnula, 2025; Taieihagh, 2025).

The absence of tailored frameworks for AI adopters rather than AI developers has left many organizations without a clear roadmap for establishing proportionate governance structures (Hickok, 2022; Kuehnert et al.; 2025; Oliveira, 2023; Taeihagh, 2021). Without adaptation, they risk compliance gaps, ethical blind spots, and stakeholder mistrust when implementing AI systems procured from third parties (Agbadamasi et al., 2025; Hickok, 2022; Taeihagh, 2021). This chapter seeks to address this gap by proposing a practical governance approach designed for organizations that consume AI technology; helping them translate high-level standards into actionable processes for evaluating, procuring, and overseeing AI solutions throughout their lifecycle. The resulting roadmap provides stepwise guidance; from establishing oversight structures to operational integration and continuous improvement; tailored to organizations adopting AI systems.

SIGNIFICANCE OF PROJECT

This perspective paper addresses a critical and underexplored gap in the field of AI governance: the lack of practical, operational guidance for organizations that adopt and integrate third-party AI systems rather than develop them internally (Hickok, 2022; Kuehnert et al.; 2025; Oliveira, 2023; Taeihagh, 2021). While numerous governance frameworks provide detailed direction for model developers and technical creators, they offer limited applicability to organizations purchasing AI solutions and embedding them into existing workflows (Batool et al., 2023; Benraouane, 2024; Birkstedt et al., 2023; Hickok, 2022; Kilian et al., 2025; Oliveira, 2023; Ribeiro et al., 2025; Taeihagh, 2021; Themann, 2025). These adopters face unique challenges related to procurement, vendor accountability, transparency, operational integration, and ongoing monitoring, yet existing guidance rarely extends to these operational realities (Hickok, 2022; Kuehnert et al.; 2025; Oliveira, 2023; Taeihagh, 2021). This chapter addresses the context of organizations that adopt and integrate third-party AI systems rather than develop them internally.

By focusing on the adoption context, this perspective paper advances both scholarly understanding and industry practice. It bridges the gap between conceptual governance principles and practical implementation, offering a structured roadmap that organizations can apply to ensure responsible, transparent, and accountable AI use. The project's phased design; moving from conceptual synthesis to applied roadmap development and pilot implementation; creates a rare continuum between academic theory and real-world application.

Ultimately, this work contributes to building organizational capacity for responsible AI adoption, enabling decision-makers to integrate governance processes that align with ethical standards, regulatory expectations, and operational constraints. By doing so, it lays the foundation for scalable, evidence-based governance practices that can be adapted across sectors and maturity levels, advancing the responsible and trustworthy deployment of AI technologies in industry. Our operational model, designed to guide organizations in adopting and governing third-party AI systems in a responsible manner, translates existing theory into concrete, implementable steps, guiding responsible AI adopters across sectors.

METHODOLOGY

The purpose of this study is to advance the practical implementation of AI governance by translating the AI Governance Implementation Framework (AGIF), a conceptual model developed in our earlier work, into a step-by-step, actionable roadmap for organizations that adopt and integrate third-party artificial intelligence (AI) systems. This roadmap will fill an important gap that most existing AI governance frameworks are designed for AI developers rather than adopters (Batool et al., 2023; Hickok, 2022; Kuehnert et al., 2025; Oliveira, 2023; Ribeiro et al.). Our work is an early-stage reflection on implementing AI governance frameworks in adopting organizations. We are drawing lessons learned, conceptual insights, and observations from our hands-on experience to offer guidance to others beginning this process. We aim to answer the following questions:

1. How can the conceptual AGIF be translated into a step-by-step, actionable roadmap?
2. What sequence of activities enable repeatable implementation in adopting organizations?

The output of this study is a strategic and practical roadmap that defines how organizational leaders, governance practitioners, and cross-functional teams can deploy an AI governance oversight program.

This perspective paper employs an embedded practitioner-researcher approach, drawing on the methodological traditions of Action Design Research (ADR). We work directly with a healthcare organisation's AI-governance implementation team, iteratively applying our conceptual AI Governance Implementation Framework (AGIF), developed in a previous study (currently under review for publication), to produce a practical roadmap for AI governance implementation. The work is conceptual and reflective in nature, grounded in the authors' applied industry experience in building cybersecurity and governance programs. It relies on observations, lessons learned, and theoretical interpretation from the implementation process. The approach aligns with action research principles, emphasizing iterative learning, practitioner collaboration, and reflection on implementation-in-progress (Castro et al., 2025; Cedergren & Hassel, 2022; Sein et al., 2011.) Working closely with this industry partner allows for real-time translation of research concepts into organizational practice.

Action design research is a practice-inspired research activity that looks at problems as knowledge-creation opportunities (Castro et al., 2025; Cedergren & Hassel, 2022; Sein et al., 2011). In ADR, during the design and implementation of the solution to the defined problem, researchers and practitioners work together in an interactive process, continuously evaluating the solution and learning throughout the process (Castro et al., 2025; Cedergren & Hassel, 2022; Sein et al., 2011). This approach enables us to both advance theory and generate knowledge with high practical relevance and theoretical foundations, and therefore combining scientific rigour and practical value in supporting organisations to solve problems in practice (Cedergren & Hassel, 2022; Sein et al., 2011).

This study frames AI governance as an adaptive, learning-oriented process rather than a static compliance system. Rather than presenting new empirical data, this chapter focuses on conceptual synthesis and practice-informed insight, examining the early stages of implementation through the dual theoretical lenses of Organizational Learning Theory and Adaptive Governance Theory. Organizational Learning Theory (Argyris & Schön, 1978; Senge, 1990) provides the foundation for interpreting AI governance implementation as a "learning-by-doing" process, in which organizational structures, norms, and behaviors evolve through cycles of reflection, feedback, and adaptation. This perspective positions governance not as a fixed compliance exercise, but as a dynamic capacity that matures through experience and dialogue across functions.

Complementing this view, Adaptive Governance Theory (Folke et al., 2005; Chaffin et al., 2014) offers a framework for understanding how organizations respond to evolving technological, ethical, and regulatory environments. Adaptive governance emphasizes flexibility, distributed decision-making, and feedback-driven adjustment; principles particularly relevant to the governance of AI systems, where complexity and uncertainty are inherent. Applying this lens allows the authors to conceptualize AI governance as a dynamic system that must continuously evolve alongside advances in technology and shifting accountability demands.

Taken together, these theoretical foundations guide an interpretive, practice-based inquiry that focuses on how organizations can iteratively develop and refine governance mechanisms as they operationalize responsible AI principles. The perspective draws from ongoing collaborative reflection between researchers and practitioners to generate insights and practical lessons for organizations beginning their AI governance journey.

In the broader context of our work, this chapter represents the second phase of a larger, multi-phase initiative focused on developing and validating a practical roadmap for implementing AI governance across organizational settings. The overall research program combines cross-industry analysis, applied conceptual innovation and development (i.e. this book chapter), and empirical testing to build an evidence-based, scalable approach to operationalizing AI governance. The broader study is implemented in 3 phases depicted in Figure 1. In phase 1, we identified our guiding conceptual framework, AGIF. In phase 2 (this chapter), informed by our conceptual AGIF framework, we develop a conceptual innovation in the form of an AI governance implementation roadmap. In phase 3, we will test our roadmap by validating it through primary data collection.

Figure 1. Research questions, methods, and outputs of the 3 phases of our research program. This chapter discusses phase 2, the conceptual innovation of RAIG

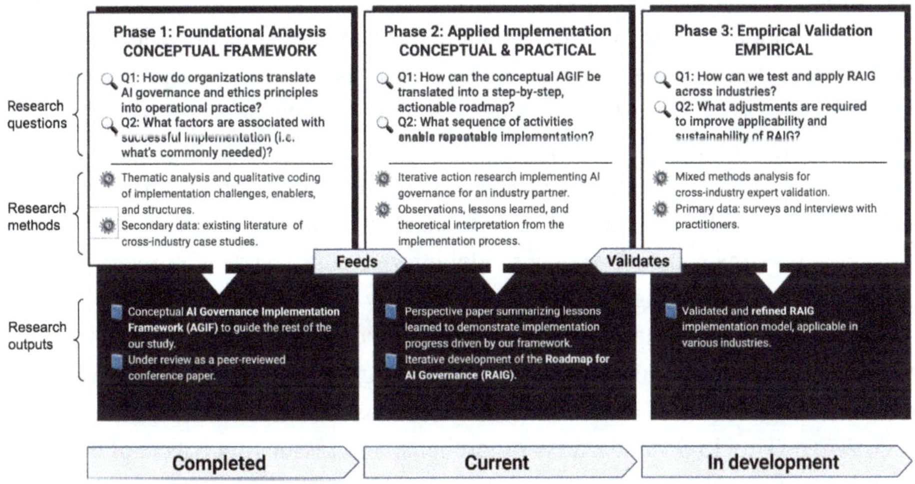

LITERATURE REVIEW

A growing body of work and multiple international frameworks have defined the contours of "responsible AI" and propose concrete governance mechanisms for reducing technological, ethical, and legal risks (Batool et al., 2023; Cloud Security Alliance, 2025; European Union, 2024; International Organization for Standardization, 2023; ISACA, 2024; NIST, 2025a). However, this content is uneven in its intended audience: many influential standards and guidance documents are framed around the life-cycle activities of creating AI (design, data curation, model training, validation, and testing), which leaves a practical gap for organizations that primarily acquire and operate third-party AI solutions rather than develop models internally (Hickok, 2022; Oliveira, 2023; Taeihagh, 2021).

Foundational reviews of ethics guidelines and governance solutions show a broad consensus on high-level principles (fairness, transparency, accountability, privacy), but repeatedly note a weakness in operational, stakeholder-specific guidance and in translating high-level principles into organizational practices. The mapping conducted by Jobin et al. of AI ethics guidelines showed wide convergence on principles but also identified limited clarity on implementation and stakeholder roles (Jobin et al., 2019). Subsequent systematic reviews similarly find calls for clearer, operational governance approaches across contexts, including guidance for AI adopters, not just AI providers (Batool et al., 2023; Benraouane, 2024; Birkstedt et al., 2023; Hickok, 2022; Kilian et al., 2025; Oliveira, 2023; Ribeiro et al., 2025; Taeihagh, 2021; Themann, 2025).

Major standards and regulatory initiatives confirm the developer orientation. The NIST AI Risk Management Framework (AI RMF) is explicitly designed to help organizations incorporate trustworthiness considerations into the design, development, use, and evaluation of AI products, services, and systems, with detailed mappings to development/testing activities and risk measurement processes (NIST, 2025a). While NIST's guidance is useful for adopters in principle, much of its technical discussion presumes influence over model internals and the development pipeline; capabilities that procuring organizations typically do not possess.

Similarly, international technical standards such as ISO/IEC TR 24028 (an overview of trustworthiness in AI) emphasize engineering, testing, and mitigation techniques targeting those responsible for system construction and lifecycle assurance (ISO, 2020). This ISO standard is comprehensive on issues such as explainability, robustness, and data pitfalls, but again assumes actors who can change algorithms, training data, or model architectures. ISO/IEC 42001:2023 extends this by defining a certifiable management system for AI, similar to ISO 27001, but the high-level recommendations still pose difficulties for adoption across industries (Benraouane, 2024; ISO, 2023).

Regulations are beginning to acknowledge differences between providers (those who develop and place systems on the market) and deployers or adopters (organizations who put systems into use). The EU AI Act, for example, distinguishes a range of obligations across providers, importers, distributors and deployers of high-risk AI systems; placing stricter obligations on providers but also assigning duties to deployers, such as requirements for human oversight, logging, informing users, cooperation with authorities (European Union, 2024). This distinction is important because it recognizes deployers as a legally relevant category but still leaves many practical governance questions unresolved for typical adopters, notably expectations related to procurement evaluation criteria, contractual enforcement, or ongoing monitoring of third-party models.

Practice-oriented guidance that explicitly targets procuring organizations is emerging but remains limited and fragmented. The World Economic Forum's procurement guideline for responsible AI adoption document is a notable example that directly addresses procurement and vendor management challenges for buyers, offering procurement checklists and practical controls (World Economic Forum, 2023). This guideline, however, is still limited to what buyers should do during the procurement process, such as administering vendor questionnaires, procurement checklists, contractual clauses, and post-deployment monitoring; without specific recommendations for deeper, technical standards for integration into existing systems.

The literature and standards ecosystem establishes two linked observations that motivate this study. First, the dominant core of standards and technical guidance concentrates on the development pipeline and engineering controls related to data, modeling and validation; content that presumes control over model internals and developer-side practices (European Union, 2024; Hickok, 2022; ISO, 2020; NIST, 2025a Oliveira, 2023). Second, the realities of adopting organizations; ranging from a limited ability to inspect the usually "black box" AI models to operational integration roadblocks across workflows; require a distinct, operational governance approach that is not yet synthesized into a cohesive, evidence-based roadmap (Hickok, 2022; Oliveira, 2023; Papagiannidis et al., 2022; Taeihagh, 2021; Themann, 2025). This gap justifies a focused investigation into operationalizing AI governance for adopting organizations. Our perspective paper proposes to fill this gap between the theoretical guidelines and practical implementation. To guide this work, we are relying on Organizational Learning Theory and Adaptive Governance Theory.

Organizational Learning Theory offers a foundational lens for understanding how organizations adapt, evolve, and institutionalize new knowledge through experience. Pioneered by Argyris and Schön in 1978, the theory posits that learning is not merely the accumulation of knowledge but the continuous transformation of organizational routines, behaviors, and mental models (Argyris & Schön, 1978; Fiol & Lyles, 1985; Schwengber, 2024). Learning occurs through iterative cycles of action and reflection, allowing organizations to respond to changing environments and to develop new competencies. Within the context of AI governance, this perspective highlights that embedding responsible AI practices is not a one-time implementation effort but an ongoing organizational learning process that requires adaptation, reflection, and continuous feedback.

Garvin further explained this theory through the Five Building Blocks of Organizational Learning: systematic problem solving, experimentation with new approaches, learning from past experience, learning from others, and transferring knowledge (Garvin, 1993). Together, these components describe how organizations cultivate the structures and mindsets necessary for continuous improvement. Garvin's knowledge transfer ties to inter-organizational learning, that addresses the sharing of information as a value creation mechanism in an interconnected, digitally driven economy (Schwengber, 2024). Within the context of AI governance, these building blocks highlight the importance of structured reflection mechanisms for embedding responsible AI practices across teams and functions. Learning internally, and also sharing our learning with the broader community, will allow other organizations to enhance their AI governance implementation practices.

A key mechanism within Organizational Learning Theory is double-loop learning, which extends beyond corrective action to question the fundamental norms, assumptions, and goals that shape decision-making (Argyris, 1976; Argyris & Schön, 1978, 1996; Basten & Haamann, 2018; Fiol & Lyles, 1985). Whereas single-loop learning involves correcting errors within existing policies or processes, double-loop learning challenges the governing values themselves, enabling deeper transformation and innovation (Argyris, 1976; Argyris & Schön, 1996; Basten & Haamann, 2018). In the context of AI governance, this learning mode is essential to managing emerging risks and ethical dilemmas. It enables organizations to move from compliance-oriented governance toward adaptive governance, characterized by ongoing reflection, shared learning, and responsive evolution of policies and practices as technologies and contexts change.

These underlying principles directly support our second grounding theory, the concept of Adaptive Governance, particularly in complex, uncertain domains such as AI. Adaptive Governance emphasizes flexibility, continuous feedback, and responsiveness to evolving social, technical, and regulatory conditions (Folke et al., 2005; Chaffin et al., 2014). These same qualities are enabled by the learning capacities described in Organizational Learning Theory: leadership that encourages inquiry, systems that capture and disseminate insights, and cultures that support experimentation and reflection. Double-loop learning, in particular, provides the cognitive and structural foundation for adaptive governance by enabling organizations to question assumptions, reinterpret principles, and adjust governance mechanisms in light of new challenges. Thus, adaptive governance can be viewed as the organizational expression of mature learning processes, where governance evolves not through static compliance, but through iterative cycles of sensemaking, feedback, and refinement.

Adaptive Governance Theory provides a framework for managing complex, uncertain, and rapidly evolving systems through fast, flexible, iterative, learning-oriented institutional arrangements. Originating in environmental and sustainability studies, the theory emphasizes responsiveness, collaboration and dialogue, and continuous feedback among diverse stakeholders (Brunner et al, 2005; Dietz et al., 2003; Folke et al., 2005; Van Assche et al., 2022; Wyborn, 2015). Adaptive governance promotes iterative decision-making, distributed authority, and the capacity to adjust rules and processes as new information and conditions emerge. Adaptive governance is especially useful in problems assessing risk, which is a core component of cybersecurity governance programs in general (Van Assche et al., 2022).

Parallel to how environmental and sustainability issues have global consequences, the broad impacts of AI (from workplaces to health outcomes) necessitate organizations to apply adaptive governance approaches to manage its effects on larger systems and our society as a whole (Reuel & Undheim, 2024). Applied to AI governance, this perspective highlights the need for organizations to evolve governance mechanisms in response to technological advances, shifting ethical expectations, and emerging regulatory requirements. Governance for AI technologies is challenging due to its technical complexity and rapidly evolving nature, which requires industry collaboration and an adaptive governance approach (Reuel & Undheim, 2024).

Drawing on the framework proposed by Melaku (2023), we adopt a layered, adaptive governance implementation model that spans strategic, tactical and operational levels. At the strategic level, governance sets the vision, business alignment and governance architecture for the AI/technology domain. At the tactical level, governance translates strategy into processes that bridge high-level policy into implementable frameworks. At the operational level, governance becomes embedded into day-to-day activities and manifests in the execution of controls, monitoring and reporting, incident management and feedback. A critical feature of the framework is a continuous feedback loop: operational outcomes and metrics inform tactical refinement and strategic realignment, hence making the governance system dynamic and adaptive (Melaku, 2023). Employing this same flow enables us to map our conceptual framework into distinct governance levels and derive a sequential roadmap for AI governance implementation.

Melaku's adaptive governance approach resonates with the findings of our previous study (submitted to an international conference for peer review), where we established the conceptual AI Governance Implementation Framework (AGIF) through a thematic analysis of cross-industry case studies of AI governance implementations. The AGIF (Figure 2) proposed that successful AI governance emerges through the interaction of three interdependent domains:

1. **Oversight mechanisms** that establish accountability, policy direction, and decision-making structures;
2. **Operationalization tools** and processes that embed governance into day-to-day workflows, technical procedures and activities; and

3. **Continuous feedback loops** that monitor system performance, capture ethical or compliance issues, and drive iterative improvement.

Figure 2. The conceptual AI Governance Implementation Framework (AGIF). Highlighted in the diagram is our current scope of implementation for AI governance Oversight Mechanisms. (The original diagram without the highlight is currently under review for an international conference)

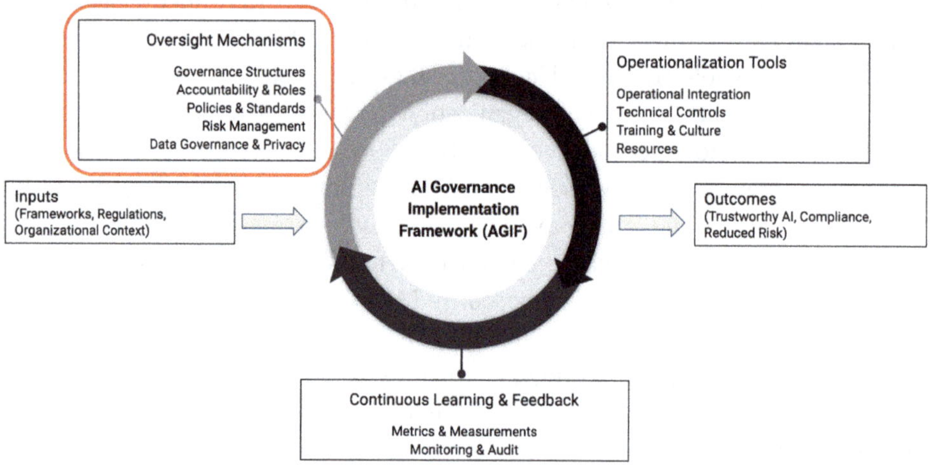

AGIF conceptualizes AI governance not as a single compliance activity but as a dynamic, organization-wide capability of constant learning. It provides a foundation for understanding the mechanisms by which governance principles can be operationalized, and it serves as the conceptual driver for this chapter. Throughout this project, the conceptual elements of AGIF were translated into practical actions and decision points forming the Roadmap for AI Governance (RAIG). Whereas AGIF conceptualized the "what" (i.e. "what is needed?") for AI governance, RAIG focuses on the "how": translating conceptual mechanisms into actionable, step-by-step guidance. This chapter explains the steps necessary for designing and building the oversight mechanisms (highlighted in Figure 2) for AI governance, which includes establishing governance structures, identifying accountability and roles, defining policies and standards, and synchronizing the AI governance program with its existing risk management and data governance efforts. The project remains ongoing, with future stages to document the transition from oversight design to full operational integration.

In summary, the gap in literature is clear: there is a pressing need to develop practical tools that can guide organizational implementation of AI governance programs. Within this study, organizational learning theory and adaptive governance theory provide the conceptual foundation for understanding AI governance not as a static compliance framework, but as a dynamic, evolving process. This has been confirmed by our previous study's findings, where the clear requirement for continuous learning emerged as part of AGIF. Combining AGIF with these theories, we iteratively developed our proposed Roadmap for AI Governance (RAIG), detailed in the next section.

RESULTS

Step 1: Establish a Formal AI Governance Oversight Body

As observed by AGIF, governance structures are crucial in building out an AI governance program. AI governance must be approached holistically at a strategic level, with formal governance structures in place (AlGhamdi et al., 2020; Hickok, 2022; ISACA, 2018; Selig, 2016; Taeihagh, 2021). Support from senior leadership is important in developing AI oversight and governance (AlGhamdi et al., 2020; Kuehnert et al., 2025; Themann, 2025). Many organizations have elected AI committees or similar structures as a means to foster leadership commitment and collaboration (Agbadamasi et al., 2025; AlGhamdi et al., 2020; Ribeiro et al., 2025, Themann, 2025). Our findings indicate that a top-down approach for endorsement paired with a consultative, cross-departmental approach is best, and this is confirmed by our study (AlGhamdi et al., 2020; Hickok, 2022; Kuehnert et al., 2025; Ribeiro et al., 2025; Themann, 2025). The implementation organization adopted a leadership-driven AI committee as an early governance structure. It was discovered that, while executive leadership plays a central role in setting vision and accountability for governance, their required involvement in the definition of a governance function is most effective when complemented by individual contributors with specialised AI domain knowledge.

Due to the complexity and quickly changing landscape, AI expertise can sit deeper in the organization than traditional leadership hierarchies expect. This means that senior leaders and the AI governance program will benefit from close partnerships with individual contributors who have deep working knowledge with the various dimensions of AI: technical, ethical, regulatory, risk, etc. (AlGhamdi et al.; Hickok, 2022; Kuehnert et al., 2025; Ribeiro et al., 2025; Themann, 2025). This requires collaboration that crosses managerial lines and bridges large gaps in hierarchy, potentially connecting individual contributors with directors, C-level leadership, or VP's. This is non-traditional for most organizations, but the complexity of AI demands a shift towards expert-informed leadership. By crossing managerial lines and collaborating vertically, as well as horizontally, the AI governance function will be informed by both the strategic oversight of leadership and the operational realities of the field, reducing the likelihood of well-intentioned but impractical policy design.

Cross-functional teams facilitate complex problem solving and organizational learning by combining a wide range of expertise across units (Basten & Haamann, 2018; Huang & Newell, 2003). They can facilitate double-loop learning by generating new ideas and solutions for the organizational context (Basten & Haamann, 2018; Huang & Newell, 2003). Adaptive governance systems tend to self-organize, creating diverse teams and stakeholder groups, and integrating multiple forms of knowledge and experience to build shared understanding and coordinated policies (Folke et al., 2005). These key actors play a crucial role by fostering leadership, trust, shared vision, and collective meaning, helping transform management structures into environments that enable continuous learning (Folke et al., 2005).

Based on this, our first recommended and most critical step in operationalizing AI governance is to create a dedicated oversight structure: a formal body responsible for coordinating AI strategy, risk management, and ethical oversight across the organization (Batool et al., 2023; ISACA, 2018; Ribeiro et al., 2025; Themann, 2025). This structure may take different forms depending on organizational culture and maturity; such as an AI Governance Committee, Responsible AI Council, or AI Center of Excellence (AICoE); but its function is consistent: to serve as the centralized point of accountability and coordination for all AI-related activities (Ribeiro et al., 2025; Themann, 2025). Similar to how many organizations established Cloud Centers of Excellence to guide cloud adoption, this body should define governance standards, approve AI use cases, and ensure alignment between business objectives, regulatory obligations, and ethical principles (Agbadamasi et al., 2025; Ribeiro et al., 2025; Themann, 2025). Establishing this entity early creates a clear governance anchor from which operational policies, technical controls, and compliance processes can later evolve.

Figure 3 visualizes a possible scenario that many organizations, such as our partner company, may consider implementing. The overall AI governance program is responsible for setting the general direction and strategy for AI governance. The AICoE is the "translator" between governance and operations: guiding strategic directions for the program, while operationalizing the strategy into practice, and defining standards and best practices for AI use. Finally, the AI Operations segment implements those standards in the everyday operational setting.

Figure 3. Hierarchy of the AI governance program

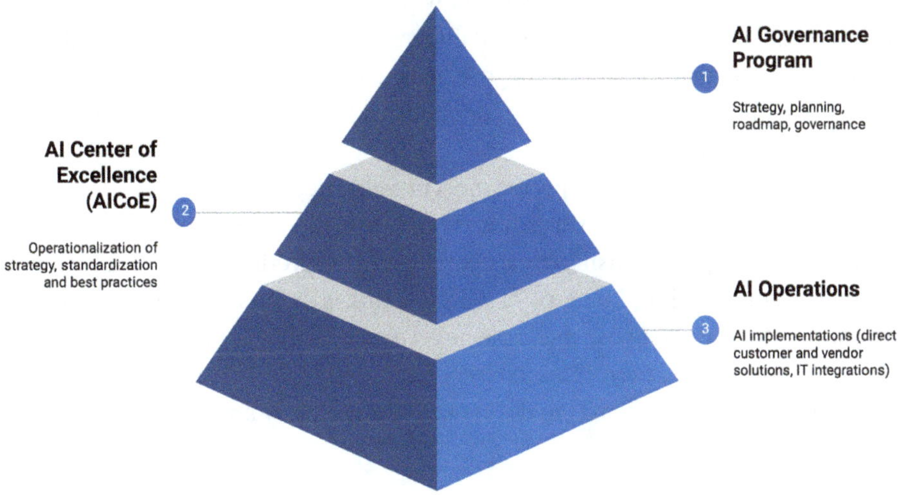

Step 2: Scoping

When scoping an AI governance program, organizations must evaluate how heavily they depend on AI/ML, the magnitude of investment, integration with business, and their regulatory exposure (Hickok, 2022; Selig, 2016). For this, however, they must first define what is considered to be AI. The first problem with the implementation organization's initial AI committee and review process was a broad scope. Technology that included AI in any capacity was considered subject for review by the committee, however the term "AI" is exceptionally broad and fluid. For scoping the governance program, it is suggested that organizations select and tailor their approach based on their environment, priorities, capabilities and resources (Mäntymäki et al., 2022; Melaku, 2023; Mökander & Floridi, 2022; Oliveira, 2023; Selig, 2016; Themann, 2025).

Artificial intelligence, in one form or another, dates back to the 1950's with one of the earliest examples of a chatbot being ELIZA in 1966 (Bassett, 2018; Kaul et al., 2020). The 1970's AI expert system MYCIN was developed to identify bacteria and recommend antibiotics (Kaul et al., 2020). While these early systems meet technical definitions of artificial intelligence, the average person, including those technically adept, may not consider these systems to be AI by today's standards. These systems were deterministic; they could be described as "hard-coded", meaning the systems contained no learning nor reasoning capabilities and operated off of a set of rule based statements and if/then logic (Bassett, 2018; Kaul et al., 2020).

This historical context highlights a fundamental point: an organization's perception of what constitutes AI depends on who you ask, what they know, and how they define it. Without a clear and shared understanding, every individual and every team will interpret the scoping of AI governance slightly differently. This problem escalates quickly when we consider related terms such as machine learning, deep learning, and generative AI.

If an organization simply adopts the most broad understanding of AI - "machines that can perform tasks that would previously have required human (or other biological) brainpower to accomplish" - then nearly every AI product would fall within its governance scope (Gajjar, 2023, p. 7). Clearly, this is an undesired result, as early rule-based systems do not pose the same governance challenges and risks as today's modern AI systems. To resolve this, an important starting point for the development of an AI oversight mechanism is to define key terms clearly and consistently across the organization.

Definitions

The quick advances in the AI industry and the wide educational gaps across individuals make mere chatter of AI difficult, much less a dialogue concerning AI governance. Crafting definitions is not just a chance to make sure everyone is using the same terminology, but serves to establish boundaries for AI governance and ensure stakeholders have similar understandings of core AI concepts (Fernández-Llorca et al., 2024; Stahl et al., 2023). Thus, definitions are more than semantics, it is an activity in which the organization and its stakeholders must ask foundational questions:

- What are we really governing?
- Why does AI technology require special governance where others do not?
- What distinguishes legacy AI from today's AI systems?

In our project implementation, the concept of non-determinism defines the boundary between today's AI systems and governance requirements from legacy AI systems. Non-determinism describes the probabilistic nature of modern AI systems (Cohen, 1979; Cooper et al., 2022; Williams, 2025). That is, they are composed of algorithms that, when given the same input, can produce different outputs or follow different paths through its execution on different runs. Just like human thinking can vary when you ask multiple people about the same opinion: non-deterministic AI tools may generate different results for the same question (Cohen, 1979; Cooper et al., 2022; Williams, 2025). It is this unpredictability and opacity that creates new risks, complexities, and the need for a dedicated governance process.

Table 1 defines our definition of four levels of AI terminology by increasing levels of non-determinism. The objectives of the table are to remove confusion on AI concepts, ensure all stakeholders are using the same language, and to scope the AI governance function to systems of level 3 and 4 (systems that are non-deterministic).

Table 1. Four levels of AI terminology by increasing levels of non-determinism

Level	Name	Technology	Examples
1	"Legacy" Artificial Intelligence (AI)	Deterministic Rule-based logic, hard coded logic, decision trees, if/then rule maps, and similar.	Signature based antivirus, basic thermostat controls, MYCIN expert system, ELIZA chatbot
2	Machine Learning (ML)	Typically deterministic Predictions and pattern identification from structured data based on statistical techniques such as regression analysis.	SAS Analytics, predictive modeling tools
3	Deep Learning (DL)	Typically non-deterministic Modeling complex, non-linear relationships of unstructured data using neural networks.	Google DeepMind AlphaFold, Nuance Dragon Medical One (speech to text), Aidoc (medical imaging analysis)
4	Generative AI (GenAI)	Non-deterministic Synthesizes novel text, images, or output with large scale neural networks trained on large, typically mixed, datasets.	ChatGPT, Microsoft Copilot, Nuance DAX Copilot, Hippocratic AI.

While the definitions in Table 1 were developed with industry standards in mind, the primary objective was to balance technical accuracy with practical usability. The table was designed not only as an educational tool for stakeholders, but also as a practical guide to determine scope within the AI governance program. As such, greater emphasis was placed on making the definitions intuitive and easy to map to the types of SaaS systems and AI applications the implementation organization is likely to encounter, rather than adhering strictly to technical or academic delineations.

Additional terms to consider defining in the scoping phase, together with the implementation organization's own definition for these, are listed below:

- Autonomy levels: The levels and capabilities of AI to act without human interaction, informed by the American Medical Association's CPT Appendix S: AI taxonomy for medical services & procedures (2024).
    - Assistive: AI system identifies or highlights relevant data or patterns, but does not draw conclusions or make decisions.
    - Augmentative: AI system processes, analyzes, and summarizes data to produce structured and decision ready outputs, but still requires human interpretation and action.

- Autonomous: AI system independently interprets data and takes action or makes decisions without needing real-time human input or validation.

- AI Actors: Individuals involved in the deployment, management, security, maintenance, and use of AI systems.
    - Decision maker: Members of the AI governance structure (e.g., AI committee, etc.) and other stakeholders who influence decisions regarding AI systems.
    - Developer: Individuals responsible for the development, configuration, deployment, and technical maintenance of AI systems.
    - System owner: Individual responsible for a given instance and implementation of an AI system with responsibility for certain maintenance and management activities.
    - User: Individuals who use and interact with AI systems.
    - Impacted individuals: Individuals who are impacted or affected by the outputs or actions of the AI system.
- AI Control Owners: Adopted in alignment with the Cloud Security Alliances' AI Controls Matrix, control owners define the level of ownership of AI systems and controls (Cloud Security Alliance, 2025).
    - Model Provider: Entities that develop, train, and distribute foundational and fine-tuned AI models for various applications. They create the underlying AI capabilities that other actors build upon. Example: OpenAI (e.g., GPT 5).
    - Orchestrated Service Provider: Entities that create the technical building blocks and management tools that enable AI implementation. This can include platforms, frameworks, and tools that facilitate the integration, deployment, and management of AI models within enterprise workflows. These providers focus on model orchestration and offer services like API access, automated scaling, prompt management, workflow automation, monitoring, and governance. Example: AWS Bedrock.
    - Application Provider: Entities that build and offer end-user applications that leverage generative AI models for specific tasks such as content creation, chatbots, code generation, and enterprise automation. These applications are often delivered as software-as-a-service (SaaS) solutions. Examples: OpenAI (e.g., ChatGPT app), Adobe Firefly.
    - AI Customer: Entities that consume AI services or products.
- Foundational Models: Commonly referred to as general-purpose AI, foundational models are AI systems capable of a range of general tasks such as text synthesis, image generation, and audio generation (Fernández-Llorca et al., 2024; Triguero et al., 2024).

- Frontier Models: Cutting-edge AI models that have newer and better capabilities than foundational models, but pose dangerous and risky capabilities (Anderljung et al., 2023; Phuong et al., 2024).
- Agents / Agentic AI: AI systems that pursue goals and take actions autonomously with little to no human action. Agents interact with external systems and take autonomous actions within those systems, not just produce outputs. These systems are called agentic because the AI has agency to make decisions and perform actions (Schneider et al., 2022; Taeihagh, 2021).

Program Objectives

The implementation organization defined the objective of their AI governance program as identifying and promoting the trustworthiness of AI systems and their responsible development, use, and maintenance. Trustworthiness, as articulated in chapter 3 of the NIST AI RMF encompasses seven characteristics: valid & reliable, safe, secure & resilient, accountable & transparent, explainable & interpretable, privacy-enhanced, and fair with harmful bias managed (NIST, 2025a). The implementation organization adopted these characteristics as foundational objectives of its AI governance framework. Each characteristic was examined to identify actionable steps the organization could take to achieve and demonstrate it. As an example, the "valid and reliable" component of AI trustworthiness was mapped to organizational action items such as (1) evaluation of incoming AI technologies for use case and context, and (2) ongoing testing of AI systems. Table 2 contains the action items required for each AI characteristic.

Table 2. Sample of organizational action items required for each AI characteristic.

Characteristic	Action Item
Valid and reliable	(1) Evaluation of incoming AI technologies for use case and context. (2) Initial and ongoing testing of AI systems.
Safe	(1) Define and ensure appropriate levels of human oversight. (2) Initial and ongoing testing of AI systems (3) Training for AI actors.
Secure and resilient	(1) Evaluation of incoming AI technologies for security components and data handling. (2) Integrate AI governance with data governance (3) Initial and ongoing testing of AI systems.
Accountable and transparent	(1) Develop RACI to define clear roles and accountability. (2) Conduct user-driven testing and feedback of AI systems.
Explainable and interpretable	(1) Provide clear information, documentation, and training for AI actors. (2) Conduct user-driven testing and feedback of AI systems.

continued on following page

Table 2. Continued

Characteristic	Action Item
Privacy-enhanced	(1) Evaluation of incoming AI technologies for legal, privacy, and compliance components. (2) Review AI for regulatory conformance.
Fair, with harmful bias managed	(1) Initial and ongoing testing of AI systems. (2) Define and ensure appropriate levels of human oversight. (3) Define high risk AI systems and restricted AI use cases.

Step 3: Risk Management with the Risk and Control Matrix (RACM)

Successful governance must manage risk, and risks are managed through controls (Batool et al., 2023; Melaku, 2023; Themann, 2025). Therefore, to effectively govern AI, an understanding of present risks and applicable controls is necessary and can be accomplished through the development of a risk and control matrix (RACM). The RACM informs many of the oversight mechanisms in the AGIF, such as accountability & roles, policies & standards, and risk management. Because of this, it is recommended to begin the development of a RACM early in the oversight development process but only after scoping since the bounds set in step two will inform the depth and breadth of the RACM.

At its core, an RACM is a list of relevant controls and risks mapped to each other (Gutfraind, 2025; KPMG, 2018; Tjoa et al., 2022). Each risk may be mitigated by several controls and each control may apply to many risks. This mapping enables the organization to analyze problems and support evaluations and audits from both the risk and control side. When a particular risk is of concern to stakeholders, the RACM allows quick identification of the controls required to mitigate that risk. Conversely, if an AI system under evaluation lacks a specific control, the organization can readily determine which risks are heightened as a result.

In building its RACM, the implementation team referenced three main sources; ISACA's Artificial Intelligence Audit Toolkit, the Cloud Security Alliance's AI Controls Matrix, and the MITRE ATLAS Matrix; to aggregate a list of AI related risks and controls (Cloud Security Alliance, 2025; ISACA, 2024; MITRE, n.d.). From the controls perspective, ISACA's Artificial Intelligence Audit Toolkit and the Cloud Security Alliance's (CSA) AI Controls Matrix contained a combined 494 controls, each reviewed for applicability to the implementation organization. Many controls were duplicated between the two sources and others deemed out of scope due to their relation to the development and training of AI systems; a practice not occurring in adopting organizations. Additionally, many controls in the CSA's matrix were cloud-specific controls not inherently tied to AI and therefore excluded.

After identifying applicable controls, the granularity requirements of the matrix must be evaluated. While the RACM should be comprehensive, it should not be burdensome to use and maintain. As this is the implementation organization's first formalization of an RACM and AI governance function, practicality and usability was emphasized. To facilitate quick deployment and ease of use, the controls were presented at an aggregate level, combining similar controls and developing higher-order control statements. As of the writing of this chapter, 34 control statements were defined.

From the risk perspective, the 34 control statements were reviewed and evaluated to determine what risks would logically result from a lack of controls. For example, from the controls related to logging and monitoring (e.g., logging AI inputs and output, access control logs, security and policy violation logs, etc.) a risk statement regarding insufficient logging was developed. To ensure no applicable risks were missed, the MITRE ATLAS Matrix was reviewed. Many tactics and techniques inspired the creation of risk statements for the implementation organization. For example, AML.T0070 and AML.T0071, retrieval-augmented generation (RAG) poisoning and false RAG entry injection, highlighted the risk associated with providing AI with supplemental documents, knowledge bases, or other data repositories. Similar to the creation of control statements, the risk statements were written at an aggregate level. As of the writing of this paper, 12 fundamental risk statements were written and mapped back to mitigating controls.

In our RACM, we do not assign severity to any AI associated risk. The severity of a risk is determined by its likelihood and impact. Since both of these factors are context-dependent (varying based on the data accessed by or contained within the AI tool, as well as the scope and use case of the system), scores were not allocated to the risks in this step. Rather, the RACM serves as an inventory of risks that team members can reference as they onboard tools in the organization. Subsequent phases of the framework (steps 4 - AI evaluation, 5 - inherent risk, and 6 - TEVV) will provide the information needed to assess likelihood and impact, and step 8 will formalize risk scoring for each identified risk.

The RACM is not a static document and should be updated regularly with new risks and controls. Regular reviews of the RACM will be scheduled periodically by the governing body, especially as AI technologies and use cases advance and change quickly.

Step 4: AI Evaluation

Before developing the evaluation process, it was important to establish a foundational understanding of AI-related risks and the corresponding controls available to address them. The organization's RACM served as key input for designing the evaluation questionnaire, as it defined the primary areas of concern to investigate and controls to require in AI solutions.

Readers familiar with the NIST AI RMF may recognize the term "evaluation" from the acronym TEVV: Testing, Evaluation, Verification, and Validation. As of the writing of this paper, NIST has not yet fully defined standards for TEVV (NIST, 2025b). Using what guidance and verbiage was available in the NIST AI RMF and the current understanding of TEVV in NIST's Proposed Zero Draft for a Standard on AI TEVV, definitions and scope for each term were defined by the implementation organization (NIST, 2025 a & b). We defined and scoped each phase of TEVV for their use case of evaluating purchased, third-party AI solutions.

Evaluation was defined as the quantitative or qualitative determination if, or to what extent, the AI system meets or exceeds a set of characteristics or criteria. This definition was informed by the current understanding of Evaluation as defined by NIST (NIST, 2025b). Evaluation was implemented in the implementation organization's governance program by defining a questionnaire to be answered by internal stakeholders and external vendors for prospective AI solutions. To ensure a comprehensive evaluation was developed, eight question categories spanning key areas of AI governance were developed, listed in Table 3.

Table 3. The eight question categories of the evaluation questionnaire.

Question Category	Focus	Purpose
Use Case & Context	Can We?	Clarify what problems the AI solves, who will use it, and how it fits into existing workflows.
Ethics & Responsible Use	Should We?	Enables us to understand if we should use AI. Ensure the AI's design and deployment align with our ethical standards and do no unintended harm.
Technology & Model Components	How does it work?	Break down the AI's architecture, frameworks and pre-trained components, for technical understanding, integration support, and risk analysis.
Human Impact & Augmentation	What about people?	Understand how people interact with, verify, and transition alongside the AI.
Governance & Accountability	Who is accountable?	Define who's responsible for decisions, approvals, audit trails, and ongoing oversight of the AI.
AI Controls & Accuracy	Is the model safe?	Verify the model's outputs are reliable, safe from adversarial inputs, and meet defined quality thresholds.

continued on following page

Table 3. Continued

Question Category	Focus	Purpose
Data Ownership & Usage	How is our data used?	Understand what data is used, how it is protected, and if training processes use internal data.
Legal, Privacy, & Compliance	Are we covered?	Confirm the solution satisfies all regulatory, contractual, and privacy requirements.

As of the writing of this chapter, a set of 58 questions were defined and most questions were mapped to a risk or control from the RACM to ensure coverage of all risks and controls. Some questions were foundational, such as inquiring on the use case and function of the AI, therefore not mapping to a specific risk or control. The volume of questions is burdensome for most AI evaluations and would slow down many procurement processes. The questionnaire was designed to be flexible so that only certain subsets of questions are asked depending on the inherent risk of the solution and the required respondent.

The first 9 questions are context and scoping questions applicable to all requested AI applications. These questions help evaluators first understand if the solution falls within the scope of governance, second determine the context and business case for the requested technology, and third determine the inherent risk level of the AI.

Inherent risk is "the risk to an entity in the absence of any direct or focused actions by management to alter its severity" (NIST, 2020, pp. 61-62). In the context of AI evaluation, we propose an adapted definition for inherent risk as the initial understanding of risk the AI solution poses as determined by the 9 context and scoping questions. From this understanding, an initial/inherent risk score is derived which is used to determine how much additional evaluation and testing of the solution is necessary.

The remaining 49 questions are categorized by their applicable inherent risk level and the required respondent; internal or vendor. The inherent risk level determined by the first 9 questions defines which of the remaining 49 questions must be evaluated. Questions designated Low+ indicate the question applies to all AI systems (i.e., all systems are rated at least a low or higher), whereas High+ indicates a question is applicable to AI systems designated with a high or critical inherent risk.

Systems with a lower inherent risk do not need the same depth of evaluation as critical systems, making the questionnaire increase in length with the inherent risk level of the evaluated system (European Union, 2024; Mökander & Floridi, 2022; Themann, 2025; Stahl et al., 2023). For example, an AI system used for triaging patients is defined by the organization as having a critical inherent risk, requiring much more oversight and evaluation than an AI system used for summarizing business emails which has a low inherent risk and does not require expansive levels of oversight. For low risk systems, only two additional questions are required, whereas for critical systems, all remaining 49 are required. Strategically defining the various inherent risk levels can reduce the number of evaluation questions for the average requested AI system. For example, in the implementation organization, a requirement of low risk systems is the lack of RAG, MCP servers, or other integrations with company data or system. That requirement eliminates many data protection and security questions.

To further reduce the volume of questions for any one party, the questionnaire was further segmented into questions required to be answered internally and questions required to be answered by vendors. Questions regarding business case and context are typically answered internally whereas questions regarding AI guardrails and bias require vendor response. When combining the inherent risk level and required respondent question categories, a medium risk solution would only require 15 questions to be answered by the vendor and 8 by internal resources.

Step 5: Inherent Risk

As we defined earlier, inherent risk is the initial understanding of risk posed by an AI solution as a means of determining how much additional evaluation and testing is required of the AI system. As seen in the previous section, defining inherent risk levels can help structure evaluation questionnaires into management segments. However, based on the organization's experience, defining inherent risk doesn't just help with evaluation, it sets the foundation for the larger risk management program and prompts the AI governance committee to consider their risk tolerance and which AI use cases exceed those tolerances.

Because of the close relation with AI evaluation, defining inherent risk is an activity organizations may wish to conduct alongside the development of the evaluation questionnaire. If an organization chooses to not tie inherent risk to their evaluation questionnaire, the exact order matters less, but based on our experience it is still recommended to do so after building the RACM. The RACM provides a comprehensive overview of applicable risk and controls that can enable a more informed determination of low, medium, high, or critical levels of inherent risk (Gutfraind, 2025; KPMG, 2018; Tjoa et al., 2022).

In our case, the EU AI Act's definition of high risk AI systems served as a foundational starting point for the development of inherent risk levels. Even though the implementation organization resides outside of EU jurisdiction, the high risk use cases and AI systems listed in Annex III of the EU AI act (such as systems using biometrics, or involved in critical infrastructure and employment related processes) helped establish a border frame for reference for defining inherent risk levels (European Union, 2024). Even though not all use cases, such as migration and asylum, were applicable to the implementation organization, the EU AI Act encouraged a more holistic perspective for defining high level AI use cases.

Using the EU AI Act's high risk systems as a starting point, critical, medium, and low risk use cases were then defined. The development of inherent risk levels was informed by both the RACM and the evaluation questionnaire. The insights from the RACM and questionnaire highlighted the distinctions between low, medium, high, and critical risk systems. Care was taken to consider how the inherent risk definitions fit with the questionnaire and through an iterative approach, the inherent risk levels were informed by the RACM and aligned with the evaluation questionnaire.

In addition, human-in-the-loop controls are an important consideration for organizations looking to deploy AI systems (Mosqueira-Rey et al., 2022; Ribeiro et al., 2025; Themann, 2025). The level of human oversight was deemed significant by the implementation organization's AI governance committee and was therefore given special consideration and included in the defining inherent risk levels. Using CPT Appendix S: AI Taxonomy for Medical Services and Procedures as a guide, three levels of AI autonomy (the inverse of human oversight) were defined: Assistive, Augmentative, and Autonomous (American Medical Association, 2024). The CPT's definitions were altered to better fit the organization's context and potential AI use cases. The level of autonomy was then mapped to the inherent risk levels.

Table 4 is a non-exhaustive list of sample use cases and features mapped to their inherent risk level as defined by the implementation organization. For comparison, a financial services company may elect to define AI tools that can assist in loan applications as high risk.

Table 4. Sample use cases and features mapped to their inherent risk level, as defined by the implementation organization

Inherent Risk Level	Example Use Cases & Features	Autonomy
Low	● Basic productivity tools ● Spam filters	Assistive
Medium	● Staff scheduling assistants ● Meeting summarization ● Integration with external systems, potentially using a model context protocol (MCP) server	Assistive, Augmentative
High	● Employee and workforce management (e.g., resume screening) ● Basic medical use (e.g., summarization of patient care materials)	Assistive, Augmentative, Autonomous
Critical	● Safety components of medical products ● Emergency services triaging	Augmentative, Autonomous

Each inherent risk level was accompanied by a descriptive risk statement outlining:

- General characteristics: example use cases and scope of AI systems, how outputs will be used, if the system is customer facing, if the AI is agentic, etc.
- Degree of human involvement: statements regarding if the AI system runs autonomously, supports decision making, or assists with general tasks.
- Extent of technological integration: does the system leverage RAG, connect to MCP servers, access sensitive data, etc.

Each inherent risk level is also accompanied by failure statements characterising potential consequences of systems across four dimensions. Note, failure is not limited to system downtime or failure to operate, but includes any failure of trustworthiness, including failure to uphold fairness or failure to maintain proper security.

- Disruption: to what level would failure disrupt business operations.
- Harm: to what level would failure impact the rights, fairness, dignity, and safety of individuals.
- Security: to what level would the cybersecurity of IT systems be impacted.
- Compliance: to what level would the business be exposed to compliance, legal, or regulatory violations.

Step 6: TEVV

The evaluation phase of TEVV was defined in step four and the remaining phases - testing, validation, and verification - are picked up in step 6. As mentioned earlier, the statement in the evaluation section concerning the current lack of a defined TEVV process by NIST applies here as well, therefore, our definitions of testing, validation, and verification were developed in-house using what sources were available at the time (NIST, 2025b).

As a reminder to readers, the testing, validation, and verification processes defined herein are for the purposes of organizations purchasing AI applications such as SaaS applications and other pre-trained AI models. The goals of testing for this paper are limited to ensuring the purchased AI system meets the vendors claims and adheres to internal requirements. Therefore, the means of testing and validation presented are through prompting the AI with questions and observing results. Advanced means of testing AI models and tools such as Fairlearn, LIME, Adversarial Robustness Toolbox, LM Evaluation Harness, and others are recognized but out of scope for the purposes of this AI governance program.

Testing

Testing, informed by NIST's current documentation, is a procedure that determines one or more measurable and operational characteristics of the AI system (NIST, 2025a). For the implementation organization, that means probing the AI with prompts to determine its accuracy, fairness/bias, reliability (includes testing the system's susceptibility to hallucination, efficacy of guardrails, and handling of poor or inaccurate data), and toxicity (J. Marpet, personal communication, October 1 & 7, 2025).

The primary means of testing is conducted by providing the AI with hundreds of prompts from a database and analyzing the responses to calculate the accuracy of the system as well as signs of harm, toxicity, enforcement of guardrails, and bias (J. Marpet, personal communication, October 1 & 7, 2025). The prompt database is a living document with new prompts added regularly. In addition to general prompts, use-case-specific prompts will be developed for individual AI systems. For example, custom HR-related questions for evaluating an HR related AI system. In the database, but not revealed to the AI, are success and failure criteria to help analysts determine if an AI's generated response adheres to acceptable boundaries.

Testing for the impact of non-determinism is defined by a procedure in which the AI is prompted with the same question repeatedly (J. Marpet, personal communication, October 1 & 7, 2025). After dozens or hundreds of repeated prompts, the generated answers are evaluated for consistency. In all tests, but especially the repeated test, it is important to ensure prompts are given to the AI separately in different context windows to ensure previous prompts and answers do not influence the testing of future prompts.

Primarily due to model drift, testing is a recurring activity, not a single activity (NIST, 2025a; J. Marpet, personal communication, October 1 & 7, 2025; Stahl et al., 2023). The risk level and use case of each AI will inform which tests are performed, the depth to which they are performed, and the recurrence of testing (weekly, monthly, quarterly, or annually). For ease of testing and to automate a continuous testing program, it is recommended to leverage scripts and API connections to the AI (if made available) to automate the delivery of prompts and collection of responses (J. Marpet, personal communication, October 1 & 7, 2025).

Metrics for accuracy, harm, bias, reliability, toxicity, and other organizational concerns and priorities should be defined and tracked on subsequent tests (NIST, 2025a; Palumbo et al., 2024; Waters, 2025) . A procedure to address AI systems that exceed defined tolerances for each metric should be established (Mökander & Floridi, 2022; Xia et al., 2024). All of these are currently ongoing efforts that the organization is currently working through as additional standards are being developed.

Validation

Occurring alongside testing, we are implementing an end user-driven validation process to ensure that each AI system meets the organization's requirements and operates effectively within its expected context. Ideally, this would involve providing end users with controlled access to test environments, enabling them to interact with the system and provide structured feedback on its functionality, accuracy, and usability (Hickok, 2022; J. Marpet, personal communication, October 1 & 7, 2025; Kuehnert et al., 2025). Members of the AI governance team could supplement this by conducting user interviews or observing their interactions with the AI system to ensure intended functionality and that its outputs align with organizational expectations.

In addition, a recommendation is being developed for the AI governance committee to establish a formal mechanism for user feedback and issue reporting, allowing employees to flag performance concerns, ethical issues, or unexpected system behaviors (Hickok, 2022; Kuehnert et al., 2025; Oliveira, 2023; Themann, 2025). This process would strengthen continuous evaluation and alert governance teams to emerging risks or user-identified issues that may not surface during technical testing. To support ongoing performance monitoring, key performance indicators (KPIs) should also be defined to measure whether the AI system effectively achieves its intended business objectives (Hickok, 2022; Melaku, 2023; Oliveira, 2023; Stahl et al., 2023; Themann, 2025). These metrics should focus on real-world outcomes rather than technical model performance alone (Hickok, 2022; Kuehnert et al., 2025; Themann, 2025).

These recommendations will be reviewed for feasibility as implementation progresses, acknowledging that available resources, budget, and organizational capacity may require adjustments. For example, while structured user interviews and detailed feedback cycles represent the ideal approach, more streamlined validation methods may be adopted if resource constraints arise. The key objective is to balance rigor with practicality, ensuring that validation activities remain proportionate to each system's risk level, use case, and organizational context. Furthermore, just like in the case of testing, the complexity and depth of validation methods used will be highly influenced by the risk level and use case of each AI system (European Union, 2024; Mökander & Floridi, 2022; Themann, 2025; Stahl et al., 2023).

Verification

Verification is the process by which the designers or developers of AI systems confirm the AI system they are building meets the specifications of the internal customer (NIST, 2025b). This process is appropriately reserved for AI systems that require design, development, or configuration by teams other than the end users.

For an organization primarily procuring pre-built AI applications, verification is not a key activity for the governance process. In instances where custom AI applications are built using pre-trained models, verification serves an important purpose for internal development teams.

Currently, the implementation organization's process to verify that AI applications being built adhere to the customer's requirements is delegated to the appropriate internal development teams. Future iterations may see verification processes defined within the AI governance oversight process.

Step 7: RACI

In governance, clearly defined roles, responsibilities, and ownership, including risk ownership, are crucial (AlGhamdi et al., 2020; ISACA, 2018; Selig, 2016). Shared accountability, designation of business and IT roles, and executive sponsorship are important factors that can set organizations up for success (AlGhamdi et al., 2020). RACI is a valuable tool that can help outline who is responsible (R), accountable (A), consulted (C), and informed (I) in the governance program. More specifically, RACI can help define decision rights (who approves algorithmic deployment), responsibilities (who owns the models), consultative partners (such as legal and ethics team members and data-owners), and stakeholders needing to be informed about actions and decision points, such as cross-functional business stakeholders and regulators (Selig, 2016).

In the implementation organization, the RACI framework was planned on being defined early to establish clarity of ownership and decision-making authority. However, as implementation progressed, it became evident to the organization that developing a RACI prematurely, before the underlying AI governance scope and definitions were fully understood, was counterproductive. The organization recognized that the novelty of AI-related activities, the evolving definitions of evaluation and TEVV processes, and the lack of established internal expertise made it difficult to assign clear accountability at the outset. As an example: initially, the organization designated the Chief Information Officer (CIO) as the sole representative for the IT function on the AI governance committee. This decision, while suitable during early formation, later proved limiting as the exclusion of cybersecurity highlighted the need for periodic reassessment of governance representation and scope in response to the evolving understanding of AI risk.

Consequently, the sequencing was adjusted: instead of creating a RACI at the program's inception, the organization prioritized defining process boundaries and key governance components first. Only once these foundational elements involved in

AI governance (especially those defined in scoping, AI evaluation, and TEVV) were articulated could roles and responsibilities be meaningfully assigned. This sequencing helps avoid a pitfall of assigning accountability before the definitions and boundaries are well understood. This adaptive approach reflects a pragmatic lesson learned: that in emerging domains such as AI governance, clarity (what do we govern?) must precede accountability (who owns what?). As a next crucial milestone to clarify ownership and accountability across the AI governance framework, the organization is in the process of refining its RACI.

Step 8: Risk Scoring

The implementation organization has not yet defined the calculations for risk scoring but has intentionally placed risk scoring as a later step due to its reliance on earlier phases (Stahl et al., 2023). Specifically, risk scoring depends on understanding the risk and controls defined in step three (RACM) and the risk levels defined in step five (Mökander & Floridi, 2022; Stahl et al., 2023). While the exact scoring methodology has not yet been formalized, the organization anticipates that risk scoring will incorporate several inputs, including the evaluation results (step four) and TEVV results (step six).

While the precise methodology remains under development, it is understood that to develop an accurate and complete understanding of risk, the prior steps must be well defined (Melaku, 2023; Mökander & Floridi, 2022; Stahl et al., 2023). Positioning this step after the establishment of controls, classification of risk levels by use case, and execution of TEVV activities results in a risk scoring system that encompasses many aspects of AI governance.

Ultimately, the AI risk scoring process will be integrated into the organization's overarching risk management program, ensuring that risks associated with AI systems are evaluated, prioritized, and monitored alongside other enterprise risks. This alignment promotes consistency in risk reporting, facilitates executive oversight, and embeds AI governance within the organization's established risk governance structure.

Steps 1-8: Overarching Considerations Across the AI Governance Lifecycle

Data Governance and Privacy

Artificial intelligence systems are inherently data-dependent, making data governance and privacy foundational to trustworthy AI use (Batool et al., 2023; Mosqueira-Rey et al., 2022; Oliveira, 2023; Taeihagh, 2021). While we begin by defining these concepts during the scoping phase, data governance extends across every stage of the AI governance lifecycle. More precisely, data governance is an established enterprise function that must be aligned and mapped to the AI governance program to ensure consistent data quality, protection, and accountability. The integration of data classification, data ownership, and privacy management within the AI governance framework can assure compliance with privacy regulations and protection of sensitive assets (AlGhamdi et al., 2020). This assumption is confirmed in the article published by Mäntymäki et al., which places AI governance in partial overlap with data governance (2022). Since AI systems deal with data as input and output, data governance must be an overarching consideration in AI governance as a whole.

The mapping of data governance to AI governance is a bidirectional process that occurs throughout multiple implementation phases:

- Risk and Control Matrix: The risks defined in the RACM will inform data governance. Conversely, existing data governance controls will inform the RACM and treatment of risks.
- AI Evaluation: Data governance requirements and policies will inform the intake questions and tasks of the evaluation phase.
- Inherent Risk: AI use cases are mapped to data governance requirements and policies.
- TEVV: Data governance processes inform testing criteria.
- RACI: Unique data use and handling aspects of AI, including data for training, RAG, and handling of AI outputs, require consideration by data governance to assign appropriate data ownership and responsibilities.
- Risk Scoring: The data-governance-informed evaluation and TEVV phases will inform risk scoring.
- User Document: From the RACI, data governance will inform what aspects of data handling are the responsibility of end users.

Due to this inherent synergy between AI governance and data governance, it is best practice to integrate AI-related policies with the components of an (ideally) already existing data governance program, such as data-loss-prevention (DLP) processes, data classifications, role-based access controls, etc. Furthermore, organizations are advised to assign data stewards or owners for critical information systems to assure appropriate ownership and accountability (AlGhamdi et al., 2020; Mäntymäki et al., 2022; Papagiannidis et al., 2022; Themann, 2025). AI and data governance programs must be mapped to each other due to their overlapping nature touching organizational data: AI governance data controls should be mapped to the organization's overall data governance program.

Risk Management

Risk management is not a discrete or isolated activity within the AI governance process but rather a continuous, cross-cutting function that informs decision-making throughout all phases of implementation (AlGhamdi et al., 2020; Kuehnert et al., 2025; Stahl et al., 2023; Themann, 2025). For AI systems, this means identifying risks (model bias, reputation, regulatory, data leakage), assessing magnitude relative to business dependency, integrating risk assessment into the governance lifecycle (monitoring, metrics), and building contingency/resilience plans and incident response (Selig, 2016). Furthermore, risk ownership and risk appetite must be explicitly assigned by management (AlGhamdi et al., 2020; ISACA, 2018).

Within our proposed roadmap, risk considerations begin at the early stages of governance design, when the Risk and Control Matrix (RACM) is established. The RACM defines the organizational risk taxonomy, and outlines the control environment in which AI systems will be assessed and monitored (Gutfraind, 2025; KPMG, 2018; Tjoa et al., 2022). By embedding risk thinking at this initial stage, organizations can ensure that governance mechanisms are not reactive but proactively structured to identify, evaluate, and mitigate risks before AI systems are acquired or deployed.

As implementation progresses, risk management remains a central thread through subsequent activities, particularly during AI evaluation and the remainder of the TEVV processes (Kuehnert et al., Mökander & Floridi, 2022; 2025; Stahl et al., 2023; Themann, 2025). These stages operationalize risk governance by applying structured assessments to AI tools, such as the scoring questionnaire developed in our implementation organization. This continuous assessment framework allows organizations to map identified risks to control actions within the RACM, ensuring traceability between governance principles and operational safeguards.

Finally, the governance process culminates in risk scoring and active risk management of deployed AI systems. At this stage, identified risks are quantified, prioritized, and integrated into the organization's enterprise risk management program (Melaku, 2023; NIST, 2025a; Stahl et al., 2023; Themann, 2025). In the operational phase of an AI system, controls will be monitored and recalibrated based on observed system behavior, incident reports, and performance data (Agbadamasi et al., 2025; Mökander & Floridi, 2022; Stahl et al., 2023). The overall risk management process should be supported with regular internal audits, performance evaluations, and scenario testing (AlGhamdi et al., 2020; Selig, 2016). Measurement, metrics and performance reporting are a great means to monitor and control risk exposure and respond to change as the organization's AI maturity evolves (Melaku, 2023; Oliveira, 2023; Selig, 2016; Themann, 2025).

In summary, risk management must be embedded across all stages of AI governance (from oversight design to continuous monitoring) rather than assigned to a single sequential step (Kuehnert et al., 2025; Mökander & Floridi, 2022; Stahl et al., 2023; Themann, 2025). Treating risk as a pervasive governance dimension enables organizations to maintain an adaptive, responsive posture in the face of rapidly evolving AI technologies and regulatory expectations.

Policies and Standards

Policies and standards represent another foundational and cross-cutting dimension of AI governance, functioning as the connective core that translates organizational intent into consistent operational practice (Agbadamasi et al., 2025; NIST, 2025a; Schneider et al., 2022). Formal, enforced policies aligned with organizational strategies, undergoing regular updates, training, and compliance monitoring are critical to ensuring evolving AI-related threats are mitigated (AlGhamdi et al., 2020; NIST, 2025a; Schneider et al., 2022). From the earliest stages (when governance structures are established), policy development serves to formalize expectations and assign responsibilities for ethical and compliant AI use (Agbadamasi et al., 2025; NIST, 2025a; Schneider et al., 2022). Well-defined policies provide the authority under which governance committees operate, articulate decision rights, and set the parameters for how AI systems are evaluated, approved, and monitored (Batool et al., 2023; NIST, 2025a; Schneider et al., 2022). Without clear policy direction, governance activities risk becoming fragmented or dependent on ad hoc decisions, undermining consistency and accountability.

As implementation progresses, the development of standards becomes critical to operationalizing these policies (Mökander & Floridi, 2022; Schneider et al., 2022; Themann, 2025). During evaluation, testing, and assurance phases, standards guide how AI systems are assessed for reliability, fairness, and security (Agbadamasi et al., 2025; Schneider et al., 2022; Themann, 2025). They establish uniform criteria for TEVV activities, and ensure that vendor assessments, procurement due diligence, and ongoing monitoring follow consistent benchmarks. In this way, standards serve as the operational expression of policy, bridging high-level governance intent with the practical activities that occur across business and technical domains.

Like risk management, the development and maintenance of policies and standards span the entire AI governance lifecycle; they cannot be confined to a single phase. Rather, they operate in parallel with all roadmap activities, ensuring that the implementation of AI systems remains structured, auditable, and aligned with organizational values and compliance obligations (Agbadamasi et al., 2025; NIST, 2025a; Schneider et al., 2022). Accordingly, in our implementation organization, policies and standards were not developed in isolation; rather, they evolved progressively alongside implementation activities. As each governance step has matured, corresponding policies and standards have been drafted to support those functions.

Synthesis of Findings: The Roadmap for AI Governance (RAIG)

Table 5 and Figure 4 summarize the previous eight interconnected steps that comprise our proposed Roadmap for AI Governance (RAIG). The process begins with establishing a governance structure and defining program scope, which together set the foundation for all subsequent activities. The development of the Risk and Control Matrix (RACM) operationalizes this framework by mapping AI-specific risks to corresponding controls, guiding later phases of evaluation, inherent risk assessment, and the Testing, Verification, and Validation components of TEVV. These steps collectively ensure that AI systems are assessed for fairness and compliance before final risk scoring determines their overall risk posture. The RACI framework then defines clear accountability and oversight roles to support consistent execution across functions. Together, these elements create a structured yet adaptive approach to operationalizing AI governance. Each step builds upon and informs the others, forming an iterative process that evolves as organizational maturity and technological complexity increase.

Figure 4. The Roadmap for AI Governance (RAIG).

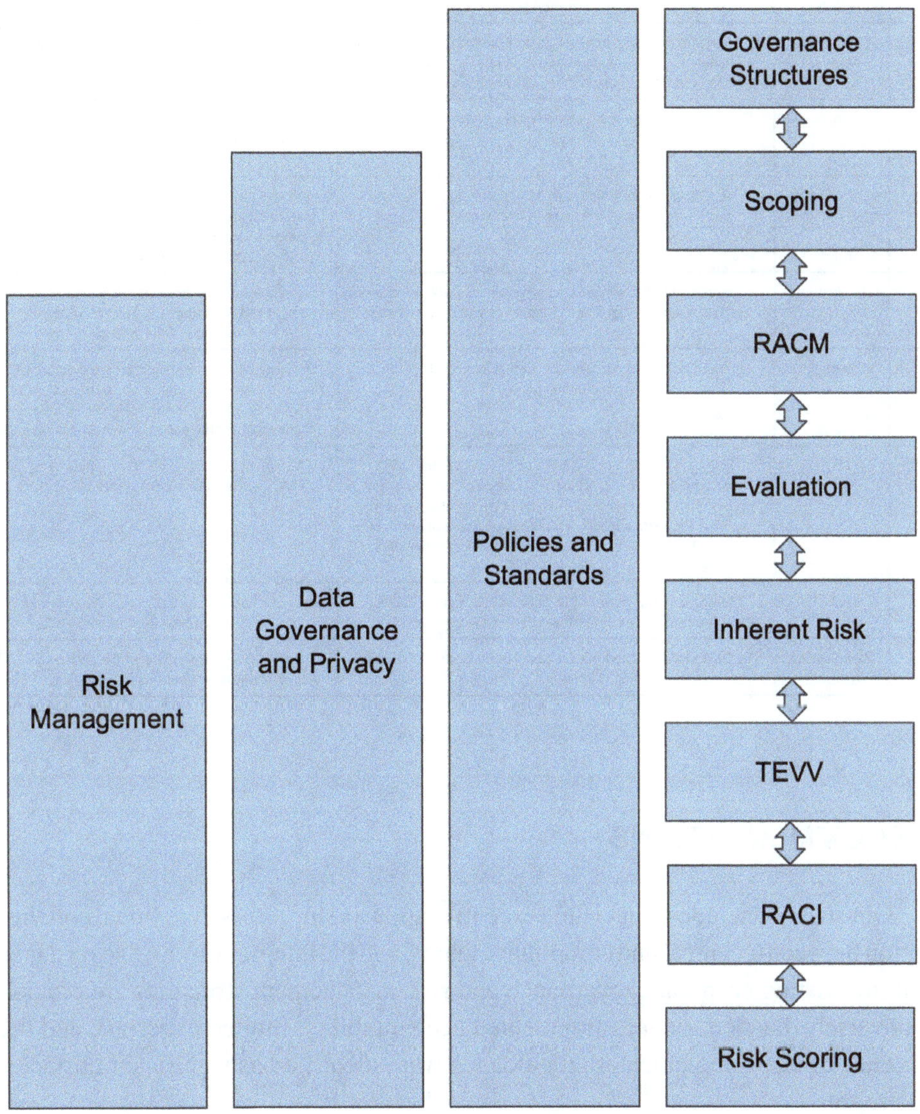

Table 5. The explanation of steps of the Roadmap for AI Governance (RAIG).

#	Item	Summary	What it supports/informs
1	Governance Structure	Procurement of leadership support and formalization of a cross functional group of leaders and individual contributors to inform the development of an AI Governance program.	A governance structure supports all subsequent stages.
2	Scoping	The definition of program objectives, key terms, and in scope AI systems.	Informs the bounds of what AI systems, and therefore what risks and controls, are applicable to the program.
3	RACM	A risk and control matrix (RACM) is a mapped list of applicable AI risks and controls.	Informs the evaluation questionnaire, TEVV processes, and risk scoring by clarifying what aspects of vendor solutions to evaluate and test, and define risks to score against.
4	Evaluation	An assessment of whether an AI system meets defined criteria for performance, safety, and compliance within its intended use.	Evaluation informs inherent risk score of the AI system and, subsequently, the level of testing required of the system.
5	Inherent Risk	An initial risk score of an AI system as a result of the evaluation phase.	Defining inherent risk supports the creation of risk levels and consideration for restricted use of AI systems. The evaluated inherent risk informs the level of testing needed of the AI solution.
6	TEVV	Testing, Verification, and Validation (evaluation having been completed in step 4) are the defined processes to test the accuracy, fairness, reliability, and toxicity of AI systems, validate the system meets organizational requirements, and verify that internally developed systems meet stakeholder requirements.	Along with inherent risk, the outputs of AI TEVV are used to inform a final risk score.
7	RACI	The definition of responsible, accountable, consulted, and informed members of the AI governance process.	The governance structure, evaluation processes, and TEVV processes inform the RACI.
8	Risk Scoring	The final likelihood and impact calculations of the AI solution.	Risk scoring is informed by the outputs of evaluation, inherent risk, and TEVV.

RECOMMENDATIONS

Our study concludes that visible executive sponsorship, cross-functional collaboration between technical and compliance teams, and the integration of AI governance within existing corporate governance and risk-management structures are crucial. Conversely, barriers such as fragmented accountability, limited expertise, and the absence of clear implementation guidance were identified as significant obstacles to progress.

During this initial phase of AI governance development, our partner organization has encountered a range of implementation challenges that remain under active resolution, reflecting the complexity of translating governance principles into operational practice. Integrating AI governance within existing enterprise processes has proven complex, as the initiative intersects with many established structures.

As an example, for the evaluation of AI systems, an appropriate intake process is critical. Procurement and evaluation (even without considering AI) is broken across many tools and functions and visibility is poor. When new vendors are onboarded, they go through third-party risk assessments (or TPRM, handled by the cybersecurity team), technical assessments (led by the technical architects and involving various IT teams), procurement checks, and now an AI review. Procurement uses one tool, TPRM uses another, and the technical architectural reviews are conducted in a third tool. A significant challenge is combining these functions in a way that the process is streamlined and makes onboarding smooth for end users.

Efforts to streamline these functions have surfaced institutional barriers, organizational silos and competing agendas, illustrating the political and procedural challenges inherent in large organizations. This highlights that early stakeholder engagement and process alignment across these domains are essential prerequisites for effective AI governance implementation. Developing an AI governance program in isolation is insufficient; success depends on proactively engaging these adjacent stakeholders early and harmonizing governance workflows before formal implementation begins.

Another challenge observed involves organizational resistance to change, which can significantly hinder the adaptability of AI governance structures. Given the rapid evolution of AI technologies, governance models established under earlier assumptions may quickly lose relevance. For instance, at the time of initial design, the organization designated the Chief Information Officer (CIO) as the sole representative for the entire IT function within the AI governance committee. While this arrangement appeared appropriate during early formation, it inadvertently excluded key domains such as cybersecurity from active participation in governance decision-making.

As the organizational understanding of AI risk has matured, this exclusion has become increasingly problematic, demonstrating the need for periodic reassessment of governance representation and scope. More broadly, institutional reluctance to revisit prior decisions can cause AI governance programs to become outdated or misaligned with emerging technological, regulatory, and risk landscapes. Sustaining an effective governance function therefore requires a commitment to continuous review, flexibility, and structural adaptation as the AI ecosystem evolves.

Finally, another key lesson learned is that clarity must precede accountability. While many governance programs begin by defining a RACI framework early to establish ownership, the organization found that doing so before fully understanding the scope, processes, and technical dimensions of AI governance was premature. The evolving nature of AI-related activities and limited initial expertise made early role assignment impractical and potentially misleading. Instead, sequencing the RACI after defining core governance components (such as scoping, evaluation, and TEVV) proved more effective, ensuring that responsibilities were grounded in a clear understanding of what was being governed. This experience highlights the importance of allowing governance structures to mature iteratively as organizational understanding deepens.

CONCLUSIONS

This study set out to address a central gap in the AI governance landscape: how organizations that adopt AI systems can establish proportionate and effective oversight mechanisms. Through the applied development of the Roadmap for AI Governance (RAIG), this work operationalized our conceptual AI Governance Implementation Framework (AGIF), demonstrating how theory can be translated into practice. This applied study confirms the AGIF's first domain (oversight mechanisms) and provides practical insight into how these structures can be implemented in complex, regulated environments. The implication of the current conceptual and practical RAIG includes providing a transferable governance model that enhances accountability, transparency, and trust in AI-enabled decision-making, thereby supporting the responsible and ethical use of AI technologies across sectors.

The findings confirm that responsible AI adoption requires both structural readiness and iterative learning with governance processes that evolve through practice, feedback, and collaboration. The study shows that the foundations of successful AI governance are established through clear accountability, adaptive oversight, and integration with existing enterprise risk and data governance functions. Governance maturity emerges when these mechanisms move beyond static policy documents to living systems of evaluation, testing, and feedback.

For practitioners, the study highlights that AI governance must begin with clearly defined oversight mechanisms before progressing toward operational controls and continuous feedback. Building the foundational structures (leadership committees, clear scoping definitions, and risk mapping) creates the organizational readiness required to translate principles into practice. Attempting to embed detailed processes or accountability structures prematurely can create friction and confusion. AI governance is an evolving organizational capability rather than a one-time compliance activity that requires integration into existing enterprise structures (such as data governance and risk management) and alignment across business functions. Following these 7 recommendations, executives and governance leaders can successfully operationalize AI oversight within their own organizations:

1. Establish a formal AI governance oversight structure early. Create a cross-functional AI Governance Committee, Council, or Center of Excellence that brings together leadership, compliance, risk, data governance, and technical experts. This structure should anchor accountability and serve as the central body for approving AI use cases and setting standards.
2. Define scope and terminology before building controls. Establish clear organizational definitions for "AI," "machine learning," "deep learning," and "generative AI," identifying which systems fall within governance scope. This

shared language prevents confusion, streamlines review processes, and aligns policy boundaries.

3. Develop a practical Risk and Control Matrix (RACM) as the foundation of AI risk management. Map AI-specific risks to mitigating controls early in program development. This enables traceability, supports evaluation and audit processes, and ensures consistent risk treatment across AI systems.
4. Implement proportionate evaluation processes linked to inherent risk. Use structured evaluation questionnaires to assess AI systems based on risk level. Align the depth of assessment, testing, and approval workflows with each system's inherent risk classification to maintain efficiency and proportionality.
5. Integrate AI governance with existing enterprise programs. Align AI oversight with current risk, cybersecurity, data governance, and procurement processes. This minimizes duplication, ensures consistent data protection practices, and embeds AI governance into familiar organizational workflows.
6. Adopt an iterative, feedback-driven implementation model. Treat governance as an evolving capability that matures through learning. Regularly review and refine processes, RACMs, and evaluation tools to adapt to changing technologies and organizational realities.
7. Embed continuous review and alignment across stakeholders. Periodically reassess governance representation, committee membership, and policy applicability as AI use expands. Governance programs should remain flexible, ensuring representation of technical, ethical, and operational perspectives as the landscape evolves. This will also help set up change management success as the operational activities are launched.

Collectively, RAIG and these recommendations offer a pragmatic roadmap for transforming abstract AI principles into implementable governance practice, bridging the gap between conceptual frameworks and real-world implementation. By situating governance within the operational realities of AI adopters, it provides a roadmap for institutions across sectors to deploy AI responsibly, advancing both organizational accountability and societal trust in an era defined by intelligent systems.

Beyond immediate applications, the broader implication of this research is that AI governance should be understood as an organizational learning system that develops through reflection, testing, and iteration. Embedding adaptive oversight mechanisms enables organizations to remain resilient in the face of evolving technologies and regulatory landscapes. In doing so, AI governance becomes not merely a risk-containment function, but a foundation for trustworthy innovation.

The findings of this study also carry significant implications for AI policy and regulatory design. As organizations grapple with translating abstract governance principles into operational practice, it becomes evident that effective AI policy must move beyond prescriptive compliance checklists toward adaptive, capability-oriented frameworks that enable contextual implementation. Policies should encourage organizations to establish governance mechanisms that are responsive to continuous learning and feedback, mirroring the adaptive cycles observed in our implementation roadmap. Regulators and policymakers can support this evolution by promoting interoperability between governance standards, fostering transparency in AI system procurement and oversight, and incentivizing cross-sector learning through shared repositories of governance practices. In doing so, policy can act not as a static constraint but as an enabler of adaptive governance, ensuring that accountability, fairness, and transparency are sustained across the AI lifecycle while leaving room for innovation and organizational maturity to evolve.

RECOMMENDATIONS FOR FUTURE RESEARCH

In this chapter, we addressed how governance principles can be translated into practical oversight mechanisms for organizations functioning primarily as AI consumers. At the time of submission of this chapter, our focus centered around the oversight mechanisms of AGIF that determine operational practice. The findings suggest that while AGIF's dimensions for governance oversight remain valid, their application and future iterations should emphasize adaptive sequencing, resource feasibility, and stakeholder alignment to better support real-world implementation. The findings also indicate that governance maturity evolves through practice; structures, policies, and accountability must be refined iteratively as understanding deepens and risks emerge.

As the next phase of our roadmapping work explores the operationalization (technical translation) and feedback components (learning and measurement) of AGIF, these findings will inform refinements to both AGIF and RAIG, ensuring it evolves from a conceptual model into a fully tested, practical framework that guides organizations through the full lifecycle of AI governance implementation. This will also strengthen our ability to assess its practicality, adaptability, and effectiveness in guiding AI governance implementation. Through continuous monitoring of this applied study, the research will evaluate how the roadmap performs under operational conditions, including how governance mechanisms function within existing compliance structures, what barriers emerge in daily use, and how feedback loops can be optimized for continuous learning and improvement.

The final phase of our broader research (Phase 3) will focus on practitioner validation of our proposed roadmap across diverse industry contexts for further scalability and practicality. It will ensure practical relevance and usability by further validating AGIF and RAIG through engagement with industry practitioners. Participants will include representatives from organizations in various sectors, as well as members of AI governance committees and CISOs. Practitioner feedback will be gathered through online surveys and semi-structured interviews. These discussions will provide additional structured feedback on the proposed roadmap elements, such as governance roles, implementation sequencing, and metrics for oversight. The purpose of this engagement is to refine the roadmap through expert validation, ensuring that it reflects the realities of the broader organizational governance practice and aligns with existing operational processes across industry contexts.

In addition, comparative data between sectors (healthcare, finance, manufacturing, aviation) will help determine which components of AI governance are universally applicable and which must be contextually adapted. Future inquiry may also explore organizational maturity models, linking the roadmap's stages to measurable indicators of AI governance readiness. In addition, practitioner-led studies can deepen understanding of how human factors (such as culture, leadership commitment, and workforce capability) affect the successful adoption of governance mechanisms. Deeper mapping with existing high-level frameworks (NIST, ISO, etc.) would provide even more clarity for practitioners hoping to translate these findings into organizational governance plans and processes.

By integrating these next steps, the broader research program will move from theoretical and conceptual development toward a tested and refined implementation model for AI governance, ensuring that our framework evolves through iterative feedback and empirical validation. This continued work will not only strengthen the evidence base but also support the creation of actionable guidance and toolkits that organizations can readily apply to govern AI responsibly in complex, real-world settings.

ACKNOWLEDGMENT

This research was partially supported by the Embry-Riddle Aeronautical University Faculty Research Development Program.

REFERENCES

Agbadamasi, T. O., Opoku, L. K., Adukpo, T. K., & Mensah, N. (2025). Artificial Intelligence Governance in U.S. corporations: Legal and ethical implications for business intelligence and regulatory compliance. *International Journal of Research Publication and Reviews*, *6*(3), 3083–3089. DOI: 10.55248/gengpi.6.0325.11124

AlGhamdi, S., Win, K. T., & Vlahu-Gjorgievska, E. (2020). Information security governance challenges and critical success factors: Systematic review. *Computers & Security*, *99*, 102030. Advance online publication. DOI: 10.1016/j.cose.2020.102030

American Medical Association. (2024, December 30). *CPT Appendix S: AI taxonomy for medical services & procedures*. https://www.ama-assn.org/practice-management/cpt/cpt-appendix-s-ai-taxonomy-medical-services-procedures

Anderljung, M., Barnhart, J., Korinek, A., Leung, J., O'Keefe, C., Whittlestone, J., Avin, S., Brundage, M., Bullock, J., Cass-Beggs, D., Chang, B., Collins, T., Fist, T., Hadfield, G., Hayes, A., Ho, L., Hooker, S., Horvitz, E., Kolt, N., . . . Wolf, K. (2023). *Frontier AI Regulation: Managing Emerging Risks to Public Safety*. https://doi.org//arXiv.2307.03718DOI: 10.48550

Argyris, C. (1976). Single-loop and double-loop models in research on decision making. *Administrative Science Quarterly*, *21*(3), 363–375. DOI: 10.2307/2391848

Argyris, C., & Schön, D. A. (1978). *Organizational learning: A theory of action perspective*. Addison-Wesley.

Argyris, C., & Schön, D. A. (1996). *Organizational learning II: Theory, method, and practice*. Addison-Wesley.

Bassett, C. (2018). The computational therapeutic: Exploring Weizenbaum's eliza as a history of the present. *AI & Society*, *34*(4), 803–812. DOI: 10.1007/s00146-018-0825-9

Basten, D., & Haamann, T. (2018). Approaches for organizational learning: A literature review. *SAGE Open*, *8*(3), 2158244018794224. Advance online publication. DOI: 10.1177/2158244018794224

Batool, A., Zowghi, D., & Bano, M. (2023). Responsible AI governance: A systematic literature review. *arXiv:2401.10896*. https://doi.org//arXiv.2401.10896DOI: 10.48550

Batool, A., Zowghi, D., & Bano, M. (2025). AI governance: A systematic literature review. *AI and Ethics*, *5*(3), 3265–3279. DOI: 10.1007/s43681-024-00653-w

Benraouane, S. A. (2024). *AI management system auditing and compliance according to ISO/IEC 42001*. Routledge.

Birkstedt, T., Minkkinen, M., Tandon, A., & Mäntymäki, M. (2023). AI governance: Themes, knowledge gaps and future agendas. *Internet Research*, *33*(7), 133–167. DOI: 10.1108/INTR-01-2022-0042

Bracken, A., Reilly, C., Feeley, A., Sheehan, E., Merghani, K., & Feeley, I. (2025). Artificial Intelligence (AI) – Powered Documentation Systems in Healthcare: A Systematic Review. *Journal of Medical Systems*, *49*(1), 28. Advance online publication. DOI: 10.1007/s10916-025-02157-4 PMID: 39966286

Brunner, R., Steelman, T. A., Coe-Juell, L., Cromley, C. M., Edwards, C. M., & Tucker, D. W. (2005). *Adaptive governance: Integrating science, policy, and decision making*. Columbia University Press.

Castro, V. D., Martín-Peña, M. L., Martínez, E. M., & Salgado, M. (2025). Combining action research with design science as a qualitative research methodology. An application to service (operations) management research. *International Journal of Qualitative Methods*, *24*, 1–15. DOI: 10.1177/16094069241312018

Cedergren, A., & Hassel, H. (2022). Using action design research for developing and implementing a method for risk assessment and continuity management. *Safety Science*, *151*, 105727. Advance online publication. DOI: 10.1016/j.ssci.2022.105727

Chaffin, B. C., Gosnell, H., & Cosens, B. A. (2014). A decade of adaptive governance scholarship: Synthesis and future directions. *Ecology and Society*, *19*(3), art56. https://www.jstor.org/stable/26269646. DOI: 10.5751/ES-06824-190356

Cloud Security Alliance. (2025). *AI controls matrix*. https://cloudsecurityalliance.org/artifacts/ai-controls-matrix#

Cohen, J. (1979). Non-deterministic algorithms. *ACM Computing Surveys*, *11*(2), 79–94. DOI: 10.1145/356770.356773

Cooper, A. F., Frankle, J., & De Sa, C. (2022). Non-determinism and the lawlessness of machine learning code. *Proceedings of the 2022 Symposium on Computer Science and Law*, 1–8. DOI: 10.1145/3511265.3550446

Deloitte. (2024). *Governance of AI: A critical imperative for today's boards.* https://www2.deloitte.com/content/dam/Deloitte/mx/Documents/risk/2024/DI_Governance-of-AI_A-critical-imperative-for-todays-boards.pdf

Dietz, T., Ostrom, E., & Stern, P. C. (2003). The struggle to govern the commons. *Science, 302*(5652), 1907–1912. DOI: 10.1126/science.1091015 PMID: 14671286

European Union. (2024). *Regulation 2024/1689 Artificial Intelligence Act.* https://eur-lex.europa.eu/legal-content/EN/TXT/?uri=CELEX%3A32024R1689

Fernández-Llorca, D., Gómez, E., Sánchez, I., & Mazzini, G. (2024). An interdisciplinary account of the terminological choices by EU policymakers ahead of the Final Agreement on the AI Act: AI system, general purpose AI system, Foundation model, and Generative AI. *Artificial Intelligence and Law, 33*(4), 875–888. DOI: 10.1007/s10506-024-09412-y

Fiol, C. M., & Lyles, M. A. (1985). Organizational learning. *Academy of Management Review, 10*(4), 803–813. https://www.proquest.com/scholarly-journals/organizational-learning/docview/230008225/se-2. DOI: 10.2307/258048

Folke, C., Hahn, T., Olsson, P., & Norberg, J. (2005). Adaptive governance of social-ecological systems. *Annual Review of Environment and Resources, 30*(1), 441–473. DOI: 10.1146/annurev.energy.30.050504.144511

Gajjar, D. (2023). *Artificial Intelligence: An Explainer.* DOI: 10.58248/PB57

Ganesh, N. B., Siddineni, D., & Reddy, B.N Balaji Ganesh. (2025). Corporate governance in the age of AI: Ethical oversight and accountability frameworks. *Journal of Information Systems Engineering & Management, 10*(35s), 1141–1148. Advance online publication. DOI: 10.52783/jisem.v10i35s.6285

Garvin, D. A. (1993). Building a learning organization. *Harvard Business Review, 71*(4), 78–91. PMID: 10127041

Gutfraind, A. (2025). *On Strategies for Risk Management and Decision Making under Uncertainty Shared across Multiple Fields.* https://doi.org//arXiv.2309.03133DOI: 10.48550

Hickok, M. (2022). Public Procurement of Artificial Intelligence Systems: New risks and future proofing. *AI & Society, 39*(3), 1213–1227. DOI: 10.1007/s00146-022-01572-2 PMID: 36212228

Huang, J. C., & Newell, S. (2003). Knowledge integration processes and dynamics within the context of cross-functional projects. *International Journal of Project Management, 21*(3), 167–176. DOI: 10.1016/S0263-7863(02)00091-1

IBM. (2024, January 10). *Data suggests growth in enterprise adoption of AI is due to widespread deployment by early adopters, but barriers keep 40% in the exploration and experimentation phases*. https://www.prnewswire.com/news-releases/data-suggests-growth-in-enterprise-adoption-of-ai-is-due-to-widespread-deployment-by-early-adopters-but-barriers-keep-40-in-the-exploration-and-experimentation-phases-302030592.html

International Organization for Standardization. (2020). *ISO/IEC TR 24028:2020, Information technology — Artificial intelligence — Overview of trustworthiness in artificial intelligence*. https://www.iso.org/standard/77608.html

International Organization for Standardization. (2023). *ISO/IEC 42001:2023, Information technology — Artificial intelligence — Management system*. https://www.iso.org/standard/42001

ISACA. (2018). *COBIT® 2019 Framework: Introduction & methodology*. ISACA.

ISACA. (2024). *Artificial intelligence audit toolkit*. ISACA.

Jobin, A., Ienca, M., & Vayena, E. (2019). The global landscape of AI ethics guidelines. *Nature Machine Intelligence*, *1*(9), 389–399. DOI: 10.1038/s42256-019-0088-2

Kaul, V., Enslin, S., & Gross, S. A. (2020). History of artificial intelligence in medicine. *Gastrointestinal Endoscopy*, *92*(4), 807–812. DOI: 10.1016/j.gie.2020.06.040 PMID: 32565184

Kilian, R., Jäck, L., & Ebel, D. (2025). European AI standards - Technical standardization and implementation challenges under the EU AI Act. *European Journal of Risk Regulation*, *16*(3), 1038–1062. DOI: 10.1017/err.2025.10032

KPMG LLP (UK). (2018). *AI Risk and Controls Matrix*. https://assets.kpmg.com/content/dam/kpmgsites/uk/pdf/2018/09/ai-risk-and-controls-matrix.pdf

Kuehnert, B., Kim, R., Forlizzi, J., & Heidari, H. (2025). The "who", "what", and "how" of responsible AI governance: A systematic review and meta-analysis of (actor, stage)-specific tools. *Proceedings of the 2025 ACM Conference on Fairness, Accountability, and Transparency*, 2991–3005. DOI: 10.1145/3715275.3732191

Mäntymäki, M., Minkkinen, M., Birkstedt, T., & Viljanen, M. (2022). Defining organizational AI governance. *AI and Ethics*, *2*(4), 603–609. DOI: 10.1007/s43681-022-00143-x

Martinez-Requejo, S., Jimenez García, E., Redondo Duarte, S., Ruiz Lázaro, J., Puertas Sanz, E., & Mariscal Vivas, G. (2024). AI-Driven Student Assistance: Chatbots Redefining University Support. *INTED Proceedings*, *1*, 617–625. DOI: 10.21125/inted.2024.0221

McKinsey & Company. (2025). *The state of AI: Global survey 2025.* https://www.mckinsey.com/capabilities/quantumblack/our-insights/the-state-of-ai

Melaku, H. M. (2023). A dynamic and adaptive cybersecurity governance framework. *Journal of Cybersecurity and Privacy*, *3*(3), 327–350. DOI: 10.3390/jcp3030017

MITRE. (n.d.). *ATLAS Matrix.* https://atlas.mitre.org/matrices/ATLAS

Mökander, J., & Floridi, L. (2022). Operationalising AI governance through Ethics-based auditing: An industry case study. *AI and Ethics*, *3*(2), 451–468. DOI: 10.1007/s43681-022-00171-7 PMID: 35669570

Mosqueira-Rey, E., Hernández-Pereira, E., Alonso-Ríos, D., Bobes-Bascarán, J., & Fernández-Leal, Á. (2022). Human-in-the-loop machine learning: A state of the art. *Artificial Intelligence Review*, *56*(4), 3005–3054. DOI: 10.1007/s10462-022-10246-w

National Institute of Standards and Technology [NIST]. (2020). *Integrating Cybersecurity and Enterprise Risk Management (ERM).* DOI: 10.6028/NIST.IR.8286

National Institute of Standards and Technology [NIST]. (2025a). *AI risk management framework.* https://www.nist.gov/itl/ai-risk-management-framework

National Institute of Standards and Technology [NIST]. (2025b). *Outline: Proposed zero draft for a standard on AI testing, evaluation, verification, and validation.* https://www.nist.gov/system/files/documents/2025/07/15/Outline_%20Proposed%20Zero%20Draft%20for%20a%20Standard%20on%20AI%20TEVV-for-web.pdf

Odeyemi, O., Mhlongo, N. Z., Nwankwo, E. E., & Soyombo, O. T. (2024). Reviewing the role of AI in Fraud Detection and Prevention in Financial Services. *International Journal of Science and Research Archive*, *11*(1), 2101–2110. DOI: 10.30574/ijsra.2024.11.1.0279

OECD. (2024). *Explanatory memorandum on the updated OECD definition of an AI system.* https://www.oecd.org/content/dam/oecd/en/publications/reports/2024/03/explanatory-memorandum-on-the-updated-oecd-definition-of-an-ai-system_3c815e51/623da898-en.pdf

Oliveira, D. (2023). Navigating responsible AI adoption. *Proceedings of the 15th International Joint Conference on Knowledge Discovery, Knowledge Engineering and Knowledge Management*, 339–345. DOI: 10.5220/0012262600003598

Palumbo, G., Carneiro, D., & Alves, V. (2024). Objective metrics for ethical AI: A systematic literature review. *International Journal of Data Science and Analytics, 20*(2), 247–267. DOI: 10.1007/s41060-024-00541-w

Panchagnula, V. D. (2025). Ethical AI and responsible automation: Building trust in GenAI-powered systems. *Hampton Global Business Review.* https://hgbr.org/research_articles/ethical-ai-and-responsible-automation-building-trust-in-genai-powered-systems/

Papagiannidis, E., Enholm, I. M., Dremel, C., Mikalef, P., & Krogstie, J. (2022). Toward AI governance: Identifying best practices and potential barriers and outcomes. *Information Systems Frontiers, 25*(1), 123–141. DOI: 10.1007/s10796-022-10251-y PMID: 35464171

Phuong, M., Aitchison, M., Catt, E., Cogan, S., Kaskasoli, A., Krakovna, V., Lindner, D., Rahtz, M., Assael, Y., Hodkinson, S., Howard, H., Lieberum, T., Kumar, R., Abi Raad, M., Webson, A., Ho, L., Lin, S., Farquhar, S., Hutter, M., . . . Shevlane, T. (2024). *Evaluating Frontier Models for Dangerous Capabilities.* https://doi.org//arXiv.2403.13793DOI: 10.48550

Reuel, A., & Undheim, T. A. (2024). Generative AI needs adaptive governance. *arXiv preprint.* https://doi.org//arXiv.2406.04554DOI: 10.48550

Ribeiro, D., Rocha, T., Pinto, G., Cartaxo, B., Amaral, M., Davila, N., & Camargo, A. (2025). Toward effective AI governance: A review of principles. *arXiv.* https://doi.org//arXiv.2505.23417DOI: 10.48550

Schneider, J., Abraham, R., Meske, C., & Vom Brocke, J. (2022). Artificial intelligence governance for businesses. *Information Systems Management, 40*(3), 229–249. DOI: 10.1080/10580530.2022.2085825

Schwengber, J. G. (Ed.). (2024). *Organizational learning as relational governance.* Springer., DOI: 10.1007/978-3-031-52015-0

Sein, M. K., Henfridsson, O., Purao, S., Rossi, M., & Lindgren, R. (2011). Action design research. *Management Information Systems Quarterly, 35*(1), 37–56. DOI: 10.2307/23043488

Selig, G. J. (2016). IT governance-An integrated framework and roadmap: How to plan, deploy and sustain for improved effectiveness. *Journal of International Technology and Information Management, 25*(1), 55–76. DOI: 10.58729/1941-6679.1252

Senge, P. M. (1990). *The fifth discipline: The art and practice of the learning organization.* Doubleday.

Stahl, B. C., Antoniou, J., Bhalla, N., Brooks, L., Jansen, P., Lindqvist, B., Kirichenko, A., Marchal, S., Rodrigues, R., Santiago, N., Warso, Z., & Wright, D. (2023). A systematic review of Artificial Intelligence Impact Assessments. *Artificial Intelligence Review, 56*(11), 12799–12831. DOI: 10.1007/s10462-023-10420-8 PMID: 37362899

Taeihagh, A. (2021). Governance of artificial intelligence. *Policy and Society, 44*(2), 137–157. DOI: 10.1080/14494035.2021.1928377

Themann, S. (2025). Challenges and strategies used in implementing AI governance: A systematic literature review. *Stockholm University.* https://su.diva-portal.org/smash/get/diva2:1983756/FULLTEXT01.pdf

Tjoa, S., Temper, P. K., Temper, M., Zanol, J., Wagner, M., & Holzinger, A. (2022). Airman: An artificial intelligence (AI) Risk Management System. *2022 International Conference on Advanced Enterprise Information System (AEIS)*, 72–81. DOI: 10.1109/AEIS59450.2022.00017

Triguero, I., Molina, D., Poyatos, J., Del Ser, J., & Herrera, F. (2024). General Purpose Artificial Intelligence Systems (GPAIS): Properties, definition, taxonomy, societal implications and responsible governance. *Information Fusion, 103*, 102135. DOI: 10.1016/j.inffus.2023.102135

Van Assche, K., Valentinov, V., & Verschraegen, G. (2022). Adaptive governance: Learning from what organizations do and managing the role they play. *Kybernetes, 51*(5), 1738–1758. DOI: 10.1108/K-11-2020-0759

Waters, G. (2025). *Testing, Evaluation, Verification and Validation (TEVV) of Digital Twins: A Comprehensive Framework. arXiv* https://doi.org//arXiv.2507.04555DOI: 10.48550

Williams, J. (2025, August 19). *Agentic AI: Understanding and security the next wave of AI systems.* [Webinar]. IANS, Virtual.

World Economic Forum. (2023). *Adopting AI responsibly: Guidelines for procurement of AI solutions by the private sector.* https://www3.weforum.org/docs/WEF_Adopting_AI_Responsibly_Guidelines_for_Procurement_of_AI_Solutions_by_the_Private_Sector_2023.pdf

Wyborn, C. (2015). Co-productive governance: A relational framework for adaptive governance. *Global Environmental Change, 30*, 56–67. DOI: 10.1016/j.gloenvcha.2014.10.009

Xia, B., Lu, Q., Zhu, L., Lee, S. U., Liu, Y., & Xing, Z. (2024). Towards a responsible AI metrics catalogue: A collection of metrics for AI accountability. *Proceedings of the IEEE/ACM 3rd International Conference on AI Engineering - Software Engineering for AI*, 100–111. DOI: 10.1145/3644815.3644959

Chapter 7
The Cyberpsychological Dimensions of Healthcare Cybersecurity Crime Risks

Adina Lundy
https://orcid.org/0000-0001-7564-2110
University of Rhode Island, USA

Darrell Norman Burrell
https://orcid.org/0000-0002-4675-9544
Marymount University, USA & Pellegrino Center for Clinical Bioethics, Georgetown University, USA

Allison Huff
https://orcid.org/0000-0001-6102-8013
College of Medicine-Tucson, University of Arizona, USA

ABSTRACT

This study examines the cyberpsychological dimensions of cybersecurity risks in healthcare, emphasizing how human cognition, emotion, and organizational culture shape vulnerability within digitally transformed care environments. As healthcare integrates electronic health records, AI diagnostics, and telehealth systems, leaders, often trained in clinical or administrative domains, remain largely untrained in human factors psychology, limiting their capacity to address behavioral risk. Cyberattacks increasingly exploit cognitive biases such as urgency, authority, and trust, while clinicians under high cognitive load and ethical pressure frequently bypass protocols perceived as obstructive to patient care. Through an integrative,

DOI: 10.4018/979-8-3373-9918-8.ch007

evidence-based framework grounded in cyberpsychological theory, this research aims to align technical controls with user behavior, leadership awareness, and institutional culture. The goal is to transition healthcare cybersecurity from a reactive, technology-centric model to a proactive, human-centered paradigm that fosters resilience, ethical responsibility, and trust across clinical and digital ecosystems.

INTRODUCTION

The healthcare sector is undergoing a profound transformation driven by the integration of advanced digital technologies, including electronic health records (EHRs), telehealth platforms, wearable biosensors, and artificial intelligence-enabled diagnostic tools (Turuk, 2020; Hermes et al., 2020; Yogev et al., 2023). While these technologies promise significant gains in care efficiency, personalization, and clinical precision, they also expose the healthcare environment to a distinct and escalating category of cyberpsychological risksrisks shaped not only by technological vulnerabilities but also by human cognitive behavior, emotional bias, and institutional culture.

This risk landscape is particularly complex in healthcare because the decision-makers responsible for cybersecurity policy, executives, administrators, and physician-leaders, are typically trained in clinical or operational disciplines, not in human factors psychology or behavioral science. As a result, many cybersecurity interventions are designed with insufficient consideration for how employees actually perceive, interpret, and respond to cyber threats. For instance, while machine learning systems may enhance anomaly detection, their deployment often fails to account for how clinicians interact with alert fatigue or how social engineering tactics exploit emotional urgency and hierarchical deference, factors well documented in cyberpsychological literature (Kioskli et al., 2023; Klimburg-Witjes & Wentland, 2021).

In an environment where time pressure, clinical acuity, and moral responsibility dominate professional behavior, human error becomes a persistent and predictable vector for compromise. The most common breaches stem not from technical exploits but from cognitive and psychological manipulation, phishing emails that mimic trusted sources, fake credential prompts that play on urgency, or subtle behavioral cues that lead to over-disclosure (Barlow et al., 2020). These attacks succeed not merely because systems are misconfigured, but because staff are cognitively overloaded, behaviorally conditioned to bypass controls, and psychologically unprepared to detect deception.

THE CYBERSECURITY PARADOX AND THE COGNITIVE BURDEN OF DIGITAL TRANSFORMATION

As healthcare organizations expand their digital ecosystems, they inadvertently broaden the psychological and behavioral attack surface. The shift toward data-driven, real-time care has significantly increased reliance on digital interfaces, often without corresponding increases in staff cyberliteracy or resilience to manipulation (Cartwright, 2023). The paradox is stark: the same technologies that promise operational modernization also increase exposure to threat actors who weaponize human cognition. This makes security transformation not only a technological imperative, but also a behavioral and psychological one.

The challenge is exacerbated by healthcare's unique informational burden. With healthcare producing nearly 30% of the world's total data (Gopal et al., 2019), clinicians and staff must routinely navigate vast, high-stakes datasets under intense time constraints. The cognitive load required to manage complex patient information is further strained by multilayered security procedures, which are often perceived as obstructive rather than protective. Leaders untrained in cyberpsychology may misinterpret noncompliance as negligence rather than what it often is, an adaptive response to system design that ignores human limitations.

Healthcare leadership often underestimates how deeply culture, stress, and perceptual framing influence behavior in digital spaces. For example, if a nurse bypasses multi-factor authentication during a code blue scenario, it is not a rejection of policy but a reflection of embedded cultural assumptions that prioritize immediate patient care above all else. These assumptions, rarely articulated, but deeply felt, are precisely the type of latent vulnerabilities that must be identified and reshaped through cyberpsychological awareness and leadership retraining.

THE PSYCHOLOGICAL VALUE OF HEALTH DATA

The heightened value of healthcare data in illicit markets further complicates the landscape. Protected health information (PHI) and personally identifiable information (PII) are not only sensitive but psychologically significant; they represent core aspects of identity, vulnerability, and trust (Argaw et al., 2020). A breach is not merely a privacy event, it is a psychological betrayal with long-term consequences. Victims may experience anxiety, loss of trust in their provider, and a reluctance to disclose critical medical information in future encounters, which in turn can undermine diagnostic accuracy and continuity of care (Playing with Lives, 2021).

Healthcare leaders, lacking formal training in cyberpsychological dynamics, may focus disproportionately on encryption, access controls, or compliance frameworks, without addressing the emotional, cognitive, and behavioral underpinnings of both cyber risk and response. An effective cybersecurity strategy must therefore integrate both technical and psychological protections, aligning user behavior with institutional safeguards through empathetic design, trust-building communication, and psychologically informed risk messaging.

PROBLEM STATEMENT

Cybersecurity risks in healthcare are not merely technological in origin, they are deeply rooted in human behavior, perception, and organizational culture. Despite the growing frequency, cost, and operational disruption caused by cyberattacks, most healthcare leaders lack formal training in the behavioral sciences underpinning cyberpsychological vulnerabilities. While the sector continues to invest in advanced tools and infrastructures, leadership's limited exposure to human factors psychology hinders their ability to design and implement interventions that align with the behavioral realities of clinical practice (Coventry et al., 2020). This disconnect is evidenced by the persistent prevalence of breaches, the growing sophistication of social engineering attacks, and the limited effectiveness of traditional compliance-based training models.

From 2022 to 2023, the number of cyber incidents in U.S. healthcare systems rose by 9.4%, with average breach costs surpassing $10 million, double the average across other sectors (Tin et al., 2023; Alanazi, 2023). On black markets, PHI is worth exponentially more than financial credentials because of its longitudinal permanence and cross-functional utility (Pool et al., 2024). Despite this, the prevailing governance frameworks remain largely technocratic, failing to consider how staff attitudes, decision-making heuristics, and organizational climate contribute to risk. Without deliberate psychological integration, even the most sophisticated digital defenses remain vulnerable to human error and manipulation.

SIGNIFICANCE STATEMENT

The psychological toll of cybercrime in healthcare extends far beyond the loss of data, it undermines the foundational trust that enables effective care. Ransomware events disrupt hospital operations, delay life-saving treatments, and engender public fear, but their impact also resonates on a cognitive and emotional level among patients and providers alike (Neprash et al., 2022; Okafor et al., 2023). The frequent bypassing of cybersecurity protocols by clinicians is not simply defiance, it is often a rational response to competing priorities, poor system design, or cultural conditioning. Recognizing and addressing these dynamics requires a shift in leadership consciousness, from viewing cybersecurity as an IT function to treating it as an enterprise-wide, human-centered challenge.

Integrating cyberpsychological principles into organizational strategy, by investing in user-centric training, behaviorally informed policies, and leadership development, can mitigate both technical and emotional fallout. By reframing cybersecurity as a shared ethical responsibility and aligning it with patient-centered values, organizations can build resilience at the cognitive and cultural levels, not just the technological one.

PURPOSE OF THE STUDY

This study seeks to develop an integrative, evidence-based framework that enables healthcare leaders to address cybersecurity threats not only through technical fortification but through cyberpsychologically informed leadership, communication, and culture change. The aim is to close the existing gap between digital transformation and human-centric cybersecurity practices by equipping decision-makers, most of whom are clinically trained but behaviorally uninitiated, with the knowledge and tools necessary to manage human factors risk in digital environments.

Specifically, the study will identify actionable practices that align technical controls with user psychology, institutional culture, and leadership awareness. By doing so, it aims to support a transition from reactive breach containment to proactive behavioral risk mitigation, ensuring that security efforts are perceived as enablers of care rather than obstacles to it.

NATURE OF THE STUDY

Adopting a multidisciplinary, practice-focused lens, this study examines healthcare cybersecurity through the intersecting domains of information systems, behavioral science, and organizational leadership. Using cyberpsychological theory as its central analytical scaffold, the study will synthesize empirical research, behavioral incident patterns, and organizational case studies to develop a practical framework for secure, psychologically aligned digital transformation in healthcare.

The methodology follows a design science orientation, privileging the development of real-world, actionable interventions over abstract theorizing. The inquiry explores how user behavior, cognitive stressors, leadership biases, and institutional culture influence cybersecurity outcomes. It will assess how psychological blind spots among clinical leaders contribute to system-level vulnerabilities and offer strategic solutions for cultivating cyber-aware leadership, trust-building communication, and behaviorally optimized system design.

Ultimately, the research aspires to equip healthcare institutions with a roadmap for building resilient cybersecurity ecosystems that protect not only data and infrastructure, but also the human actors who remain their most unpredictable, yet most essential, guardians.

IMPACT ON EMPLOYEES: CYBERPSYCHOLOGY AT THE FRONT LINE

Healthcare employees now perform high-stakes clinical and administrative work through densely networked digital tools, placing human cognition squarely within the threat surface. Cyber adversaries systematically exploit cognitive shortcuts, social norms, and emotional triggers, urgency, authority, reciprocity, to manipulate attention and decision-making under time pressure (Klimburg-Witjes & Wentland, 2021). Empirical patterns are unambiguous: human-factor vectors such as spear-phishing and social engineering account for the overwhelming majority of successful intrusions (Barlow et al., 2020; Kioskli et al., 2023). This duality, employees as both primary vulnerability and first line of defense, explains why capability building must extend beyond technical skills to include perception, judgment, and stress-resilient behavior (Alahmari et al., 2023; Prasad et al., 2023).

In practice, the same psychological mechanisms that enable rapid, compassionate care can be weaponized. A convincingly crafted "stat" email spoofing a surgeon-in-chief, a fraudulent VPN prompt timed to a shift change, or a help-desk voice pretext exploiting hierarchical deference can each elicit a single errant click that cascades into PHI exfiltration and clinical downtime. Conversely, when staff are trained to recognize persuasion cues, verify identity out-of-band, and apply micro-pauses before credential entry, they materially reduce breach likelihood. Effective programs therefore combine threat simulations with reflective debriefs that surface cognitive biases and reframe cybersecurity as inseparable from patient safety (Reeves et al., 2021).

BARRIERS TO COMPLIANCE: COGNITIVE LOAD, CULTURE, AND LEADERSHIP GAPS

Sustained compliance falters less from ignorance than from cognitive overload and competing moral priorities. Clinicians operate amid chronic time scarcity, alarm fatigue, and administrative demand, leaving diminished bandwidth for effortful security tasks (Javaid et al., 2023). Under the "patient-first" ethos, bypassing MFA during an emergency or sharing a workstation to expedite triage is perceived as prosocial, not risky, revealing how culture and context shape risk perception (Jalali & Kaiser, 2018).

A central, under-addressed driver is the leadership expertise gap. Many healthcare leaders are deeply trained in clinical science but have limited exposure to human-factors psychology and cyberbehavioral risk. As a result, security controls are often designed as if users were error-free operators rather than stressed humans with bounded attention. Policies that add logins, password rotations, and modal warnings without ergonomic redesign predictably meet workarounds, behavioral adaptations misread as resistance rather than signals of misaligned system design. Closing this gap requires leaders to internalize how heuristics (e.g., urgency, authority), social identity, and workload intensity interact with security tasks, and to sponsor controls that subtract friction at critical moments rather than merely exhort vigilance.

HOW HUMAN FACTORS SCALE TO SYSTEMIC HARM

Organizational losses from cyber incidents, averaging millions per breach and representing a substantial share of all reported events, are the visible outcomes of invisible cognitive dynamics that play out at scale (Kotte et al., 2020; Dhawan et al., 2023). An attacker needs only to succeed with one persuasive pretext; an organization must succeed every time, across every shift, device, and handoff. Once initial access is gained through a human vector, effects propagate far beyond IT: postponed surgeries, manual chemotherapy orders, ambulance diversions, liquidity stress, and prolonged operational backlog (Wasserman & Wasserman, 2022).

FINANCIAL COSTS

Ransom is only the headline. True costs include emergency protocol activation, forensics and incident-response retainers, infrastructure rebuilds, public communication and legal expenses, regulatory exposure, insurance premium hikes, and lost revenue from canceled procedures, all while paying overtime for command-center operations (Wasserman & Wasserman, 2022). A cognitively engineered phish that compromises an anesthesia documentation account can idle operating rooms for days, converting a single moment of human error into multi-million-dollar losses.

DATA LOSS

From 2010–2019, theft and loss comprised roughly 37.65% of healthcare breaches; in 2016–2021 only ~20% of affected organizations restored data successfully from backups (Seh et al., 2020; Neprash et al., 2022). Even when "recovered," data must be treated as permanently compromised due to unobservable alteration or resale risk (Wasserman & Wasserman, 2022). Facilities that pair immutable, offline backups with quarterly restoration drills convert psychological preparedness into technical resilience, reconstituting EHRs in days rather than weeks.

REPUTATION AND TRUST

Breach aftermath produces measurable trust erosion and patient anger; patients may withhold stigmatized histories essential for safe prescribing, elevating risk for avoidable harm (Wasserman & Wasserman, 2022). Reputation loss also undermines clinician recruitment and payer negotiations, long-tail effects triggered by short-horizon cognitive manipulation.

CYBERSECURITY STRATEGIES RECAST THROUGH A HUMAN-FACTORS LENS

The CIA triad, confidentiality, integrity, availability, remains foundational (Abdelghani, 2019). Yet in healthcare, how controls are experienced cognitively determines whether they are followed. Defense-in-depth must therefore be redesigned as defense-with-mind, integrating behavioral science at each layer:

- Confidentiality: Pair encryption and access controls with choice architecture that defaults to safer actions (e.g., secure messaging pre-selected over email for PHI) and with context-aware MFA that relaxes friction during verified emergencies while preserving strong assurance at routine access points.
- Integrity: Complement hashing and audit trails with attentional safeguards, salient verification banners for high-risk actions (bulk record access, external data export) and just-in-time prompts that cue verification without inducing alert fatigue.
- Availability: Combine redundancy and tested failover with cognitive continuity, downtime playbooks rehearsed in clinical drills, role-based job aids at the point of care, and cross-training that reduces stress-induced errors during EHR outages.

Leadership's role is pivotal: translate clinical mastery into cyberpsychological literacy. That means sponsoring usability testing with frontline staff, funding simulation-based phishing exercises with reflective debriefs, measuring human-risk indicators (e.g., simulated phish click-through, reporting latency), and holding executives accountable for friction budgets, targets to reduce unnecessary cognitive steps in critical workflows. In short, sustainable security in healthcare emerges when technical architecture and human architecture are designed together, so that doing the clinically right thing is also the securely easy thing.Top of Form

DEFENSE-IN-DEPTH (DID): A CYBERPSYCHOLOGICAL REFRAMING

Traditional models of defense-in-depth (DiD) emphasize layered technological, procedural, and administrative safeguards designed to reduce the probability of compromise through redundancy and segmentation (Abdelghani, 2019). However, in healthcare, where digital transformation intersects with cognitive overload, emotional fatigue, and behavioral heuristics, the effectiveness of DiD depends as much on psychological alignment as on technical sophistication. The model must therefore evolve from a purely architectural construct to one that deliberately incorporates human factors psychology, acknowledging that perception, cognition, and social behavior are themselves control layers in the defense system.

Healthcare leaders, though often highly proficient in clinical governance, typically possess limited formal training in behavioral science or cyberpsychology. This expertise gap results in protective strategies that assume rational, consistent compliance with security controls rather than recognizing how stress, moral priorities, or habituation shape decision-making. For example, clinicians under cognitive strain may unintentionally circumvent multi-factor authentication (MFA) or share credentials to expedite patient care, interpreting these behaviors as compassionate efficiency rather than noncompliance. A psychologically informed DiD framework thus requires leadership literacy in cognitive ergonomics, the capacity to design controls that fit human behavior rather than demand behavioral adaptation.

CONTROL LAYERS: INTEGRATING PSYCHOLOGICAL AND TECHNICAL DIMENSIONS

- **Physical Controls** Traditional controls such as badge access, mantraps, and alarms remain foundational (Keshta & Odeh, 2021). Yet their psychological dimension, how secure spaces influence staff vigilance, should not be overlooked. For instance, visibly controlled access zones can serve as behavioral anchors, reinforcing perceptions of cybersecurity importance. Environmental design that subtly primes secure conduct (e.g., privacy signage, visual reminders near terminals) complements physical safeguards with cognitive cues that sustain awareness.

- **Technical Controls** Firewalls, encryption, endpoint detection, and access management are essential (Keshta & Odeh, 2021), but these tools only perform optimally when user interaction aligns with their design. Cognitive load theory suggests that over-complex authentication processes or ambiguous warning prompts increase error rates and user workarounds. Leaders must therefore collaborate with behavioral scientists to test usability under realistic clinical conditions, ensuring that secure behaviors are intuitive rather than resisted.
- **Administrative Controls** Policy frameworks, vendor contracts, and training programs form the administrative layer (Keshta & Odeh, 2021). However, conventional training often emphasizes compliance over comprehension. Cyberpsychologically informed education reframes this approach by explaining why controls exist and demonstrating how attackers manipulate psychological vulnerabilities, authority bias, fear appeals, or social trust, to elicit risky actions. By embedding emotional and cognitive awareness into policy rollout, leaders can convert abstract mandates into meaningful, behaviorally resonant practices.

SYSTEM SECURITY LAYERS: DESIGNING FOR HUMAN-TECHNOLOGY INTERACTION

A cyberpsychological perspective expands the traditional data–device–network view by considering how human users cognitively and emotionally engage with these systems under clinical pressure.

- **Network Protection** Intrusion detection and prevention (IDS/IPS) technologies can generate high false-positive rates that overwhelm analysts and erode trust. Applying principles of cognitive psychology, such as signal-to-noise optimization and attentional filtering, helps calibrate alert systems to maintain operator confidence and responsiveness (Akbaş, 2023; Ramadan et al., 2021).
- **System Protection** Security information and event management (SIEM) and automated response platforms (SOAR) should include human-in-the-loop designs where critical decisions are structured to prevent automation bias.

Brief, structured prompts that request operator reflection ("verify intent before execution") can disrupt impulsive confirmation actions during incident triage.

- **Data Protection** Encryption, hashing, and tokenization safeguard data integrity (Ramadan et al., 2021), but leaders must also address the psychological aftermath of data breaches. Communicating transparently and empathetically with staff and patients post-incident reduces trust erosion and mitigates the collective anxiety that often undermines organizational recovery.
- **Access Control** Least privilege and MFA are effective only when friction is minimized. Adaptive authentication mechanisms that recognize context (e.g., emergency status, device type) align security rigor with the clinician's psychological and temporal constraints, reducing policy evasion driven by urgency.
- **Device Protection** Biomedical devices, especially legacy systems, require not only virtual patching but also user-interface awareness. Staff frequently interact with device alerts; if notifications are poorly designed, desensitization occurs. Human factors psychology can inform alert frequency, color coding, and escalation protocols to sustain attention without fatigue.

A practical example illustrates the integration: In a radiology department, cognitive load testing is conducted before MFA rollout to ensure login prompts do not delay image retrieval during emergencies. Technologists receive scenario-based training on phishing tactics specific to imaging workflows, linking their daily routines to the psychological tactics adversaries exploit. This combination of human-centered design and technical rigor strengthens both compliance and competence.

ZERO TRUST STRATEGY: COGNITIVE VERIFICATION AS CONTINUOUS ASSURANCE

The Zero Trust paradigm, "never trust, always verify," embodies not only a technological framework but a cognitive model of skepticism (Yeoh et al., 2023). Its effectiveness in healthcare depends on embedding *situational awareness* and *decision hygiene* among users. Zero Trust's continuous verification principles parallel psychological vigilance: rather than relying on static trust assumptions, users and systems remain dynamically alert to anomalies.

Leadership unfamiliar with cognitive biases often underestimate how trust heuristics, habitual reliance on known colleagues, familiar email templates, or assumed legitimacy of internal requests, can subvert Zero Trust principles. Consequently, behavioral reinforcement mechanisms must accompany technical enforcement. For example:

- **Users**: Adaptive MFA can incorporate behavioral biometrics (typing rhythm, mouse movement) to authenticate unobtrusively, reducing fatigue and frustration.
- **Devices**: Automated profiling should be complemented by user prompts that reinforce awareness of authorized device scope, combating complacency.
- **Workloads and Networks**: Segmentation logic can mirror psychological compartmentalization, users access only what they truly need, reinforcing mental models of limited exposure.
- **Visibility & Analytics**: User and Entity Behavior Analytics (UEBA) not only detect anomalies but should feed back into awareness programs, transforming detected behavioral deviations into training narratives that humanize risk patterns.

Zero Trust's ultimate strength lies in harmonizing machine-driven vigilance with human cognitive discipline. When users perceive verification as protective collaboration rather than surveillance, compliance becomes self-sustaining.

SYNTHESIS FOR PRACTICE: BUILDING PSYCHOLOGICALLY AWARE DEFENSE ARCHITECTURES

The integration of the CIA triad, defense-in-depth, and Zero Trust illustrates a conceptual evolution, from static protection principles toward dynamic, human-centered cybersecurity ecosystems. Yet healthcare's leadership gap in human factors psychology remains a critical vulnerability. Leaders must be retrained to think of cybersecurity not as an engineering problem but as a behavioral ecosystem, where every click, decision, and habit contributes to collective defense (Abdelghani, 2019; Akbaş, 2023; Ramadan et al., 2021; Yeoh et al., 2023).

By institutionalizing behavioral metrics, such as cognitive load assessments, phishing susceptibility rates, and adaptive response times, alongside technical KPIs, organizations can measure their psychological resilience as rigorously as their digital resilience. Cyberpsychological literacy at the executive level transforms defense frameworks from reactive compliance structures into living systems that anticipate, absorb, and adapt to the ever-evolving interplay between human cognition and malicious intent.

In essence, sustainable healthcare cybersecurity depends not solely on firewalls or algorithms, but on leaders who understand that defending digital integrity begins with understanding the mind behind the keyboard.

SCHEIN'S THREE LEVELS OF ORGANIZATIONAL CULTURE: A CYBERPSYCHOLOGICAL FRAMEWORK

Schein's model of organizational culture provides a powerful lens for understanding how shared cognition, perception, and emotion shape institutional behavior. In the context of healthcare cybersecurity, the model's diagnostic depth illuminates how human factors and collective mental models influence compliance, risk perception, and resilience. Schein's framework comprises three interdependent levels, artefacts, espoused values, and underlying assumptions, which together define how an organization collectively interprets and responds to cybersecurity threats (Braathe, 2021).

At Level 1 – Artefacts, culture is revealed in visible, behavioral, and environmental expressions of shared norms. In healthcare, artefacts are often encoded in routine actions: clinicians hurriedly entering data into EHRs under cognitive overload, staff propping open secure doors for convenience, or teams informally sharing login credentials to maintain workflow continuity. These behaviors are not mere procedural lapses, they are psychological artefacts of a culture that implicitly rewards expedience and patient-centered responsiveness over procedural vigilance. The physical layout of open nursing stations, the ambient urgency of clinical settings, and the visible presence (or absence) of cybersecurity prompts all function as symbolic cues communicating whether digital safety is integral or peripheral to care delivery.

Level 2 – Espoused Values captures the organization's declared priorities, its stated commitments to patient welfare, quality, and safety. However, these ideals often exist in tension with the lived experience of frontline staff. Leadership may publicly emphasize "data integrity" and "digital compliance," yet without behavioral framing, these principles remain abstract. Clinicians, motivated by ethical imperatives and time-sensitive pressures, often interpret cybersecurity tasks as secondary to patient care. This perceptual dissonance arises because leadership, often clinically trained and steeped in biomedical reasoning, rarely integrates insights from human factors psychology when developing cybersecurity policies. Consequently, leaders may misjudge resistance as negligence rather than as a behaviorally rational adaptation to conflicting demands (Braathe, 2021).

At Level 3 – Underlying Assumptions, the deepest and most enduring cultural beliefs reside, those unconscious convictions that govern how employees interpret authority, risk, and trust. In healthcare, a common but dangerous assumption persists:

"If security delays care, security must yield." This belief, deeply rooted in the moral hierarchy of clinical priorities, explains why even sophisticated technical controls fail when confronted with real-world exigencies. Correcting these assumptions requires leaders to engage in reflective inquiry, probing how clinicians perceive cybersecurity's relationship to patient safety and rearticulating it as an ethical extension of the healing mission rather than an administrative imposition.

APPLYING SCHEIN'S MODEL TO THE CYBERPSYCHOLOGY OF HEALTHCARE LEADERSHIP

Negative staff perceptions of cybersecurity are not primarily technical failures, they are manifestations of organizational cognition shaped by leadership blind spots in human psychology (Coventry et al., 2020). Leaders in healthcare, trained predominantly in clinical reasoning and operational management, often lack formal expertise in the psychological sciences that explain why humans misjudge risk, succumb to social engineering, or normalize unsafe shortcuts. Schein's model allows them to surface and correct these cultural blind spots.

At the artefact level, leaders should conduct behavioral ethnographies, structured observations of daily practices, to uncover where and why employees deviate from policy. A clinician who leaves a workstation unlocked during an emergency is not demonstrating disregard but revealing a cognitive hierarchy that prioritizes immediacy over protocol. These observations can then inform environmental and procedural redesign, such as implementing biometric reauthentication that aligns with clinical tempo rather than opposes it.

At the espoused values level, leaders must use structured dialogue and reflective inquiry to explore how employees interpret organizational priorities. When clinicians equate cybersecurity with administrative burden, this perception indicates a semantic gap between leadership rhetoric and frontline cognition. Leaders who reframe security as a moral obligation, "protecting data protects the patient," translate abstract compliance into meaningful professional identity, aligning cybersecurity with intrinsic motivation.

At the underlying assumptions level, leadership must interrogate the unconscious belief systems that justify risk normalization. This involves psychologically sophisticated conversations that invite clinicians to articulate their implicit reasoning and emotional trade-offs. For instance, asking, "What would it mean for patient safety if a cyberattack delayed access to their critical data?" encourages cognitive reframing that situates security within the continuum of clinical ethics.

KOTTER'S CHANGE MANAGEMENT THEORY: OPERATIONALIZING CYBERPSYCHOLOGICAL TRANSFORMATION

While Schein's model diagnoses cultural architecture, Kotter's Eight-Step Change Model provides a methodical pathway to reshape it into a security-conscious mindset (Ovington, 2018). In healthcare, this transformation must acknowledge both the emotional and cognitive barriers to change, resistance rooted not in obstinacy, but in stress, habituation, and limited psychological literacy among leaders themselves (Burrell et al., 2023).

1. **Create a Sense of Urgency.** Leaders must employ emotionally salient storytelling, using case studies of ransomware-related care delays or compromised medical devices, to trigger affective engagement, not just intellectual concern. Awareness campaigns grounded in real human consequences activate empathy and moral responsibility (Ovington, 2018).
2. **Build a Powerful Coalition.** Transformation requires psychological diversity within the coalition, bringing together clinicians, IT professionals, behavioral scientists, and administrators to model cross-domain collaboration. This corrects the cognitive siloing that often isolates cybersecurity as an "IT issue" (Ovington, 2018).
3. **Develop a Vision for Change.** The vision must appeal to both logic and emotion, integrating clinical purpose with cyberpsychological insight. A compelling narrative, "Every secure login saves a life," connects data protection with caregiving identity, a critical bridge for clinicians accustomed to valuing tangible patient outcomes.
4. **Communicate the Vision.** Effective communication requires repetition, transparency, and psychological safety. Town halls, simulation-based workshops, and nonpunitive reporting systems allow employees to surface anxieties and cognitive dissonance about cybersecurity without fear of reprisal (Ovington, 2018).
5. **Remove Obstacles.** Leaders must identify both technical and psychological barriers, cumbersome authentication procedures, alert fatigue, or fear of discipline, and replace them with usability-centered designs and positive reinforcement. Cognitive ergonomics should guide the redesign of processes to ensure that compliance aligns with human capability, not idealized rationality (Ovington, 2018).
6. **Create Short-Term Wins.** Celebrating behavioral achievements, such as reduced phishing susceptibility or faster secure login compliance, taps into the neuropsychological reward circuits that sustain motivation and collective pride.

7–8. **Build on Change and Anchor It in Culture.** Institutionalizing cybersecurity requires continuous psychological reinforcement. Embedding behavioral metrics into governance, integrating cyberpsychological education into leadership development, and aligning performance evaluations with secure behavior norms ensures that the change persists as shared identity rather than transient policy (Ovington, 2018).

INTEGRATING SCHEIN AND KOTTER: TOWARD A CYBERPSYCHOLOGICALLY INFORMED SECURITY CULTURE

Together, Schein's cultural diagnosis and Kotter's change framework provide complementary instruments for transforming cybersecurity from a compliance regime into a cognitive culture. Schein identifies the mental schemas and implicit assumptions that drive unsafe practices; Kotter offers the mechanism for reshaping them through structured behavioral reinforcement.

For example, if Schein's analysis reveals that clinicians bypass authentication because "patient care cannot wait," Kotter's steps guide leaders in reframing that belief, first by creating urgency around the human consequences of data breaches, then by forming cross-functional coalitions that model secure yet agile workflows. Over time, these behaviors become artefacts of a new culture: where quick response and secure access coexist, and cybersecurity is viewed not as a barrier but as a dimension of ethical care.

This synthesis underscores a critical truth: healthcare leadership cannot defend digital infrastructures without understanding the psychological infrastructures of their workforce. To cultivate enduring resilience, leaders must evolve from clinically proficient decision-makers into cyberpsychologically literate stewards who understand that the mind is both the target and the shield in modern cyber defense. In a sector where compassion drives action, the next frontier of patient safety lies in cultivating the same depth of empathy and insight toward the human factors that shape digital security.

ACTIONABLE RECOMMENDATIONS FOR STRENGTHENING CYBERSECURITY CULTURE IN HEALTHCARE

Address Human Factors and Cyberpsychological Risks

1. **Implement Continuous Behavioral Awareness Training.** Develop recurring, scenario-based training programs that emphasize real-world examples

of phishing, social engineering, and insider threat behavior. Training should include simulations that mirror actual healthcare workflows (e.g., simulated phishing messages disguised as urgent patient updates) to reinforce vigilance under realistic conditions (Reeves et al., 2021; Kioskli et al., 2023).

2. **Integrate Cognitive Load Management into Cybersecurity Design.** Reduce the mental and temporal strain on healthcare workers by designing security processes that accommodate the fast-paced clinical environment. For instance, use biometric logins or context-aware authentication during emergencies to replace repetitive password entry, thereby minimizing cognitive fatigue and compliance shortcuts (Javaid et al., 2023).
3. **Adopt Human-Centered Security Engineering (HCSE).** Involve clinicians, nurses, and administrative staff in co-designing cybersecurity workflows. Conduct usability testing on new security tools to ensure they complement, rather than disrupt, patient care. This participatory approach enhances perceived usefulness and decreases resistance, aligning with the Technology Acceptance Model's principles of ease-of-use and utility (Reeves et al., 2021).
4. **Embed Cyberpsychology-Informed Support Mechanisms.** Establish confidential support channels or debriefing sessions after cyber incidents to address anxiety, blame, or burnout that may result from security breaches or false alarms. This mitigates defensive avoidance behaviors and fosters psychological resilience in frontline employees (Fauzi et al., 2021).
5. **Gamify Cyber Hygiene Reinforcement.** Introduce recognition systems, leaderboards, or small incentives for employees who demonstrate consistent cybersecurity compliance. Gamified approaches leverage intrinsic motivation and create positive reinforcement loops that enhance both engagement and retention of secure practices.

Strengthen Organizational Culture and Leadership Engagement

6. **Apply Schein's Three-Level Diagnostic Approach. Level 1 (Artefacts):** Conduct periodic cultural audits observing daily routines, physical security habits, and informal communication patterns that reveal implicit security priorities.

    Level 2 (Espoused Values): Facilitate structured discussions and surveys to gauge discrepancies between leadership's intended cybersecurity message and employees' lived perceptions.

    Level 3 (Underlying Assumptions): Hold leadership-led reflective sessions to uncover deeply held beliefs, such as "security slows care," and replace them with the principle that "cybersecurity protects patient lives" (Braathe, 2021; Coventry et al., 2020).

7. **Reframe Cybersecurity as Patient Safety.** Incorporate cybersecurity objectives into patient safety initiatives, emphasizing that data integrity directly influences care accuracy. For example, showcase incidents where corrupted patient data led to medical errors to highlight the ethical linkage between cybersecurity and patient welfare (Jalali & Kaiser, 2018).
8. **Model Secure Behavior at the Leadership Level.** Executives, department heads, and senior clinicians should actively demonstrate compliance, using secure logins, completing training, and discussing cybersecurity openly during staff meetings. Leadership modeling shapes cultural norms and helps translate espoused values into visible action (Braathe, 2021).
9. **Integrate Cybersecurity Metrics into Organizational Performance Dashboards.** Include cybersecurity compliance indicators, such as phishing resilience scores or MFA adoption rates, within key performance measures to communicate that security is a shared institutional responsibility, not solely an IT concern.

Apply Change Management to Drive Sustainable Transformation

10. **Follow Kotter's Eight-Step Change Framework for Cyber Readiness.** Use Kotter's model to operationalize cybersecurity culture change:

    Step 1: Create urgency through storytelling, share local examples of breaches disrupting patient care.
    Step 2: Build a multidisciplinary coalition of IT, clinical, and operational leaders.
    Step 3: Craft a clear vision connecting security to ethical care.
    Step 4: Communicate consistently across all communication channels.
    Step 5: Eliminate friction points that discourage compliance (e.g., redundant logins).
    Step 6: Publicly celebrate short-term wins, such as reductions in phishing-click rates.
    Step 7: Expand change by integrating feedback from frontline staff.
    Step 8: Institutionalize success by embedding cybersecurity into governance structures and annual training cycles (Ovington, 2018; Burrell et al., 2023).

11. **Align Cybersecurity Goals with Organizational Mission and Values.** Embed cybersecurity objectives within the institution's strategic plan. When employees see that protecting digital assets supports their overarching mission to deliver

ethical, safe, and compassionate care, resistance to change diminishes (Braathe, 2021).

12. **Develop Cybersecurity Change Champions.** Identify respected clinicians and administrative staff to serve as internal ambassadors for cybersecurity initiatives. These individuals can translate technical policies into relatable narratives, bridging the communication gap between IT and clinical teams (Burrell et al., 2023).

Adopt Proactive and Preventive Strategies

13. **Conduct Routine Cyber Resilience Simulations.** Pair traditional IT tabletop exercises with clinical workflow drills that test continuity of care under simulated cyber incidents (e.g., EHR downtime, ransomware lockdown). Involving clinical staff directly reinforces preparedness and underscores interdependence between technology and care delivery.
14. **Institutionalize a Continuous Learning Ecosystem.** Establish regular cybersecurity briefings, micro-learning modules, and feedback loops so that lessons from incidents are immediately incorporated into practice. For example, after a phishing attempt, debrief teams to analyze root causes and share prevention strategies across departments (Hermes et al., 2020).
15. **Measure and Report Human Risk Indicators.** Move beyond technical metrics by tracking human-centered indicators such as security awareness assessment scores, click rates on simulated phishing campaigns, and incident reporting frequency. Use these analytics to target high-risk units for additional coaching or redesign interventions (Akbaş, 2023; Yeoh et al., 2023).
16. **Establish "Security Rounds" Modeled on Clinical Rounds.** Implement routine interdisciplinary "cyber rounds," where cybersecurity professionals and clinicians jointly review vulnerabilities, discuss recent incidents, and co-create improvement strategies. This normalizes security dialogue within clinical contexts and breaks down departmental silos.
17. **Integrate Cybersecurity into Clinical Onboarding and Continuing Education.** New employee orientation should include cybersecurity fundamentals contextualized to clinical roles, demonstrating how data protection directly supports patient care outcomes. Annual recertification can use scenario-based evaluations to ensure sustained competence.

CONCLUSION

A secure healthcare ecosystem cannot be sustained by technology alone. True cybersecurity resilience emerges at the intersection of human cognition, organizational culture, and adaptive leadership. The integration of cyberpsychology into cybersecurity strategy reframes defense not merely as the prevention of digital compromise, but as the preservation of clinical integrity and ethical care.

The human mind, its perceptions, biases, stress responses, and heuristics, functions as both a vulnerability and a vector of resilience. When leaders acknowledge this duality, they can design systems where compliance is not coerced but cognitively natural; where controls are not impediments but enablers of care. The recasting of the CIA triad, Defense-in-Depth, and Zero Trust through a behavioral lens transforms cybersecurity from a static architecture into a living ecosystem, one that senses, learns, and adapts alongside its human participants.

By embedding behavioral metrics into technical key performance indicators, tracking cognitive load, attention fatigue, and trust dynamics alongside encryption strength and patch latency, healthcare organizations can evolve from reactive posture to anticipatory defense. The ultimate insight is simple yet profound: cybersecurity is not only about protecting data but about protecting the minds that protect data. When leadership recognizes that human factors are the true operational substrate of digital safety, cyber resilience becomes synonymous with organizational vitality and ethical continuity.

The future of healthcare cybersecurity depends on a profound cultural awakening: recognizing that technology alone cannot secure what psychology misunderstands. Every secure login, every correctly handled alert, every vigilant pause reflects not a rule followed but a mind trained, supported, and ethically engaged. By uniting technical precision with psychological insight, leadership vision with staff empathy, and business continuity with cognitive continuity, the healthcare sector can achieve what no firewall can ensure alone, a culture of mindful resilience where digital security and human care coexist seamlessly.

Leadership Implications

Healthcare leadership stands at the fulcrum between clinical care and digital defense. The next generation of leaders must possess cyberpsychological literacy, an understanding of how human cognition and behavior interact with system design under stress. Leadership's primary task is not to command compliance but to engineer environments where secure behavior aligns with intuitive, ethical decision-making.

1. **Cultivate Behavioral Insight as a Core Competency.** Executives and department heads must develop proficiency in cognitive ergonomics and risk perception theory. This literacy allows them to sponsor human-centered security testing, measure cognitive friction in workflows, and interpret noncompliance not as defiance but as an adaptive response to misaligned design.
2. **Translate Clinical Mastery into Cyberpsychological Stewardship.** Leaders who frame cybersecurity as an extension of patient safety transform moral priorities into protective reflexes. By embedding phrases like "protecting data protects the patient" into institutional dialogue, they realign ethical motivation with cyber vigilance.
3. **Model Accountability and Transparency.** Psychological safety must underpin all cyber initiatives. Leaders who openly discuss breaches, near-misses, and recovery lessons cultivate collective ownership of security outcomes. Transparency reframes cybersecurity from an IT concern into a shared cultural enterprise.
4. **Champion Friction Budgets and Cognitive Efficiency.** Leadership must hold themselves accountable for reducing unnecessary cognitive burdens that drive risky workarounds. A "friction budget" should become a governance metric alongside uptime and cost, signaling that usability is a security imperative.

Ultimately, leadership maturity in cybersecurity is measured not by control enforcement but by the ability to make the secure choice the easy choice.

Organizational Implications

Organizational resilience in healthcare cybersecurity now depends on aligning cultural architecture with human cognition. Drawing on Schein's model, institutions must examine how artefacts, espoused values, and underlying assumptions collectively shape cybersecurity behavior.

1. **Redefine Security as an Expression of Care.** Organizations should formally integrate cybersecurity into their patient safety and quality frameworks, positioning digital integrity as a direct determinant of care outcomes. This reframing dissolves the false dichotomy between security and compassion.
2. **Institutionalize Behavioral Metrics in Risk Governance.** Beyond traditional compliance audits, organizations must assess psychological indicators, such as alert fatigue, phishing susceptibility, and perceived security climate, to identify latent vulnerabilities in human performance.
3. **Embed Psychological Continuity into Business Continuity Planning.** Business continuity protocols must address not only system recovery but cognitive recovery, staff stress, decision fatigue, and post-incident anxiety that can impair

operational judgment. Including psychological first-aid measures and transparent communication plans strengthens both recovery speed and morale.

4. **Normalize Cross-Functional Collaboration.** Security cannot remain siloed within IT. Creating interdisciplinary "security rounds," modeled after clinical rounds, fosters a shared sense of vigilance and facilitates the mutual translation of technical and clinical priorities.
5. **Anchor Cultural Change through Symbolic and Structural Reinforcement.** Security signage, secure-by-default interfaces, and visible leadership participation signal that cybersecurity is not peripheral but integral to care delivery. Over time, these artefacts crystallize new shared assumptions about responsibility and trust.

Through this transformation, organizations evolve from rule-based compliance systems to learning ecosystems that self-correct and adapt under pressure.

Training and Development Implications

Traditional cybersecurity training in healthcare, dominated by compliance checklists and technical instruction, fails to engage the emotional and cognitive dimensions of behavior. A cyberpsychologically informed training and development strategy must instead cultivate emotional intelligence, situational awareness, and resilience under stress.

1. **Adopt Continuous, Scenario-Based Learning.** Training should simulate real-world cognitive challenges, such as responding to phishing during high clinical load or maintaining procedural accuracy under EHR downtime. Immersive, emotionally realistic scenarios foster the kind of experiential memory that sustains behavioral change.
2. **Integrate Cognitive Load Management.** Instruction should include strategies for managing attention, multitasking, and fatigue. Teaching clinicians how stress and overload distort judgment enhances both cybersecurity and patient safety performance.
3. **Build Reflective Practice and Emotional Debriefing.** After incidents or drills, structured reflection allows staff to articulate emotions, errors, and insights without stigma. This psychological processing strengthens resilience and reduces avoidance behaviors that often lead to concealment of mistakes.
4. **Gamify Cyber Hygiene and Reward Secure Behavior.** Recognition systems that celebrate secure habits tap into intrinsic motivation and reinforce security as an element of professional pride, not punishment.

5. **Develop Leadership Pipelines with Cyberpsychological Education.** Leadership programs should embed modules on cognitive bias, social engineering, and behavioral economics, equipping emerging leaders to interpret and influence human behavior in digital contexts.
6. **Integrate Training with Business Continuity Exercises.** Cyber resilience drills should not end with system restoration. They must evaluate team communication, role adaptability, and stress regulation, ensuring that psychological endurance is recognized as a key continuity asset.

When cybersecurity training evolves from rote compliance to cognitive competence, organizations shift from reactive awareness to proactive vigilance. Employees cease to be the "weakest link" and become the first line of adaptive defense.

REFERENCES

Abdelghani, T. (2019). Implementation of defense in depth strategy to secure industrial control system in critical infrastructures. *American Journal of Artificial Intelligence, 3*(2), 17. DOI: 10.11648/j.ajai.20190302.11

Akbaş, E. (2023). *The importance of real-time detection and correlation in SIEM/UEBA solutions and criticality for SOAR*. Unpublished. DOI: 10.13140/RG.2.2.12607.69285

Alahmari, S., Renaud, K., & Omoronyia, I. (2023). Moving beyond cyber security awareness and training to engendering security knowledge sharing. *Information Systems and e-Business Management, 21*(1), 123–158. DOI: 10.1007/s10257-022-00575-2

Alanazi, A. (2023). Clinicians' perspectives on healthcare cybersecurity and cyber threats. *Cureus, 15*(10). Advance online publication. DOI: 10.7759/cureus.47026 PMID: 37965389

Argaw, S. T., Troncoso-Pastoriza, J. R., Lacey, D., Florin, M.-V., Calcavecchia, F., Anderson, D., Burleson, W., Vogel, J.-M., O'Leary, C., Eshaya-Chauvin, B., & Flahault, A. (2020). Cybersecurity of Hospitals: Discussing the challenges and working towards mitigating the risks. *BMC Medical Informatics and Decision Making, 20*(1), 146. Advance online publication. DOI: 10.1186/s12911-020-01161-7 PMID: 32620167

Barlow, L., Bendiab, G., Shiaeles, S., & Savage, N. (2020). A novel approach to detect phishing attacks using binary visualisation and machine learning. *2020 IEEE World Congress on Services (SERVICES)*. DOI: 10.1109/SERVICES48979.2020.00046

Braathe, R. (2021, January 23). *The Schein model of organization culture: Three levels of a robust organization culture*. Robert Braathe's HR & Albany Jobs Blog. https://www.albany.com/hr/2021/01/the-schein-model-of-organization-culture-three-levels-of-a-robust-organization-culture/

Burrell, D. N., Burton, S. L., Nobles, C., Springs, D., Huff, A. J., Brown-Jackson, K. L., Richardson, K., Wright, J. B., Muller, S. R., & Jones, A. J. (2023). The managerial ethical and operational challenges of hospital cybersecurity. In *Transformational Interventions for Business, Technology, and Healthcare* (pp. 444–458). IGI Global. DOI: 10.4018/979-8-3693-1634-4.ch026

Cartwright, A. J. (2023). The elephant in the room: Cybersecurity in healthcare. *Journal of Clinical Monitoring and Computing, 37*(5), 1123–1132. DOI: 10.1007/s10877-023-01013-5 PMID: 37088852

Coventry, L., Branley-Bell, D., Sillence, E., Magalini, S., Mari, P., Magkanaraki, A., & Anastasopoulou, K. (2020). Cyber-Risk in Healthcare: Exploring Facilitators and Barriers to Secure Behaviour. *HCI for Cybersecurity, Privacy and Trust*, 105–122. DOI: 10.1007/978-3-030-50309-3_8

Dhawan, M., Purohit, L., & Gupta, Dr. N. (2023). A comprehensive study on the latest trends of cyber security in the medical management. *SSRN Electronic Journal*. DOI: 10.2139/ssrn.4361044

Fauzi, M. A., Yeng, P., Yang, B., & Rachmayani, D. (2021). Examining the Link Between Stress Level and Cybersecurity Practices of Hospital Staff in Indonesia. *The 16th International Conference on Availability, Reliability and Security*. DOI: 10.1145/3465481.3470094

Gopal, G., Suter-Crazzolara, C., Toldo, L., & Eberhardt, W. (2019). Digital transformation in healthcare – architectures of present and future information technologies. *Clinical Chemistry and Laboratory Medicine*, *57*(3), 328–335. DOI: 10.1515/cclm-2018-0658 PMID: 30530878

Hermes, S., Riasanow, T., Clemons, E. K., Böhm, M., & Krcmar, H. (2020). The digital transformation of the healthcare industry: Exploring the rise of emerging platform ecosystems and their influence on the role of patients. *Business Research*, *13*(3), 1033–1069. DOI: 10.1007/s40685-020-00125-x

Jalali, M. S., & Kaiser, J. P. (2018). Cybersecurity in Hospitals: A Systematic, Organizational Perspective. *Journal of Medical Internet Research*, *20*(5), e10059. DOI: 10.2196/10059 PMID: 29807882

Javaid, M., Haleem, A., Singh, R. P., & Suman, R. (2023). Towards insighting cybersecurity for healthcare domains: A comprehensive review of recent practices and trends. *Cyber Security and Applications*, *1*(100016), 100016. DOI: 10.1016/j.csa.2023.100016

Keshta, I., & Odeh, A. (2021). Security and privacy of electronic health records: Concerns and challenges. *Egyptian Informatics Journal*, *22*(2), 177–183. DOI: 10.1016/j.eij.2020.07.003

Kioskli, K., Fotis, T., Nifakos, S., & Mouratidis, H. (2023). The importance of conceptualising the human-centric approach in maintaining and promoting cybersecurity-hygiene in healthcare 4.0. *Applied Sciences (Basel, Switzerland)*, *13*(6), 3410. DOI: 10.3390/app13063410

Klimburg-Witjes, N., & Wentland, A. (2021). Hacking humans? Social engineering and the construction of the “deficient user” in cybersecurity discourses. *Science, Technology & Human Values*, *46*(6), 1316–1339. DOI: 10.1177/0162243921992844

Kotte, D., Venkatesh, R., Satish Kumar, B., Rao, U., & Kshatra, P. (2020). Analysis of data breaches and its impact on organizations. *International Journal of Emerging Trends in Engineering Research*, *8*(10), 6989–6994. DOI: 10.30534/ijeter/2020/588102020

Neprash, H. T., McGlave, C. C., Cross, D. A., Virnig, B. A., Puskarich, M. A., Huling, J. D., Rozenshtein, A. Z., & Nikpay, S. S. (2022). Trends in Ransomware Attacks on US Hospitals, Clinics, and Other Health Care Delivery Organizations, 2016-2021. *JAMA Health Forum*, *3*(12), e224873. DOI: 10.1001/jamahealthforum.2022.4873 PMID: 36580326

Okafor, C., Kolade, A., Onunka, T., Daraojimba, C., Eyo-Udo, N., & Omotosho, A. (2023). Mitigating Cybersecurity Risks in the U.S. Healthcare Sector [Review of Mitigating Cybersecurity Risks in the U.S. Healthcare Sector]. *International Journal of Innovation and Scientific Research*, *10*(9), 177–194. DOI: 10.51244/IJRSI

Ovington, T. (2018, December 16). *How to use Kotter’s 8-step model: The key to change success*. The Change Management Blog; Change Management. https://change.walkme.com/kotters-8-step-change-model/

Prasad, G., Gujjar, P., Naveen Kumar, H. N., Anand Kumar, M., & Chandrappa, S. (2023). Advances of cyber security in the healthcare domain for analyzing data. In *Advances in Information Security, Privacy, and Ethics* (pp. 1–14). IGI Global.

Ramadan, R. A., Aboshosha, B. W., Alshudukhi, J. S., Alzahrani, A. J., El-Sayed, A., & Dessouky, M. M. (2021). Cybersecurity and countermeasures at the time of pandemic. *Journal of Advanced Transportation*, *2021*, 1–19. DOI: 10.1155/2021/6627264

Reeves, A., Delfabbro, P., & Calic, D. (2021). Encouraging Employee Engagement With Cybersecurity: How to Tackle Cyber Fatigue. *SAGE Open*, *11*(1), 215824402110000. DOI: 10.1177/21582440211000049

Seh, A. H., Zarour, M., Alenezi, M., Sarkar, A. K., Agrawal, A., Kumar, R., & Khan, R. A. (2020). Healthcare data breaches: Insights and implications. *Healthcare*, *8*(2), 133. NCBI. DOI: 10.3390/healthcare8020133

Tin, D., Hata, R., Granholm, F., Ciottone, R. G., Staynings, R., & Ciottone, G. R. (2023). Cyberthreats: A primer for healthcare professionals. *The American Journal of Emergency Medicine*, *68*, 179–185. Advance online publication. DOI: 10.1016/j.ajem.2023.04.001 PMID: 37061434

Turuk, M. (2020). Digital strategy. *International Journal of Contemporary Business and Entrepreneurship*, *1*(1), 62–76. DOI: 10.47954/ijcbe.1.1.5

Wasserman, L., & Wasserman, Y. (2022). Hospital cybersecurity risks and gaps: Review (for the non-cyber professional). *Frontiers in Digital Health*, *4*, 862221. Advance online publication. DOI: 10.3389/fdgth.2022.862221 PMID: 36033634

Yeoh, W., Liu, M., Shore, M., & Jiang, F. (2023). Zero trust cybersecurity: Critical success factors and A maturity assessment framework. *Computers & Security*, *133*(103412), 103412. DOI: 10.1016/j.cose.2023.103412

Yogev, D., Goldberg, T., Arami, A., Tejman-Yarden, S., Winkler, T. E., & Maoz, B. M. (2023). Current state of the art and future directions for implantable sensors in medical technology: Clinical needs and engineering challenges. *APL Bioengineering*, *7*(3), 031506. Advance online publication. DOI: 10.1063/5.0152290 PMID: 37781727

Chapter 8

SEO Poisoning as a Hidden Vector of Cyber Risk and Organizational Compromise

Laura A. Jones
https://orcid.org/0000-0002-0299-370X
Capitol Technology University, USA

ABSTRACT

SEO poisoning has commonly been seen as a consumer cyber risk; recent attacks highlight its threat to enterprise networks. This study examines how SEO poisoning exploits user trust, hybrid work models, and browser synchronization to circumvent traditional firewalls. Real-world incidents demonstrate how attackers manipulate search rankings and leverage browser integrations to deliver malware and steal credentials within work environments. These attack techniques blur the line between external and internal risks, creating hidden dangers typically just outside an organization's main security perimeter that can easily slip through the barrier to evade conventional detection. The research concludes that SEO poisoning is now a critical risk for organizations reliant on SaaS, remote work, and search engines. This study recommends AI-driven detection, enhanced user training, and sector-wide collaboration to counteract these evolving threats and better protect digital trust for cyber professionals, researchers, and policymakers.

DOI: 10.4018/979-8-3373-9918-8.ch008

INTRODUCTION

The digital transformation of the global workforce has fundamentally redrawn the boundaries of organizational cybersecurity. No longer contained within the rigid walls of on-premises data centers, today's enterprise environments are distributed, virtualized, and porous, defined by hybrid workforces, Software-as-a-Service (SaaS) adoption, and the ubiquity of cloud-syncing browser profiles (Somé et al., 2025). Cybercriminals employ AI in contemporary attacks, enabling the creation of highly targeted and scalable attack vectors, such as AI-driven spear-phishing and automated hacking that can breach most modern security measures (Syed, 2022). The Threat Report 2024 found that 67% of workers use personal mobile devices for work-related tasks (Morgan, 2024). This trend has only accelerated since 2020. The modern organizational environment is predominantly digital, with many workers and contractors operating remotely and managing corporate data on personal devices, creating a progressively intricate technological ecosystem that underscores the escalating risk of insider attacks. This profound shift has diluted, and in some cases dissolved, the lines between internal. This challenges the premise that a technical firewall serves as a singular barrier to unauthorized access from external systems. Web application firewalls (WAFs) are employed to identify and prevent attacks on susceptible web applications. These advanced website shields are a prevailing defense against common threats such as hacking, deception, and cross-site scripting (Lasopoulou, 2025); they can protect against a wide range of vulnerabilities (Jadhav, 2023; Kizza, 2024). Although frequently used as a secondary line of defense, WAFs are essential for securing a company's web environment (Nagendran et al., 2020).

In parallel, the cyber threat landscape has evolved with equal dynamism. While much contemporary scholarship examines credential phishing and direct network breaches, an insidious class of attack, search engine optimization (SEO) poisoning, has reemerged with renewed potency (Banerjee & Roy, 2024; Fortinet, 2024; Shaharia, 2025). SEO increases the volume and quality of organic traffic to a website by improving its presence in search engines (Wallenius, 2024); accordingly, attackers use "search poisoning," an abuse of SEO tactics, to target search phrases that drive traffic to their malicious websites. Vectra (2024) defines SEO poisoning as a cyber-attack strategy in which adversaries manipulate search engine rankings to prominently feature malicious websites in search results, either to distribute malware or to extract credentials from visitors who mistakenly perceive these sites as legitimate.

Unlike conventional exploits that directly target the corporate perimeter, SEO poisoning manipulates public search engine algorithms (Ganguli, 2024) to place malicious or spoofed websites at the top of organic search results (Banerjee & Roy, 2024; Vectra, 2024). *Search engine optimization (SEO)* is the deliberate process of shaping online content, website architecture, and digital reputation to improve a webpage's standing in the organic, or unpaid, results delivered by search engines such as Google, Bing, or Baidu. Shaharia (2025) defines SEO as *"the process of optimizing digital content to rank higher on search engines like Google."* Tasin (2025) advances that SEO is integral to online success. Albeit in an era of increasingly sophisticated cyberattacks, attackers craft keyword-rich domains or compromise trusted web properties (Sarkar et al., 2024), turning routine user queries, ranging from software documentation to administrative utilities, into high-risk encounters.

Recent industry and peer-reviewed research have documented these trends with growing alarm. Fortinet's 2025 global threat analysis uncovered sophisticated multilingual malware campaigns in which compromised sites deployed JavaScript payload controllers and delivered weaponized installers (such as *Hiddengh0st* and *Winos*) (IBM X-Force, 2025) to unsuspecting professionals (Fortinet, 2024). These attacks are not merely opportunistic; they are precisely engineered to harvest credentials, hijack browser sessions, and exploit cached authentication tokens, often persisting across browser-synced devices and authenticated cloud sessions. Palo Alto Networks' "Operation Rewrite" investigation in 2025 revealed that attackers increasingly use hijacked legitimate servers as proxies to launder malicious traffic, making it exponentially harder for standard security controls to detect and block these incursions (Zemah, 2025).

Critical to this new era of cyber risk is understanding that insiders, trusted employees, contractors, and partners can unknowingly bypass even the strongest technical defenses (Burton, 2022; Jones & Burrell, 2025). Corporate firewalls, while effective at blocking incoming threats, are often ineffective against outbound movement and attackers spreading to other computers inside a company once access is obtained, which is usually facilitated by modern workplace behaviors (Fritts, 2021; Ngo Higgins, 1999). These digital pitfalls are designed to lure users into misinformation or malicious content by manipulating trusted online sources, a phenomenon also referred to as *information eco-traps*. Limited egress controls, combined with employees' regular need to access external resources, create opportunities for attackers to gain entry through subtle and indirect methods. A single click on a poisoned search result can lead to the download of trojanized tools or scripts that allow attackers to steal VPN credentials, set up hidden command-and-control tunnels, and move laterally through mapped drives or shared resources (Wu et al., 2025).

What makes this vector particularly urgent is its alignment with current organizational and technical trends (Fortinet, 2024). Hybrid networking, such as split-tunnel VPNs, creates overlapping zones where internal and external traffic coexist, magnifying the opportunities for malicious code to leap across supposed barriers (Shi et al., 2021; Zohaib et al., 2024). VPNs are essential for assured tunneling and continuous observation of network traffic for suspicious movement (Lasopoulou, 2025). Despite the longstanding existence of remote work in various forms and the rapid advancement of supporting technological infrastructure over the past fifty years, it only became a focal point in societal discourse with the onset of the COVID-19 pandemic, which prompted governments globally to impose restrictions on physical mobility (Leonardi et al., 2024). The convergence of remote work, SaaS reliance, and the blurring of personal and corporate browsing behaviors forms a threat landscape in which conventional perimeter defenses are demonstrably insufficient (Leonardi et al., 2024).

The urgency surrounding this attack vector is inextricably linked to profound organizational and technological upheavals that have unfolded since the onset of the COVID-19 pandemic. The global public health crisis not only catalyzed an unprecedented shift toward remote work (Leonardi et al., 2024) but also established distributed, digital-first operations as a permanent fixture of corporate life (Burrell, 2024; Dahiya et al., 2021). Practically overnight, organizations were compelled to dismantle legacy notions of the secure, centralized office and instead enable a workforce that operates fluidly across home offices, co-working spaces, and geographically dispersed teams.

This pivot necessitated the rapid deployment of hybrid networking models, with split-tunnel VPNs becoming prevalent to enable employees to access corporate networks and the broader internet seamlessly (Abbas et al., 2023; Korty et al., 2021). In these hybrid settings, internal and external data streams intermingle, a phenomenon that multiplies the pathways by which malicious code can traverse what were once secure boundaries. The explosive adoption of SaaS solutions and reliance on cloud-hosted applications (Lasopoulou, 2025) has removed data, workflows, and authentication far beyond the walls and oversight of any single enterprise perimeter. Exploitation of cloud computing has become pervasive across industries (Alouffi et al., 2021).

Moreover, the pandemic-era normalization of personal devices for work, often with minimal IT oversight, has blurred the lines between corporate and individual digital behaviors (Burrell, 2024; Burton, 2022). Employees regularly toggle between business applications and personal browsing, often within a single session or even the same browser window (Kamruzzaman et al., 2022). The cumulative effect is a security environment in which traditional perimeter defenses, built to repel threats at distinct, predictable ingress points, have lost much of their efficacy. In this new landscape, the opportunity for adversaries to exploit human behavior and technical ambiguity is greater than ever, requiring organizations to fundamentally rethink cyber resilience.

Bridging these developments is a pivotal shift in the cyber threat landscape: adversaries now harness the combined force of advanced automation, adaptive artificial intelligence, and nuanced psychological profiling to exploit organizational transformation (Dehghantanha et al., 2023). Rather than relying solely on brute-force attacks or static malware, contemporary threat actors deploy AI-driven reconnaissance and adaptive content generation, allowing social engineering tactics to mirror the tempo and logic of today's distributed, digital-first workplaces (Syed, 2022). Leveraging machine learning, attackers can identify and predict employee routines, crafting tailored traps, such as AI-generated phishing sites and dynamically ranked malicious content (Eze & Shamir, 2024) that surface precisely when users are most vulnerable: during information searches, tool downloads, or unsanctioned troubleshooting beyond the safety of the enterprise perimeter.

The ubiquitous integration of AI across collaboration platforms, search algorithms, and endpoint devices further complicates defensive boundaries, enabling cybercriminals to automate the escalation of privilege, steal behavioral telemetry, and orchestrate deception operations at unprecedented speed and scale (Syed, 2022). In a fluid environment, strategies like tricking search engines into directing users to dangerous or fake websites no longer require brute-force assaults; instead, malicious actors deploy machine-optimized payloads, waiting for unsuspecting insiders to bridge the final gap. Thus, risks are silently transported from the chaotic, AI-influenced expanse of public search results into the most protected segments of corporate networks. This convergence of artificial intelligence, behavioral susceptibility, and technical ambiguity defines a new, and critically underestimated, frontier for cyber risk management (Dehghantanha et al., 2023).

Nevertheless, despite the increasing risk, the research literature continues to underestimate the importance of SEO poisoning as a boundary-crossing attack. There is a clear gap, a critical lack of systematic, peer-reviewed research into how these indirect attacks propagate through trusted environments, how insiders enable such breaches, and how strategic countermeasures can prevent future damage. This study addresses that gap. By integrating the latest threat intelligence, behavioral data, and enterprise case studies, it offers an urgently needed reassessment of cyber risk in the era of hybrid networks and human-mediated vulnerabilities.

In this context, the present research contends that SEO poisoning is not merely a technical nuisance confined to casual internet use, but a strategically significant, perimeter-adjacent threat to organizational integrity. Only by recognizing its true nature, and tracing precisely how insiders can, often unknowingly, act as bridges over the firewall, can organizations develop effective, modern defenses fit for the realities of 2025 and beyond.

PROBLEM STATEMENT

A rapidly escalating cybersecurity problem is the surge in SEO poisoning attacks, which exploit trusted search engines and employee browsing habits to distribute malware and steal sensitive data. Security researchers documented that corporate firewalls are bypassed in 49% of remote connections, exposing internal systems directly to the internet (Ramirez, 2025) and a staggering 60% increase in SEO poisoning incidents in just six months in 2025, resulting in the compromise of over 15,000 legitimate websites (Vectra, 2024). Targeted campaigns, such as Operation Rewrite, infiltrated enterprises through manipulated search rankings and fake administrative tool downloads (Lakshmanan, 2025; Zemah, 2025). Notably, over 8,500 IT administration systems were compromised in one such campaign, as SEO poisoning increasingly targets the daily routines of knowledge workers who rely on web search for software, documentation, and troubleshooting (Vectra, 2024). These attacks are not isolated to technical staff: industries including healthcare, legal, and finance have faced ongoing, sector-specific SEO poisoning campaigns, placing vast pools of confidential information and critical business operations at risk.

Data breaches are a significant method of assaulting a corporation's or government agency's website or server; however, individuals' home networks are also attacked (Vagal & Dillon, 2021). Remote and hybrid work environments have intensified this threat, as employees often bypass traditional organizational firewalls by using personal devices and unsecured home networks (Ganguli, 2024). Remote work-related breaches now carry an average cost of $4.56 million, and small- to medium-sized businesses lose approximately $25,000 per SEO poisoning incident (Ramirez, 2025; Vectra, 2024). Over half of Chief Information Security Officers (CISOs) reported a spike in credential theft associated with remote access tools, with 62% of breaches exploiting weak or stolen credentials just this year (Ramirez, 2025). The rapid proliferation of misconfigured VPNs and unpatched personal devices serves as a fertile ground for threat actors, making perimeter-focused security strategies insufficient to contend with the breadth and speed of modern search-driven attacks. This union of work patterns and evolving search-based threats fundamentally challenges classical cyber defense models and demands adaptive, evidence-driven approaches to prevent persistent compromise and costly breaches.

PURPOSE OF THE STUDY

The purpose of this research is to conduct a thorough review and critical analysis of current cyber risk studies, focusing specifically on the indirect threat of SEO poisoning as it intersects with insider behavior and hybrid enterprise setups. This study draws on peer-reviewed research, global threat intelligence reports, and recent case studies to demonstrate how SEO poisoning, often seen as a public-facing threat, now exploits organizational weaknesses created by remote work and blurred network boundaries (Leonardi et al., 2024). This book chapter aims to fill that knowledge gap by mapping the mechanisms, behavioral enablers, and real-world effects of SEO poisoning that crosses the firewall, and by assessing the effectiveness of existing countermeasures. In doing so, the research pursues two related goals: (1) to raise awareness of SEO poisoning as a significant organizational risk, and (2) to provide practical recommendations for rethinking cyber resilience strategies to address current urgent challenges. The results are intended to help security leaders, policymakers, and scholars update the necessary controls to manage a rapidly evolving, boundary-blurring cyber threat.

SIGNIFICANCE AND RATIONALE FOR THE STUDY

The importance of this study lies in its focus on the growing cyber threat posed by SEO poisoning. As organizations increasingly depend on search results to find technical resources, troubleshoot issues, or download legitimate software, attackers have learned to weaponize SEO itself. Between August 2023 and January 2024, industry analysis from ReliaQuest documented a 10% month-over-month increase in SEO poisoning attack detections, culminating in an overall 60% surge in cases during those six months (Sestieri, 2024). This dramatic rise highlights the accelerating threat landscape and signals why SEO poisoning now demands focused mitigation strategies. According to Vectra, SEO poisoning attacks have grown by over 60% in the past six months, affecting 8,500 enterprise systems worldwide in a single campaign targeting IT professionals searching for PuTTY and WinSCP tools (Vectra, 2024).

Further, academic research cited by Vectra AI found that small and medium enterprises suffer average losses of $25,000 per SEO poisoning incident (Vectra, 2024). When attacks escalate to ransomware or major data breaches, costs can reach millions of dollars. These figures sharply contrast with the typical average global data breach cost of $4.88 million in 2024, per IBM's latest statistics, underscoring the significance of sector-specific impacts and the need for industry-tailored responses (Vectra, 2024). These incidents highlight how covert the attack is: by hijacking users' trust in search engines, arguably the most common way to access information, threat actors can bypass traditional security measures, allowing malicious tools or payloads to evade even the most advanced firewalls and endpoint protections. Human activities, such as seeking solutions, downloading updates, or verifying technical advice, become the very channels through which risk is introduced (Ganguli, 2024). This ability to exploit cognitive trust, curiosity, and professional independence exposes a significant vulnerability in cyber defenses that existing perimeter security models were never designed to address.

The rationale for this research stems from the growing gap between technical defenses and human vulnerability. While cybersecurity efforts continue to focus on firewalls (Scheeres, 2008; Venkitanarayanan, 2025), endpoint detection (Kaur & Tiwari, 2021), and zero-trust architecture (Rose et al., 2020), campaigns like Operation Rewrite and Fortinet's BadIIS attacks reveal how these measures fall short against adversaries who manipulate the "search layer" of human activity. Attackers exploit human behavior and AI-enhanced deception (Syed, 2022), creating legitimate-looking pages that adapt to search trends and evade signature-based detection (Knowles, 2025). This shift turns SEO poisoning into a boundary-blurring threat, making it harder to distinguish between external malvertising and internal compromise. This study aims to fill this critical gap by explaining how SEO poisoning uses human behavior to bypass technical defenses, and by framing it as a key case for rethinking digital trust, awareness training, and the future of AI-driven cyber resilience strategies.

NATURE OF THE STUDY

The nature of this study is qualitative and integrative, using a structured literature review to synthesize current research, leading threat intelligence reports, and industry analyses related to the emerging phenomenon of SEO poisoning within organizational cybersecurity ecosystems. This approach is well-suited to the study's goal: to examine an underexplored digital threat vector, analyze its behavioral and technical aspects, and interpret how it operates within established security models through user interaction and hybrid networking environments.

Rooted in constructivist and interpretivist philosophical foundations, the study aims to understand how meaning and significance are constructed around the issue of firewall circumvention through human-mediated actions. This workaround is also known as *firewall evasion,* or ways attackers get around the primary digital defense. Instead of testing predetermined hypotheses, it interprets the evolving discourse and perspectives across academic and practitioner domains to identify common patterns, conceptual frameworks, and gaps in the existing literature. This approach recognizes that modern cyber risk, particularly social-engineering-based threats like SEO poisoning, cannot be fully understood through numerical metrics alone but must be viewed within a broader context as part of a complex human-technology interface.

The data collection process involves systematically gathering peer-reviewed articles, cybersecurity frameworks, government advisories, and organizational case analyses published between 2020 and 2025. Key databases include IEEE Xplore, ScienceDirect, and Google Scholar, supplemented by authoritative sources such as ENISA, Fortinet, IBM, Palo Alto Networks, and the World Economic Forum.

Selection criteria focus on sources that address hybrid network security, insider risk dynamics (Jones, 2021), and social engineering through search manipulation. Literature was filtered using keywords such as SEO poisoning, boundary-crossing threats, hybrid work cybersecurity, firewall bypass, and human-mediated cyber vulnerabilities.

A thematic synthesis analysis was used to identify relationships across studies, focusing on four areas: (1) the technical mechanics of SEO poisoning, (2) the behavioral enablers within corporate settings, (3) the systemic weaknesses of traditional firewall models, and (4) the strategic countermeasures proposed in modern cybersecurity policy and design. This analytical approach facilitates convergence between academic insight and operational practice, ensuring that the study's findings are conceptually rigorous and practically relevant.

Finally, this study uses an integrative literature review method, combining descriptive analysis with interpretive synthesis to map the intellectual and operational landscape of SEO poisoning. By placing this inquiry at the crossroads of technology, organizational behavior, and cyber risk strategy, the study seeks to build a clear and practical comprehension of how an outwardly indirect cyber threat breaches the protected core of enterprise environments through human interaction.

METHODOLOGY AND RESEARCH DESIGN

This study employs a qualitative, integrative research design, grounded in a structured literature review methodology. The primary aim is to synthesize, interpret, and critically evaluate the complex interplay of behavioral, technical, and organizational factors that give rise to SEO poisoning and its circumvention of traditional enterprise cybersecurity. This approach is particularly well-suited for topics where emergent threats and evolving best practices outpace quantitative measurement and where rich, contextual knowledge is needed to inform future research, policy, and operational recommendations (Cronin & George, 2023).

The literature review follows a systematic, multi-stage process to ensure rigor, transparency, and reproducibility. Sources were identified through targeted searches of scholarly databases (including IEEE Xplore, ScienceDirect, and Google Scholar) as well as industry-leading threat intelligence repositories, white papers, and government advisories from 2020 to 2025. Search terms included combinations of "SEO poisoning," "human firewall," "social engineering," "zero trust," "hybrid work cybersecurity," and "boundary-crossing attack." Selection criteria prioritized works that addressed the convergence of human behavior, technological vulnerability, and hybrid organizational environments, emphasizing case studies, empirical research, and foundational theoretical analysis.

After initial identification, studies were screened for relevance, methodological quality, and publication credibility, and any work that did not directly examine the mechanics, risks, or organizational context of SEO poisoning or similar perimeter-blurring threats was excluded. The included literature was subjected to a thematic synthesis: findings and insights were coded and categorized according to recurring constructs, including user trust, technical defenses, insider threat risk (Jones, 2021), perimeter dissolution, and adaptive adversary behavior. This enabled the identification of prevailing patterns, critical gaps, and points of theoretical integration across disparate sources.

Limitations of the research design include relying on secondary data and the risk of publication bias in rapidly changing threat landscapes. To address this, the search strategy included gray literature, technical threat advisories, and the latest industry reports, ensuring that emerging risks, often underrepresented in academic journals, were considered. The overall result is an integrated synthesis that aims not only to describe the current state of knowledge but also to highlight actionable pathways for organizational and scholarly progress in cyber risk management.

THEORETICAL FOUNDATIONS

The theoretical foundation is essential to understanding why SEO poisoning, a technique that manipulates technology and human behavior, remains so effective at circumventing enterprise defenses. This study draws upon three interrelated frameworks, Social Engineering Theory (augmented by the Human Firewall Construct), the Zero Trust Security Paradigm, and Socio-Technical Systems Theory. These frameworks explain how digital deception operates across human and technical areas. Each theory provides a distinct but complementary lens through which to interpret how attackers exploit trust, how organizations misplace confidence in their perimeter security, and how the interplay between human decision-making and system architecture creates exploitable gaps in defense.

Social Engineering Theory and the Human Construct

Social Engineering Theory forms the core of this research. It proposes that cyber adversaries exploit psychological tendencies like trust, authority, fear, and curiosity to manipulate individuals into actions that compromise security protocols. This era of cyberattacks extends beyond traditional IT issues; attacks are now shaped by economies, geopolitics, and public trust (Microsoft, 2024). In the context of SEO poisoning, these manipulations often happen when employees, acting on genuine professional intent, click on compromised links ranked highly by familiar search engines (Petelka et al., 2019). As Fortinet and Vectra note, this dynamic exposes the most significant vulnerability in cybersecurity: the human element. The "*human firewall*" concept extends this idea, reimagining employees as a defensive layer and a potential point of failure (Venkitanarayanan, 2025); staff who know how to spot and block online tricks. A human firewall is an alert, vigilant workforce capable of spotting and stopping deceptive cues. However, it also emphasizes that even well-trained individuals can remain vulnerable to fatigue, urgency, or overconfidence. Within this framework, human judgment is viewed as the frontline of cyber resilience and the most commonly exploited vulnerability.

Zero Trust Security Paradigm

NIST Special Publication 800-207 defines *zero trust* as a set of cybersecurity principles that shift defenses from static, network-based perimeters to focus on users, assets, and resources (Rose et al., 2020). The Zero Trust model provides the architectural counterpart to social engineering theory by challenging the outdated assumption that internally originated activity is inherently safe (Li et al., 2025). It asserts that "never trust, always verify" must be the operational principle in a threat landscape where deception can originate from inside or outside network perimeters (Kang et al., 2023). In the context of SEO poisoning, this paradigm demonstrates why traditional firewalls and perimeter-based models are insufficient; malware introduced by an authorized user through a legitimate-seeming web search bypasses the static barrier entirely. Zero Trust reframes security as continuous verification: access should be transactional, context-aware, and behavior-driven, even for authenticated users. Zero-trust frameworks, which continuously verify who is who and whether they are inside or outside the organization's system, can enhance cybersecurity by continuously validating access and constraining implicit trust, thereby safeguarding user privacy from unauthorized exposure (Paul et al., 2024; Rose et al., 2020). These frameworks enhance data reliability by implementing stringent authentication and robust access controls, ensuring that only authorized entities access critical information (Li et al., 2025). Applied here, the framework justifies the argument that defending against SEO poisoning requires sustained validation of user actions, content sources, and browsing pathways, not merely endpoint isolation or antivirus scanning.

Socio-Technical Systems Theory

Where the first two frameworks describe attack vectors, Socio-Technical Systems Theory integrates them into a holistic view of organizational vulnerability. This theory explains cybersecurity as the product of dynamic interactions between people, technical systems, and institutional structures (Münch et al, 2022). Socio-Technical Systems theory contends that failures like SEO poisoning arise not from a single flaw but from misalignments between human behavior, organizational policy, and security technology. Within this framework, effective defense requires recognizing that technical controls are only as strong as the human workflows and cultural norms in which they are embedded. Given that an organization comprises various interdependent components that interact in intricate manners, it is crucial to evaluate potential repercussions when designing or modifying any segment of the system; failure to do so may result in systems that hinder effectiveness.

Together, these frameworks form an interdisciplinary foundation for analyzing SEO poisoning as a hybrid phenomenon, simultaneously technological, behavioral, and organizational. Social Engineering Theory identifies the human cognitive vectors that attackers target; the Zero Trust Paradigm exposes the fallacy of implicit digital trust; and Socio-Technical Systems Theory unites concepts within a broader ecosystemic model. The Theoretical Integration Framework for SEO Poisoning Analysis depicts the integration of the three frameworks for SEO poisoning analysis.

Figure 1. Theoretical Integration Framework for SEO Poisoning Analysis

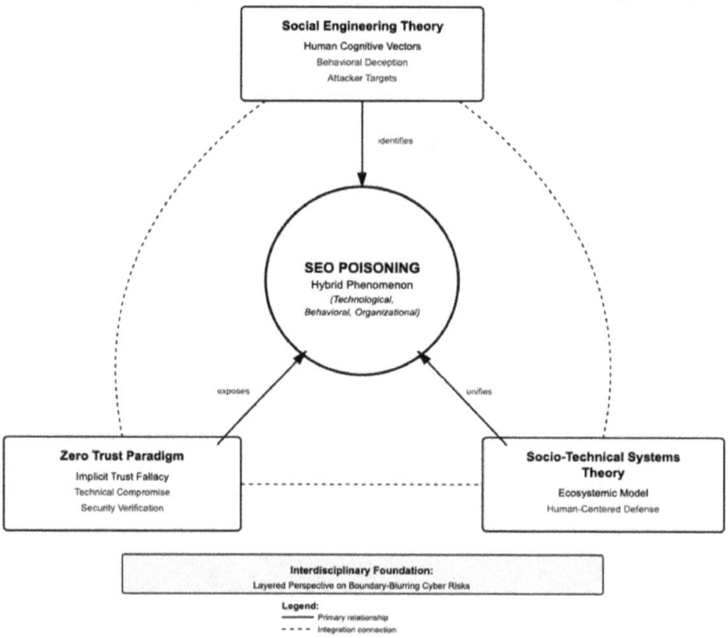

Note. The author of this paper created this visual representation.

By combining these lenses, this study moves beyond single-factor explanations of cyber incidents. It offers a layered perspective that aligns with current cybersecurity research and emphasizes adaptive, human-centered defense strategies. This integration not only reinforces the study's conceptual rigor but also situates it within the emerging discourse on boundary-blurring cyber risks, where behavioral deception and technical compromise converge to redefine organizational security.

LITERATURE REVIEW

Evolution of SEO

The evolution of search engine optimization (SEO) reflects the rapid advancement of the digital landscape and the growing sophistication of online content discovery mechanisms (Guelailia & Bouziane, 2024; Shaharia, 2025). In the earliest years, SEO was primarily about gaming simple search algorithms through techniques such as keyword stuffing, meta tag manipulation, and bulk directory submissions. During the 1990s, webmasters quickly discovered that by repeating keywords frequently and manipulating hidden tags, they could significantly improve search engine rankings on AltaVista and Yahoo (Dobbala & Lingolu, 2023). As search volume grew and the number of websites expanded exponentially, early SEO practices focused almost exclusively on keyword density, with little attention to user intent or content quality. The late 1990s witnessed the emergence of Google, whose PageRank algorithm shifted emphasis toward external link authority, making inbound link-building a core competitive strategy. This marked a pivot away from simplistic content manipulation, demanding that websites cultivate genuine credibility to earn top rankings (Dobbala & Lingolu, 2023).

Over the next two decades, SEO matured in step with advances in search engine algorithms that increasingly emphasized user-centric design, content quality, and semantic understanding. Algorithm updates such as Google's Panda, Penguin, and Hummingbird forced marketers to shift from keyword-heavy tactics to strategies that prioritize user experience, relevant backlinks, and comprehensive information architecture (Sarkar et al., 2024). By the mid-2010s, mobile compatibility and site speed became essential ranking factors, reflecting the shift to mobile browsing.

SEO Classification Types

SEO strategies are generally divided into categories that reflect the ethical framework and goals behind their implementation (Banerjee &Roy, 2024). These approaches not only influence how search engines rank a website but also impact the site's long-term reputation and digital standing. According to Banerjee and Roy (2024), SEOs can be classified into two types:

Whitehat SEO Techniques – Sanctioned Practices

Many companies may hire marketing consultants to boost their website's search engine ranking and prepare it for indexing. Conversely, some might use unethical techniques to achieve the same goal. While the website's design primarily targets end users, it is also structured to allow search engine crawlers to navigate easily and quickly. White-hat techniques that follow search engine optimization best practices for quality include creating a sitemap and using relevant headers and subheadings (Banerjee &Roy, 2024; Lu et al., 2011). Banerjee and Roy (2024) contend that traffic quality is the primary objective of advanced SEO approaches. The intent is to attract visitors genuinely interested in the products offered on the website. These visitors are often considered quality traffic (Wallenius, 2024).

Blackhat SEO Techniques – Illicit Practices

These tactics aim to manipulate rankings rather than follow search engine criteria. Black-hat techniques include redirects, hidden text and links, keyword stuffing (crowding the page with irrelevant phrases), and participation in link farms. Black-hat SEO employs aggressive strategies that contravene search engine guidelines to manipulate algorithms and unjustly enhance website rankings in search results (Wu et al., 2025). These strategies are not acceptable to search engines, and if they are found, a website may be removed from their index (Banerjee &Roy, 2024; Lu et al., 2011).

SEO and the Organizational Context

The history of search engine optimization in organizational contexts has moved far beyond the early ambition of simply driving traffic or increasing brand visibility. In the 2000s, enterprises invested heavily in SEO to maximize market reach, leveraging authoritative content and organic search rankings to attract prospective clients and partners. As SEO became integral to business strategies, attackers recognized and exploited this reliance, turning search engines into vectors for malware distribution and social engineering. Organizations began to experience significant risks not just from misconfigured infrastructure, but also from compromised third-party links or reputation-based poisoning campaigns that leveraged their legitimate web assets (CrowdStrike, 2025a).

By the late 2010s and early 2020s, SEO poisoning became a prominent tactic in advanced cyber threats specifically targeting business environments. Contemporary campaigns exploit human behavior within the enterprise by manipulating search results that employees trust in their daily workflows. Attackers employ sophisticated black-hat SEO tactics, such as keyword cannibalization, typosquatting (Fake websites with small spelling errors meant to catch people making mistakes), and cloaking, to push malicious sites to the top of high-value organizational queries, such as software downloads or IT troubleshooting (Fortinet, 2025; Vectra, 2024). When employing typosquatting, the assailant initially registers a typosquatted domain, which consists of slightly misspelled or otherwise misleading variations of legitimate software websites, such as putty[.]run or puttyy[.]org (Crowdstrike, 2025a; HHS Cybersecurity Program, 2023; Wung et al., 2025).

These websites are optimized for search engine optimization and often feature deceptive ads, boosting their visibility when people seek download links. The URL can contain misspellings, such as using a "1" instead of an "I," thereby tricking users searching for information (HHS Cybersecurity Program, 2023). Once an employee unknowingly visits a poisoned site, malware is frequently downloaded, circumventing the firewall since the interaction is perceived as user-initiated and legitimate. Recent incidents have shown that browser synchronization, credential reuse, and hybrid network configurations expose organizations to risks that firewalls alone cannot address. Security teams now contend with attackers leveraging SEO to move attacks from public to private networks, effectively bypassing perimeter controls and establishing persistent threats deep within enterprise infrastructure (Zscaler, 2025; Precursor Security, 2024).

Modern SEO

Shaharia (2025) posits that present-day SEO focuses on authority, context, and user value. Semantic search, which considers user behavior and the meaning of words and phrases, has advanced beyond simple keyword matching (Keever 2024; Sarkar et al., 2024; Shaharia 2025). Further, researchers posit that AI now powers search engines, so emphasizing quality signals and contextual understanding should be the main priority. AI has exacerbated cybercrime, enhancing its complexity, scalability, and difficulty of prevention. AI-based risks are not as static as previous cyber threats, rendering them nearly impossible to mitigate with current security methods (Syed, 2022). AI systems are engineered for real-time data processing, pattern identification, and decision-making, rendering them suitable for both cybersecurity and the perpetration of cybercrime (Syed, 2022).

AI-driven ranking systems now consider contextual user intent, search behavior, and content sentiment, requiring SEO practitioners to design content for both human engagement and algorithmic clarity. According to Shaharia (2025, p. 4), the five new signals for prioritization are: "1. Topical authority (full coverage on niche topics), 2. Semantic search & vector-based indexing, 3. User engagement signals: dwell time, scroll depth, 4. Visual content SEO (image + video schema), and 5. Structured data (rich results, FAQs, how-to events)." Contemporary SEO shows evolution and presents clear patterns, with factors such as increased human engagement in pursuit of more information and the rise of artificial intelligence and natural language processing (Syed, 2022) within search engines driving SEO toward even greater sophistication and cybersecurity concerns. The data is unmistakable: Attackers make significant investments in scalable operations, automation, and reconnaissance (Fortinet, 2024). While far too many organizations remain overloaded with reactive patch cycles and static security policies, attackers' tactics strongly emphasize speed, stealth, and scalability.

SEO POISONING: TWO CYBER-CONTEXTUAL CASE STUDIES

Case Study 1. ReliaQuest's 2025 "Mimicked Payroll Portal"

In May 2025, ReliaQuest investigated a notable example of SEO poisoning that exploited human behavior outside the organizational perimeter within a manufacturing environment (Knowles, 2025). An employee, needing access to the company's payroll portal, chose convenience and searched from a mobile device instead of using secure bookmarks and authorized login methods. Attackers created a convincing phishing site that mimicked the legitimate payroll login page and ranked it highly in mobile search results through targeted search engine manipulation and SEO tactics, including sponsored Google Ads. The employee, trusting the fraudulent link, entered their organizational credentials into the fake site (Knowles, 2025).

With access credentials in hand, adversaries logged into the legitimate payroll system, modified direct deposit information, and then redirected employee paychecks to attacker-controlled accounts. The targeted use of personal, non-corporate devices, often on home or public Wi-Fi networks, allowed threat actors to bypass enterprise threat detection, network logging, and security filtering typically enforced within corporate environments. Notably, this poisoned result and the corresponding phishing portal evaded detection when users performed company-related searches on devices protected by network defenses, highlighting the critical role of user context and device targeting in the attack's success.

This campaign highlights the serious risks that arise when employees use personal or unsecured devices to access sensitive company resources outside of company firewalls. These SEO poisoning tactics exploit the fact that hybrid and remote workers often use unauthorized methods for business tasks. The incident underscores the need for multifactor authentication, which ReliaQuest urged organizations to pay closer attention to (Knowles, 2025), strong access controls, comprehensive user training, and clear policies to prevent staff from accessing critical business portals through unapproved search methods (Al Qwaid, 2025). It also demonstrates how cyber attackers are becoming more adaptable, combining SEO manipulation with targeted phishing, which makes traditional enterprise defenses focused on firewalls insufficient in today's world of remote work and diverse devices.

Case Study 2. Palo Alto Networks' 2025 "Operation Rewrite"

SEO directly influences cybersecurity, as search engines penalize sites compromised by malware or harmful content, making strong site security an essential part of modern SEO strategies. Consequently, organizations can be exploited through SEO manipulations. An example illustrating SEO poisoning via enterprise infrastructure is provided in Palo Alto Networks' 2025 "Operation Rewrite." In this operation, Chinese-speaking threat actors used a malicious IIS (Internet Information Services) module, BadIIS, to infiltrate legitimate, high-reputation corporate web servers (Vectra, 2024; Zemah, 2025). After gaining access to the IIS request pipeline, BadIIS (Hromcová & Cherepanov, 2021; Unit 42 by Palo Alto Networks) was installed as a native module, granting the attackers extensive privileges and control over incoming and outgoing web traffic.

In this case, the SEO poisoning tactic was remarkably sophisticated. Instead of establishing their own domains, the attackers exploited the trust of hijacked enterprise websites to manipulate search engines. BadIIS dynamically injected keyword-rich (Hromcová & Cherepanov, 2021; Unit 42 by Palo Alto Networks; Sarkar et al., 2024), attacker-controlled HTML content retrieved in real time from a remote command-and-control (C2) (CISA, 2023) server whenever search engine crawlers visited the compromised site (Zemah, 2025). Content was tailored to rank for popular or profitable searches (such as gambling, pirated streaming, or malware-infected software utilities), enabling the poisoned company's domain to appear prominently in organic search results for a variety of queries.

For ordinary users and automated crawlers that did not meet the attacker's targeting criteria, the site behaved as usual. But when an actual victim, often an enterprise user searching for trusted software or documentation, clicked the newly poisoned search result and landed on the legitimate corporate domain, BadIIS triggered the second stage of the attack (Unit 42 by Palo Alto Networks; Zemah, 2025). It performed additional checks (such as inspecting the HTTP referrer and user-agent headers) and, if a match was found, redirected the user or proxied the scam content directly from the attacker's infrastructure. In the process, these users often encountered malware, fell for phishing attempts, or were directed to fraudulent services, all while their browsers indicated they were visiting a reputable organization's site. Contrasting email-based phishing, which disseminates harmful content to potential victims, SEO poisoning uses a pull tactic, anticipating that people will search for specific information. Vectra (2024) notes that the transition from push to pull attacks signifies a strategic advancement in cybercrime.

In "Operation Rewrite," the operational impact went even further: attackers were able to pivot within compromised organizations, deploying web shells, creating new user accounts, accessing source code, and moving laterally to other production servers and domain controllers (Zemah, 2025). This enabled not just SEO poisoning but full-scale espionage or monetization attacks, all while leveraging the trusted reputation and IP space of compromised victims.

Operation Rewrite illustrates a modern, two-phase SEO poisoning attack: first, a lure is created by using trusted, legitimate web assets to manipulate search rankings; second, users who rely on those search results are tricked and redirected into the attacker's ecosystem, bypassing not only technical defenses but also organizational trust. This case underscores the sophistication and the boundary-crossing nature of today's SEO poisoning, where the interaction between human trust, technical privileges, and attacker automation generates unique and wide-ranging risks for organizations.

CONCLUSIONS AND RECOMMENDATIONS

This section synthesizes the study's findings, discusses the broader implications, particularly regarding organizational, technical, and policy responses, and addresses the need for updated governance and risk management frameworks. Including legal and ethical analysis here aligns with the paper's practice of drawing strategic implications and proposing next steps for institutions, policymakers, and practitioners. This placement ensures the argument about liability, ethical duties, and regulatory evolution is framed within the overall narrative's call to adapt and reform digital risk strategies in response to threat evolution.

SEO poisoning presents multifaceted legal, ethical, and regulatory challenges as attackers manipulate search results to drive unwitting users to malicious websites, often leading to data breaches, financial losses, and erosion of digital trust. Legally, organizations are increasingly liable under frameworks such as the Regulation (EU) 2016/679 of the European Parliament and of the Council of 27 April 2016 (General Data Protection Regulation) (Europe) and the California Consumer Privacy Act of 2018 (CCPA) (California), if such incidents result in data loss; breaches stemming from SEO poisoning can trigger stiff fines, lawsuits, and regulatory investigations, especially if sensitive user information is compromised. Ethically, both malicious actors and negligent site operators can face criticism, threat actors for deliberately exploiting users' trust in search engines, and organizations for failing to implement adequate controls and user education that could have prevented exposure to these risks. Regulatory responses are intensifying globally: Beyond enforcing mandatory data protection, the EU's Digital Services Act and similar proposed U.S. legislation increasingly press search engines to quickly delist poisoned results and bolster preemptive verification of advertised content, as seen in recent policy discussions and in the fallout from real-world manipulations during major events like the COVID-19 pandemic and the World Cup. For example, during the COVID-19 pandemic, SEO poisoning led to the dissemination of malware via fake information sites and exposed companies to significant reputational and financial damage, underscoring the escalating scrutiny and the need for legal and policy reforms.

Cybercriminals employ AI in contemporary attacks, enabling the creation of highly targeted and scalable attack vectors, such as AI-driven spear-phishing and automated hacking, which can breach most modern security measures (Syed, 2025). In 2025, SEO poisoning emerged as a prominent threat that straddles the intersection of technological vulnerability and human fallibility. The attack does not seek to breach firewalls or directly penetrate private networks through conventional vectors. Instead, it thrives on employees' behavioral patterns as they routinely navigate between protected corporate environments and the public internet (Champa et al., 2025; Vakulov, 2025). By manipulating search engine algorithms and creating compelling, malicious sites, adversaries have discovered a powerful way to subvert the so-called human firewall, which represents the last line of defense in a distributed, digitally transformed organization (Das Guptta et al., 2024; Fortinet, 2025).

The risk posed by SEO poisoning is multidimensional, affecting not only the technical integrity of information systems but also the organization's and operational continuity. It is now well documented that poisoned clones of corporate sites have diverted customer interactions, degraded brand authority, and polluted analytics critical to strategic business decisions (CrowdStrike, 2025b). The damage does not end at external compromise. Attackers have leveraged backdoored administrative tools downloaded by unsuspecting IT staff, allowing malware and advanced persistent threats to bypass network boundaries and establish a foothold deep within internal systems.

Furthermore, keeping bookmarks, passwords, and settings the same across attacks and credential reuse has paved additional pathways for intrusion (Vakulov, 2025). Modern attackers exploit synchronized browsing profiles and user extensions to effectively clone and transfer malicious artifacts or compromised credentials between personal and professional endpoints. Stolen session tokens or VPN credentials further enable adversaries to pivot from a seemingly inconspicuous web search to a high-value organizational domain, rendering traditional threat intelligence and perimeter monitoring insufficient (Vectra, 2024). This dynamic reveals SEO poisoning as not only a precursor but a multiplier of compound risks within complex environments.

SEO poisoning campaigns follow a sophisticated *kill chain*, the stages hackers go through to launch an attack, that maximizes reach and evasion. Recommendations provide responses to address each stage of the contemporary SEO poisoning kill chain (Microsoft, 2024):

1. Keyword Research and Selection As adversaries continue to implement AI, cyber defenders must do the same (Microsoft, 2024). Defenders should employ threat intelligence platforms to monitor which keywords are being targeted within their sector, especially those linked to administrative tools, corporate portals, or trending organizational topics. Proactive monitoring for suspicious domain registrations and rapid analysis of keyword trends can provide early warning of possible targeting.
2. Infrastructure Preparation Network defenders should leverage domain monitoring and rapid takedown services to detect suspicious domains that closely resemble legitimate business assets. IT teams should work with registrars to quickly identify and eliminate malicious domains or hosting environments that appear early in attack planning.
3. Content Generation Organizations can use AI content detection tools to identify and report synthetically generated webpages that mimic legitimate content or brands. Regular scanning for unauthorized duplication of official content helps spot and address malicious clones before they gain traction with search engines or end-users.
4. SEO Optimization Proactively monitor for aggressive link-building, keyword stuffing, and other artificial ranking signals associated with malicious actors. Establish partnerships with digital risk vendors specializing in detecting and disrupting link-farm networks and fake authority schemes that manipulate search engine algorithms.
5. Search Engine Indexing Set up automated routines that routinely check major search engines for new high-ranking pages using variations of critical keywords, brand names, and service terms. Promptly report any findings to the relevant search providers to achieve quick delisting of malicious content before it is widely accessed.
6. Victim Targeting Deploy web proxy and browser isolation technologies to restrict what information can be fingerprinted by external sites. User sessions should be anonymized or segmented to limit the amount of device and environment data provided to web servers, making precise targeting by attackers more difficult.
7. Payload Delivery Ensure that all endpoints are protected by advanced endpoint detection and response (EDR) platforms that can identify and block drive-by downloads, suspicious installers, and phishing attempts. Mandate regular user training, including simulated *incident response exercises*, the plan and actions

taken to deal with and recover from a cybersecurity attack, to reduce the likelihood of successful credential harvesting or malware installation.

8. **Post-compromise Activity** Implement a zero-trust architecture by restricting lateral movement through microsegmentation and least-privilege access to minimize the reach of risks from abuse of power and curtail the scope of threats (Kang et al., 2023; Rose et al., 2020). Use behavioral analytics on endpoints and networks to detect unauthorized persistence or unusual account activity and ensure that post-infection recovery includes comprehensive forensics to remove hidden backdoors and persistence mechanisms.

The strategic implications reach into trust, resilience, and digital policy. As organizations adopt hybrid work and expand SaaS solutions, the risk of adversaries operating in the gray area between private and public spaces increases. This shift makes SEO poisoning a key example of a "boundary-layer" threat, highlighting how behavioral and technological weaknesses reinforce each other. As cybersecurity and digital trust are critical concepts in this contemporary era, organizations urgently need to update their understanding of digital trust (Malik, 2024). Relying on perimeter-based security without strong behavioral monitoring and ongoing verification creates significant gaps. Scholars and security experts recommend investing in user training, real-time browser isolation, AI-powered detection tools (Syed, 2022), and integrated incident response plans that cover both technical and social aspects of deception (IBM X-Force, 2025).

Organizations benefit from establishing effective responses to counter SEO poisoning. These plans should be organized into short-, mid-, and long-term priorities. Recommended examples include:

Short-Term Priorities

Organizations must take immediate action to combat SEO poisoning by increasing employee awareness and deploying rapid-response technical controls. Implementing organization-wide security training focused on identifying poisoned search results, suspicious downloads, and lookalike domains should become a top priority.

1. Conduct simulated phishing and SEO poisoning exercises to prepare employees for real incidents and reinforce vigilance. "Phishing employee trick or organizational treat" highlights the key difference between a malicious cyberattack and an opportunity for security education (Champa et al., 2025). Phishing attacks have been a significant concern for many years; however, advancements in technology, particularly the integration of artificial intelligence, have made them more frequent and sophisticated (Syed, 2022). Conventional phishing involves

sending emails or messages designed to deceive the recipient into disclosing personal information. AI phishing extends beyond simple phishing by leveraging artificial intelligence and natural language processing to generate highly realistic messages that closely resemble corporate communications. A phishing attack can pose serious risks to an organization; however, a security team can use a simulated phishing campaign as a harmless educational tool to boost employee awareness and strengthen defenses. Discourage cyber leaders from viewing phishing exercises as "tricking employees"; instead, see the simulations as a way to identify common behaviors that need attention to help prevent successful exploits. Additionally, Eze & Shamir (2024) argue that, since phishing email attacks often involve sending fraudulent emails to many recipients, a defense is to detect a high volume of identical emails received by the mail server within a short timeframe.

2. Enforce browser isolation policies for accessing untrusted websites and require endpoint protection solutions on corporate devices to reduce initial exposure (CrowdStrike, 2025b). Browser isolation policies isolate dangerous web activity from the core IT environment and endpoints, providing proactive defense. When a company requires browser isolation, all browsing sessions to untrusted, unknown, or high-risk websites are done in a remote or virtualized environment. This prevents poisoned search results from running malicious programs, scripts, or drive-by downloads on company machines. Instead, the user interacts with an isolated website rendering, reducing the risk of malicious code compromising device security or accessing internal network resources.
3. Incident response teams should monitor the IT help desk and user reports for abnormal system behavior or credential loss, enabling faster containment of suspected attacks. IT administrators must regularly update browser extensions, plugins, and endpoint software to close vulnerabilities exploited by SEO poisoning tactics (Vectra, 2024). Quickly deploying domain-monitoring tools that alert the security team to brand impersonation or unexpected changes in search engine rankings is crucial (Fortinet, 2025).

Mid-Term Priorities

1. Organizations should evolve their security models to embrace zero-trust principles that emphasize continuous authentication, least-privilege access, and real-time network monitoring (Palo Alto Networks Unit 42, 2025). Implementing AI-augmented detection tools that analyze web, DNS, and endpoint telemetry will empower security teams to detect novel attack patterns and automate blocking actions before malware reaches internal systems (Al Qwaid, 2025).

2. To strengthen cross-functional defense, organizations need to foster collaboration among IT, security, legal, and communications staff to develop coordinated response plans for SEO poisoning-related incidents. Regular tabletop and live simulation exercises involving technical and non-technical stakeholders should be used to test scenarios such as credential theft, browser synchronization attacks, or brand impersonation. Periodic reviews of third-party vendor, marketing, and SaaS application policies ensure that external actors do not unintentionally expose the organization to poisoned assets (IBM Security X-Force, 2025).

Long-Term Priorities

1. Long-term, enterprises must invest in building AI-powered security operations centers (SOCs) that leverage autonomous monitoring and detection at scale. Organizations should support sector-wide sharing of threat intelligence, including joint action on takedown requests for SEO-poisoned domains impersonating their brands. Actively participating in cross-industry alliances and collaborating with regulators can drive the adoption of standards for secure search engine practices and domain registration protocols (ENISA, 2025).
2. Long-term resilience depends on embedding digital risk management and adaptive cyber defense into organizational culture and governance. Leadership must establish a structure for continuous learning, from both simulated and real-world incidents, and adapt policies as attackers innovate. Moving beyond the perimeter, digital trust must be cultivated at every level (Ei et al., 2023; Hasan, 2025), recognizing that boundary-blurring threats like SEO poisoning will persist as the Internet and enterprise environments continue to converge.
3. Organizations must promptly implement measures to counteract SEO poisoning by enhancing employee knowledge and instituting swift technology controls. The longer the delay in responding, the greater the impact of an incident can become. Comprehending the human experience and the social aspects of critical incident management is essential for formulating comprehensive plans that meet both the immediate practical demands of individuals and foster long-term community resilience and well-being (Baraldo & Di Franco, 2024). Reputational damage worsens when customers and partners lose trust in a brand (Burton, 2024; Jones, 2020), as seen after evidence of SEO manipulation or credential theft. The ripple effects from information traps include legal issues, regulatory review, and unexpected business disruptions. As attack scenarios become more autonomous and digital transformation accelerates, security needs to be flexible and integrated rather than static or isolated.

SEO poisoning has disrupted many long-standing beliefs about organizational boundaries and layered defenses. Generative AI has significantly transformed content creation and SEO optimization (Keever, 2024). The rise of AI-driven attack automation, seamless web browser synchronization, and user-driven behavioral risks now requires a re-evaluation of cyber risk strategies (Vakulov, 2025). Organizations that do not see SEO poisoning as a direct threat to both their technical and human systems risk increased financial and reputational damage. Future research and leadership must view SEO poisoning not as a minor inconvenience but as a critical challenge in the evolution of digital risk.

RECOMMENDATIONS FOR FUTURE RESEARCH

AI-assisted security frameworks exist to address AI-based cyber risks. The IDS, anomaly detection systems, and reaction generators are powered by artificial intelligence. Artificial intelligence enables security systems to monitor network activities, identify alterations in operational characteristics, and promptly detect potential threats (Syed, 2022). Future research on SEO poisoning should focus on innovative methods and expanding empirical evidence, emphasizing the need to bridge the gap between advanced, evolving attacker tactics and practical organizational responses. As current evidence indicates, the changing nature of SEO poisoning, which includes AI-generated content and legitimate business domains, requires a research agenda that is reactive to new threats and proactive in anticipating shifts in attacker and defender strategies. The following three methodological approaches are outlined; each is designed to uncover new insights and provide practical guidance for academic research and enterprise defense.

Longitudinal Behavioral Analytics, User Simulation, and Autonomous Detection

Next-generation studies should pair longitudinal behavioral analytics with simulated enterprise environments and autonomous monitoring technologies. For example, simulated "red team" scenarios can be augmented by AI-powered behavioral anomaly detection (Syed, 2022) that tracks how employees engage with search engines, interact with suspicious download prompts, and respond to new browser extensions over extended periods. Conduct simulations that mirror disruptive threats. Embedding autonomous endpoint analytics and user- and entity-behavior analytics (UEBA) enables researchers to monitor and automatically flag suspicious activity, such as unexpected downloads from newly registered domains or rapid privilege escalations following web-based interactions (Khan et al., 2022). Integrating deception technology, such as honeypot poisoned search results, can further support rich empirical analysis while fueling defense innovation.

Key Steps:

- Design AI-assisted simulations with adaptive poisoned search scenarios and browser-injected telemetry.
- Deploy and calibrate *autonomous detection platforms,* computer systems that detect attacks autonomously, to capture and flag user behaviors and system events indicative of SEO poisoning.
- Analyze results across employee groups, functional roles, and organizational privileges to tune technical and human-centric responses.
- Leverage findings to guide implementation of context-aware browser isolation, real-time sandboxing, and instant remediation workflows.

Cross-Sectional Case Analysis and AI-Informed Risk Mapping

Future cross-sectional studies must move beyond static attack case summaries to dynamic, industry-wide mapping of SEO poisoning threats, infused with real-time threat intelligence feeds and AI-based web crawler surveillance. Researchers should establish federated partnerships among cybersecurity teams across sectors to enable collective monitoring of brand impersonation, lookalike domains, and anomalous spikes in search engine rankings for industry-critical keywords. AI-powered digital risk protection platforms can be deployed to continuously scan and classify newly registered domains and rapidly surface "brandjacking" trends or emerging threat actors.

Key Steps:

- Aggregate and analyze domain telemetry, threat intelligence, and case data with autonomous classification models.
- Use machine learning to correlate attack methods, threat actor signatures, and defense gaps across sectors.
- Generate adaptive "attack surface maps" for at-risk industries to guide coordinated early warning and response.
- Develop guidelines for automated takedown requests, DNS filtering, and regulator collaboration informed by ongoing AI analysis.

Design Science, Participatory Action, and AI-Driven Defense Co-Development

The imperative for participatory, action-oriented research is heightened by the speed and adaptability of AI-driven SEO poisoning. Future design science efforts should co-create, pilot, and refine security solutions with practitioners at every stage, prioritizing innovations such as AI-powered web filtering algorithms, zero-day domain detection engines, automated detonation chambers for suspicious downloads, and workflow-integrated browser isolation protocols. AI-enabled SOAR (Security Orchestration, Automation, and Response) platforms should be optimized for continuous, autonomous aggregation of weak digital signals, with dynamic adaptation informed by real-world detection experience (Felix & Claudia, 2021; Kolosnjaji, 2024).

Key Steps:

- Collaborate with enterprise SOCs to iteratively deploy and improve autonomous threat monitoring and AI-driven deception infrastructure.
- Establish real-time feedback loops in which detection errors and success stories directly inform algorithmic logic and user training content.
- Conduct cross-enterprise tabletop and live attack simulations using AI adversary emulation to benchmark defense agility and resilience.
- Document resulting defense playbooks and automation templates for wide dissemination and uptake.

Notably, despite the growing use of online platforms to collect data, researchers have raised several concerns about their use and the quality of the data obtained (Newman et al., 2021; Smith). Therefore, internal validity, construct validity, external validity, and statistical conclusion validity must be considered (Newman et al., 2021). However, advancing the research and defense of SEO poisoning requires moving decisively toward multidisciplinary, AI-augmented, and automation-empowered inquiry. Artificial intelligence is revolutionizing search engine optimization by enhancing search precision, streamlining content development, and prioritizing user intent. Integrating AI tools while maintaining human expertise is essential in this era (Keever, 2024). By combining autonomous detection, sector-wide intelligence collaboration, and user-centric adaptive controls, scholars, policymakers, and practitioners alike can preempt, rather than merely react to, the shifting balance of adversarial innovation. Only through such forward-looking, technologically infused research can organizations maintain cyber resilience in the face of relentless, AI-enabled boundary-blurring attacks.

REFERENCES

Abbas, H., Emmanuel, N., Amjad, M. F., Yaqoob, T., Atiquzzaman, M., Iqbal, Z., & Shafqat, N. Bin Shahid., Tanveer, A., & Ashfaq, U. (2023). Security assessment and evaluation of VPNs: a comprehensive survey. *ACM Computing Surveys, 55*(13s), 1-47. https://dl-acm-org.captechu.idm.oclc.org/doi/full/10.1145/3579162

Al Qwaid, M. (2025). Cybersecurity threats: Ransomware, phishing, and social engineering. In *Complexities and Challenges for Securing Digital Assets and Infrastructure* (pp. 399–434). IGI Global Scientific Publishing., DOI: 10.4018/979-8-3373-1370-2.ch018

Alouffi, B., Hasnain, M., Alharbi, A., Alosaimi, W., Alyami, H., & Ayaz, M. (2021). A systematic literature review on cloud computing security: Threats and mitigation strategies. *IEEE Access : Practical Innovations, Open Solutions*, *9*, 57792–57807. DOI: 10.1109/ACCESS.2021.3073203

Banerjee, R., & Roy, R. (2024). Deception in the digital age: How SEO poisoning undermines online trust. https://multiarticlesjournal.com/uploads/articles/IJCRM-2024-3-3-45.pdf (accessed on 23 October 2025)

Baraldo, M., & Di Franco, P. D. G. (2024). Place-centred emerging technologies for disaster management: A scoping review. *International Journal of Disaster Risk Reduction, 112*, 104782. DOI: 10.1016/j.ijdrr.2024.104782

Burrell, D. N. (Ed.). (2024). *Multisector Insights in Healthcare, Social Sciences, Society, and Technology*. IGI Global. DOI: 10.4018/979-8-3693-3226-9

Burton, S. L. (2022). Strategy: A Business and Cybersecurity Intertwined Necessity. [IJSEUS]. *International Journal of Smart Education and Urban Society, 13*(1), 1–12. DOI: 10.4018/IJSEUS.312232

Burton, S. L. (2024). Business resilience in a cyber world: protect against attacks, part 2. In *Innovations, securities, and case studies across healthcare, business, and technology* (pp. 1–25). IGI Global Scientific Publishing., DOI: 10.4018/979-8-3693-1906-2.ch001

Champa, A. I., Rabbi, M. F., Eishita, F., & Zibran, M. (2025, August). Trick or Treat: A Study of Human Detection of Manipulative Tactics in Phishing Emails. In *International Conference on Computer Safety, Reliability, and Security* (pp. 299-311). Cham: Springer Nature Switzerland. DOI: 10.1007/978-3-032-02018-5_22

Cronin, M. A., & George, E. (2023). The why and how of the integrative review. *Organizational Research Methods, 26*(1), 168–192. DOI: 10.1177/1094428120935507

CrowdStrike. (2025a). 2025 Global Threat Report. https://www.crowdstrike.com/en-us/global-threat-report/ (accessed 20 October 2025)

CrowdStrike. (2025b, August 11). What is SEO poisoning? https://www.crowdstrike.com/en-us/cybersecurity-101/social-engineering/seo-poisoning/ (accessed 16 Sep 2025)

Cybersecurity & Infrastructure Security Agency (CISA). (2023, January 26). Protecting against malicious use of remote monitoring and management software. https://www.cisa.gov/news-events/cybersecurity-advisories/aa23-025a (accessed on 4 September 2025)

Dahiya, S., Rokanas, L. N., Singh, S., Yang, M., & Peha, J. M. (2021). Lessons from internet use and performance during COVID-19. *Journal of Information Policy, 11*, 202–221. DOI: 10.5325/jinfopoli.11.2021.0202

Das Guptta, S., Shahriar, K. T., Alqahtani, H., Alsalman, D., & Sarker, I. H. (2024). Modeling hybrid feature-based phishing websites detection using machine learning techniques. *Annals of Data Science*, *11*(1), 217–242. DOI: 10.1007/s40745-022-00379-8

Dehghantanha, A., Yazdinejad, A., & Parizi, R. M. (2023, November). Autonomous cybersecurity: Evolving challenges, emerging opportunities, and future research trajectories. In *Proceedings of the Workshop on Autonomous Cybersecurity* (pp. 1-10). https://doi-org.captechu.idm.oclc.org/10.1145/3689933.3690832

Dobbala, M. K., & Lingolu, M. S. S. (2023). New trends and ideas SEO: A Multivocal Literature Review. *European Journal of Advances in Engineering and Technology*, *10*(10), 33–41.

Ei, C. H., Tan, J., & Soon, C. (2023). Digital trust and why it matters. https://ctic.nus.edu.sg/resources/CTIC-WP-05(2023).pdf (accessed 20 Oct 2025)

ENISA. (2025, September 30). ENISA Threat Landscape 2025. European Union Agency for Cybersecurity. https://www.enisa.europa.eu/publications/enisa-threat-landscape-2025 (accessed 12 October 2025)

Eze, C. S., & Shamir, L. (2024). Analysis and prevention of AI-based phishing email attacks. *Electronics (Basel)*, *13*(10), 1839. DOI: 10.3390/electronics13101839

Felix, N., & Claudia, W. (2021). Automated Security Operations: Scaling Threat Response with SOAR and AI-Driven Playbooks. *International Journal of Trend in Scientific Research and Development*, *5*(2), 1317–1323.

Fortinet. (2024, December 31). Fortinet 2025 Global Threat Landscape Report. https://www.fortinet.com/resources/reports/threat-landscape-report (accessed 14 July 2025)

Fortinet. (2025a, September 11). SEO poisoning attack targets Chinese-speaking users with fake software sites. https://www.fortinet.com/blog/threat-research/seo-poisoning-attack-targets-chinese-speaking-users-with-fake-software-sites (accessed 7 October 2025)

Fortinet. (2025b, January 16). Top IT trends in disaster recovery to watch in 2025. https://www.datamotive.io/blog/top-it-trends-in-disaster-recovery-to-watch-in-2025

Fritts, B. (2021). *Firewall: Configuration deficiencies* (master's thesis, Utica College). https://www.proquest.com/docview/2531533020?pq-origsite=gscholar&fromopenview=true (accessed 25 October 2025)

Ganguli, P. (2024, November 2). From Utility to Exploitation: Rethinking SEO in a Misinformed World. *Available at SSRN* 5007988. DOI: 10.2139/ssrn.5007988

Guelailia, R., & Bouziane, M. (2024). Enhancing Search Engine Optimization through Artificial Intelligence. *Beam Journal of Economic Studies*, *8*(2), 489–500. DOI: 10.54666/2334-008-002-030

Hasan, R. (2025). Enhancing market competitiveness through AI-powered SEO and digital marketing strategies in e-commerce. *ASRC Procedia: Global Perspectives in Science and Scholarship*, *1*(01), 465–500. DOI: 10.63125/31tpjc54

HHS Cybersecurity Program. (2023, June 21). June 22 HC3 Analyst Note — SEO poisoning. https://www.hhs.gov/sites/default/files/june-2023-seo-poisoning-analyst-note-tlpclear.pdf (accessed on 5 August 2025)

Hromcová, Z., & Cherepanov, A. (2021). Anatomy of native IIS malware. https://eset-info.canon-its.jp/files/user/malware_info/images/special/211020/us-21-Anatomy-Of-Native-Iis-Malware-wp.pdf (accessed on 20 October 2025)

IBM Security X-Force. (2025, April 15). IBM X-Force 2025 Threat Intelligence Index. https://www.ibm.com/thought-leadership/institute-business-value/en-us/report/2025-threat-intelligence-index (accessed 8 August 2025)

Jadhav, A. S. (2023). *An Analytic Approach to Improve Security Features of Web Application using Freeware WAF* (Doctoral dissertation, Dublin, National College of Ireland). https://norma.ncirl.ie/6522/2/akshaysatishjadhavconfigurationmanual.pdf (accessed 23 Sep 2025)

Jones, L. A. (2020). *Reputation risk and potential profitability: Best practices to predict and mitigate risk through amalgamated factors*. Capitol Technology University. https://www.proquest.com/docview/2466047018/DFF9754EFF284F6DPQ/1?accountid=44888&sourcetype=Dissertations%20&%20Theses (accessed on 17 Sep 2025)

Jones, L. A. (2021). A content analysis review of literature to create a usable framework for reputation risk management. In *Handbook of Research on Multidisciplinary Perspectives on Managerial and Leadership Psychology*, 91-133. DOI: 10.4018/978-1-7998-3811-1.ch006

Jones, L. A., & Burrell, D. N. (2025). Illegal cybersecurity threats created by organizational arsonists in healthcare organizations. *Law. Economics and Society*, *1*(1), 93. DOI: 10.30560/les.v1n1p93

Kamruzzaman, A., Ismat, S., Brickley, J. C., Liu, A., & Thakur, K. (2022, December). A comprehensive review of endpoint security: Threats and defenses. In *2022 International Conference on Cyber Warfare and Security (ICCWS)* (pp. 1-7). IEEE. DOI: 10.1109/ICCWS56285.2022.9998470

Kang, H., Liu, G., Wang, Q., Meng, L., & Liu, J. (2023). Theory and application of zero trust security: A brief survey. *Entropy (Basel, Switzerland)*, *25*(12), 1595. DOI: 10.3390/e25121595

Kaur, H., & Tiwari, R. (2021, November). Endpoint detection and response using machine learning. In *Journal of Physics: Conference Series* (Vol. 2062, No. 1, p. 012013). IOP Publishing. DOI: 10.1088/1742-6596/2062/1/012013

Keever, S. (2024, February 2). AI is driving the future of SEO: How to adapt. *Forbes*. https://www.forbes.com/councils/forbesagencycouncil/2024/02/02/ai-is-driving-the-future-of-seo-how-to-adapt/ (accessed 30 July 2025)

Khan, M. M., & Arshad, J. (2022, December). Anomaly detection and enterprise security using user and entity behavior analytics (UEBA). In *2022 3rd International Conference on Innovations in Computer Science & Software Engineering (ICONICS)* (pp. 1-9). IEEE. DOI: 10.1109/ICONICS56716.2022.10100596

Kizza, J. M. (2024). Firewalls. In *Guide to Computer Network Security* (pp. 265–294). Springer International Publishing., DOI: 10.1007/978-3-031-47549-8_12

Knowles, C. (2025, May 22). SEO poisoning attack diverts wages using fake payroll websites. *Security Brief*. https://securitybrief.in/story/seo-poisoning-attack-diverts-wages-using-fake-payroll-websites (accessed 15 August 2025)

Kolosnjaji, B., Xiao, H., Xu, P., & Zarras, A. (2024). *Artificial intelligence for cybersecurity: develop AI approaches to solve cybersecurity problems in your organization*. Packt Publishing Ltd.

Korty, A., Calarco, D., & Spencer, M. (2021). Balancing risk with virtual private networking during a pandemic. *Business Horizons, 64*(6), 757–761. DOI: 10.1016/j.bushor.2021.07.011

Lakshmanan, R. (2025, September, 23). BadIIS malware spreads via SEO poisoning – redirects traffic, plants web shells. The Hacker News. https://thehackernews.com/2025/09/badiis-malware-spreads-via-seo.html (accessed 26 September 2025)

Lasopoulou, V. (2025). *Cloud security and privacy* (Master's thesis, Πανεπιστήμιο Πειραιώς). https://dione.lib.unipi.gr/xmlui/bitstream/handle/unipi/17502/Lasopoulou_mte2213.pdf?sequence=1&isAllowed=y (accessed 18 October 2025)

Leonardi, P. M., Parker, S. H., & Shen, R. (2024). How remote work changes the world of work. *Annual Review of Organizational Psychology and Organizational Behavior, 11*(1), 193–219. DOI: 10.1146/annurev-orgpsych-091922-015852

Li, K., Li, C., Yuan, X., Li, S., Zou, S., Ahmed, S. S., Wei, N., Niyato, D., Jamalipour, A., Dressler, F., & Akan, Ö. B. (2025). Zero-trust foundation models: A new paradigm for secure and collaborative artificial intelligence for internet of things. *IEEE Internet of Things Journal*. https://ieeexplore.ieee.org/stamp/stamp.jsp?tp=&arnumber=11143153 (accessed 25 Oct 2025)

Lu, L., Perdisci, R., & Lee, W. (2011, October). Surf: detecting and measuring search poisoning. In *Proceedings of the 18th ACM conference on Computer and Communications Security* (pp. 467-476).

Malik, P. K. (2024). The role of digital trust in enhancing cyber security resilience. *Transforming Industry using Digital Twin Technology*, 59. DOI: 10.1007/978-3-031-58523-4_4

Microsoft. (2024, December 31). Microsoft Digital Defense Report 2025. https://www.microsoft.com/en-us/security/security-insider/threat-landscape/microsoft-digital-defense-report-2025 (accessed 23 June 2025)

Morgan, S. (2024, January 19). Data has never been more vulnerable to insider threats. *Cybercrime Magazine*. https://cybersecurityventures.com/insider-threat-report-2024/#:~:text=67%20percent%20of%20employees%20have%20used%20their%20personal%20mobile%20devices (accessed 25 October 2025)

Münch, C., Marx, E., Benz, L., Hartmann, E., & Matzner, M. (2022). Capabilities of digital servitization: Evidence from the socio-technical systems theory. *Technological Forecasting and Social Change*, *176*, 121361. DOI: 10.1016/j.techfore.2021.121361

Nagendran, K., Balaji, S., Raj, B. A., Chanthrika, P., & Amirthaa, R. G. (2020, March). Web application firewall evasion techniques. In *2020 6th International Conference on Advanced Computing and Communication Systems (ICACCS)* (pp. 194-199). IEEE. DOI: 10.1109/ICACCS48705.2020.9074217

Newman, A., Bavik, Y. L., Mount, M., & Shao, B. (2021). Data collection via online platforms: Challenges and recommendations for future research. *Applied Psychology*, *70*(3), 1380–1402. DOI: 10.1111/apps.12302

Ngo Higgins, H. (1999). Corporate system security: Towards an integrated management approach. *Information Management & Computer Security*, *7*(5), 217–222. DOI: 10.1108/09685229910292817

Paul, E. M., Mmaduekwe, U., Kessie, J. D., & Dolapo, M. (2024). Zero trust architecture and AI: A synergistic approach to next-generation cybersecurity frameworks. *International Journal of Science and Research Archive*, *13*(2), 4159–4169. DOI: 10.30574/ijsra.2024.13.2.2583

Petelka, J., Zou, Y., & Schaub, F. (2019, May). Put your warning where your link is: Improving and evaluating email phishing warnings. In *Proceedings of the 2019 CHI conference on human factors in computing systems* (pp. 1-15). https://doi-org.captechu.idm.oclc.org/10.1145/3290605.3300748

Ramirez, S. (2025, October 7). Remote work cybersecurity statistics 2025: VPN, shadow IT, cloud, and more. SQ Magazine. https://sqmagazine.co.uk/remote-work-cybersecurity-statistics/ (accessed 16 Oct 2025)

Regulation (EU) 2016/679 of the European Parliament and of the Council of 27 April 2016 on the protection of natural persons with regard to the processing of personal data and on the free movement of such data (General Data Protection Regulation). Official Journal of the European Union, L119, 1–88. https://eur-lex.europa.eu/eli/reg/2016/679/oj (accessed 9 September 2025)

Rose, S., Borchert, O., Mitchell, S., & Connelly, S. (2020). *Zero Trust Architecture. National Institute of Technology*. NIST., DOI: 10.6028/NIST.SP.800-207

Sarkar, U., Paul, S., Gowrav, M. R., & Mitra, A. (2024, August). Optimizing SEO with AI: Achieving Success Through Responsible Innovation. In *International Conference on Technology Advances for Green Solutions and Sustainable Development* (pp. 51-62). Cham: Springer Nature Switzerland. DOI: 10.1007/978-3-031-94997-5_6

Sestieri, G. (2024, April 2). The dark side of SEO: Understanding SEO poisoning. ReliaQuest. https://reliaquest.com/blog/seo-poisoning/ (accessed 12 November 2025)

Shaharia, S. (2025, June 21). Is SEO Dead in 2025? A data-driven reality check. Zenodo (Version 1). https://doi.org./DOI: 10.5281/zenodo.15712794

Shi, J., Leau, Y. B., Li, K., & Obit, J. H. (2021). A comprehensive review on a hybrid network traffic prediction model. *International Journal of Electrical and Computer Engineering*, *11*(2), 1450. DOI: 10.11591/ijece.v11i2.pp1450-1459

Somé, D. F., Airan, M., Durumeric, Z., & Staicu, C. A. (2025). User Profiles: The Achilles' Heel of Web Browsers. *arXiv preprint arXiv:2504.17692*. https://doi.org// arXiv.2504.17692DOI: 10.48550

Syed, S. A. (2022). AI-powered cybercrime: The new frontier of digital threats. [IJETRM]. *International Journal of Engineering Technology Research & Management*, *6*(02).

Unit 42 by Palo Alto Networks. (2025, August 1). 2025 Unit 42 Global Incident Response Report: Social engineering edition. https://unit42.paloaltonetworks.com/ 2025-unit-42-global-incident-response-report-social-engineering-edition/ (accessed 14 September 2025)

Vagal, V., & Dillon, R. (2021). Reducing cyber risk in remote working. In *Digital Transformation in a Post-Covid World* (pp. 155–170). CRC Press. DOI: 10.1201/9781003148715-8

Vakulov, A. (2025, January 31). *New browser syncjacking attack gives hackers full device control.* Forbes. https://www.forbes.com/sites/alexvakulov/2025/01/31/ new-browser-syncjacking-attack-gives-hackers-full-device-control/ (accessed on 23 October 2025)

Vectra. (2024, February 25). SEO poisoning attacks: Detection & defense. https:// www.vectra.ai/topics/seo-poisoning (accessed on 16 October 2025)

Venkitanarayanan, A. (2025). Behind the Screen: Understanding the Human Firewall in Cybersecurity. DOI: 10.54014/GWQ8-MWP8

Wallenius, S. (2024). Recommended SEO-techniques to increase organic traffic for a website: a scoping review. https://www.theseus.fi/bitstream/handle/10024/876381/ Wallenius_Susanne.pdf?sequence=2&isAllowed=y (accessed on 19 July 2025)

Wu, M., Hong, G., Mai, W., Wu, X., Zhang, L., Pu, Y., Chai, H., Ying, L., Duan, H., & Yang, M. (2025, March). Exposing the Hidden Layer: Software Repositories in the Service of Seo Manipulation. In *2025 IEEE/ACM 47th International Conference on Software Engineering (ICSE)* (pp. 684-684). IEEE Computer Society. https://ieeexplore.ieee.org/stamp/stamp.jsp?tp=&arnumber=11029819 (accessed 25 October 2025)

Wung, W. S., Kranig, C., Pauley, E., Barford, P., Crovella, M., & Sommers, J. (2025, May). Squatspotting: Towards the systematic measurement of typosquatting techniques. IFIP. https://www.cs.bu.edu/faculty/crovella/paper-archive/wung-ifip-networking25-dns.pdf (accessed on 13 August 2025)

Zemah, Y. (2025, September 21). Operation Rewrite: Chinese-speaking threat actors deploy BadIIS in a wide SEO poisoning campaign. Palo Alto Networks Unit. 42. https://unit42.paloaltonetworks.com/operation-rewrite-seo-poisoning-campaign/ (accessed 17 October 2025)

Zohaib, S. M., Sajjad, S. M., Iqbal, Z., Yousaf, M., Haseeb, M., & Muhammad, Z. (2024). Zero trust vpn (zt-vpn): A systematic literature review and cybersecurity framework for hybrid and remote work. *Information (Basel)*, *15*(11), 734. DOI: 10.3390/info15110734

Zscaler. (2025, June 23). Black hat SEO poisoning search engine results for AI. https://www.zscaler.com/blogs/security-research/black-hat-seo-poisoning-search-engine-results-ai-distribute-malware (accessed 3 August 2025)

KEY TERMS AND DEFINITIONS

Behavioral security: The practice of monitoring and analyzing user actions to spot unusual behavior that could signal a security threat.

Browser isolation: Separating web browsing activity from the local computer or network to prevent dangerous content from causing harm.

Browser Synchronization: Keeping browser data such as bookmarks, history, and passwords up-to-date across multiple devices.

Cyberattack: An intentional attempt to disrupt, damage, or gain unauthorized access to computers, networks, or data.

Cyber risk: The potential for loss or harm resulting from cyber threats, vulnerabilities, or attacks on digital systems.

Domain: A website's unique address or name on the internet used to identify and access it.

Firewall evasion: Techniques used to bypass or trick a protective network barrier so that unauthorized traffic or threats can get through.

Human factors: The influence of human behavior, habits, and decisions on technology safety and security.

Hybrid work: A workplace model where employees split their time between remote locations and a physical office.

Information eco-traps: Digital pitfalls created to lure users into misinformation or malicious content by manipulating trusted online sources.

Malware: Harmful software designed to damage, disrupt, or steal data from computers or networks.

Search Engine Optimization: (**SEO**): The process of improving a website's visibility in search engine results to attract more relevant visitors.

SEO poisoning: The act of manipulating search engine results to promote malicious or deceptive websites that target unsuspecting users.

Zero trust: A security approach that requires every user and device to be continuously verified, regardless of their location or network

Compilation of References

Abbas, H., Emmanuel, N., Amjad, M. F., Yaqoob, T., Atiquzzaman, M., Iqbal, Z., & Shafqat, N. Bin Shahid., Tanveer, A., & Ashfaq, U. (2023). Security assessment and evaluation of VPNs: a comprehensive survey. *ACM Computing Surveys, 55*(13s), 1-47. https://dl-acm-org.captechu.idm.oclc.org/doi/full/10.1145/3579162

Abdelghani, T. (2019). Implementation of defense in depth strategy to secure industrial control system in critical infrastructures. *American Journal of Artificial Intelligence*, *3*(2), 17. DOI: 10.11648/j.ajai.20190302.11

Abdullah-Poulos, L. (2015). Turning "Other" Into "Another": Valuing Diverse Knowledge Through the Standpoint Theory. *Transformative Science Teaching in Higher Education Journal of Transformative Education, 13 (2), April 2015, p. 154, 13*(2), 11.

Adler-Milstein, J., Kvedar, J., & Bates, D. W. (2014). Telehealth among US hospitals: Several factors, including state reimbursement and licensure policies, influence adoption. *Health Affairs (Project Hope)*, *33*(2), 207–215. DOI: 10.1377/hlthaff.2013.1054

Agbadamasi, T. O., Opoku, L. K., Adukpo, T. K., & Mensah, N. (2025). Artificial Intelligence Governance in U.S. corporations: Legal and ethical implications for business intelligence and regulatory compliance. *International Journal of Research Publication and Reviews*, *6*(3), 3083–3089. DOI: 10.55248/gengpi.6.0325.11124

Aijaz, M., Lewis, V. A., & Murray, G. F. (2024). Advancing equity in challenging times: A qualitative study of telehealth expansion and changing patient–provider relationships in primary care settings during the COVID-19 pandemic. *Digital Health*, *10*, 20552076241233148. DOI: 10.1177/20552076241233148

Ajzen, I. (1991). The theory of planned behavior. *Organizational Behavior and Human Decision Processes*, *50*(2), 179–211. DOI: 10.1016/0749-5978(91)90020-T

Ajzen, I. (2020). The theory of planned behavior: Frequently asked questions. *Human Behavior and Emerging Technologies, 2*(4), 314–324. DOI: 10.1002/hbe2.195

Akbaş, E. (2023). *The importance of real-time detection and correlation in SIEM/UEBA solutions and criticality for SOAR*. Unpublished. DOI: 10.13140/RG.2.2.12607.69285

Akhavan, S., & Redmond, N. (2023). Medical assistants' telehealth roles and skills in primary care during the COVID-19 pandemic. *Center for Health Workforce Studies, University of Washington*. https://familymedicine.uw.edu/chws/wp-content/uploads/sites/5/2023/05/MAs-Telehealth-Roles-During-COVID-19-FR-2023-May.pdf

Al Qwaid, M. (2025). Cybersecurity threats: Ransomware, phishing, and social engineering. In *Complexities and Challenges for Securing Digital Assets and Infrastructure* (pp. 399–434). IGI Global Scientific Publishing., DOI: 10.4018/979-8-3373-1370-2.ch018

Alahmari, S., Renaud, K., & Omoronyia, I. (2023). Moving beyond cyber security awareness and training to engendering security knowledge sharing. *Information Systems and e-Business Management, 21*(1), 123–158. DOI: 10.1007/s10257-022-00575-2

Alanazi, A. (2023). Clinicians' perspectives on healthcare cybersecurity and cyber threats. *Cureus, 15*(10). Advance online publication. DOI: 10.7759/cureus.47026 PMID: 37965389

Alex, & Anastasija. (2025). *Applying neuromarketing to digital banking apps and fintech design*. UXDA. Retrieved July 26, 2025, from https://www.theuxda.com/blog/category/ux-trends

AlGhamdi, S., Win, K. T., & Vlahu-Gjorgievska, E. (2020). Information security governance challenges and critical success factors: Systematic review. *Computers & Security, 99*, 102030. Advance online publication. DOI: 10.1016/j.cose.2020.102030

Allied Market Research. (2022). Sustainable Finance Market by Component, End-User, and Region: Global Opportunity Analysis and Industry Forecast, 2022–2031.

Alouffi, B., Hasnain, M., Alharbi, A., Alosaimi, W., Alyami, H., & Ayaz, M. (2021). A systematic literature review on cloud computing security: Threats and mitigation strategies. *IEEE Access : Practical Innovations, Open Solutions, 9*, 57792–57807. DOI: 10.1109/ACCESS.2021.3073203

Alsharif, A. H., Salleh, N. Z. M., Hashem, E. A. R., Khraiwish, A., Putit, L., & Arif, L. S. M. (2023). Exploring factors influencing neuromarketing implementation in Malaysian universities: Barriers and enablers. *Sustainability (Basel)*, *15*(5), 4603. Advance online publication. DOI: 10.3390/su15054603

American College of Obstetricians and Gynecologists. (2024). Addressing social and structural determinants of health in the delivery of reproductive health care: ACOG Committee Statement No. 11. *Obstetrics and Gynecology*, *144*(5), e113–e120. DOI: 10.1097/AOG.0000000000005721

American Medical Association. (2024, December 30). *CPT Appendix S: AI taxonomy for medical services & procedures*. https://www.ama-assn.org/practice-management/cpt/cpt-appendix-s-ai-taxonomy-medical-services-procedures

American Society for Reproductive Medicine Ethics Committee. (2024). Ethical considerations for telemedical delivery of fertility care: An Ethics Committee opinion. *Fertility and Sterility*, *121*(3), 434–438. DOI: 10.1016/j.fertnstert.2023.12.005

Ananny, M., & Crawford, K. (2018). Seeing without knowing: Limitations of the transparency ideal and its application to algorithmic accountability. *New Media & Society*, *20*(3), 973–989. https://journals.sagepub.com/doi/10.1177/1461444817736645. DOI: 10.1177/1461444816676645

Anawade, P. A., Sharma, D., Gahane, S., Anawade, P. A.Sr, & Sharma, D. S. (2024). A comprehensive review on exploring the impact of telemedicine on healthcare accessibility. *Cureus*, *16*(3). Advance online publication. DOI: 10.7759/cureus.55996

Anderljung, M., Barnhart, J., Korinek, A., Leung, J., O'Keefe, C., Whittlestone, J., Avin, S., Brundage, M., Bullock, J., Cass-Beggs, D., Chang, B., Collins, T., Fist, T., Hadfield, G., Hayes, A., Ho, L., Hooker, S., Horvitz, E., Kolt, N., . . . Wolf, K. (2023). *Frontier AI Regulation: Managing Emerging Risks to Public Safety*. https://doi.org//arXiv.2307.03718DOI: 10.48550

Anderson, K., Coskun, R., Jimenez, P., & Omurtag, K. (2022). Satisfaction with new patient telehealth visits for reproductive endocrinology patients in the era of COVID-19. *Journal of Assisted Reproduction and Genetics*, *39*(7), 1571–1576. DOI: 10.1007/s10815-022-02539-4

Andino, J. J., Eyrich, N. W., & Boxer, R. J. (2023). Overview of telehealth in the United States since the COVID-19 public health emergency: A narrative review. *mHealth*, *9*, 26. DOI: 10.21037/mhealth-23-15

Andreou, C., & Veliz, C. (2020). Targeted advertising and the right to mental integrity. *Minds and Machines*, *30*(3), 427–444. DOI: 10.1007/s11023-020-09525-8

Argaw, S. T., Troncoso-Pastoriza, J. R., Lacey, D., Florin, M.-V., Calcavecchia, F., Anderson, D., Burleson, W., Vogel, J.-M., O'Leary, C., Eshaya-Chauvin, B., & Flahault, A. (2020). Cybersecurity of Hospitals: Discussing the challenges and working towards mitigating the risks. *BMC Medical Informatics and Decision Making*, *20*(1), 146. Advance online publication. DOI: 10.1186/s12911-020-01161-7 PMID: 32620167

Argyris, C. (1976). Single-loop and double-loop models in research on decision making. *Administrative Science Quarterly*, *21*(3), 363–375. DOI: 10.2307/2391848

Argyris, C., & Schön, D. A. (1978). *Organizational learning: A theory of action perspective*. Addison-Wesley.

Argyris, C., & Schön, D. A. (1996). *Organizational learning II: Theory, method, and practice*. Addison-Wesley.

Argyris, C., & Schön, D. A. (1997). Organizational learning: A theory of action perspective. *Revista Española de Investigaciones Sociológicas*, (77/78), 345–348. DOI: 10.2307/40183951

Ariely, D. (2008). *Predictably irrational: The hidden forces that shape our decisions*. HarperCollins.

Ariely, D., & Berns, G. (2010). Neuromarketing: The hope and hype of neuroimaging in business. *Nature Reviews. Neuroscience*, *11*(4), 284–292. DOI: 10.1038/nrn2795

Arya, K., Bhardwaj, V., Kumari, V., & Singh, D. (2025). From brain to business: The role of neuroscience in marketing, hr, and finance, along with ethical issues. *Academy of Marketing Studies Journal*, *29*(S5), 1–20.

Astari, D., Ana, H., & Setiawan, P. A. H. (2025). Legal Certainty of Sustainable Finance Provisions in Relation to Corporate Social Responsibility (CSR) Programs at Financial Services Institutions. *International Journal of Research and Innovation in Social Science*, *9*(1), 372–376. DOI: 10.47772/IJRISS.2025.9010034

Azzone, G., & Broccardo, L. (2021). *Sustainable Finance: The Road Ahead*. Springer International Publishing.

Bakker, A. B., & Demerouti, E. (2017). Job demands–resources theory: Taking stock and looking forward. *Journal of Occupational Health Psychology*, *22*(3), 273–285. DOI: 10.1037/ocp0000056 PMID: 27732008

Banerjee, R., & Roy, R. (2024). Deception in the digital age: How SEO poisoning undermines online trust. https://multiarticlesjournal.com/uploads/articles/IJCRM-2024-3-3-45.pdf (accessed on 23 October 2025)

Bank of America. (2023). *Green bond campaign*. https://www.bankofamerica.com/greenbondcampaign

Bank, D. B. S. (2023). *Case study: DBS Bank's use of biometrics for ESG investor profiling*. https://www.dbs.com/sustainability/biometrics-esg-investor-profiling

Baraldo, M., & Di Franco, P. D. G. (2024). Place-centred emerging technologies for disaster management: A scoping review. *International Journal of Disaster Risk Reduction, 112*, 104782. DOI: 10.1016/j.ijdrr.2024.104782

Barlow, L., Bendiab, G., Shiaeles, S., & Savage, N. (2020). A novel approach to detect phishing attacks using binary visualisation and machine learning. *2020 IEEE World Congress on Services (SERVICES)*. DOI: 10.1109/SERVICES48979.2020.00046

Barocas, S., Hardt, M., & Narayanan, A. (2019). *Fairness and machine learning: Limitations and opportunities*. MIT Press. https://fairmlbook.org/

Barocas, S., & Selbst, A. D. (2016). Big data's disparate impact. *California Law Review, 104*(3), 671–732. https://www.californialawreview.org/print/big-datas-disparate-impact/. DOI: 10.15779/Z38BG31

Bashshur, R., Doarn, C. R., Frenk, J. M., Kvedar, J. C., & Woolliscroft, J. O. (2020). Telemedicine and the COVID-19 pandemic, lessons for the future. *Telemedicine Journal and e-Health, 26*(5), 571–573. DOI: 10.1089/tmj.2020.29040.rb

Bassett, C. (2018). The computational therapeutic: Exploring Weizenbaum's eliza as a history of the present. *AI & Society, 34*(4), 803–812. DOI: 10.1007/s00146-018-0825-9

Basten, D., & Haamann, T. (2018). Approaches for organizational learning: A literature review. *SAGE Open, 8*(3), 2158244018794224. DOI: 10.1177/2158244018794224

Batool, A., Zowghi, D., & Bano, M. (2025). AI governance: A systematic literature review. *AI and Ethics, 5*(3), 3265–3279. DOI: 10.1007/s43681-024-00653-w

Benraouane, S. A. (2024). *AI management system auditing and compliance according to ISO/IEC 42001*. Routledge.

Berger, J., Fisek, M. H., Norman, R. Z., & Zelditch, M. (1972). *Status characteristics and social interaction*. Elsevier. DOI: 10.2307/2093465

Berlińska, E., & Kaszycka, I. (2016). Neuromarketing–Chance or Danger for Consumers in the Opinion of MSU's Students.

Biewendt, M., Blaschke, F., & Böhnert, A. (2021). A review of contemporary challenges in business culture. *International Journal of Applied Research in Business and Management*, *2*(1), 1–12. DOI: 10.51137/ijarbm.2021.2.1.1

Bijker, W. E., Hughes, T. P., & Pinch, T. (Eds.). (1987). *The social construction of technological systems: New directions in the sociology and history of technology*. MIT Press., https://mitpress.mit.edu/9780262521376/, DOI: 10.7551/mitpress/6348.001.0001

Bini, S. A. (2018). Artificial intelligence, machine learning, deep learning, and cognitive computing: What do these terms mean and how will they impact health care? *The Journal of Arthroplasty*, *33*(8), 2358–2361. DOI: 10.1016/j.arth.2018.02.067

Binns, R. (2018). Algorithmic accountability and public reason. *Philosophy & Technology*, *31*(4), 543–556. https://link.springer.com/article/10.1007/s13347-017-0263-5. DOI: 10.1007/s13347-017-0263-5 PMID: 30873342

Biondi, A., Laiou, P., Bruno, E., Viana, P. F., Schreuder, M., Hart, W., Nurse, E., Pal, D. K., & Richardson, M. P. (2021). Remote and long-term self-monitoring of electroencephalographic and noninvasive measurable variables at home in patients with epilepsy (EEG@HOME): Protocol for an observational study. *JMIR Research Protocols*, *10*(3), e25309. DOI: 10.2196/25309

Birkstedt, T., Minkkinen, M., Tandon, A., & Mäntymäki, M. (2023). AI governance: Themes, knowledge gaps and future agendas. *Internet Research*, *33*(7), 133–167. DOI: 10.1108/INTR-01-2022-0042

Bond, B. (2024, October 28). *Best practices for change management in healthcare*. Prosci. IT. https://www.prosci.com/blog/change-management-healthcare-it

Borges do Nascimento, I. J., Abdulazeem, H., Vasanthan, L. T., Martinez, E. Z., Zucoloto, M. L., Østengaard, L., Azzopardi-Muscat, N., Zapata, T., & Novillo-Ortiz, D. (2023). Barriers and facilitators to utilizing digital health technologies by healthcare professionals. *NPJ Digital Medicine*, *6*(1), 161. DOI: 10.1038/s41746-023-00899-4

Bosnjak, M., Ajzen, I., & Schmidt, P. (2020). The theory of planned behavior: Selected recent advances and applications. *Europe's Journal of Psychology*, *16*(3), 352–356. DOI: 10.5964/ejop.v16i3.3107 PMID: 33680187

Braathe, R. (2021, January 23). *The Schein model of organization culture: Three levels of a robust organization culture*. Robert Braathe's HR & Albany Jobs Blog. https://www.albany.com/hr/2021/01/the-schein-model-of-organization-culture-three-levels-of-a-robust-organization-culture/

Bracken, A., Reilly, C., Feeley, A., Sheehan, E., Merghani, K., & Feeley, I. (2025). Artificial Intelligence (AI) – Powered Documentation Systems in Healthcare: A Systematic Review. *Journal of Medical Systems*, *49*(1), 28. Advance online publication. DOI: 10.1007/s10916-025-02157-4 PMID: 39966286

Bradford, A. (2020). *The Brussels effect: How the European Union rules the world*. Oxford University Press., https://global.oup.com/academic/product/the-brussels-effect-9780190088583, DOI: 10.1093/oso/9780190088583.001.0001

Bratton, K. A. (2005). Critical mass theory revisited: The behavior and success of token women in state legislatures. *Politics & Gender*, *1*(1), 97–125. DOI: 10.1017/S1743923X0505004X

Brommeyer, M., Whittaker, M., & Liang, Z. (2024). Organizational Factors Driving the Realization of Digital Health Transformation Benefits from Health Service Managers: A Qualitative Study. *Journal of Healthcare Leadership*, *16*, 455–472. DOI: 10.2147/JHL.S487589

Brunner, R., Steelman, T. A., Coe-Juell, L., Cromley, C. M., Edwards, C. M., & Tucker, D. W. (2005). *Adaptive governance: Integrating science, policy, and decision making*. Columbia University Press.

Buchanan, N. T., & Settles, I. H. (2019). Managing (in) visibility and hypervisibility in the workplace. *Journal of Vocational Behavior*, *113*, 1–5. DOI: 10.1016/j.jvb.2018.11.001

Bucher, T. (2018). *If...then: Algorithmic power and politics*. Oxford University Press., https://global.oup.com/academic/product/ifthen-9780190493028, DOI: 10.1093/oso/9780190493028.001.0001

Burrell, D. N., Burton, S. L., Nobles, C., Springs, D., Huff, A. J., Brown-Jackson, K. L., Richardson, K., Wright, J. B., Muller, S. R., & Jones, A. J. (2023). The managerial ethical and operational challenges of hospital cybersecurity. In *Transformational Interventions for Business, Technology, and Healthcare* (pp. 444–458). IGI Global. DOI: 10.4018/979-8-3693-1634-4.ch026

Burrell, D. N. (2022). Creating inclusive, diverse, and psychologically safe workplaces for African-American women working in public health response supply chain and logistics. *Land Forces Academy Review*, *27*(2), 134–140. DOI: 10.2478/raft-2022-0018

Burrell, D. N. (2023). Understanding telemedicine strategies through field-based observations, interviews and benchmarking activities. *Health Economics and Management Review*, *4*(4), 58–68. DOI: 10.61093/hem.2023.4-05

Burrell, D. N. (2024). Telehealth Technologies, Disruptions, and Health Literacy. *Health Economics and Management Review*, *5*(4), 33–46. DOI: 10.61093/hem.2024.4-03

Burrell, D. N. (Ed.). (2024). *Multisector Insights in Healthcare, Social Sciences, Society, and Technology*. IGI Global. DOI: 10.4018/979-8-3693-3226-9

Burton, S. L., Burrell, D. N., & Nobles, C. (2023). Adapting to the cyber-driven workforce: a battle for the discouraged worker. In *Real-World Solutions for Diversity, Strategic Change, and Organizational Development: Perspectives in Healthcare, Education, Business, and Technology* (pp. 130-152). IGI Global. DOI: 10.4018/978-1-6684-8691-7.ch009

Burton, S. L. (2022). Strategy: A Business and Cybersecurity Intertwined Necessity. [IJSEUS]. *International Journal of Smart Education and Urban Society*, *13*(1), 1–12. DOI: 10.4018/IJSEUS.312232

Burton, S. L. (2024). Business resilience in a cyber world: protect against attacks, part 2. In *Innovations, securities, and case studies across healthcare, business, and technology* (pp. 1–25). IGI Global Scientific Publishing., DOI: 10.4018/979-8-3693-1906-2.ch001

Callon, M. (1986). Some elements of a sociology of translation: Domestication of the scallops and the fishermen of St Brieuc Bay. *The Sociological Review*, *32*(1), 196–233. https://journals.sagepub.com/doi/10.1111/j.1467-954X.1984.tb00813.x. DOI: 10.1111/j.1467-954X.1984.tb00813.x

Calo, R. (2017). Artificial intelligence policy: A primer and roadmap. *University of California Davis Law Review*, *51*, 399–435. https://lawreview.law.ucdavis.edu/issues/51/2/Symposium/51-2_Calo.pdf

Carolan, K., Grabowski, D. C., Mehrotra, A., & Hatfield, L. A. (2020). Use of telemedicine for emergency triage in an independent senior living community: Mixed methods study. *Journal of Medical Internet Research*, *22*(12), e23014. DOI: 10.2196/23014

Carroll, A. B. (1991). The pyramid of corporate social responsibility: Toward the moral management of organisational stakeholders.

Cartwright, A. J. (2023). The elephant in the room: Cybersecurity in healthcare. *Journal of Clinical Monitoring and Computing*, *37*(5), 1123–1132. DOI: 10.1007/s10877-023-01013-5 PMID: 37088852

Castro, V. D., Martín-Peña, M. L., Martínez, E. M., & Salgado, M. (2025). Combining action research with design science as a qualitative research methodology. An application to service (operations) management research. *International Journal of Qualitative Methods, 24*, 1–15. DOI: 10.1177/16094069241312018

Cedergren, A., & Hassel, H. (2022). Using action design research for developing and implementing a method for risk assessment and continuity management. *Safety Science, 151*, 105727. Advance online publication. DOI: 10.1016/j.ssci.2022.105727

Cerroni, S., Watson, V., & Macdiarmid, J. (2019). Consumers' rationality and home-grown values for healthy and environmentally sustainable food. 8(2). DOI: 10.13128/bae-8927

Chaffin, B. C., Gosnell, H., & Cosens, B. A. (2014). A decade of adaptive governance scholarship: Synthesis and future directions. *Ecology and Society, 19*(3), art56. https://www.jstor.org/stable/26269646. DOI: 10.5751/ES-06824-190356

Champa, A. I., Rabbi, M. F., Eishita, F., & Zibran, M. (2025, August). Trick or Treat: A Study of Human Detection of Manipulative Tactics in Phishing Emails. In *International Conference on Computer Safety, Reliability, and Security* (pp. 299-311). Cham: Springer Nature Switzerland. DOI: 10.1007/978-3-032-02018-5_22

Chen, C. H., Lan, Y. L., Yang, W. P., Hsu, F. M., Lin, C. L., & Chen, H. C. (2019). Exploring the impact of a telehealth care system on organizational capabilities and organizational performance from a resource-based perspective. *International Journal of Environmental Research and Public Health, 16*(20), 3988. DOI: 10.3390/ijerph16203988

Childs, S., & Krook, M. L. (2009). Analysing women's substantive representation: From critical mass to critical actors. *Government and Opposition, 44*(2), 125–145. DOI: 10.1111/j.1477-7053.2009.01279.x

Citron, D. K., & Pasquale, F. (2014). The scored society: Due process for automated predictions. *Washington Law Review (Seattle, Wash.), 89*, 1–33. https://digitalcommons.law.uw.edu/wlr/vol89/iss1/2/

Cloud Security Alliance. (2025). *AI controls matrix*. https://cloudsecurityalliance.org/artifacts/ai-controls-matrix#

Coglianese, C., & Lehr, D. (2017). Regulating by robot: Administrative decision making in the machine-learning era. *The Georgetown Law Journal, 105*, 1147–1223. https://www.law.georgetown.edu/georgetown-law-journal/in-print/volume-105/

Cohen, J. (1979). Non-deterministic algorithms. *ACM Computing Surveys, 11*(2), 79–94. DOI: 10.1145/356770.356773

Cohen, J. E. (2019). *Between truth and power: The legal constructions of informational capitalism*. Oxford University Press., https://global.oup.com/academic/product/between-truth-and-power-9780190246693, DOI: 10.1093/oso/9780190246693.001.0001

Congressional Research Service. (2024). *Artificial intelligence: Background and policy considerations*. Washington, DC: Library of Congress. https://crsreports.congress.gov/product/pdf/R/R46795

Cooper, A. F., Frankle, J., & De Sa, C. (2022). Non-determinism and the lawlessness of machine learning code. *Proceedings of the 2022 Symposium on Computer Science and Law*, 1–8. DOI: 10.1145/3511265.3550446

Coventry, L., Branley-Bell, D., Sillence, E., Magalini, S., Mari, P., Magkanaraki, A., & Anastasopoulou, K. (2020). Cyber-Risk in Healthcare: Exploring Facilitators and Barriers to Secure Behaviour. *HCI for Cybersecurity, Privacy and Trust*, 105–122. DOI: 10.1007/978-3-030-50309-3_8

Crespo-Pereira, V., Legerén-Lago, B., & Arregui-McGullion, J. (2020, November 27). Implementing neuromarketing in the enterprise: Factors that impact the adoption of neuromarketing in major Spanish corporations. *Frontiers in Communication*, *5*, 576789. Advance online publication. DOI: 10.3389/fcomm.2020.576789

Cronin, M. A., & George, E. (2023). The why and how of the integrative review. *Organizational Research Methods*, *26*(1), 168–192. DOI: 10.1177/1094428120935507

Crossan, M. M., Lane, H. W., White, R. E., & Djurfeldt, L. (1995). Organizational learning: Dimensions for a theory. *The International Journal of Organizational Analysis*, *3*(4), 337–360. DOI: 10.1108/eb028835

CrowdStrike. (2025a). 2025 Global Threat Report. https://www.crowdstrike.com/en-us/global-threat-report/ (accessed 20 October 2025)

CrowdStrike. (2025b, August 11). What is SEO poisoning? https://www.crowdstrike.com/en-us/cybersecurity-101/social-engineering/seo-poisoning/ (accessed 16 Sep 2025)

Ćwiklicki, M., Duplaga, M., & Klich, J. (Eds.). (2021). *The digital transformation of healthcare: Health 4.0*. Routledge., M., Duplaga, M., & Klich, J. (Eds.). (2021). *The digital transformation of healthcare: Health 4.0*. Routledge.

Cybersecurity & Infrastructure Security Agency (CISA). (2023, January 26). Protecting against malicious use of remote monitoring and management software. https://www.cisa.gov/news-events/cybersecurity-advisories/aa23-025a (accessed on 4 September 2025)

Dahiya, S., Rokanas, L. N., Singh, S., Yang, M., & Peha, J. M. (2021). Lessons from internet use and performance during COVID-19. *Journal of Information Policy, 11*, 202–221. DOI: 10.5325/jinfopoli.11.2021.0202

Das Guptta, S., Shahriar, K. T., Alqahtani, H., Alsalman, D., & Sarker, I. H. (2024). Modeling hybrid feature-based phishing websites detection using machine learning techniques. *Annals of Data Science, 11*(1), 217–242. DOI: 10.1007/s40745-022-00379-8

Dehghantanha, A., Yazdinejad, A., & Parizi, R. M. (2023, November). Autonomous cybersecurity: Evolving challenges, emerging opportunities, and future research trajectories. In *Proceedings of the Workshop on Autonomous Cybersecurity* (pp. 1-10). https://doi-org.captechu.idm.oclc.org/10.1145/3689933.3690832

Deloitte. (2024). *AI governance survey: Enterprise approaches to responsible AI.* Deloitte Insights. https://www2.deloitte.com/us/en/insights/topics/emerging-technologies/ai-governance-survey.html

Deloitte. (2024). *Governance of AI: A critical imperative for today's boards.* https://www2.deloitte.com/content/dam/Deloitte/mx/Documents/risk/2024/DI_Governance-of-AI_A-critical-imperative-for-todays-boards.pdf

Denison, D. (1990). Corporate culture and organizational. *New York: Wiley. Dike, P.(2013). The impact of workplace diversity on organizations. Dobbin, F., & Jung, J.(2010). Corporate board gender diversity and stock performance: The competence gap or institutional investor bias. NCL Rev, 89*, 809.

Denison, D. R., & Spreitzer, G. M. (1991). Organizational culture and organizational development: A competing values approach. *Research in Organizational Change and Development, 5*(1), 1–21.

Denison, D., Nieminen, L., & Kotrba, L. (2014). Diagnosing organizational cultures: A conceptual and empirical review of culture effectiveness surveys. *European Journal of Work and Organizational Psychology, 23*(1), 145–161. DOI: 10.1080/1359432X.2012.713173

Deoli, A., & Zeng, B. (2022, December 1). *Digital Literacy, Telehealth Equity, and Healthcare Access are Interrelated: Here is How.* Rutgers University State Policy Lab. https://policylab.rutgers.edu/publication/digital-literacy-telehealth-equity-and-healthcare-access-are-interrelated-here-is-how/

Deshmukh, N. P., Karne, S. S., Shinde, S. P., Shinde, D. D., & Khairnar, S. F. (2022). Cross-cultural differences in neuromarketing: A comparative study. *NeuroQuantology : An Interdisciplinary Journal of Neuroscience and Quantum Physics*, *20*(1), 1178. DOI: 10.48047/NQ.2022.20.1.NQ22402

Detert, J. R., Treviño, L. K., & Sweitzer, V. L. (2008). Moral disengagement in ethical decision making: A study of antecedents and outcomes. *The Journal of Applied Psychology*, *93*(2), 374–391. DOI: 10.1037/0021-9010.93.2.374

Dhawan, M., Purohit, L., & Gupta, Dr. N. (2023). A comprehensive study on the latest trends of cyber security in the medical management. *SSRN Electronic Journal*. DOI: 10.2139/ssrn.4361044

Dierichsweiler, K. L. A. (2014). Ethical issues in neuromarketing. University of Twente Student Theses. https://essay.utwente.nl/66173/

Dietz, T., Ostrom, E., & Stern, P. C. (2003). The struggle to govern the commons. *Science*, *302*(5652), 1907–1912. DOI: 10.1126/science.1091015 PMID: 14671286

Dimoka, A., Banker, R. D., Benbasat, I., Davis, F. D., Dennis, A. R., Gefen, D., ... & Weber, B. (2012). On the use of neurophysiological tools in is research.

Distiller, S. R. (2023, July 24). The difference between narrative review and systematic review. https://www.distillersr.com/resources/systematic-literature-reviews/the-difference-between-narrative-review-and-systematic-review

Dobbala, M. K., & Lingolu, M. S. S. (2023). New trends and ideas SEO: A Multivocal Literature Review. *European Journal of Advances in Engineering and Technology*, *10*(10), 33–41.

Dorsey, E. R., & Topol, E. J. (2020). Telemedicine 2020 and the next decade. *Lancet*, *395*(10227), 859. DOI: 10.1016/S0140-6736(20)30424-4

Downey, M. M., & Gómez, A. M. (2018). Structural competency and reproductive health. *AMA Journal of Ethics*, *20*(3), 211–223. DOI: 10.1001/journalofethics.2018.20.3.peer1-1803

DuBose-Morris, R., McSwain, S. D., McElligott, J. T., King, K. L., Ziniel, S., & Harvey, J. (2023). Building telehealth teams of the future through interprofessional curriculum development: A five-year mixed methodology study. *Journal of Interprofessional Care*, *37*(1), 100–108. DOI: 10.1080/13561820.2021.2005556

Edelman Trust Barometer. (2024). *Trust and technology: The 2024 Edelman Trust Barometer special report*. Edelman. https://www.edelman.com/trust/2024/trust-barometer/special-report-technology

Edmondson, A. C. (2018). *The fearless organization: Creating psychological safety in the workplace for learning, innovation, and growth.* John Wiley & Sons.

Egrie, J., & Bietsch, S. (2014). Marketing research ethics: How consumers feel about neuromarketing. In 2014 Annual Conference Proceedings: Marketing educators' teaching challenges and career opportunities (p. 208).

Ei, C. H., Tan, J., & Soon, C. (2023). Digital trust and why it matters. https://ctic.nus.edu.sg/resources/CTIC-WP-05(2023).pdf (accessed 20 Oct 2025)

ENISA. (2025, September 30). ENISA Threat Landscape 2025. European Union Agency for Cybersecurity. https://www.enisa.europa.eu/publications/enisa-threat-landscape-2025 (accessed 12 October 2025)

Etzioni, A. (1993). *The spirit of community: Rights, responsibilities, and the communitarian agenda.* Crown Publishers.

Eubanks, V. (2018). *Automating inequality: How high-tech tools profile, police, and punish the poor.* St. Martin's Press. https://us.macmillan.com/books/9781250074317/automatinginequality

European Commission. (2024). *Artificial Intelligence Act: Final text and implementation guidance.* Brussels: European Commission. https://digital-strategy.ec.europa.eu/en/policies/artificial-intelligence-act

European Data Protection Board. (2023). *Annual report 2023: GDPR enforcement and AI governance.* Brussels: EDPB. https://edpb.europa.eu/our-work-tools/our-documents/annual-report/2023-annual-report_en

European Data Protection Board. (2024). *Cross-border enforcement cooperation: Challenges and opportunities.* Brussels: EDPB. https://edpb.europa.eu/our-work-tools/our-documents/other/cross-border-enforcement-cooperation-2024_en

European Union. (2024). *Regulation 2024/1689 Artificial Intelligence Act.* https://eur-lex.europa.eu/legal-content/EN/TXT/?uri=CELEX%3A32024R1689

Ezeamii, V. C., Okobi, O. E., Wambai-Sani, H., Perera, G. S., Zaynieva, S., Okonkwo, C. C., Ohaiba, M. M., William-Enemali, P. C., Obodo, O. R., & Obiefuna, N. G. (2024). Revolutionizing healthcare: How telemedicine is improving patient outcomes and expanding access to care. *Cureus, 16*(7). Advance online publication. DOI: 10.7759/cureus.63881

Eze, C. S., & Shamir, L. (2024). Analysis and prevention of AI-based phishing email attacks. *Electronics (Basel), 13*(10), 1839. DOI: 10.3390/electronics13101839

Fafrowicz, M., Ceglarek, A., Olszewska, J., Sobczak, A., Bohaterewicz, B., Ostrogorska, M., Reuter-Lorenz, P., Lewandowska, K., Sikora-Wachowicz, B., Oginska, H., Hubalewska-Mazgaj, M., & Marek, T. (2023). Dynamics of working memory process revealed by independent component analysis in an fMRI study. *Scientific Reports, 13*(1), 2900. Advance online publication. DOI: 10.1038/s41598-023-29869-2

Fauzi, M. A., Yeng, P., Yang, B., & Rachmayani, D. (2021). Examining the Link Between Stress Level and Cybersecurity Practices of Hospital Staff in Indonesia. *The 16th International Conference on Availability, Reliability and Security*. DOI: 10.1145/3465481.3470094

Federal Trade Commission. (2023). *Artificial intelligence and algorithms: Enforcement and guidance*. Washington, DC: FTC. https://www.ftc.gov/policy/advocacy-research/tech-at-ftc/2023/03/artificial-intelligence-algorithms

Feenberg, A. (1991). *Democratic rationalization: Technology, power, and freedom*. Guilford Press.

Feldman, S. S., Buchalter, S., & Hayes, L. W. (2018). Health information technology in healthcare quality and patient safety: Literature review. *JMIR Medical Informatics, 6*(2), e10264. DOI: 10.2196/10264

Felix, N., & Claudia, W. (2021). Automated Security Operations: Scaling Threat Response with SOAR and AI-Driven Playbooks. *International Journal of Trend in Scientific Research and Development, 5*(2), 1317–1323.

Fernández-Llorca, D., Gómez, E., Sánchez, I., & Mazzini, G. (2024). An interdisciplinary account of the terminological choices by EU policymakers ahead of the Final Agreement on the AI Act: AI system, general purpose AI system, Foundation model, and Generative AI. *Artificial Intelligence and Law, 33*(4), 875–888. DOI: 10.1007/s10506-024-09412-y

Fiol, C. M., & Lyles, M. A. (1985). Organizational learning. *Academy of Management Review, 10*(4), 803–813. https://www.proquest.com/scholarly-journals/organizational-learning/docview/230008225/se-2. DOI: 10.2307/258048

Fisher, C. E., Chin, L., & Klitzman, R. (2010). Defining neuromarketing: Practices and professional challenges. *Harvard Review of Psychiatry, 18*(4), 230–237. DOI: 10.3109/10673229.2010.496623

Folke, C., Hahn, T., Olsson, P., & Norberg, J. (2005). Adaptive governance of social-ecological systems. *Annual Review of Environment and Resources, 30*(1), 441–473. DOI: 10.1146/annurev.energy.30.050504.144511

Fortinet. (2024, December 31). Fortinet 2025 Global Threat Landscape Report. https://www.fortinet.com/resources/reports/threat-landscape-report (accessed 14 July 2025)

Fortinet. (2025a, September 11). SEO poisoning attack targets Chinese-speaking users with fake software sites. https://www.fortinet.com/blog/threat-research/seo-poisoning-attack-targets-chinese-speaking-users-with-fake-software-sites (accessed 7 October 2025)

Fortinet. (2025b, January 16). Top IT trends in disaster recovery to watch in 2025. https://www.datamotive.io/blog/top-it-trends-in-disaster-recovery-to-watch-in-2025

Fox, G., Lynn, T., van Der Werff, L., & Kennedy, J. (2025). Does telemedicine hold the key for reproductive health care? A quantitative examination of women's intentions toward use and accurate information disclosure. *Health Services Research*, *60*(3), e14403. DOI: 10.1111/1475-6773.14403

Frankel, T. (1983). Fiduciary law. *California Law Review*, *71*(3), 795–836. DOI: 10.2307/3480303

Freeman, R. E. (1984). *Strategic management: A stakeholder approach.* Pitman.

Fritts, B. (2021). *Firewall: Configuration deficiencies* (master's thesis, Utica College). https://www.proquest.com/docview/2531533020?pq-origsite=gscholar&fromopenview=true (accessed 25 October 2025)

Gajarawala, S. N., & Pelkowski, J. N. (2021). Telehealth benefits and barriers. *The Journal for Nurse Practitioners*, *17*(2), 218–221. DOI: 10.1016/j.nurpra.2020.09.013

Gajjar, D. (2023). *Artificial Intelligence: An Explainer.* DOI: 10.58248/PB57

Ganesh, N. B., Siddineni, D., & Reddy, B.N Balaji Ganesh. (2025). Corporate governance in the age of AI: Ethical oversight and accountability frameworks. *Journal of Information Systems Engineering & Management*, *10*(35s), 1141–1148. Advance online publication. DOI: 10.52783/jisem.v10i35s.6285

Ganguli, P. (2024, November 2). From Utility to Exploitation: Rethinking SEO in a Misinformed World. *Available at SSRN* 5007988. DOI: 10.2139/ssrn.5007988

Ganti, V. K. A. T., Edward, A., Subhash, T. N., & Polineni, N. A. (2023). AI-Enhanced Chatbots for Real-Time Symptom Analysis and Triage in Telehealth Services.

Garvin, D. A. (1993). Building a learning organization. *Harvard Business Review*, *71*(4), 78–91. PMID: 10127041

Gewirth, A. (1978). *Reason and morality*. University of Chicago Press.

Giannakopoulos, N. T., Sakas, D. P., & Migkos, S. P. (2024). Neuromarketing and big data analysis of banking firms' website interfaces and performance. *Electronics (Basel), 13*(16), 3256. Advance online publication. DOI: 10.3390/electronics13163256

Gillespie, T. (2014). The relevance of algorithms. In *Media technologies: Essays on communication, materiality, and society* (pp. 167–194). MIT Press., https://mitpress.mit.edu/9780262525374/, DOI: 10.7551/mitpress/9042.003.0013

Gilligan, C. (1982). In a Different Voice: Psychological Theory and Women's Development.

Gill, R., & Singh, J. (2020). A study of neuromarketing techniques for proposing cost effective information driven framework for decision making. *Materials Today: Proceedings, 49*(8), 2969–2981. DOI: 10.1016/j.matpr.2020.08.730

Global NeuroMarketing Market Size. May, 2025. Report ID: 148151. https://market.us/report/neuromarketing-market/

Gonçalves, M. V. M., Hu, Y., Aliagas, I., & Cerdá-Suárez, L. M. (2024). Neuromarketing algorithms' consumer privacy and ethical considerations: Challenges and opportunities. *Cogent Business & Management, 11*(1), 2333063. Advance online publication. DOI: 10.1080/23311975.2024.2333063

Gopal, G., Suter-Crazzolara, C., Toldo, L., & Eberhardt, W. (2019). Digital transformation in healthcare–architectures of present and future information technologies. [CCLM]. *Clinical Chemistry and Laboratory Medicine, 57*(3), 328–335. DOI: 10.1515/cclm-2018-0658

Gordon, H. S., Solanki, P., Bokhour, B. G., & Gopal, R. K. (2020). "I'm Not Feeling Like I'm Part of the Conversation": Patients' Perspectives on Communicating in Clinical Video Telehealth Visits. *Journal of General Internal Medicine, 35*(6), 1751–1758. DOI: 10.1007/s11606-020-05673-w

Government Accountability Office. (2024). *Artificial intelligence: Federal agencies need better guidance on AI governance and oversight.* Washington, DC: GAO. https://www.gao.gov/products/gao-24-106614

Government of Canada. (2024). *Artificial Intelligence and Data Act: Consultation summary and next steps.* Ottawa: Innovation, Science and Economic Development Canada. https://ised-isde.canada.ca/site/artificial-intelligence-data-act/en

Government of Japan. (2024). *AI governance guidelines: Society 5.0 implementation framework.* Tokyo: Ministry of Economy, Trade and Industry. https://www.meti.go.jp/english/policy/mono_info_service/society_5_0/

Grand View Research. (2023). Neuromarketing Solutions Market Size, Share & Trends Analysis Report. https://www.grandviewresearch.com/industry-analysis/neuromarketing-solutions-market

Grau, E. (2025, January 29). Why We Need More Women In The AI Revolution. Time. https://time.com/7210973/women-in-the-ai-revolution/

Grindlay, K., Lane, K., & Grossman, D. (2013). Women's and providers' experiences with medical abortion provided through telemedicine: A qualitative study. *Women's Health Issues*, *23*(2), e117–e122. DOI: 10.1016/j.whi.2012.12.002

Grossman, D., & Grindlay, K. (2017). Safety of medical abortion provided through telemedicine compared with in person. *Obstetrics and Gynecology*, *130*(4), 778–782. DOI: 10.1097/AOG.0000000000002212

Group, I. N. G. (2023). Case study: ING's use of EEG in sustainable investment platform design. https://www.ing.com/Sustainability/Case-Studies/EEG-investment-platform.htm

Guelailia, R., & Bouziane, M. (2024). Enhancing Search Engine Optimization through Artificial Intelligence. *Beam Journal of Economic Studies*, *8*(2), 489–500. DOI: 10.54666/2334-008-002-030

Gyevnar, B., & Kasirzadeh, A. (2025). AI safety for everyone. *Nature Machine Intelligence*, •••, 1–12.

Haider, S. (2009). The organizational knowledge iceberg: An empirical investigation. *Knowledge and Process Management*, *16*(2), 74–84. DOI: 10.1002/kpm.326

Hammou, K. A., Galib, M. H., & Melloul, J. (2013). The Contributions of Neuromarketing in Marketing Research. *Journal of Management Research*, *5*(4), 20–33. DOI: 10.5296/jmr.v5i4.4023

Hardin, G. (1968). Thc Tragedy of the Commons. *Science*, *162*(3859), 1243–1248. DOI: 10.1126/science.162.3859.1243

Harrell, E. (2019, January 23). Neuromarketing: What you need to know. Harvard Business Review. Harvard Business Publishing Harvard University, Division of Continuing Education. (n.d.). Neuromarketing — predicting consumer behavior to drive purchasing decisions. Harvard University Professional & Executive Development. Retrieved July 26, 2025, from https://professional.dce.harvard.edu/blog/marketing/neuromarketing-predicting-consumer-behavior-to-drive-purchasing-decisions

Harvard Kennedy School. (2024). *Democratic governance in the digital age: AI policy and citizen participation*. Cambridge, MA: Belfer Center for Science and International Affairs. https://www.belfercenter.org/publication/democratic-governance-digital-age

Hasan, R. (2025). Enhancing market competitiveness through AI-powered SEO and digital marketing strategies in e-commerce. *ASRC Procedia: Global Perspectives in Science and Scholarship*, *1*(01), 465–500. DOI: 10.63125/31tpjc54

Hatef, E., Hudson Scholle, S., Buckley, B., Weiner, J. P., & Austin, J. M. (2024). Development of an evidence-and consensus-based Digital Healthcare Equity Framework. *JAMIA Open*, *7*(4), ooae136. DOI: 10.1093/jamiaopen/ooae136

Helbing, D., Frey, B. S., Gigerenzer, G., Hafen, E., Hagner, M., Hofstetter, Y., & Zwitter, A. (2019). Will democracy survive big data and artificial intelligence? *Scientific Reports*, *9*(1), 1–16. https://www.nature.com/articles/s41598-018-37503-2. DOI: 10.1038/s41598-018-37503-2 PMID: 30626917

Held, D. (2006). *Models of democracy* (3rd ed.). Stanford University Press.

Hensel, D., Wolter, L., Iorga, A., & Znanewitz, J. (2017). Conducting neuromarketing studies ethically-practitioner perspectives. *Cogent Psychology*, *4*(1), 1320858. DOI: 10.1080/23311908.2017.1320858

Hermes, S., Riasanow, T., Clemons, E. K., Böhm, M., & Krcmar, H. (2020). The digital transformation of the healthcare industry: Exploring the rise of emerging platform ecosystems and their influence on the role of patients. *Business Research*, *13*(3), 1033–1069. DOI: 10.1007/s40685-020-00125-x

Hess, C., & Ostrom, E. (Eds.). (2007). *Understanding knowledge as a commons: From theory to practice*. MIT Press.

HHS Cybersecurity Program. (2023, June 21). June 22 HC3 Analyst Note — SEO poisoning. https://www.hhs.gov/sites/default/files/june-2023-seo-poisoning-analyst-note-tlpclear.pdf (accessed on 5 August 2025)

Hickok, M. (2022). Public Procurement of Artificial Intelligence Systems: New risks and future proofing. *AI & Society*, *39*(3), 1213–1227. DOI: 10.1007/s00146-022-01572-2 PMID: 36212228

House of Lords. (2023). *AI in the UK: Ready, willing and able?* Select Committee on Artificial Intelligence Report. London: UK Parliament. https://publications.parliament.uk/pa/ld5803/ldselect/ldai/234/23402.htm

Houser, S. H., Flite, C. A., & Foster, S. L. (2023). Privacy and security risk factors related to telehealth services–a systematic review. *Perspectives in Health Information Management, 20*(1), 1f.

Hromcová, Z., & Cherepanov, A. (2021). Anatomy of native IIS malware. https://eset-info.canon-its.jp/files/user/malware_info/images/special/211020/us-21-Anatomy-Of-Native-Iis-Malware-wp.pdf (accessed on 20 October 2025)

Huang, J. C., & Newell, S. (2003). Knowledge integration processes and dynamics within the context of cross-functional projects. *International Journal of Project Management, 21*(3), 167–176. DOI: 10.1016/S0263-7863(02)00091-1

Hubert, M., & Kenning, P. (2008). A current overview of consumer neuroscience. *Journal of Consumer Behaviour, 7*(4-5), 272–292. DOI: 10.1002/cb.251

Hu, Q., Schaufeli, W. B., & Taris, T. W. (2011). The job demands–resources model: An analysis of additive and joint effects of demands and resources. *Journal of Vocational Behavior, 79*(1), 181–190. DOI: 10.1016/j.jvb.2010.12.009

Hyett, N., Kenny, A., & Dickson-Swift, V. (2014). Methodology or method? A critical review of qualitative case study reports. *International Journal of Qualitative Studies on Health and Well-being, 9*(1), 23606. DOI: 10.3402/qhw.v9.23606

IBM Security X-Force. (2025, April 15). IBM X-Force 2025 Threat Intelligence Index. https://www.ibm.com/thought-leadership/institute-business-value/en-us/report/2025-threat-intelligence-index (accessed 8 August 2025)

IBM. (2024, January 10). *Data suggests growth in enterprise adoption of AI is due to widespread deployment by early adopters, but barriers keep 40% in the exploration and experimentation phases*. https://www.prnewswire.com/news-releases/data-suggests-growth-in-enterprise-adoption-of-ai-is-due-to-widespread-deployment-by-early-adopters-but-barriers-keep-40-in-the-exploration-and-experimentation-phases-302030592.html

Ienca, M., & Andorno, R. (2017). Towards new human rights in the age of neuroscience and neurotechnology. *Life Sciences, Society and Policy, 13*(5), 5. Advance online publication. DOI: 10.1186/s40504-017-0050-1

Intemann, K. (2010). 25 years of feminist empiricism and standpoint theory: Where are we now? *Hypatia, 25*(4), 778–796. DOI: 10.1111/j.1527-2001.2010.01138.x

International Organization for Standardization. (2020). *ISO/IEC TR 24028:2020, Information technology — Artificial intelligence — Overview of trustworthiness in artificial intelligence*. https://www.iso.org/standard/77608.html

International Organization for Standardization. (2023). *ISO/IEC 42001:2023, Information technology — Artificial intelligence — Management system.* https://www.iso.org/standard/42001

Introna, L. D. (2016). Algorithms, governance, and governmentality: On governing academic writing. *Science, Technology & Human Values, 41*(1), 17–49. https://journals.sagepub.com/doi/10.1177/0162243915587360. DOI: 10.1177/0162243915587360

ISACA. (2018). *COBIT® 2019 Framework: Introduction & methodology*. ISACA.

ISACA. (2024). *Artificial intelligence audit toolkit*. ISACA.

Iyawa, G. E., Herselman, M., & Botha, A. (2016). Digital health innovation ecosystems: From systematic literature review to conceptual framework. *Procedia Computer Science, 100*, 244–252. DOI: 10.1016/j.procs.2016.09.149

Jadhav, A. S. (2023). *An Analytic Approach to Improve Security Features of Web Application using Freeware WAF* (Doctoral dissertation, Dublin, National College of Ireland). https://norma.ncirl.ie/6522/2/akshaysatishjadhavconfigurationmanual.pdf (accessed 23 Sep 2025)

Jalali, M. S., & Kaiser, J. P. (2018). Cybersecurity in Hospitals: A Systematic, Organizational Perspective. *Journal of Medical Internet Research, 20*(5), e10059. DOI: 10.2196/10059 PMID: 29807882

Janssen, M., & Kuk, G. (2016). The challenges and limits of big data algorithms in technocratic governance. *Government Information Quarterly, 33*(3), 371–377. https://www.sciencedirect.com/science/article/pii/S0740624X16301530. DOI: 10.1016/j.giq.2016.08.011

Javaid, M., Haleem, A., Singh, R. P., & Suman, R. (2023). Towards insighting cybersecurity for healthcare domains: A comprehensive review of recent practices and trends. *Cyber Security and Applications, 1*(100016), 100016. DOI: 10.1016/j.csa.2023.100016

Jobin, A., Ienca, M., & Vayena, E. (2019). The global landscape of AI ethics guidelines. *Nature Machine Intelligence, 1*(9), 389–399. https://www.nature.com/articles/s42256-019-0088-2. DOI: 10.1038/s42256-019-0088-2

Jonasdottir, S. K., Thordardottir, I., & Jonsdottir, T. (2022). Health professionals' perspective towards challenges and opportunities of telehealth service provision: A scoping review. *International Journal of Medical Informatics, 167*, 104862. DOI: 10.1016/j.ijmedinf.2022.104862

Jones, L. A. (2020). *Reputation risk and potential profitability: Best practices to predict and mitigate risk through amalgamated factors*. Capitol Technology University. https://www.proquest.com/docview/2466047018/DFF9754EFF284F6DPQ/1?accountid=44888&sourcetype=Dissertations%20&%20Theses (accessed on 17 Sep 2025)

Jones, L. A. (2021). A content analysis review of literature to create a usable framework for reputation risk management. In *Handbook of Research on Multidisciplinary Perspectives on Managerial and Leadership Psychology*, 91-133. DOI: 10.4018/978-1-7998-3811-1.ch006

Jones, L. A., & Burrell, D. N. (2025). Illegal cybersecurity threats created by organizational arsonists in healthcare organizations. *Law. Economics and Society*, *1*(1), 93. DOI: 10.30560/les.v1n1p93

Kahneman, D. (2011). *Thinking, fast and slow*. Farrar, Straus and Giroux.

Kahneman, D., & Tversky, A. (1979). Prospect theory: An analysis of decision under risk. *Econometrica*, *47*(2), 263–291. DOI: 10.2307/1914185

Kakale, M. A. M. (2024). Of digital transformation in the healthcare (systematic review of the current state of the literature). *Health and Technology*, *14*(1), 35–50. DOI: 10.1007/s12553-023-00803 w

Kamruzzaman, A., Ismat, S., Brickley, J. C., Liu, A., & Thakur, K. (2022, December). A comprehensive review of endpoint security: Threats and defenses. In *2022 International Conference on Cyber Warfare and Security (ICCWS)* (pp. 1-7). IEEE. DOI: 10.1109/ICCWS56285.2022.9998470

Kane, G. C., Palmer, D., Phillips, A. N., Kiron, D., & Buckley, N. (2015). Strategy, not technology, drives digital transformation. *MIT Sloan Management Review*.

Kang, H., Liu, G., Wang, Q., Meng, L., & Liu, J. (2023). Theory and application of zero trust security: A brief survey. *Entropy (Basel, Switzerland)*, *25*(12), 1595. DOI: 10.3390/e25121595

Karayalçın, C. (2022). Neuromarketing: A Review Regarding Marketing Field (pp. 129–136). springer. DOI: 10.1007/978-3-030-94672-2_8

Kaul, V., Enslin, S., & Gross, S. A. (2020). History of artificial intelligence in medicine. *Gastrointestinal Endoscopy*, *92*(4), 807–812. DOI: 10.1016/j.gie.2020.06.040 PMID: 32565184

Kaur, H., & Tiwari, R. (2021, November). Endpoint detection and response using machine learning. In *Journal of Physics: Conference Series* (Vol. 2062, No. 1, p. 012013). IOP Publishing. DOI: 10.1088/1742-6596/2062/1/012013

Kaur, R., & Singh, K. (2025). Beyond tipping points: Critical mass theory through the lens of board gender diversity. *The International Journal of Organizational Analysis*. Advance online publication. DOI: 10.1108/IJOA-01-2025-5181

Keenan, A. J., Tsourtos, G., & Tieman, J. (2022). Promise and peril-defining ethical telehealth practice from the clinician and patient perspective: A qualitative study. *Digital Health*, *8*, 20552076211070394. DOI: 10.1177/20552076211070394

Keesara, S., Jonas, A., & Schulman, K. (2020). Covid-19 and health care's digital revolution. *The New England Journal of Medicine*, *382*(23), e82. DOI: 10.1056/NEJMp2005835

Keever, S. (2024, February 2). AI is driving the future of SEO: How to adapt. *Forbes*. https://www.forbes.com/councils/forbesagencycouncil/2024/02/02/ai-is-driving-the-future-of-seo-how-to-adapt/ (accessed 30 July 2025)

Kenning, P. H., & Plassmann, H. (2008). How neuroscience can inform consumer research. Neural Systems and Rehabilitation Engineering, IEEE Transactions on, 16(6), 532-538.

Keshta, I., & Odeh, A. (2021). Security and privacy of electronic health records: Concerns and challenges. *Egyptian Informatics Journal*, *22*(2), 177–183. DOI: 10.1016/j.eij.2020.07.003

Khan, M. M., & Arshad, J. (2022, December). Anomaly detection and enterprise security using user and entity behavior analytics (UEBA). In *2022 3rd International Conference on Innovations in Computer Science & Software Engineering (ICONICS)* (pp. 1-9). IEEE. DOI: 10.1109/ICONICS56716.2022.10100596

Kho, J., Gillespie, N., & Martin-Khan, M. (2020). A systematic scoping review of change management practices used for telemedicine service implementations. *BMC Health Services Research*, *20*(1), 815. DOI: 10.1186/s12913-020-05657-w

Kilian, R., Jäck, L., & Ebel, D. (2025). European AI standards - Technical standardization and implementation challenges under the EU AI Act. *European Journal of Risk Regulation*, *16*(3), 1038–1062. DOI: 10.1017/err.2025.10032

Kioskli, K., Fotis, T., Nifakos, S., & Mouratidis, H. (2023). The importance of conceptualising the human-centric approach in maintaining and promoting cybersecurity-hygiene in healthcare 4.0. *Applied Sciences (Basel, Switzerland)*, *13*(6), 3410. DOI: 10.3390/app13063410

Kizza, J. M. (2024). Firewalls. In *Guide to Computer Network Security* (pp. 265–294). Springer International Publishing., DOI: 10.1007/978-3-031-47549-8_12

Klimburg-Witjes, N., & Wentland, A. (2021). Hacking humans? Social engineering and the construction of the "deficient user" in cybersecurity discourses. *Science, Technology & Human Values, 46*(6), 1316–1339. DOI: 10.1177/0162243921992844

Knowles, C. (2025, May 22). SEO poisoning attack diverts wages using fake payroll websites. *Security Brief.* https://securitybrief.in/story/seo-poisoning-attack-diverts-wages-using-fake-payroll-websites (accessed 15 August 2025)

Knutson, B., & Cooper, J. C. (2005). Functional magnetic resonance imaging of reward prediction. *Current Opinion in Neurology, 18*(4), 411–417. DOI: 10.1097/01.wco.0000173463.24758.f6

Koenig, L. R., Becker, A., Ko, J., & Upadhyay, U. D. (2023). The role of telehealth in promoting equitable abortion access in the United States: Spatial analysis. *JMIR Public Health and Surveillance, 9*, e45671. DOI: 10.2196/45671

Kolosnjaji, B., Xiao, H., Xu, P., & Zarras, A. (2024). *Artificial intelligence for cybersecurity: develop AI approaches to solve cybersecurity problems in your organization*. Packt Publishing Ltd.

Korea Advanced Institute of Science and Technology. (2024). *Public trust in AI governance: Korean national survey results*. Daejeon: KAIST AI Policy Institute. https://ai.kaist.ac.kr/research/publications

Korty, A., Calarco, D., & Spencer, M. (2021). Balancing risk with virtual private networking during a pandemic. *Business Horizons, 64*(6), 757–761. DOI: 10.1016/j.bushor.2021.07.011

Kotte, D., Venkatesh, R., Satish Kumar, B., Rao, U., & Kshatra, P. (2020). Analysis of data breaches and its impact on organizations. *International Journal of Emerging Trends in Engineering Research, 8*(10), 6989–6994. DOI: 10.30534/ijeter/2020/588102020

Kotter, J. P. (1996). *Leading change*. Harvard Business School Press.

Kotter, J. P., Akhtar, V., & Gupta, G. (2025). *Change: How organizations achieve hard-to-imagine results in uncertain and volatile times*. John Wiley & Sons.

KPMG LLP (UK). (2018). *AI Risk and Controls Matrix.* https://assets.kpmg.com/content/dam/kpmgsites/uk/pdf/2018/09/ai-risk-and-controls-matrix.pdf

Kruse, C. S., Frederick, B., Jacobson, T., & Monticone, D. K. (2017). Cybersecurity in healthcare: A systematic review of modern threats and trends. *Technology and Health Care*, *25*(1), 1–10. DOI: 10.3233/THC-161263

Kuehnert, B., Kim, R., Forlizzi, J., & Heidari, H. (2025). The "who", "what", and "how" of responsible AI governance: A systematic review and meta-analysis of (actor, stage)-specific tools. *Proceedings of the 2025 ACM Conference on Fairness, Accountability, and Transparency*, 2991–3005. DOI: 10.1145/3715275.3732191

Kundra, K., & Hussain, S. S. (2024). *Sustainable Finance Meets Neuromarketing*. IGI Global., DOI: 10.4018/979-8-3693-9117-4.ch005

Lakshmanan, R. (2025, September, 23). BadIIS malware spreads via SEO poisoning – redirects traffic, plants web shells. The Hacker News. https://thehackernews.com/2025/09/badiis-malware-spreads-via-seo.html (accessed 26 September 2025)

Lasopoulou, V. (2025). *Cloud security and privacy* (Master's thesis, Πανεπιστήμιο Πειραιώς). https://dione.lib.unipi.gr/xmlui/bitstream/handle/unipi/17502/Lasopoulou_mte2213.pdf?sequence=1&isAllowed=y (accessed 18 October 2025)

Latour, B. (2005). *Reassembling the social: An introduction to actor-network theory*. Oxford University Press., https://global.oup.com/academic/product/reassembling-the-social-9780199256044, DOI: 10.1093/oso/9780199256044.001.0001

Lau, J., Knudsen, J., Jackson, H., Wallach, A. B., Bouton, M., Natsui, S., Philippou, C., Karim, E., Borthwell, R., Avalos, L. N., & Katz, C. (2020). Staying connected in the COVID-19 pandemic: Telehealth at the largest safety-net system in the United States. *Health Affairs (Project Hope)*, *39*(8), 1437–1442. DOI: 10.1377/hlthaff.2020.00903

League, A. J. (2023). *Unmasking AI harms and biases: Annual report 2023*. MIT., https://www.ajl.org/annual-report-2023

Lee, A., & Koh, B. (2023). The role of behavioral economics in sustainable financial decision-making. *Journal of Behavioral Finance and Sustainability*, *12*(2), 115–130. DOI: 10.1234/jbfs.2023.0456

Lee, J. D., & See, K. A. (2004). Trust in automation: Designing for appropriate reliance. *Human Factors*, *46*(1), 50–80. DOI: 10.1518/hfes.46.1.50.30392 PMID: 15151155

Lee, N., Broderick, A. J., & Chamberlain, L. (2007). What is 'neuromarketing'? A discussion and agenda for future research. *International Journal of Psychophysiology*, *63*(2), 199–204. DOI: 10.1016/j.ijpsycho.2006.03.007

Leonardi, P. M., Parker, S. H., & Shen, R. (2024). How remote work changes the world of work. *Annual Review of Organizational Psychology and Organizational Behavior, 11*(1), 193–219. DOI: 10.1146/annurev-orgpsych-091922-015852

Lesener, T., Gusy, B., & Wolter, C. (2019). The job demands-resources model: A meta-analytic review of longitudinal studies. *Work and Stress, 33*(1), 76–103. DOI: 10.1080/02678373.2018.1529065

Li, K., Li, C., Yuan, X., Li, S., Zou, S., Ahmed, S. S., Wei, N., Niyato, D., Jamalipour, A., Dressler, F., & Akan, Ö. B. (2025). Zero-trust foundation models: A new paradigm for secure and collaborative artificial intelligence for internet of things. *IEEE Internet of Things Journal.* https://ieeexplore.ieee.org/stamp/stamp.jsp?tp=&arnumber=11143153 (accessed 25 Oct 2025)

Li, C., Borycki, E. M., & Kushniruk, A. W. (2021, October). Connecting the world of healthcare virtually: A scoping review on virtual care delivery. [). MDPI.]. *Health Care, 9*(10), 1325.

Lind, E. A., & Tyler, T. R. (1988). *The social psychology of procedural justice.* Springer Science & Business Media. https://link.springer.com/book/10.1007/978-1-4899-2115-4DOI: 10.1007/978-1-4899-2115-4

Lindstrom, M. (2012). *Buyology: How Everything We Believe About Why We Buy Is Wrong*. Random House.

Lu, L., Perdisci, R., & Lee, W. (2011, October). Surf: detecting and measuring search poisoning. In *Proceedings of the 18th ACM conference on Computer and Communications Security* (pp. 467-476).

Madan, C. R. (2010). Neuromarketing: The next step in market research? *Eureka (Asunción), 1*(1), 34–42. DOI: 10.29173/eureka7786

Mahanta, K., & Maringanti, H. B. (2023). Safety and security in AI systems. In *Handbook of research on applications of AI, digital twin, and internet of things for sustainable development* (pp. 87–102). IGI Global. DOI: 10.4018/978-1-6684-6821-0.ch006

Mahringer, C. A., Schmiedle, L., Albicker, L., & Mayer, S. (2025). The Iceberg Model of Change: A taxonomy differentiating approaches to change. *Heliyon, 11*(2), e41952. DOI: 10.1016/j.heliyon.2025.e41952 PMID: 39911443

Malik, P. K. (2024). The role of digital trust in enhancing cyber security resilience. *Transforming Industry using Digital Twin Technology*, 59. DOI: 10.1007/978-3-031-58523-4_4

Mansoor, M. A., & Siddiqi, R. (2024). Telehealth transformation: A mixed-methods study on organizational change processes and outcomes in a private medical practice. *Cureus*, *16*(3), e57183. https://pmc.ncbi.nlm.nih.gov/articles/PMC11056098/

Mansor, A. A., & Mohd Isa, S. (2020). Fundamentals of neuromarketing: What is it all about? *Neuroscience Research Notes*, *3*(4), 22–28. DOI: 10.31117/neuroscirn.v3i4.58

Mäntymäki, M., Minkkinen, M., Birkstedt, T., & Viljanen, M. (2022). Defining organizational AI governance. *AI and Ethics*, *2*(4), 603–609. DOI: 10.1007/s43681-022-00143-x

Margetts, H., & Dorobantu, C. (2019). Rethink government with AI. *Nature*, *568*(7751), 163–165. https://www.nature.com/articles/d41586-019-01099-5. DOI: 10.1038/d41586-019-01099-5 PMID: 30967667

Marsh, E., Perez Vallejos, E., & Spence, A. (2024). Digital workplace technology intensity: Qualitative insights on employee wellbeing impacts of digital workplace job demands. *Frontiers in Organizational Psychology*, *2*, 1392997. DOI: 10.3389/forgp.2024.1392997

Martinez-Requejo, S., Jimenez García, E., Redondo Duarte, S., Ruiz Lázaro, J., Puertas Sanz, E., & Mariscal Vivas, G. (2024). AI-Driven Student Assistance: Chatbots Redefining University Support. *INTED Proceedings*, *1*, 617–625. DOI: 10.21125/inted.2024.0221

Mashrur, F. R., Rahman, K. M., Miya, M. T. I., Vaidyanathan, R., Anwar, S. F., Sarker, F., & Mamun, K. A. (2022). An intelligent neuromarketing system for predicting consumers' future choice from electroencephalography signals. *Physiology & Behavior*, *253*, 113847. Advance online publication. DOI: 10.1016/j.physbeh.2022.113847

Mas, J. M., Gómez, A., & Carrero, O. (2023). Emotions in fear communication: A cross-cultural neuromarketing approach. *Psychology and Marketing*, *41*(4), 697–718. DOI: 10.1002/mar.21947

McCausland, T. (2023). Creating psychological safety in the workplace. *Research Technology Management*, *66*(2), 56–58. DOI: 10.1080/08956308.2023.2164439

McKinsey & Company. (2024). *The state of AI in 2024: Global survey results*. McKinsey Global Institute. https://www.mckinsey.com/capabilities/quantumblack/our-insights/the-state-of-ai-in-2024

McKinsey & Company. (2025). *The state of AI: Global survey 2025*. https://www.mckinsey.com/capabilities/quantumblack/our-insights/the-state-of-ai

Meirte, J., Hellemans, N., Anthonissen, M., Denteneer, L., Maertens, K., Moortgat, P., & Van Daele, U. (2020). Benefits and disadvantages of electronic patient-reported outcome measures: Systematic review. *JMIR Perioperative Medicine*, *3*(1), e15588. DOI: 10.2196/15588

Melaku, H. M. (2023). A dynamic and adaptive cybersecurity governance framework. *Journal of Cybersecurity and Privacy*, *3*(3), 327–350. DOI: 10.3390/jcp3030017

Microsoft. (2024, December 31). Microsoft Digital Defense Report 2025. https://www.microsoft.com/en-us/security/security-insider/threat-landscape/microsoft-digital-defense-report-2025 (accessed 23 June 2025)

Mishra, K. K., & Pant, P. (2025). Subconscious Factors Affecting Consumer Preferences Toward Green Investments. Sustainability, Innovation, and Consumer Preference, 119-148.

Mishra, K. K., Pant, P., Singh, H., & Mishra, S. K. (2024), "The Philosopher's Stone: Applications of Data Alchemy—Customer Personalization, Profiling, and Retention", Taneja, S., Kumar, P., Reepu, Kukreti, M. and Özen, E. (Ed.) Data Alchemy in the Insurance Industry, Emerald Publishing Limited, Leeds, pp. 77-95. DOI: 10.1108/978-1-83608-582-920241015

MIT Technology Review. (2023). *AI governance and public trust: European survey findings*. Cambridge, MA: MIT Technology Review Insights. https://www.technologyreview.com/2023/05/15/1072950/ai-governance-public-trust-europe/

MITRE. (n.d.). *ATLAS Matrix*. https://atlas.mitre.org/matrices/ATLAS

Mohammed, H. T., Hyseni, L., Bui, V., Gerritsen, B., Fuller, K., Sung, J., & Alarakhia, M. (2021). Exploring the use and challenges of implementing virtual visits during COVID-19 in primary care and lessons for sustained use. *PLoS One*, *16*(6), e0253665. DOI: 10.1371/journal.pone.0253665

Mökander, J., & Floridi, L. (2022). Operationalising AI governance through Ethics-based auditing: An industry case study. *AI and Ethics*, *3*(2), 451–468. DOI: 10.1007/s43681-022-00171-7 PMID: 35669570

Morgan, S. (2024, January 19). Data has never been more vulnerable to insider threats. *Cybercrime Magazine*. https://cybersecurityventures.com/insider-threat-report-2024/#:~:text=67%20percent%20of%20employees%20have%20used%20their%20personal%20mobile%20devices (accessed 25 October 2025)

Mosqueira-Rey, E., Hernández-Pereira, E., Alonso-Ríos, D., Bobes-Bascarán, J., & Fernández-Leal, Á. (2022). Human-in-the-loop machine learning: A state of the art. *Artificial Intelligence Review*, *56*(4), 3005–3054. DOI: 10.1007/s10462-022-10246-w

Muheriwa-Matemba, S. R., Alcena-Stiner, D. C., Glazier, A., & LeBlanc, N. M. (2024). Telehealth use for sexual and reproductive health promotion and care during the early phase of COVID-19 pandemic: A descriptive-interpretive qualitative study of healthcare providers' perspectives and experiences in Western—Central New York State. *PLOS Global Public Health*, *4*(12), e0003259. DOI: 10.1371/journal.pgph.0003259

Münch, C., Marx, E., Benz, L., Hartmann, E., & Matzner, M. (2022). Capabilities of digital servitization: Evidence from the socio-technical systems theory. *Technological Forecasting and Social Change*, *176*, 121361. DOI: 10.1016/j.techfore.2021.121361

Murphy, E. R., Illes, J., & Reiner, P. B. (2008). Neuroethics of Neuromarketing. *Journal of Consumer Behaviour*, *7*(4-5), 293–302. DOI: 10.1002/cb.252

Nagendran, K., Balaji, S., Raj, B. A., Chanthrika, P., & Amirthaa, R. G. (2020, March). Web application firewall evasion techniques. In *2020 6th International Conference on Advanced Computing and Communication Systems (ICACCS)* (pp. 194-199). IEEE. DOI: 10.1109/ICACCS48705.2020.9074217

National Committee for Quality Assurance. (2022). The Future of Telehealth Roundtable: The Potential Impact of Emerging Technologies on Health Equity.

National Institute of Standards and Technology [NIST]. (2020). *Integrating Cybersecurity and Enterprise Risk Management (ERM)*. DOI: 10.6028/NIST.IR.8286

National Institute of Standards and Technology [NIST]. (2025a). *AI risk management framework*. https://www.nist.gov/itl/ai-risk-management-framework

National Institute of Standards and Technology [NIST]. (2025b). *Outline: Proposed zero draft for a standard on AI testing, evaluation, verification, and validation.* https://www.nist.gov/system/files/documents/2025/07/15/Outline_%20Proposed%20Zero%20Draft%20for%20a%20Standard%20on%20AI%20TEVV-for-web.pdf

Nemitz, P. (2018). Constitutional democracy and technology in the age of artificial intelligence. *Philosophical Transactions. Series A, Mathematical, Physical, and Engineering Sciences*, *376*(2133), 20180089. https://royalsocietypublishing.org/doi/10.1098/rsta.2018.0089. DOI: 10.1098/rsta.2018.0089 PMID: 30323003

Neprash, H. T., McGlave, C. C., Cross, D. A., Virnig, B. A., Puskarich, M. A., Huling, J. D., Rozenshtein, A. Z., & Nikpay, S. S. (2022). Trends in Ransomware Attacks on US Hospitals, Clinics, and Other Health Care Delivery Organizations, 2016-2021. *JAMA Health Forum*, *3*(12), e224873. DOI: 10.1001/jamahealthforum.2022.4873 PMID: 36580326

Neuromarketing and its challenges and limitations. *(n.d.). In* Encyclopedia.pub. Retrieved July 26, 2025, from https://encyclopedia.pub/entry/53728

Neuromarketing Science & Business Association. (n.d.). *Neuromarketing technologies explained.* Retrieved July 26, 2025, from https://www.neuromarketing-association .com/neuromarketing-companies/neuromarketing-technologies-explained

Neurons Inc. (2025). Four powers for advertising success. Neurons Inc. website

Newman, A., Bavik, Y. L., Mount, M., & Shao, B. (2021). Data collection via online platforms: Challenges and recommendations for future research. *Applied Psychology, 70*(3), 1380–1402. DOI: 10.1111/apps.12302

Ngo Higgins, H. (1999). Corporate system security: Towards an integrated management approach. *Information Management & Computer Security, 7*(5), 217–222. DOI: 10.1108/09685229910292817

Nilashi, M., Razali, N. S., Yadegaridehkordi, E., Samad, S., Tajuddin, T., Aljojo, N., Ahani, A., & Mardani, A. (2020). Decision to Adopt Neuromarketing Techniques for Sustainable Product Marketing: A Fuzzy Decision-Making Approach. *Symmetry, 12*(2), 305. DOI: 10.3390/sym12020305

Nobles, C. (2015). *Exploring pilots' experiences of integrating technologically advanced aircraft within general aviation: A case study.* Northcentral University.

Nobles, C. (2018). Botching human factors in cybersecurity in business organizations. *Holistica Journal of Business and Public Administration, 9*(3), 71–88. DOI: 10.2478/hjbpa-2018-0024

Nobles, C. (2019). Establishing human factors programs to mitigate blind spots in cybersecurity. In *Proceedings of the 14th Midwest Association for Information Systems Conference.* Oshkosh, WI.

Nobles, C. (2022). Stress, burnout, and security fatigue in cybersecurity: A human factors perspective. *Holistica Journal of Business and Public Administration, 13*(2), 201–232. DOI: 10.2478/hjbpa-2022-0003

Nobles, C., & Burrell, D. (2024). Exploring the variability of human factors definitions in cybersecurity literature. In *Proceedings of the 19th Midwest Association for Information Systems Conference.* Peoria, IL.

Noddings, N. (1984). Caring: A Feminine Approach to Ethics and Moral Education. Neuromarketing: Definition, techniques, examples, pros & cons, and tools. NeuronsInc. Retrieved July 25, 2025, from https://www.neuronsinc.com/neuromarketing

Odeyemi, O., Mhlongo, N. Z., Nwankwo, E. E., & Soyombo, O. T. (2024). Reviewing the role of AI in Fraud Detection and Prevention in Financial Services. *International Journal of Science and Research Archive, 11*(1), 2101–2110. DOI: 10.30574/ijsra.2024.11.1.0279

OECD Digital Government Review. (2023). *Citizen participation in digital government: Trends and challenges*. Paris: OECD Publishing. https://doi.org/ https://www.oecd-ilibrary.org/governance/citizen-participation-in-digital-government_3b3b3b3b-enDOI: 10.1787/3b3b3b3b-en

OECD. (2021). *ESG Investing and Sustainability Reporting*. Organisation for Economic Co-operation and Development.

OECD. (2023). *AI governance in Asia-Pacific: Comparative analysis of democratic approaches.* Paris: OECD Publishing. https://doi.org/ https://www.oecd-ilibrary.org/science-and-technology/ai-governance-in-asia-pacific_7b3c3f5a-enDOI: 10.1787/7b3c3f5a-en

OECD. (2024). *Explanatory memorandum on the updated OECD definition of an AI system.* https://www.oecd.org/content/dam/oecd/en/publications/reports/2024/03/explanatory-memorandum-on-the-updated-oecd-definition-of-an-ai-system_3c815e51/623da898-en.pdf

Okafor, C., Kolade, A., Onunka, T., Daraojimba, C., Eyo-Udo, N., & Omotosho, A. (2023). Mitigating Cybersecurity Risks in the U.S. Healthcare Sector [Review of Mitigating Cybersecurity Risks in the U.S. Healthcare Sector]. *International Journal of Innovation and Scientific Research, 10*(9), 177–194. DOI: 10.51244/IJRSI

Oliveira, D. (2023). Navigating responsible AI adoption. *Proceedings of the 15th International Joint Conference on Knowledge Discovery, Knowledge Engineering and Knowledge Management*, 339–345. DOI: 10.5220/0012262600003598

Ostrom, E. (1990). Governing the Commons: The Evolution of Institutions for Collective Action.

Ovington, T. (2018, December 16). *How to use Kotter's 8-step model: The key to change success.* The Change Management Blog; Change Management. https://change.walkme.com/kotters-8-step-change-model/

Ozkaynak, M., Unertl, K., Johnson, S., Brixey, J., & Haque, S. N. (2022). Clinical workflow analysis, process redesign, and quality improvement. In *Clinical informatics study guide: Text and review* (pp. 103–118). Springer International Publishing. DOI: 10.1007/978-3-030-93765-2_8

Palmer, D., & Hedberg, T. (2013). The Ethics of Marketing to Vulnerable Populations. *Journal of Business Ethics*, *116*(2), 403–413. DOI: 10.1007/s10551-012-1476-2

Palumbo, G., Carneiro, D., & Alves, V. (2024). Objective metrics for ethical AI: A systematic literature review. *International Journal of Data Science and Analytics*, *20*(2), 247–267. DOI: 10.1007/s41060-024-00541-w

Panchagnula, V. D. (2025). Ethical AI and responsible automation: Building trust in GenAI-powered systems. *Hampton Global Business Review*. https://hgbr.org/research_articles/ethical-ai-and-responsible-automation-building-trust-in-genai-powered-systems/

Papagiannidis, E., Enholm, I. M., Dremel, C., Mikalef, P., & Krogstie, J. (2022). Toward AI governance: Identifying best practices and potential barriers and outcomes. *Information Systems Frontiers*, *25*(1), 123–141. DOI: 10.1007/s10796-022-10251-y PMID: 35464171

Parasuraman, R., & Riley, V. (1997). Humans and automation: Use, misuse, disuse, abuse. *Human Factors*, *39*(2), 230–253. DOI: 10.1518/001872097778543886

Parliament of Canada. (2023). *Bill C-27: An Act to enact the Consumer Privacy Protection Act and the Artificial Intelligence and Data Act*. Ottawa: House of Commons. https://www.parl.ca/DocumentViewer/en/44-1/bill/C-27/first-reading

Pasquale, F. (2015). *The black box society: The secret algorithms that control money and information*. Harvard University Press. https://doi.org/ https://www.hup.harvard.edu/catalog.php?isbn=9780674736061DOI: 10.4159/9780674736061

Patrick, G. (2025, May). Top 7 neuromarketing companies transforming consumer behavior insights. Verified Market Research.

Paul, E. M., Mmaduekwe, U., Kessie, J. D., & Dolapo, M. (2024). Zero trust architecture and AI: A synergistic approach to next-generation cybersecurity frameworks. *International Journal of Science and Research Archive*, *13*(2), 4159–4169. DOI: 10.30574/ijsra.2024.13.2.2583

Personal Data Protection Commission. (2022). Advisory guidelines on the personal data protection act for selected topics. https://www.pdpc.gov.sg

Petelka, J., Zou, Y., & Schaub, F. (2019, May). Put your warning where your link is: Improving and evaluating email phishing warnings. In *Proceedings of the 2019 CHI conference on human factors in computing systems* (pp. 1-15). https://doi-org.captechu.idm.oclc.org/10.1145/3290605.3300748

Pierre, I. (2024). Impact of the increased use of telehealth on health care management and administration: The case of new care management practices. *Doctoral Dissertations and Projects. 5148.* https://digitalcommons.liberty.edu/doctoral/5148/

Plassmann, H., Ramsøy, T. Z., & Milosavljevic, M. (2012). Branding the brain: A critical review and outlook. *Journal of Consumer Psychology*, *22*(1), 18–36. DOI: 10.1016/j.jcps.2011.11.010

Plassmann, H., Venkatraman, V., Huettel, S., & Yoon, C. (2015). Consumer neuroscience: Applications, challenges, and possible solutions. *JMR, Journal of Marketing Research*, *52*(4), 427–435. DOI: 10.1509/jmr.14.0048

Porter, M. E., & Kramer, M. R. (2006). Strategy and society: The link between competitive advantage and corporate social responsibility.

Prasad, G., Gujjar, P., Naveen Kumar, H. N., Anand Kumar, M., & Chandrappa, S. (2023). Advances of cyber security in the healthcare domain for analyzing data. In *Advances in Information Security, Privacy, and Ethics* (pp. 1–14). IGI Global.

Rahaman, M., Pappachan, P., Orozco, S. M., Bansal, S., & Arya, V. (2024). AI Safety and Security. In *Challenges in Large Language Model Development and AI Ethics* (pp. 354–383). IGI Global. DOI: 10.4018/979-8-3693-3860-5.ch011

Ramadan, R. A., Aboshosha, B. W., Alshudukhi, J. S., Alzahrani, A. J., El-Sayed, A., & Dessouky, M. M. (2021). Cybersecurity and countermeasures at the time of pandemic. *Journal of Advanced Transportation*, *2021*, 1–19. DOI: 10.1155/2021/6627264

Ramirez, S. (2025, October 7). Remote work cybersecurity statistics 2025: VPN, shadow IT, cloud, and more. SQ Magazine. https://sqmagazine.co.uk/remote-work-cybersecurity-statistics/ (accessed 16 Oct 2025)

Rawls, J. (1971). *A theory of justice*. Harvard University Press. https://www.hup.harvard.edu/catalog.php?isbn=9780674042605DOI: 10.4159/9780674042605

Rawnaque, F. S., Rahman, K. M., Anwar, S. F., Vaidyanathan, R., Chau, T., Sarker, F., & Mamun, K. A. A. (2020). Technological advancements and opportunities in neuromarketing: A systematic review. *Brain Informatics*, *7*(1), 10. Advance online publication. DOI: 10.1186/s40708-020-00109-x

Reeves, A., Delfabbro, P., & Calic, D. (2021). Encouraging Employee Engagement With Cybersecurity: How to Tackle Cyber Fatigue. *SAGE Open*, *11*(1), 215824402110000. DOI: 10.1177/21582440211000049

Regulation (EU) 2016/679 of the European Parliament and of the Council of 27 April 2016 on the protection of natural persons with regard to the processing of personal data and on the free movement of such data (General Data Protection Regulation). Official Journal of the European Union, L119, 1–88. https://eur-lex.europa.eu/eli/reg/2016/679/oj (accessed 9 September 2025)

Reimann, M., Marx, C. K., & Tisch, A. (2024). "With Kind Regards?": The Relationship Between Digital Work Communication and Mental Health. *Management Review Quarterly, 35*(2), 194–221.

Ridgeway, C. L. (2011). *Framed by gender: How gender inequality persists in the modern world.* Oxford University Press. DOI: 10.1093/acprof:oso/9780199755776.001.0001

Roberts, E. T., & Mehrotra, A. (2020). Assessment of disparities in digital access among Medicare beneficiaries and implications for telemedicine. *JAMA Internal Medicine, 180*(10), 1386–1389. DOI: 10.1001/jamainternmed.2020.2666

Robinson, N. (2023). Human factors security engineering: The future of cybersecurity teams. *EDPACS, 67*(5), 1–17. DOI: 10.1080/07366981.2023.2211429

Rose, S., Borchert, O., Mitchell, S., & Connelly, S. (2020). *Zero Trust Architecture. National Institute of Technology*. NIST., DOI: 10.6028/NIST.SP.800-207

Sainimnuan, S., Preedachitkul, R., Petchthai, P., Paokantarakorn, Y., Siriussawakul, A., & Srinonprasert, V. (2025). Low Prevalence of Adequate eHealth Literacy and Willingness to Use Telemedicine Among Older Adults: Cross-Sectional Study From a Middle-Income Country. *Journal of Medical Internet Research, 27*, e65380. DOI: 10.2196/65380

Saldanha, T. (2019). *Why digital transformations fail: The surprising disciplines of how to take off and stay ahead.* Berrett-Koehler Publishers.

Salhab, W., Ameyed, D., Jaafar, F., & Mcheick, H. (2024). A systematic literature review on ai safety: Identifying trends, challenges and future directions. *IEEE Access : Practical Innovations, Open Solutions, 12*, 131762–131784. DOI: 10.1109/ACCESS.2024.3440647

Sarah, C., & Mona, L. K. (2008). Critical mass theory and women's political representation. *Political Studies, 56*(3), 725–736. DOI: 10.1111/j.1467-9248.2007.00712.x

Sarkar, U., Paul, S., Gowrav, M. R., & Mitra, A. (2024, August). Optimizing SEO with AI: Achieving Success Through Responsible Innovation. In *International Conference on Technology Advances for Green Solutions and Sustainable Development* (pp. 51-62). Cham: Springer Nature Switzerland. DOI: 10.1007/978-3-031-94997-5_6

Sasu, A. (2016). The cultural iceberg and other cultural models. *Buletinul tiin ific al Universită ii Tehnice de Construc ii Bucure ti Seria: Limbi Străine i Comunicare, 9*(2), 79-87.

Schneider, J., Abraham, R., Meske, C., & Vom Brocke, J. (2022). Artificial intelligence governance for businesses. *Information Systems Management, 40*(3), 229–249. DOI: 10.1080/10580530.2022.2085825

Scholz, M., & Tietje, O. (2020). Ethical challenges of neuromarketing in the context of sustainable finance. *Journal of Business Ethics, 165*(3), 543–557.

Schwengber, J. G. (Ed.). (2024). *Organizational learning as relational governance*. Springer., DOI: 10.1007/978-3-031-52015-0

Seh, A. H., Zarour, M., Alenezi, M., Sarkar, A. K., Agrawal, A., Kumar, R., & Khan, R. A. (2020). Healthcare data breaches: Insights and implications. *Healthcare, 8*(2), 133. NCBI. DOI: 10.3390/healthcare8020133

Sein, M. K., Henfridsson, O., Purao, S., Rossi, M., & Lindgren, R. (2011). Action design research. *Management Information Systems Quarterly, 35*(1), 37–56. DOI: 10.2307/23043488

Selig, G. J. (2016). IT governance-An integrated framework and roadmap: How to plan, deploy and sustain for improved effectiveness. *Journal of International Technology and Information Management, 25*(1), 55–76. DOI: 10.58729/1941-6679.1252

Senge, P. M. (1990). *The fifth discipline: The art and practice of the learning organization*. Doubleday.

Sestieri, G. (2024, April 2). The dark side of SEO: Understanding SEO poisoning. ReliaQuest. https://reliaquest.com/blog/seo-poisoning/ (accessed 12 November 2025)

Shachar, C., Engel, J., & Elwyn, G. (2020). Implications for telehealth in a post-pandemic future: Regulatory and privacy issues. *Journal of the American Medical Association, 323*(23), 2375–2376. DOI: 10.1001/jama.2020.7943

Shaharia, S. (2025, June 21). Is SEO Dead in 2025? A data-driven reality check. Zenodo (Version 1). https://doi.org./DOI: 10.5281/zenodo.15712794

Shi, J., Leau, Y. B., Li, K., & Obit, J. H. (2021). A comprehensive review on a hybrid network traffic prediction model. *International Journal of Electrical and Computer Engineering, 11*(2), 1450. DOI: 10.11591/ijece.v11i2.pp1450-1459

Singh, M. A., & Zaheer, A. (2023). Review on impact of Ai on green banking towards sustainability with special reference to Indian public and private bank. *Journal of Survey in Fisheries Sciences, 10*(4S), 2475–2492.

Singh, P., Alhassan, I., & Khoshaim, L. (2023). What Do You Need to Know? A Systematic Review and Research Agenda on Neuromarketing Discipline. *Journal of Theoretical and Applied Electronic Commerce Research, 18*(4), 2007–2032. DOI: 10.3390/jtaer18040101

Sisakhti, S. A. H., Sachdev, P. S., & Batouli, S. A. H. (2021). The effect of cognitive load on the retrieval of long-term memory: An fMRI study. *Frontiers in Human Neuroscience, 15*, 700146. Advance online publication. DOI: 10.3389/fnhum.2021.700146

Slager, E. (2023). Unravelling the adoption of neuromarketing techniques in marketing organisations: Insight from (neuro)marketing professionals [Master's thesis, University of Twente]. University of Twente Student Theses. https://purl.utwente.nl/essays/97227

Smidts, A., Hsu, M., Sanfey, A. G., Boksem, M. A. S., Ebstein, R. B., Huettel, S. A., Kable, J. W., Loewenstein, G., & Yoon, C. (2014). Advancing consumer neuroscience. *Marketing Letters, 25*(3), 257–267. DOI: 10.1007/s11002-014-9306-1

Smith, A. C., Thomas, E., Snoswell, C. L., Haydon, H., Mehrotra, A., Clemensen, J., & Caffery, L. J. (2022). Telehealth for global emergencies: Implications for coronavirus disease 2019 (COVID-19). *Journal of Telemedicine and Telecare, 28*(1), 1–6. DOI: 10.1177/1357633X20916567

Solimini, R., Busardò, F. P., Gibelli, F., Sirignano, A., & Ricci, G. (2021). Ethical and Legal Challenges of Telemedicine in the Era of the COVID-19 Pandemic. *Medicina (Kaunas, Lithuania), 57*(12), 1314. DOI: 10.3390/medicina57121314

Soni, N., Zaheer, A., & Singh, R. K. (2023, October). Brain Tumor Detection and Classification Using Machine Learning Techniques. In *2023 International Conference on New Frontiers in Communication, Automation, Management and Security (ICCAMS)* (Vol. 1, pp. 1-6). IEEE. DOI: 10.1109/ICCAMS60113.2023.10525743

Spence, C. (2019). On the Ethics of Neuromarketing and Sensory Marketing (pp. 9–29). springer. DOI: 10.1007/978-3-030-27177-0_3

Stahl, B. C., Antoniou, J., Bhalla, N., Brooks, L., Jansen, P., Lindqvist, B., Kirichenko, A., Marchal, S., Rodrigues, R., Santiago, N., Warso, Z., & Wright, D. (2023). A systematic review of Artificial Intelligence Impact Assessments. *Artificial Intelligence Review, 56*(11), 12799–12831. DOI: 10.1007/s10462-023-10420-8 PMID: 37362899

Stanton, B., Theofanos, M., Prettyman, S., & Furman, S. (2016). Security fatigue. *IT Professional, 18*(5), 26–32. DOI: 10.1109/MITP.2016.84 PMID: 38566917

Stanton, S. J., Huettel, S. A., & Sinnott-Armstrong, W. (2016). Neuromarketing: Ethical Implications of Its Use and Potential Misuse. *Journal of Business Ethics, 144*(4), 799–811. DOI: 10.1007/s10551-016-3059-0

Staras, S., Tauscher, J. S., Rich, N., Samarah, E., Thompson, L. A., Vinson, M. M., Muszynski, M. J., & Shenkman, E. A. (2021). Using a clinical workflow analysis to enhance eHealth implementation planning: Tutorial and case study. *JMIR mHealth and uHealth, 9*(3), e18534. DOI: 10.2196/18534

Statista. (2024). *Artificial intelligence market size worldwide from 2020 to 2030.* Hamburg: Statista GmbH. https://www.statista.com/statistics/1365145/artificial-intelligence-market-size/

Stoumpos, A. I., Kitsios, F., & Talias, M. A. (2023). Digital transformation in healthcare: Technology acceptance and its applications. *International Journal of Environmental Research and Public Health, 20*(4), 3407. DOI: 10.3390/ijerph20043407

Surmanidze, N., Tskhadadze, K., Beridze, M., & Amashukeli, M. (2023). empowering small businesses in georgia: access to finance, economic resilience, and sustainable growth. agora international journal of economical sciences, 17(2), 158–169. DOI: 10.15837/aijes.v17i2.6453

Sussman, R., & Gifford, R. (2019). Causality in the theory of planned behavior. *Personality and Social Psychology Bulletin, 45*(6), 920–933. DOI: 10.1177/0146167218801363 PMID: 30264655

Syed, S. A. (2022). AI-powered cybercrime: The new frontier of digital threats. [IJETRM]. *International Journal of Engineering Technology Research & Management, 6*(02).

Taeihagh, A. (2021). Governance of artificial intelligence. *Policy and Society, 44*(2), 137–157. DOI: 10.1080/14494035.2021.1928377

Taiwan Digital Government. (2024). *Digital democracy and AI governance: The Taiwan model.* Taipei: National Development Council. https://www.ndc.gov.tw/en/Content_List.aspx?n=6C39A6E6F7B8A1A6

Talwar, S., Dhir, A., Islam, N., Kaur, P., & Almusharraf, A. (2023). Resistance of multiple stakeholders to e-health innovations: Integration of fundamental insights and guiding research paths. *Journal of Business Research, 166*, 114135. DOI: 10.1016/j.jbusres.2023.114135

Thaler, R. H., & Sunstein, C. R. (2008). *Nudge: Improving decisions about health, wealth, and happiness.* Yale University Press.

Themann, S. (2025). Challenges and strategies used in implementing AI governance: A systematic literature review. *Stockholm University.* https://su.diva-portal.org/smash/get/diva2:1983756/FULLTEXT01.pdf

Thomas, E. E., Haydon, H. M., Mehrotra, A., Caffery, L. J., Snoswell, C. L., Banbury, A., & Smith, A. C. (2022). Building on the momentum: Sustaining telehealth beyond COVID-19. *Journal of Telemedicine and Telecare, 28*(4), 301–308. DOI: 10.1177/1357633X20960638

Tin, D., Hata, R., Granholm, F., Ciottone, R. G., Staynings, R., & Ciottone, G. R. (2023). Cyberthreats: A primer for healthcare professionals. *The American Journal of Emergency Medicine, 68*, 179–185. Advance online publication. DOI: 10.1016/j.ajem.2023.04.001 PMID: 37061434

Tjoa, S., Temper, P. K., Temper, M., Zanol, J., Wagner, M., & Holzinger, A. (2022). Airman: An artificial intelligence (AI) Risk Management System. *2022 International Conference on Advanced Enterprise Information System (AEIS)*, 72–81. DOI: 10.1109/AEIS59450.2022.00017

Transatlantic Business Council. (2024). *Cross-border data governance: Regulatory conflicts and business impacts*. Washington, DC: TBC. https://transatlanticbusiness.org/publications/2024-data-governance-report

Traymbak, S., Shukla, A., & Dutta, M. (2024). A study of reliability and validity of constructs of neuromarketing among Indian consumers. *Annals of Neurosciences, 29*(2–3), 121–128. DOI: 10.1177/09727531231181868

Triguero, I., Molina, D., Poyatos, J., Del Ser, J., & Herrera, F. (2024). General Purpose Artificial Intelligence Systems (GPAIS): Properties, definition, taxonomy, societal implications and responsible governance. *Information Fusion, 103*, 102135. DOI: 10.1016/j.inffus.2023.102135

Turuk, M. (2020). Digital strategy. *International Journal of Contemporary Business and Entrepreneurship, 1*(1), 62–76. DOI: 10.47954/ijcbe.1.1.5

Tyler, T. R. (2006). *Why people obey the law*. Princeton University Press., https://press.princeton.edu/books/paperback/9780691126739/why-people-obey-the-law, DOI: 10.1515/9781400828609

U.S. Department of Health & Human Services. (2022). Telehealth policy changes after the COVID-19 public health emergency. https://telehealth.hhs.gov/providers/policy-changes-during-the-covid-19-public-health-emergency/

UK Government. (2023). *AI White Paper: A pro-innovation approach to AI regulation*. London: Department for Science, Innovation and Technology. https://www.gov.uk/government/publications/ai-regulation-a-pro-innovation-approach

Ulman, Y. I., Cakar, T., & Yildiz, G. (2015). Ethical Issues in Neuromarketing: "I Consume, Therefore I am!". *Science and Engineering Ethics, 21*(5), 1271–1284. DOI: 10.1007/s11948-014-9581-5

Unit 42 by Palo Alto Networks. (2025, August 1). 2025 Unit 42 Global Incident Response Report: Social engineering edition. https://unit42.paloaltonetworks.com/2025-unit-42-global-incident-response-report-social-engineering-edition/ (accessed 14 September 2025)

University of Waikato. (2024, April 18). Library guides: Writing a literature review: For researchers: Narrative literature reviews. https://libraryguides.waikato.ac.nz/c.php?g=968696&p=7042945

Vagal, V., & Dillon, R. (2021). Reducing cyber risk in remote working. In *Digital Transformation in a Post-Covid World* (pp. 155–170). CRC Press. DOI: 10.1201/9781003148715-8

Vakulov, A. (2025, January 31). *New browser syncjacking attack gives hackers full device control.* Forbes. https://www.forbes.com/sites/alexvakulov/2025/01/31/new-browser-syncjacking-attack-gives-hackers-full-device-control/ (accessed on 23 October 2025)

Valenta, S. R., Glanville, M., & Sederstrom, E. (2021). Telehealth development, implementation, and sustainability challenges: An Introduction into the telehealth service implementation model (TSIM™). *Telemedicine: Overview and Application in Pulmonary, Critical Care, and Sleep Medicine*, 61-69.

Van Assche, K., Valentinov, V., & Verschraegen, G. (2022). Adaptive governance: Learning from what organizations do and managing the role they play. *Kybernetes, 51*(5), 1738–1758. DOI: 10.1108/K-11-2020-0759

Vashishth, T. K., Sharma, V., Sharma, K. K., Kumar, B., Chaudhary, S., & Panwar, R. (2025). Securing the Cloud: Strategies for Protecting Sensitive Patient Data in Cloud-Based Healthcare Recommender Systems. *Healthcare Recommender Systems: Techniques and Recent Developments*, 185-220.

Veale, M., & Borgesius, F. Z. (2021). Demystifying the draft EU Artificial Intelligence Act. *Computer Law Review International, 22*(4), 97–112. https://www.degruyter.com/document/doi/10.9785/cri-2021-220402/htmlDOI: 10.9785/cri-2021-220402

Vecchiato, G., Astolfi, L., De Vico Fallani, F., Toppi, J., Aloise, F., Bez, F., Wei, D., Kong, W., Dai, J., Cincotti, F., Mattia, D., & Babiloni, F. (2011). On the use of EEG or MEG brain imaging tools in neuromarketing research. Computational Intelligence and Neuroscience. *Computational Intelligence and Neuroscience*, *643489*, 1–12. Advance online publication. DOI: 10.1155/2011/643489

Vectra. (2024, February 25). SEO poisoning attacks: Detection & defense. https://www.vectra.ai/topics/seo-poisoning (accessed on 16 October 2025)

Venkitanarayanan, A. (2025). Behind the Screen: Understanding the Human Firewall in Cybersecurity. DOI: 10.54014/GWQ8-MWP8

Vial, G. (2019). Understanding digital transformation: A review and a research agenda. *The Journal of Strategic Information Systems*, *28*(2), 118–144. DOI: 10.1016/j.jsis.2019.01.003

Wallenius, S. (2024). Recommended SEO-techniques to increase organic traffic for a website: a scoping review. https://www.theseus.fi/bitstream/handle/10024/876381/Wallenius_Susanne.pdf?sequence=2&isAllowed=y (accessed on 19 July 2025)

Wasserman, L., & Wasserman, Y. (2022). Hospital cybersecurity risks and gaps: Review (for the non-cyber professional). *Frontiers in Digital Health*, *4*, 862221. Advance online publication. DOI: 10.3389/fdgth.2022.862221 PMID: 36033634

Weiss, J. (2024, September 19). *Unlocking the consumer mind: The business case for neuromarketing. Marketing Mag*. Retrieved July 26, 2025, from https://www.marketingmag.com.au/featured/unlocking-the-consumer-mind-the-business-case-for-neuromarketing/

Westermeier, C. (2020). Money is data – the platformization of financial transactions. *Information Communication and Society*, *23*(14), 2047–2063. DOI: 10.1080/1369118X.2020.1770833

Williams, J. (2025, August 19). *Agentic AI: Understanding and security the next wave of AI systems.* [Webinar]. IANS, Virtual.

Wilson, R., Gaines, J., & Hill, R. P. (2008). Neuromarketing and consumer free will. *The Journal of Consumer Affairs*, *42*(3), 389–410. DOI: 10.1111/j.1745-6606.2008.00114.x

Winner, L. (1980). Do artifacts have politics? *Daedalus*, *109*(1), 121–136. https://www.jstor.org/stable/20024652

WomenTech Network. (2024). *What are the privacy concerns for women using telehealth services?* Women Tech Network. https://www.womentech.net/forum-topic/what-are-privacy-concerns-women-using-telehealth-services

World Economic Forum. (2023). *Adopting AI responsibly: Guidelines for procurement of AI solutions by the private sector.* https://www3.weforum.org/docs/WEF_Adopting_AI_Responsibly_Guidelines_for_Procurement_of_AI_Solutions_by_the_Private_Sector_2023.pdf

World Health Organization. (2021). *Global strategy on digital health 2020-2025.* https://www.who.int/publications/i/item/9789240020924

Wright, J., & Burrell, D. N. (2023). Telemedicine cybersecurity protection in reproductive healthcare. *HOLISTICA Journal of Business and Public Administration, 14*(2), 1–14. DOI: 10.2478/hjbpa-2023-0012

Wu, M., Hong, G., Mai, W., Wu, X., Zhang, L., Pu, Y., Chai, H., Ying, L., Duan, H., & Yang, M. (2025, March). Exposing the Hidden Layer: Software Repositories in the Service of Seo Manipulation. In *2025 IEEE/ACM 47th International Conference on Software Engineering (ICSE)* (pp. 684-684). IEEE Computer Society. https://ieeexplore.ieee.org/stamp/stamp.jsp?tp=&arnumber=11029819 (accessed 25 October 2025)

Wung, W. S., Kranig, C., Pauley, E., Barford, P., Crovella, M., & Sommers, J. (2025, May). Squatspotting: Towards the systematic measurement of typosquatting techniques. IFIP. https://www.cs.bu.edu/faculty/crovella/paper-archive/wung-ifip-networking25-dns.pdf (accessed on 13 August 2025)

Wyborn, C. (2015). Co-productive governance: A relational framework for adaptive governance. *Global Environmental Change, 30*, 56–67. DOI: 10.1016/j.gloenvcha.2014.10.009

Xia, B., Lu, Q., Zhu, L., Lee, S. U., Liu, Y., & Xing, Z. (2024). Towards a responsible AI metrics catalogue: A collection of metrics for AI accountability. *Proceedings of the IEEE/ACM 3rd International Conference on AI Engineering - Software Engineering for AI*, 100–111. DOI: 10.1145/3644815.3644959

Yampolskiy, R. V. (Ed.). (2018). *Artificial intelligence safety and security*. CRC Press. DOI: 10.1201/9781351251389

Yeoh, W., Liu, M., Shore, M., & Jiang, F. (2023). Zero trust cybersecurity: Critical success factors and A maturity assessment framework. *Computers & Security, 133*(103412), 103412. DOI: 10.1016/j.cose.2023.103412

Yeung, K. (2017). 'Hypernudge': Big data as a mode of regulation by design. *Information Communication and Society*, *20*(1), 118–136. https://www.tandfonline.com/doi/full/10.1080/1369118X.2016.1186713. DOI: 10.1080/1369118X.2016.1186713

Yogev, D., Goldberg, T., Arami, A., Tejman-Yarden, S., Winkler, T. E., & Maoz, B. M. (2023). Current state of the art and future directions for implantable sensors in medical technology: Clinical needs and engineering challenges. *APL Bioengineering*, *7*(3), 031506. Advance online publication. DOI: 10.1063/5.0152290 PMID: 37781727

Zaheer, A., Singh, A., & Mishra, K. K. Reepu, and Vardari, L. (2024), "The Future of Alchemy: Emerging Trends and Technologies Metaverse in Insurance – A Virtual Customer Experience", Taneja, S., Kumar, P., Reepu, Kukreti, M. and Özen, E. (Ed.) Data Alchemy in the Insurance Industry, Emerald Publishing Limited, Leeds, pp. 133-152. DOI: 10.1108/978-1-83608-582-920241021

Zaltman, G. (2003). *How customers think: Essential insights into the mind of the market.* Harvard Business School Press.

Zemah, Y. (2025, September 21). Operation Rewrite: Chinese-speaking threat actors deploy BadIIS in a wide SEO poisoning campaign. Palo Alto Networks Unit. 42. https://unit42.paloaltonetworks.com/operation-rewrite-seo-poisoning-campaign/ (accessed 17 October 2025)

Zettelmann, A., & Cano, J. A. (2024). How change management activates digital transformation in healthcare. *Health Management*, *24*(2), 101–107. https://healthmanagement.org/c/healthmanagement/issuearticle/how-change-management-activates-digital-transformation-in-healthcare

Zheng, K., Ratwani, R. M., & Adler-Milstein, J. (2020). Studying workflow and workarounds in electronic health record–supported work to improve health system performance. *Annals of Internal Medicine*, *172*(11, Supplement), S116–S122. DOI: 10.7326/M19-0871

Zohaib, S. M., Sajjad, S. M., Iqbal, Z., Yousaf, M., Haseeb, M., & Muhammad, Z. (2024). Zero trust vpn (zt-vpn): A systematic literature review and cybersecurity framework for hybrid and remote work. *Information (Basel)*, *15*(11), 734. DOI: 10.3390/info15110734

Zscaler. (2025, June 23). Black hat SEO poisoning search engine results for AI. https://www.zscaler.com/blogs/security-research/black-hat-seo-poisoning-search-engine-results-ai-distribute-malware (accessed 3 August 2025)

Zuboff, S. (2019). *The age of surveillance capitalism: The fight for a human future at the new frontier of power*. PublicAffairs. https://www.publicaffairsbooks.com/titles/shoshana-zuboff/the-age-of-surveillance-capitalism/9781610395694/

Zuboff, S. (2019). *The age of surveillance capitalism: The fight for a human future at the new frontier of power*. PublicAffairs.

About the Contributors

Darrell Norman Burrell is a visiting scholar at the Samuel DeWitt Proctor Institute for Leadership, Equity, and Justice at Rutgers University, where he is currently focusing his research on sustainability, health equity, and inclusive leadership. His work as a visiting researcher at the Pellegrino Center for Clinical Bioethics at the Georgetown University Medical Center in Washington, D.C., and as a post-doctoral public health researcher at the University of Maryland School of Pharmacy in Baltimore, MD, has provided him with a unique perspective on issues related to health disparities, health technology access, telehealth, adolescent health, and health literacy. For more than 12 years, he has also served in various roles as a doctoral faculty member, dissertation chair, and research panel participant at Marymount University, the Florida Institute of Technology, Capitol Technology University, the University of Liverpool in the U.K., and The Chicago School of Professional Psychology in Washington D.C. Dr. Burrell is a Certified Diversity Professional and a Certified Executive Coach. Dr. Burrell is an alumnus of the Presidential Management Fellows Program with the U.S. Federal Government and U.S. Nuclear Regulatory Commission, where he managed and developed leadership and diversity programs for professionals in Public Health, Environmental Health, Emergency Response, Technology, and Engineering. Academically, Dr. Burrell has three doctorate degrees and six graduate degrees, including a Master of Research in Artificial Intelligence Biotechnology Applications and Healthcare, along with additional graduate degrees in (H.R. Management, Management, Health Leadership, Sales and Marketing Management, Higher Education Administration, and Interfaith Action and Conflict Management). Dr. Burrell received his first doctoral degree in health education (DHEd), focusing on environmental public health and executive leadership coaching, at A.T. Still University in 2010. Dr. Burrell completed his 2nd doctorate, a Doctor of Philosophy (Ph.D.) in Cybersecurity Leadership at Capitol Technology University. In 2022, Dr. Burrell completed his 3rd Doctor of Business Administration (DBA) in Supply Chain Management at Capitol Technology

University. He has over 20 years of management, teaching, and training experience in academia, government, and private industry. Dr. Burrell has over 200 peer-reviewed publications and more than 1200 Google Scholar citations. Research His research focuses on the relationship between private law, economic law, EU law, economics and legal theory. He is particular interested in the intersect between consumer law, data protection, competition law, and sector specific legislation in addressing the challenges raised by technological developments in the attention economy. He is currently working on price personalization, and the use of theories of harm in consumer law with a special attention to consumer data collecion. Fabrizio is about to publish a monograph showing how to change the mainstream research paradigm at the intersect between law and economics by taking the consumer interest as core value in market regulation. Supervision Fabrizio encourages students interested in any of the above, and in particular interested in the legal structure of the attention economy to reach out and explore potential collaboration opportunities, starting with thesis supervision. Ambitious students who intend to produce publishable work in a peer-review journal and are considering interdisciplinary research and/or to pursue an academic career are particularly encouraged to reach out. Education Fabrizio graduated in law at Bocconi University in 2011. After working for two years in civil and commercial litigation, he was admitted as a researcher at the European University Institute, where he obtained an LLM in Comparative, European and International Law (2015) and his PhD in 2018 after defending his dissertation, which opens new frontiers in research about law and economics. Previous positions Before joining the NOVA School of Law, Fabrizio was a Postdoctoral Fellow at the Edmond J. Safra Center for Ethics at Tel Aviv University and Postdoctoral Fellow at the Universitè Catholique de Louvain, where he joined the PROSECO Project. He held visiting positions at the University of Helsinki and Pisa, and was a Global Visiting Fellow at UCLouvain. Publications Fabrizio publishes regularly in international journals such as: Computer Law & Security Review, the European Review of Contract Law, the Journal of Consumer Policy, the European Journal of Risk Regulation, the European Competition Journal. He has co-edited two volumes: Research Methods in Consumer Law (with H-W Micklitz and A-L Sibony; EE 2018) and Economics in Legal Reasoning (with P Cserne; Palgrave 2020). He was in charge of the legal theory section of the European Journal of Legal Studies, writes twice per year for the European Review of Contract Law about recent developments in EU contract law

***

Pratibha Gupta is working as an Assistant Professor of Management at the University School of Business, Chandigarh University, Mohali, Punjab. She has published 4 research papers and also won Best paper award. She has 4 plus years of teaching experience and also worked as an Expert for NET/JRF Coaching for 2 years. Her area of specialization is Finance.

Allison Huff focuses on technology to address complex disorders, particularly focusing on how technology impacts SDOH. Previously, she was a behavioral health clinician working with individuals with serious mental illnesses and substance use disorders. Dr. Huff is PI and Co-I on several NSF, HRSA, and industry sponsored grants and leads clinical trials and research programs. She also is a mentor for several underserved pre-professional health and pre-med students each summer and through the academic year. Dr. Huff's Doctor of Health Education is from A.T. Still University, her Master of Education in Instructional Technology is from University of Oklahoma, and her Bachelor's in Psychology is from University of West Florida.

Laura Jones is an award-winning risk management thought leader, strategist, and practitioner. She specializes in cybersecurity risk, quality assurance, and artificial intelligence. She currently serves as an adjunct faculty member at Carnegie Mellon University, Wake Forest University, and Capitol Technology University. Dr. Jones earned a PhD in Cyber Leadership, a PhD in Product Management, an MS in Quality Systems Management, and a BS in Management Studies. She has completed executive education programs at Carnegie Mellon University (Chief Risk Officer's Program), Harvard Kennedy School (Leadership Decision Making), and UC Berkeley Haas (Business Strategies and Artificial Intelligence). Dr. Jones has numerous publications on cyber and risk management. She also speaks domestically and internationally about risk management and cybersecurity. Dr. Jones previously served as a graduate school Associate Dean of Student Academic Affairs.

Kaushal Mishra is working as a Professor of Marketing at the University School of Business, Chandigarh University, Mohali, Punjab. He has published 54 research papers in Scopus-indexed journals and book chapters, and presented 31 papers at national and international conferences. He has four patent rights and three copyrights. He has 25 years of experience in teaching and research. He has supervised two PhD scholars. He has twice qualified for the UGC NET in Management. He has received the Best Faculty Award three times from the Indian Institute of Materials Management, National Headquarters, Mumbai, in 2009, 2016 and 2018, respectively. He has been conferred the Best Paper Award for the paper titled "Harnessing AI: Unveiling Educators' Intentions and Synergy in Education", presented at the 8th International Conference on Information System Design and Intelligent Applications (ISDIS 2024) in Dubai, UAE, in 2024. He has chaired technical sessions of international conferences organised by the Indian Institute of Materials Management, Mumbai, in 2016 and 2018 and OP Jindal University,

Raigarh, in 2022 and 2023. He did his PhD in "Strategy formulation for marketing services in rural Uttar Pradesh" from Uttar Pradesh Rajarshi Tandon University, Allahabad.

Pawan Pant is working as an Associate Professor of Management at the University School of Business, Chandigarh University, Mohali, Punjab. He has published eight research papers, one in a national and one in an international journal. He has 11years of teaching experience and worked as an Assistant Manager (Purchase) at Pacific Industries Ltd., Udaipur (Rajasthan) for one year. His area of specialisation is Economics.

Amalisha Sabie-Aridi, Ph.D., MBA, CMP-UNGGA, is an esteemed scholar, educator, and executive leader whose career spans over a decade of exceptional contributions to higher education, project management, organizational strategy, and leadership development. As a distinguished graduate professor and doctoral committee chair at multiple institutions, including Marymount University and Washington University of Science & Technology, she has guided countless doctoral candidates and shaped innovative curricula across disciplines such as technology, business, leadership, and project management. Dr. Sabie-Aridi's prolific scholarly output includes over 80 peer-reviewed publications covering diverse fields such as organizational behavior, artificial intelligence strategy, healthcare management, strategic leadership, diversity and inclusion, and cybersecurity. She is renowned for integrating research excellence with practical expertise drawn from her tenure as a senior project manager and executive operations leader, notably in high-stakes environments like NASA Engineering Inc. Internationally recognized, she holds honors including UN Global Goodwill Ambassador.

Azmee Zaheer is an Assistant Professor at the University School of Business, MBA department, Chandigarh University, Gharuan, Punjab. She has completed her PhD and MPhil in Management from Babasaheb Bhimrao Ambedkar University (A Central University), Lucknow, Uttar Pradesh. She received a Gold Medal for her M.Phil's exemplary work. She has four years of research experience, 3.5 years of corporate marketing experience, and 2.5 years of academic marketing experience. She has also contributed to various research journals, including those indexed in Scopus, Web of Science, and UGC Care, as well as edited books. She has participated in multiple national and international seminars.

Index

A

B

C

D

E

F

G

H

I

L

N

O

P

R

S

T

www.ingramcontent.com/pod-product-compliance
Lightning Source LLC
LaVergne TN
LVHW080903300926
849162LV00003B/540